Praise for *Cleaner, Greener, Healthier*

"David Boyd asks exactly the right questions and comes to the sad conclusion that Canada's environmental laws are far weaker than those of other countries. But he's ultimately optimistic: if government exerted some political will, most environmental threats to our health could be eliminated."

> – Gideon Forman, Executive Director, Canadian Association of Physicians for the Environment

"In this comprehensive and readable survey, David Boyd catalogues the many hazardous substances that we encounter in our environment and highlights how Canada lags far behind other developed countries with respect to regulation of many exposures. Boyd not only diagnoses the problem, he provides a scientifically robust prescription for treating it. This is a must-read for policymakers at all levels of government and for all Canadians who care about the air we breathe, the water we drink, and the food we eat."

> – Peter D. Paré, MD, Professor Emeritus of Respiratory Medicine and Pathology at the University of British Columbia and editor-in-chief of the *Canadian Respiratory Journal*

"David Boyd's latest book provides a sobering assessment of Canada's current legal framework for environmental protection and a thoughtful prescription on what can be done to improve it. An excellent read for anyone with an interest in environmental health, policy, and regulation."

> – Prof. Raymond Copes, Dalla Lana School of Public Health, University of Toronto

"This important book addresses the political failures of governments to adequately protect Canadians from environmental harm and to create more health-enhancing environments. More importantly, it shows how we can – and must – change this, using all available political, legal, and economic tools to create a cleaner, greener, and healthier future for us all."

– Prof. Trevor Hancock, School of Public Health and Social Policy, University of Victoria

"This book must be put in every politician's hands. For years, David Boyd has built a very robust diagnosis of Canada's environmental problems. Now, through this appealing and very positive book, Boyd provides the next step: a powerful prescription for achieving a healthy environment."

– Dr. François Reeves, Université de Montréal, author of *Planet Heart: How an Unhealthy Environment Leads to Heart Disease*

"Want to save thousands of lives, billions of dollars in health costs, and have a cleaner environment? Then read this book. With meticulous research and superb writing, David Boyd paints a powerful policy road map for making Canada healthy, wealthy, and wise – if we take his advice."

– Prof. Stewart Elgie, Faculty of Law, University of Ottawa

"David Boyd has once again made a monumental contribution to the scholarship of Canadian environmental law. Only rarely can it be said that a book could actually save lives; this one can. If we adopt the very reasonable approaches he suggests, we will indeed create healthier Canadians both now and in the future. A must-read for all Canadians."

– Prof. Lynda M. Collins, Faculty of Law, University of Ottawa

CLEANER, GREENER, HEALTHIER

Law and Society Series
W. Wesley Pue, General Editor

The Law and Society Series explores law as a socially embedded phenomenon. It is premised on the understanding that the conventional division of law from society creates false dichotomies in thinking, scholarship, educational practice, and social life. Books in the series treat law and society as mutually constitutive and seek to bridge scholarship emerging from interdisciplinary engagement of law with disciplines such as politics, social theory, history, political economy, and gender studies.

For a complete list of titles in the series, go to www.ubcpress.ca. Recent titles in the series include:

CLEANER, GREENER, HEALTHIER

A PRESCRIPTION FOR STRONGER CANADIAN ENVIRONMENTAL LAWS AND POLICIES

David R. Boyd

UBCPress · Vancouver · Toronto

23 22 21 20 19 18 17 16 15   5 4 3 2 1

Printed in Canada on FSC-certified ancient-forest-free paper
(100% post-consumer recycled) that is processed chlorine- and acid-free.

Library and Archives Canada Cataloguing in Publication

Boyd, David R. (David Richard), 1964-, author
    Cleaner, greener, healthier : a prescription for stronger Canadian environmental laws and policies / David R. Boyd.

(Law and society)
Includes bibliographical references and index.
Issued in print and electronic formats.
ISBN 978-0-7748-3046-1 (bound). – ISBN 978-0-7748-3047-8 (pbk.). –
ISBN 978-0-7748-3048-5 (pdf). – ISBN 978-0-7748-3049-2 (epub)

    1. Environmental law – Canada. 2. Environmental policy – Canada. 3. Environmental health – Canada. 4. Canada – Environmental conditions. I. Title. II. Series: Law and society series (Vancouver, B.C.)

| KE3619.B65 2015 | 344.7104'6 | C2015-903877-4 |
| KF3775.B65 2015 | | C2015-903878-2 |

Canadä

UBC Press gratefully acknowledges the financial support for our publishing program of the Government of Canada (through the Canada Book Fund), the Canada Council for the Arts, and the British Columbia Arts Council.

This book has been published with the help of a grant from the Canadian Federation for the Humanities and Social Sciences, through the Awards to Scholarly Publications Program, using funds provided by the Social Sciences and Humanities Research Council of Canada.

Printed and bound in Canada by Friesens
Set in Segoe and Warnock by Artegraphica Design Co. Ltd.
Copy editor and proofreader: Francis Chow

UBC Press
The University of British Columbia
2029 West Mall
Vancouver, BC V6T 1Z2
www.ubcpress.ca

Contents

Tables

Acknowledgments

I could not have written this book without the support of an amazing network of friends and colleagues. It has been in the works for eight years! Thanks to David Bates, Ray Copes, Hadi Dowlatabadi, and Milind Kandlikar for teaching me about the finer points of environmental health. Thanks to Amir Attaran, Jeanette Boyd, Kevin Chan, Stewart Elgie, Stephen Genuis, Lisa Gue, Scott Harrison, Richard Jackson, Faisal Moola, Daniel Rainham, Peter Robinson, Ann Rowan, Terre Satterfield, Meg Sears, Colin Soskolne, David Suzuki, and Scott Wallace for their helpful guidance, feedback, and support along the way. Two individuals deserve special credit for doing more than I had any right to expect: Cam Brewer, the best research assistant I've ever had; and Peter Paré, who went over the medical aspects of the book with a fine-tooth comb, offering a wealth of insight and gently correcting a few errors. This is my fourth book with UBC Press, and I'm honoured to work with their team of outstanding and passionate professionals again, including Randy Schmidt, Melissa Pitts, Ann Macklem, Laraine Coates, Kerry Kilmartin, and Frank Chow. And finally, as always, last but definitely not least, my heartfelt and abundant gratitude to Margot and Meredith, who made sure that research and writing were balanced with healthy doses of hiking, biking, kayaking, and beach time.

Abbreviations

ADHD	attention deficit hyperactivity disorder
ADR	alternative dispute resolution
AIDS	acquired immune deficiency syndrome
ASEAN	Association of Southeast Asian Nations
Bq/L	becquerels per litre
BBP	benzyl butyl phthalate
BPA	bisphenol A
CAAQS	Canadian Ambient Air Quality Standards
CAPP	Canadian Association of Petroleum Producers
CCCE	Canadian Council of Chief Executives
CDC	Centers for Disease Control and Prevention (US)
CEPA	*Canadian Environmental Protection Act, 1999*
CFC	chlorofluorocarbon
CFIA	Canadian Food Inspection Agency
CHMS	Canadian Health Measures Survey
CIHI	Canadian Institute for Health Information
CIHR	Canadian Institutes of Health Research
CIW	Canadian Index of Wellbeing
CMA	Canadian Medical Association
CO_2	carbon dioxide
COPD	chronic obstructive pulmonary disease

COSEWIC   Committee on the Status of Endangered Wildlife in Canada
CPI   consumer price index
DALY   disability adjusted life year
DBP   dibutyl phthalate
DEHP   di(2-ethylhexyl) phthalate
DIBP   diisobutyl phthalate
EAF   environmentally attributable fraction
EBD   environmental burden of disease
EFSA   European Food Safety Authority
EPA   Environmental Protection Agency (US)
ETS   Emissions Trading System (EU)
FAO   Food and Agriculture Organization
FDA   Food and Drug Administration (US)
FPTP   first past the post
FSDS   Federal Sustainable Development Strategy
GHG   greenhouse gas
GM   genetically modified
GST   Goods and Services Tax
HBCD   hexabromocyclododecane
HCB   hexachlorobenzene
HIV   human immunodeficiency virus
IARC   International Agency for Research on Cancer
IHDCYH   Institute of Human Development, Child and Youth Health
MAC   maximum acceptable concentration
MIREC   Maternal-Infant Research on Environmental Chemicals
MMP   mixed-member proportional representation
MCLG   Maximum Contaminant Level Goal
MRL   maximum residue limit
NAAQO   National Ambient Air Quality Objectives
NAAQS   National Ambient Air Quality Standards
NAFTA   North American Free Trade Agreement
NCEH   National Center for Environmental Health (US)
NCCEH   National Collaborating Centre for Environmental Health
NDP   New Democratic Party
NEHAP   National Environmental Health Action Plan
NESP   National Enteric Surveillance Program
NGO   nongovernmental organization
NHANES   National Health and Nutrition Examination Survey

NICNAS	National Industrial Chemicals Notification and Assessment Scheme (Australia)
NIEHS	National Institute of Environmental Health Sciences (US)
NOx	nitrogen oxide
NPRI	National Pollutant Release Inventory
NREL	National Renewable Energy Laboratory (US)
OECD	Organisation for Economic Co-operation and Development
OMA	Ontario Medical Association
OMB	Office of Management and Budget (US)
PAH	polycyclic aromatic hydrocarbons
PBDE	polybrominated diphenyl ether
PCB	polychlorinated biphenyl
PCPA	*Pest Control Products Act*
PFC	perfluorochemical
PFOA	perfluorooctanoic acid
PFOS	perfluorooctane sulphonate
PM	particulate matter
PMRA	Pest Management Regulatory Agency
POP	persistent organic pollutant
ppb	parts per billion
ppm	parts per million
REACH	Registration, Evaluation, Authorisation and Restriction of Chemicals
SARS	severe acute respiratory syndrome
SNUR	significant new use rules
SOx	sulphur oxide
UFFI	urea formaldehyde foam insulation
µg/dL	micrograms per decilitre
USDA	US Department of Agriculture
VOC	volatile organic compound
VSL	value of a statistical life
WHMIS	Workplace Hazardous Materials Information System
WHO	World Health Organization

PART 1

EXAMINATION

The Surprising Magnitude of Environmental
Health Problems in Canada

The area of environmental impacts on health has been seriously neglected in Canada and requires urgent investment.

– NATIONAL ADVISORY COMMITTEE ON SARS AND PUBLIC HEALTH (2003)

1

A Neglected but Vital Issue

Despite the major efforts that have been made over recent years to clean up the environment, pollution remains a major problem and poses continuing risks to health.

– DR. DAVID BRIGGS, DEPARTMENT OF EPIDEMIOLOGY AND PUBLIC HEALTH, IMPERIAL COLLEGE, LONDON (2003)

On the surface, Canada is one of the most beautiful nations in the world, with seemingly abundant fresh water, clean air, and few obvious signs of environmental contamination or degradation. However, looks can be deceiving. Canada has a relatively poor environmental record, and, as a result, Canadians are exposed to environmental hazards that cause cancer, impair the normal development of children, interfere with the respiratory, cardiovascular, reproductive, endocrine, immune, and nervous systems, and inflict damage on skin and organs.[1] Over two hundred human diseases and conditions are linked to chemical exposures, ranging from birth defects and asthma to cancer and heart disease.[2] Specific examples of adverse health outcomes that scientists link to environmental hazards are acute lymphoblastic leukemia, lung cancer, bladder cancer, skin cancer, premature birth, permanent decreases in IQ, behavioural problems, asthma, chronic obstructive pulmonary disease (COPD), Parkinson's disease, heart attacks, strokes,

reduced fertility, and acute gastrointestinal illness. The Conference Board of
Canada, a respected think tank not known for alarmist prognostications,
warned that life expectancy for today's Canadian children could be shorter
than for their parents, in part due to illnesses linked to environmental
factors.[3]

It is widely recognized that air pollution contributes to thousands of premature deaths and millions of episodes of illness in Canada annually.[4] Rates
of physician-diagnosed asthma among children in Canada quadrupled in
recent decades.[5] There have been hundreds of outbreaks of waterborne illness in Canada in the past three decades, most notably the Walkerton,
North Battleford, and Kashechewan disasters.[6] Canadian industries release
billions of kilograms of toxic substances into the air, water, and soil annually.[7] One in six Canadians lives within one kilometre of a major pollution-
producing facility.[8] The reality is that pollution is pervasive, penetrating
every ecosystem in Canada and accumulating inside every Canadian. The
bodies of adults and children across Canada are contaminated by dozens
of industrial chemicals, including pesticides, PCBs (polychlorinated biphenyls), fire retardants (polybrominated diphenyl ethers, or PBDEs), PFCs
(perfluorochemicals, found in many consumer products), volatile organic
compounds (VOCs), and phthalates (used as fragrances and plastic softeners).[9] Despite Canada's reputation as a relatively clean country, the chemical
body burden of Canadians is similar to that of Americans.[10] Recent studies
even found hundreds of toxic industrial chemicals in the cord blood of newborn infants in Canada and the United States.[11]

Twenty-first century environmental hazards in wealthy countries like
Canada are difficult for individuals to detect – often we can't see the pollution or the microbes in the air we breathe, can't taste the pathogens and
chemicals in the water we drink, and can't smell or taste the pesticides and
bacteria in the food we eat. Our senses can't tell us whether foods are genetically modified or whether consumer products contain nanoparticles. We
can't distinguish a mosquito harbouring West Nile virus from one that does
not. Some people have difficulty believing that the presence of a chemical in
their body in seemingly infinitesimal quantities could harm their health. Yet
many common prescription drugs are biologically active at similarly minuscule concentrations. Two examples are Viagra, which is active in the body at
levels as low as 30 parts per billion (ppb), and the birth control medication
Nuvaring, whose estrogen component is clinically effective at 0.035 ppb.
Despite such tiny doses, these drugs can initiate procreation or prevent it,
and also cause major side effects.[12]

Despite humanity's remarkable scientific and technological prowess, there are still enormous gaps in our knowledge and understanding of the relationships between environmental hazards and human health. Almost every week there are peer-reviewed studies published in medical and scientific journals that either strengthen our understanding of the connections between environmental factors and human health or raise troubling new questions.[13] In 2014:

- Scientists identified a gene that raises the risk of developing Parkinson's disease in people exposed to certain pesticides.[14]
- A long-term study of Inuit children enabled researchers to identify the distinct negative impacts on neurological development caused by exposure to lead, mercury, and PCBs.
- Canadian researchers revealed that exposure in the womb to chemicals found in cosmetics and other consumer products can trigger autism.[15]
- Researchers identified mechanisms by which human sperm function can be damaged by exposure to endocrine-disrupting chemicals in common consumer products.[16]

In 2013, the International Agency for Research on Cancer (IARC) designated air pollution as a human carcinogen. Three new studies link in utero exposure to organophosphate pesticides with decreased cognitive development in early childhood (deficits in IQ, working memory, and perceptual reasoning).[17] In 2010, a panel of experts appointed by US President Barack Obama concluded that environmental causes of cancer had been "grossly underestimated."[18] The lower limit at which some toxic substances have been shown to harm human health has repeatedly decreased because of new discoveries. Three classic examples are lead, a potent neurotoxin; benzene, a cancer-causing substance; and particulate air pollution. As well, researchers have discovered that exposure to some chemicals can have transgenerational health effects, meaning that your grandmother's exposure to a toxic substance could increase your vulnerability to certain diseases, and your exposure could harm your grandchildren.[19] As the authors of one article observe: "If the exposure of your grandmother at mid-gestation to environmental toxic substances can cause a disease state in you with no exposure, and you will pass it on to your grandchildren, the potential hazards of environmental toxic substances need to be rigorously assessed. Transgenerational studies need to be performed in evaluating the toxicology of environmental compounds."[20] Unfortunately, as Professor Tracy Bach recently observed, "environmental and public health laws struggle to keep pace with this growing body of environmental public health research."[21] The continuing evolution of our knowledge explains the urgency of using the precautionary principle as a fundamental guidepost in our decision-making processes. This principle acknowledges the fact that we will always be confronted by uncertainty, but taking a more cautious approach in the future will enable us to learn from, and avoid repeating, our past mistakes.

We also need to remember and build upon past successes. Many of the great public health achievements of the nineteenth and twentieth centuries were in the field of environmental health – treated drinking water, food safety, wastewater treatment, and cleaner fuels for transportation, cooking, and heating. Improvements in public infrastructure reduced preventable deaths, illnesses, and injuries. Early land-use zoning laws protected residential neighbourhoods from abattoirs, tanneries, and other sources of noxious pollution. The burning rivers, dead lakes, and choking clouds of smog that helped galvanize the modern environmental movement in the 1960s seem like distant memories in Canada today. While great strides have been made, much more remains to be done, and new challenges continue to emerge. For example, researchers continue to investigate the health implications of new scientific discoveries, from biotechnology to nanotechnology.

One of the fundamental premises of this book is that human health and environmental protection are inextricably linked. By failing to acknowledge and act upon the reality that Canadians are dependent upon the natural world for both our health and well-being, governments devote inadequate attention to resolving both health and environmental problems.

Canada's Environmental Record
Contrary to the myth of a pristine green country providing environmental leadership to the world, a large body of evidence proves beyond a reasonable doubt that Canada lags behind other nations in terms of environmental performance. According to researchers at Simon Fraser University, Canada's environmental performance ranks twenty-fourth out of the twenty-five wealthiest nations in the Organisation for Economic Co-operation and Development (OECD).[22] The OECD has published blistering critiques of Canada's weak laws and policies, perverse subsidies for unsustainable industries, and poor environmental performance.[23] In 2014, Canada ranked fifty-eighth out of sixty-one nations for its climate policies, ahead of only Kazakhstan, Iran, and Saudi Arabia. The authors concluded that "Canada

still shows no intentions to move forward on climate policy and thereby [maintains] its place as the worst performer of all western countries."[24] A 2013 study published by the Center for Global Development, a think tank in Washington, DC, ranked Canada dead last among twenty-seven wealthy countries on environmental indicators.[25] For years, the widely respected Conference Board of Canada has ranked Canada fifteenth out of seventeen large, wealthy industrialized nations on environmental performance.[26] Sweden and Norway are consistently at or near the top of the rankings. According to the Conference Board, these Scandinavian nations also outperform Canada in terms of economic competitiveness and innovation, debunking the myth that there is a trade-off between strong environmental protection and economic prosperity.

A comprehensive comparison of nations with federal governance systems concluded that "Canadian environmental quality and environmental policy are worse than one might expect in a relatively wealthy country."[27] A survey of over five thousand experts found that:

- 60 percent rated Canada's performance in protecting Canadians from the health impacts of pollution as poor or very poor.
- 65 percent rated Canada's performance in protecting fresh water as poor or very poor.
- 85 percent rated Canada's efforts to address climate change as poor or very poor.[28]

On a per capita basis, Canadians pump out more air pollution – volatile organic compounds, nitrogen oxides, sulphur dioxide, and carbon monoxide – than any other nation in the OECD.[29] Contradicting the perception that air quality is improving, Environment Canada reports that since 1990, average levels of smog are up 13 percent and ground-level ozone is up 10 percent.[30] Air pollution in Alberta's "Industrial Heartland," where oil and gas are processed, is comparable to that in the world's dirtiest megacities.[31] Canadian industries in the heavily populated Great Lakes region discharge twice as much cancer-causing pollution per facility as their American competitors.[32] Thousands of Aboriginal people living on reserves in Alberta, Manitoba, Ontario, and Quebec lack access to running water, resulting in elevated levels of waterborne illnesses.[33] Canadians have the seventh-largest per capita ecological footprint in the world.[34] If all 7 billion people on Earth consumed resources and produced waste at the prodigious rate of Canadians, we would require three additional planets.

There is some good news. Emissions of sulphur dioxide, nitrogen oxides, volatile organic compounds, mercury, and lead have come down substantially over the past thirty years. Major investments have been made to improve drinking water treatment and wastewater treatment infrastructure. Canada has eliminated the use of dozens of toxic chemicals and pesticides as a result of health and environmental concerns, resulting in lower exposures and declining body burdens of these substances (e.g., dioxins, mercury, and organochlorine pesticides). Discharges of certain toxic water pollutants, including dioxins and furans, have been reduced dramatically.

The Conservative government, elected in 2006 and re-elected in 2008 and 2011, has significantly weakened Canada's capacity for environmental protection through various actions, including:

- watering down environmental laws, including the *Fisheries Act, Navigable Waters Protection Act* (now the *Navigation Protection Act*), *Species at Risk Act,* and *Canadian Environmental Assessment Act*
- eliminating the National Round Table on the Environment and the Economy
- preventing government scientists from speaking to the media
- attacking environmental groups and seeking to revoke their charitable status
- cancelling thousands of environmental assessments
- reducing environmental protection budgets by hundreds of millions of dollars.[35]

Once internationally renowned as an environmental leader, Canada "is now a laggard in both policy innovation and environmental performance, known for inaction and obstruction."[36] Canada built a strong reputation over decades by demonstrating leadership on issues such as acid rain, ozone depletion, protection of the Arctic, and rules governing the world's oceans. As recently as the early 1990s, it was the first industrialized nation to ratify the United Nations Convention on Biological Diversity and the United Nations Framework Convention on Climate Change. Today Canada is an international environmental law outcast. For years, we have garnered countless "fossil of the day," "Colossal Fossil," and Dodo awards for blocking progress at international negotiations on climate change and biodiversity. In 2012, Canada became the only country in the world to turn its back on legal obligations under the Kyoto Protocol. In 2013, Canada became the only country in the world to withdraw from the United Nations Convention to

Combat Desertification. Despite the call of the World Health Organization (WHO) for an end to all uses of asbestos, Canada has repeatedly blocked proposals to add asbestos to the Rotterdam Convention, an international agreement that regulates trade in hazardous substances.[37] Global leaders, including Ban Ki-moon (UN secretary-general), José Manuel Barroso (former president of the European Commission), and Rajendra Pachauri (former chair of the Intergovernmental Panel on Climate Change), have criticized Canada's failure to live up to expectations in protecting the environment.[38]

Canada's Health Care Record

Just as Canadians are deeply proud of our beautiful natural environment, we also revere our health care system. However, despite universal access to health care and dedicated, highly skilled medical professionals, the health of Canadians also falls below expectations. According to the Conference Board of Canada, Canada ranks tenth out of seventeen wealthy industrialized countries on health performance, trailing environmental leaders such as Sweden, Norway, and France. Among the indicators where Canada's performance lags behind are mortality due to cancer and mortality due to diabetes, both of which are related to environmental risk factors. One in two Canadians suffers from a chronic disease, ranging from asthma to heart disease to cancer.[39]

To make matters worse, current and projected levels of spending on health care are unsustainable. The total spent by Canadians on health care is well over $200 billion annually, and these costs are rising much faster than rates of inflation or economic growth. The C.D. Howe Institute has warned that unless dramatic changes are made, health care spending could rise to 18.7 percent of GDP by 2031, crowding out spending on other government services, forcing tax increases, necessitating user fees, or decreasing the quality of services provided by the medical system.[40] Experts warn that cutting environmental budgets to fund health care will have the perverse effect of further increasing future health care costs.[41]

Canada has historically treated environmental protection and health care as separate issues, yet, as this book will demonstrate, such an approach is neither scientifically nor economically defensible. In Europe, this understanding has already taken hold: "The current, predominantly hazard-focused and compartmentalised approach to environment and health is insufficient to address interconnected and interdependent challenges, such as climate change, depletion of resources, ecosystem degradation, the obesity epidemic, and persistent social inequality."[42]

Public Concerns about Health Care and the Environment

Opinion polls conducted in Canada often identify health care as the public's top priority and a cornerstone of this country's identity.[43] Although proud of the Medicare system created in the 1960s, the majority of Canadians lack confidence in the system and believe it needs either complete rebuilding or major repairs.[44] Canadians are also profoundly worried about the state of the environment, particularly air pollution, contaminated drinking water, and toxic chemicals.[45] Most Canadians connect the dots, expressing concern that environmental degradation is harming their health, their children's health, and their grandchildren's health. The majority of both the public and health care professionals expect that the impacts of pollution, climate change, urban sprawl, and resource depletion will become more severe in the future.[46] A study of Canadians' risk perceptions found that the percentage of Canadians ranking air pollution as a "high health risk" has risen dramatically, with almost 90 percent describing air pollution as either a high or moderate health risk.[47] A poll conducted by the Canadian Medical Association (CMA) to explore public perceptions of environmental health issues found that 88 percent of Canadians were very or somewhat concerned about the potential health effects associated with inadequate inspection and monitoring of food. The CMA survey also found that:

- 82 percent of Canadians are concerned that climate change will hasten the spread of diseases.
- 75 percent are concerned about the health effects of pesticides and herbicides.
- More than one in four Canadians reported that they or a family member had sought medical treatment for an environmentally related health condition, including cancer, asthma, and other respiratory illnesses.[48]

In summary, opinion polls indicate that the environment has become one of the over-riding concerns of Canadians. Not surprisingly, most Canadians support stronger environmental laws and policies.[49]

Health care professionals share the public's concerns about environmental hazards in air, water, and food.[50] Among the expert bodies calling for greater attention and resources to be allocated to environmental health in Canada are the National Advisory Committee on SARS and Public Health, the Royal Society of Canada, the Public Health Agency of Canada, the National Round Table on the Environment and the Economy, the Commissioner of the Environment and Sustainable Development, the Canadian

Institute of Public Health Inspectors, the World Health Organization, and the Commission on the Future of Health Care in Canada.[51] A report on children's health in Canada commissioned by the federal minister of health highlighted the need to take action to protect children from environmental hazards, stating that "the physical environment – air, water, soil – all have a significant impact on the health of Canadian children and youth."[52] The Canadian Cancer Society, Canadian Lung Association, Canadian Heart and Stroke Foundation, and Canadian Public Health Association have urged governments to enact stronger laws and policies in order to reduce environmental risks.[53] A few academics, industry representatives, and conservative think tanks argue that public concerns about environmental health are overblown;[54] however, the majority of experts agree that Canadians have good reason to be concerned.

Despite high levels of public and professional concern, Canadian policymakers and pundits have neglected environmental health issues. Back in 1974, the federal government published a paper on the future of health care in Canada that was widely regarded as revolutionary for its focus on health promotion, particularly its emphasis on the importance of environmental determinants of health, including air and water pollution.[55] The Lalonde report received national and international acclaim for its forward-thinking approach to health promotion, yet for forty years Canada has effectively ignored one of its central premises: the importance of protecting the environment in achieving progress towards healthy Canadians. In 2004, thirty years after that landmark report, Canada's minister of state for public health released a discussion paper on strengthening the Canadian health care system that did not even mention environmental health.[56] Jeffrey Simpson's award-winning book *Chronic Condition*, published in 2012, explored the challenges facing the Canadian health care system but completely ignored environmental factors.[57] Similarly, a 2013 report by the Canadian Institute for Health Information (CIHI) on the drivers of rising health care costs made no reference to the environment.[58]

Defining Key Terms

Before going any further, it is essential to clarify what this book means when it uses the word "environment" and the phrase "environmental health." The failure to clearly define these terms has contributed to public misunderstanding and, in some cases, exaggerated fears about the connection between the environment and human health. The word "environment" can be defined in extremely broad terms, as illustrated by the International Epidemiological

Association: "all that which is external to the human host. Can be divided into physical, biological, social, cultural, etc., any or all of which can influence health status of populations."[59] As an example of the misunderstanding caused by this broad definition, it has been stated that at least 90 percent of cancer cases are a result of environmental factors.[60] In one sense this statement is accurate, while from another perspective it is misleading. Medical studies indicate that less than 10 percent of cancers are caused exclusively by genetic factors unique to specific individuals. In this specific context, the remaining 90 percent of cancers are described as caused by "environmental" factors, referring to all factors outside of individual genetic characteristics, such as fitness, diet, lifestyle, occupation, and socio-economic status.[61] This broad, all-encompassing definition is at odds with the narrower, conventional understanding of environmental factors, such as the definition used by the World Health Organization, in its pioneering work on environmental causes of disease: "The environment is all the physical, biological, and chemical factors external to the human host and all related behaviors, excluding those natural environments that cannot reasonably be modified."[62]

Using this narrower definition, which the public is more likely to understand, the proportion of cancer caused by environmental factors is much lower. This definition excludes factors such as genetics and culture while focusing attention on those areas where interventions can reasonably be expected to prevent or reduce mortality and illness. For these reasons, this book relies on the WHO's definition of environment. Included are contaminants in air, water, food, and consumer products, as well as radiation, noise, the impacts of built environments (housing, roads, land-use patterns), anthropogenic climate and ecosystem change, and agricultural methods. Excluded are the health effects of alcohol and tobacco consumption (except for second-hand smoke, which involves involuntary exposure), and natural disasters unmediated by human intervention.

When the phrase "environmental health" is mentioned, people may be inclined to think about the state of the environment itself, but the phrase is intended to describe the relationship between the environment and human health. The definition used by Health Canada is relied upon in this book:

> Environmental health comprises those aspects of human health, disease, injury, and wellbeing that are determined by chemical, physical, and biological factors in the environment. It includes the effects on health of the broad physical environment and related socio-economic factors. It also includes the professional practice of assessing, correcting, controlling, and

preventing environmental risks and promoting the benefits for individuals and communities.[63]

The WHO adds that environmental health is intended to address both present and future generations.[64] Thus it includes not only pollution but also the adverse health effects arising from poor urban design, human destruction and manipulation of natural ecological systems, and naturally occurring hazards such as pathogens in drinking water or radon in buildings. For example, there is evidence that urban sprawl is associated with increased Body Mass Index (an indication of obesity and its attendant health problems).[65] The recent emergence of infectious zoonotic diseases such as Ebola, West Nile virus, hantavirus pulmonary syndrome, Lyme disease, SARS (severe acute respiratory syndrome), HIV/AIDS, variant Creutzfeldt-Jakob disease (the human version of mad cow disease), and avian influenza is also incorporated in this approach to environmental health, since these diseases are influenced by anthropogenic changes to the natural environment.[66] The rise of antibiotic resistance, caused in part by excessive application of antibiotics to livestock to accelerate growth rather than treat infections, is also included.

On a brighter note, the definition of environmental health used in this book also incorporates the health benefits available from nature, such as the valuable goods and services provided by biodiversity and the health-enhancing aspects of time spent in parks, gardens, and other green spaces.[67] Not only our physical health but also our psychological health is intimately connected to the state of the environment.[68]

An Overview of the Book
The goal of this book is to comprehensively explore the landscape of environmental health in Canada, overcoming the current balkanization of information and expertise. The book strives to answer four overarching questions: What are the most serious environmental health problems in Canada? What are the economic costs of these problems? Compared with other wealthy countries, are Canada's current laws, policies, and programs adequate for reducing or minimizing the environmental burden of disease and death? What kinds of interventions – laws, policies, programs, and investments – might be introduced to reduce environmental risks, costs, and inequities in Canada? To answer these questions, this book has three parts – an examination, a diagnosis, and a prescription – similar to the three stages a doctor goes through when a patient comes in for a check-up.

Examination

Chapter 2 provides an overview of the environmental hazards – chemical, biological, and physical – that contribute to death and illness in Canada. This overview covers the full range of environmental hazards, including air pollution (outdoor and indoor), water contamination, industrial chemicals, heavy metals, pesticides, noise, radiation, consumer products, and zoonoses (diseases transmitted from other animals to humans), as well as related processes such as climate change, ozone depletion, urban sprawl, and declining native biodiversity. Chapter 2 also describes humans' fundamental dependence upon the natural world and the health benefits associated with access to ecosystem goods and services. In Chapter 3, the best available evidence is reviewed in an effort to estimate the magnitude of adverse health effects in Canada attributable to environmental hazards. How many Canadians are dying, falling ill, or becoming injured or disabled each year as a result of exposure to environmental hazards? While there are compelling reasons to be concerned about environmental impacts on health, it is important not to create unwarranted levels of concern. Other risk factors, including smoking, diet, fitness, lifestyle, and occupation, are also important determinants of health on a population-wide basis. Other significant influences include culture, income and social status, access to health and social services, education, social support networks, genetics, and personal health practices.

Chapter 4 explores the concept of environmental justice, addressing the distribution of environmental harms and benefits. Are specific Canadian communities bearing a disproportionate share of the burden of environmental risks or being denied fair access to environmental benefits? Although environmental justice has been extensively researched and debated in the United States, it is only beginning to attract attention from affected communities, activists, academics, and policymakers in Canada. Chapter 5 estimates the economic costs of the environmental burden of disease in Canada. These economic costs include the direct costs of medical care, the indirect costs caused by productivity losses, and the costs associated with premature mortality.

The results of this examination are deeply worrisome. The environmental burden of disease in Canada is much higher than generally recognized, causing thousands of premature deaths and millions of illnesses annually. To make matters worse, these harms are unfairly distributed, falling disproportionately on communities that are already economically or socially marginalized, including Aboriginal people. The economic costs resulting from the environmental burden of disease, calculated using the government's own methods, exceed $100 billion annually.

Diagnosis

Part 2 analyzes the Canadian laws and policies that are intended to prevent adverse health effects caused by environmental hazards. It seeks to answer the following questions:

- Are Canadian health and environmental laws and policies stronger or weaker than corresponding laws and policies in other wealthy nations?
- Are there successful laws, policies, and programs in other nations that have no comparable equivalents in Canada?
- Is there evidence that specific types of laws, policies, and programs are more effective in protecting human health from environmental hazards?
- Is Canada ahead of, on par with, or behind other industrialized nations in protecting its citizens from environmental threats to their health?

Chapter 6 begins the diagnosis by looking at macro-level law and policy considerations, including recognition of the right to live in a healthy environment, national environmental health policies, children's environmental health strategies, and international environmental health policies. It also identifies several crucial knowledge gaps that constrain informed policy responses to environmental health problems in Canada, including missing information about:

- the prevalence and distribution of environmental hazards
- the exposure of Canadians to environmental hazards
- the connections between exposures and adverse health outcomes
- the effectiveness of environmental health laws, policies, and programs.

Chapter 7 compares Canadian laws, policies, and standards governing air quality (indoor and outdoor), drinking water, food, consumer products, climate change, and biodiversity with environmental rules in other industrialized nations, including the United States, Europe, and Australia. These comparisons also incorporate World Health Organization recommendations. Specific case studies investigate ambient air quality standards; drinking water quality standards; pesticide registrations; maximum residue limits for pesticides on food; the regulation of five toxic substances, including chemicals that are known carcinogens and endocrine disruptors; climate change laws and regulations; and laws protecting endangered species. Chapter 8 explores the extent to which Canada is implementing the polluter-pays principle and enforcing environmental laws, again in comparison with other wealthy industrialized countries. Part 2 concludes (in Chapter 9) by probing the reasons for differences in Canada's performance vis-à-vis other industrialized nations in addressing the health risks associated with environmental hazards. Among the factors examined are political and legal institutions (including constitutional factors and national styles of regulation), culture, societal actors, and framing (the social construction of environmental health issues).

Again, the results of the comparative analysis are a source of major concern. From every perspective, the Canadian environmental laws and policies intended to protect human health lag behind those of other wealthy industrialized nations. This relative weakness applies to systemic issues such as Canada's refusal to recognize the fundamental human right to live in a healthy environment and the lack of a national environmental health strategy. It also reveals that Canada has weaker air quality guidelines and weaker drinking water guidelines, permits the use of pesticides not authorized in Europe, allows higher levels of pesticide residues, either fails to impose environmental taxes or does so at substantially lower levels, and is reluctant to enforce environmental laws rigorously. Many of these failures appear linked to an economic world-view that is outdated and unduly narrow, focused on natural resource extraction while overlooking health and environmental costs and the potential of a shift towards a green economy.

Prescription

Part 3 draws on international innovations, best practices, and success stories to chart a future course for environmental health law and policy in Canada. The concluding chapters offer a suite of recommendations intended to close existing knowledge gaps and remedy the Canadian legal and policy weaknesses identified in Part 2. Implementing these solutions will increase the health benefits provided by nature; prevent or reduce the adverse health effects of exposure to physical, chemical, and biological hazards; identify and ameliorate environmental injustices; and reduce the economic costs of environment-related illness and death. Key areas of recommendations include:

• making strategic investments in environmental health research, capacity building, knowledge exchange, and education

- developing a comprehensive national environmental health action plan that includes targets, timelines, measurable indicators, and improved surveillance of environmental hazards, exposures, and illnesses
- articulating principles, including the right to a healthy environment, to guide the implementation and enforcement of new and improved laws and regulations to reduce risks, particularly for vulnerable populations
- addressing the underlying causes of Canada's relatively poor environmental record
- ensuring that Canada plays a positive role in promoting and protecting environmental health internationally.

The recommendations in this book, based largely on proven solutions, are intended to provide Canadians with a level of protection for their health that is consistent with the highest standards found in other industrialized (i.e., OECD) nations. Based on both Canadian and international experiences with strengthening environmental laws, policies, and standards, doing so would almost certainly result in economic benefits that far outweigh the costs.

Conclusion

Two aspects of the relationship between human health and the environment should inspire optimism. First, the health benefits provided by ecosystems and access to nature can be systematically increased through strengthened laws, policies, and programs. Second, adverse environmental impacts on human health are almost entirely preventable, meaning Canada could not only reduce but virtually eliminate the majority of environmental threats to human health. Prevention is more effective because it addresses populations instead of individuals, more efficient because it is less costly than post-facto treatment or restoration, and more equitable because it reduces the heightened risks facing disadvantaged groups. Investing in a more preventive and precautionary approach is the only way that Canada will be able to afford its universal health care system in the future and eventually achieve its official health goal:

Canada is a country where:
The air we breathe, the water we drink, the food we eat, and the places we live, work and play are safe and healthy – now and for generations to come.[69]

2

Environmental Influences on
Human Health

There are many more factors that affect your health than can
be cured by a medical prescription from a doctor or even a
policy prescription from a health minister ... A clean and safe
environment is vital. Contaminants in our air, water, food, and
soil can cause everything from cancer to birth defects, to
respiratory illness and gastrointestinal ailments.

– ROY ROMANOW, CHAIR, COMMISSION ON THE
FUTURE OF HEALTH CARE IN CANADA (2003)

Discussions about the relationship between human health and the environment often emphasize the risks of pollution and toxic chemicals, while
ignoring the vital and immense benefits that healthy ecosystems provide.
Healthy environments offer clean air, safe water, and fertile soil for growing
food, which are indispensable for life and human well-being. Healthy and
diverse ecosystems provide irreplaceable services, including climate stability, pollination, and pest control. Spending time in or near natural settings
offers people both physical and psychological health benefits. Built environments that promote walking, cycling, and access to green space also have
substantial health advantages.

On the other hand, the environments where Canadians live, work, study,
and play can have negative influences on health. Adverse effects can be

caused by exposure to air pollution (indoor and outdoor), contaminated food and water, zoonotic diseases, toxic substances in consumer products, noise, and radiation. The built environment, from buildings to urban design, can also have adverse effects. Modern society's separation from Nature causes emotional and psychological harm, especially to children.

In some cases, the science connecting environmental hazards to human health consequences is clear. For example, it is known beyond a reasonable doubt that air pollution causes respiratory illness, cardiovascular disease, and cancer. However, varying degrees of uncertainty surround the relationship between other environmental risk factors and human health, such as the long-term consequences of exposure to toxic substances while in the womb or the connection between pesticides and Parkinson's disease. This chapter summarizes the state of the latest scientific evidence about the entire spectrum of environmental influences on our health.

The Health Benefits of Healthy Ecosystems

Ecosystems are natural assemblages of interconnected life forms, their environments, and associated interactions. Processes such as pollination, water filtration, and oxygen generation are referred to as ecosystem services. While often overlooked, ecosystem health is actually a cornerstone of human health and well-being.[1] There are four classes of human health benefits provided by ecosystems: basic needs such as clean air, clean water, and food; medical and genetic resources for preventing and curing disease; biological controls, which limit the spread of disease; and maintenance of mental health.[2] Because of the irreplaceable nature of ecosystems and the services they provide, protecting ecosystems is "an essential part of the survival strategy for human societies."[3]

Meeting Basic Human Needs

Oxygen is fundamental to life, constitutes approximately 21 percent of the atmosphere, and is part of a biogeochemical cycle in which it moves between the atmosphere, the biosphere, and the lithosphere. The supply of oxygen in the atmosphere is constantly replenished by ecological processes, primarily photosynthesis by plants on land and phytoplankton in the ocean. Ecosystems remove pollutants from the air, improving air quality.[4] For example, plants capture a variety of particulates from atmospheric pollution and transform polluting compounds, such as nitric oxide, into harmless ones.[5] Plants also play an essential role in the global carbon cycle by absorbing carbon dioxide.

Humans are equally dependent on water, which plays a vital role in countless physiological functions and comprises roughly 70 percent of a person's body, ranging from 33 percent of bones to 85 percent of the brain. The natural world is the source of all water consumed by humans, even if it does seem to magically flow from taps. Canadians rely on a combination of surface water (e.g., rivers and lakes) and groundwater for household uses, agriculture, industry, and electricity generation. Hydrological cycles can replenish these supplies, unless humans divert, consume, or contaminate excessive volumes of water. Ecosystems filter pollutants out of water and transform harmful substances into benign or less toxic materials. Vascular plants have the ability to concentrate toxic elements – including pesticides, medicines, industrial chemicals, and household cleaners – in ways that are not harmful to the plant but that clean up and restore contaminated areas. The extent of this phytoremediation service is significant. For example, rain in New England delivers an average of eight pounds of nitrogen annually per acre, creating a risk of eutrophication in downstream water bodies, but healthy forests remove 90 percent of the nitrogen.[6]

The timing of water flows is also important for human health. Extreme water flow events are associated with waterborne disease outbreaks. Analysis of fifty years of US data revealed that 68 percent of waterborne disease outbreaks followed precipitation events with flows above the 80th percentile.[7] Ecosystems play an important role in regulating water flows. Forests and riparian buffers, for example, allow surface water to infiltrate and become groundwater, which increases the predictability of water availability by reducing peak flows and increasing base flows.[8]

Food is the renewable energy that powers humans, providing all of the necessary nutrients – carbohydrates, proteins, vitamins, essential fatty acids, trace elements, and roughage (the indigestible components of plants). One of the most direct connections between ecosystem services and human health is the provision of food. Terrestrial food production relies upon a suite of ecosystem services, including "soil formation, biodiversity as a source of new crop varieties, pollination, pest control, climate regulation, water supply, and nitrogen fixation."[9] For example, naturally pollinated crops provide approximately one-third of the calories consumed by humans. In places where pollinators have become extinct, such as along the China-Nepal border, pollination has to be carried out by hand – a task that can take twenty to twenty-five people to accomplish the work of two bee colonies.[10] Fish contribute over 20 percent of animal protein intake for 2.6 billion people, but scientists are deeply worried about overfishing.[11]

Preventing and Curing Disease

In addition to meeting basic human needs, ecosystems also play an essential role in preventing and curing disease. Billions of years of evolution have provided de facto clinical trials on an incalculable number of substances, so that the natural world is akin to a pharmaceutical treasure trove. Plants and animals have been the most significant source of medicines in history.[12] In the developing world, as much as 80 percent of medicines come from Nature, while globally more than 50 percent of all prescription drugs are derived from natural products.[13] Traditional medicines have often provided leads to modern researchers.[14] For example, ginkgo has been used in China for centuries to treat many conditions, including asthma, diarrhea, and tuberculosis. Today ginkgo extracts are being studied for their potential to treat high-altitude sickness, tinnitus, depression, and dementia.[15]

Examples are legion. Aspirin is derived from white willow.[16] The antimalarial drug quinine comes from the bark of cinchona trees, while the anticancer drug taxol comes from the bark of Pacific yew trees.[17] An endangered plant called the Madagascar periwinkle is the source of one of the most effective chemotherapy drugs available. Remarkably, less than 1 percent of known plants have been fully analyzed for their potential to provide pharmacological benefits.[18]

Animals also provide medical science with critical insights and novel compounds. Medicinal leeches have been used for at least three thousand years and continue to be important to surgeons reattaching severed body parts and undertaking breast reconstructive therapy.[19] Naturally occurring toxins, such as snake venoms, are being explored for their anticancer potential.[20] The compounds responsible for bears' ability to maintain and grow bone mass while hibernating may lead to treatments and preventive measures for osteoporosis.[21] The ability of bears to transition from ravenous feeding to fasting may lead to new treatments for diabetes and obesity.[22] Amphibians possess a wide array of compounds, developed to defend against predators, that may have important medical uses. An alkaloid toxin from the Ecuadorian poison frog has been synthesized into a painkiller two hundred times more potent than morphine.[23] Antimicrobial peptides from another frog may be able to protect HIV/AIDS sufferers from certain life-threatening infections, and a sticky "frog glue" from another species may provide a strong and flexible adhesive for binding human tissues in surgical repairs of torn cartilage.[24]

Humans are just beginning to tap the immense pharmaceutical potential of marine ecosystems, which are home to tremendous biodiversity. For example, seven hundred species of cone snails are a source of approximately 70,000–140,000 different peptide toxins, but only about one hundred toxins have been studied in detail.[25] One of these, ziconotide, is a painkiller that is a thousand times more potent than morphine but does not result in addiction or tolerance.[26] Using these drugs for pain therapy has been called "a watershed in the history of pain management," and they may also be effective in treating head injuries and strokes, amyotrophic lateral sclerosis (Lou Gehrig's disease), spinal cord injury, urinary incontinence, and cardiac arrhythmias.[27]

Microbes are the most diverse organism on Earth and may be an important source of future pharmaceuticals. While over 99 percent of microbial flora have yet to be investigated, the small number studied thus far have yielded important medications, including penicillin, tetracycline antibiotics, doxorubicin (used for treating breast and ovarian cancers), and statins (used for treating high cholesterol).[28] A type of bacterium discovered by a Canadian scientific expedition to Easter Island in 1964 is the source of the drug sirolimus, also known as rapamycin, which has "revolutionized the treatment of solid organ transplant rejection."[29] Based on past successes, the millions of microbial species hold hope for significant discoveries.[30]

However, when a species becomes extinct, its potential for human medicine is lost forever. That is precisely what happened with gastric brooding frogs, a remarkable species that was found only in undisturbed Australian rainforests. Female gastric brooding frogs swallowed their fertilized eggs, which hatched, grew into fully developed tadpoles, and then were vomited out into the world. Scientists believe that the tadpoles secreted a substance that prevented them from being digested by their mothers. This substance could have provided insights into treating peptic ulcers, an illness afflicting tens of millions of people. Sadly, gastric brooding frogs are now believed to be extinct.[31]

Humans also rely extensively on other species for biomedical research. Many of the basic building blocks – molecules, cells, tissues, organs – of diverse and disparate species are so similar that they can be used to better understand human physiology. Humans share hundreds of our estimated twenty-five thousand genes with bacteria, thousands with yeasts, almost half our genes with fruit flies, and even more with the common mouse. Examples of medical developments based upon animal research include anesthetics, antibiotics, vaccines, blood transfusions, and kidney dialysis.

Biological Controls

Many of the diseases that afflict humans are caused by other living organisms, including influenza, malaria, West Nile virus, dengue fever, and Lyme disease. Some species act as reservoirs for infectious pathogens, while other species act as vectors, transferring pathogens from one species to another. For example, Lyme disease is caused by bacteria transmitted from a variety of vertebrate species (predominantly white-footed mice) to humans through the bites of black-legged ticks. Biological controls – predators, parasites, pathogens, and noninfective competitors to the reservoirs and vectors – serve to limit the transfer of infectious diseases, often by reducing their populations.

In order to maximize the human health benefits of infectious disease prevention through biological controls, healthy ecosystems are vital. Higher levels of native bird diversity are strongly associated with lower levels of West Nile virus prevalence in both humans and mosquitoes.[32] This is because native birds are poor hosts for some strains of the virus, while introduced birds are often better hosts, exacerbating the spread of the disease. Lyme disease, spread by tick bites, is a growing public health problem in Canada. Canadians are more likely to be infected with Lyme disease in logged forests and suburbs than in undisturbed forests.[33]

Maintaining and Restoring Mental Health

The natural environment can have beneficial effects on mental health, which is of great importance given that mental disorders are projected to account for 15 percent of the global burden of disease by 2020.[34] The World Health Organization reports that depression is the leading cause of disability worldwide.[35] Researchers have found that regular use of natural environments for physical activity is associated with a lower risk of poor mental health.[36] For example, research conducted in Toronto demonstrated a strong connection between natural areas and good mental health.[37] Interaction with nature has been shown to increase self-esteem and mood, reduce anger, and improve overall psychological well-being.[38]

There is extensive evidence that interacting with nature can improve cognitive function.[39] Exposure to nature improves performance on a range of mental tests, improves our capacity to concentrate, and increases workplace performance.[40] Nature's capacity to reduce mental fatigue appears to increase with greater species richness in green spaces.[41] Prolonged wilderness experiences restore cognitive performance, and camping trips reduce the probability of substance abuse relapse.[42]

Nature can ameliorate some of the negative psychological stressors associated with urban living.[43] Greener environments reduce aggressive behaviour and violence.[44] Spending time in natural settings can also reduce anxiety, stress, sadness, and depression.[45] Conversely, an individual's perceived stress levels increase as the amount of local green space decreases.[46] Nature in communities also assists in establishing a sense of belonging for residents: people in less green environments are more likely to report feelings of loneliness and lack of adequate social support.[47] When people experience loss, green spaces help with psychological recovery and maintaining resilience.[48]

Nature also offers a powerful boost to our mood and self-esteem. Time spent in forests, for example, may help cure burnout and depression.[49] People with views of natural settings from their office windows report greater job satisfaction, and those with views of nature from their home (or even prison cell) report greater life satisfaction.[50] Exercise in green settings, especially those that include water, has been shown to improve self-esteem and mood.[51] Negative emotions, such as anger, fatigue, and sadness, are reduced more through exercise in a natural environment than through exercise in an indoor environment.[52]

Children's psychological, cognitive, and emotional health benefit from contact with nature.[53] Nature offers settings for unstructured play and exploration, fostering imagination and creativity and contributing to healthy brain development.[54] Nature helps children moderate the impact of life stresses.[55] Children with regular access to green environments are more emotionally resilient.[56] Spending time in nature can be as effective as widely prescribed medications in treating attention deficit hyperactivity disorder (ADHD).[57] A growing number of studies suggest that "contact with nature is as important to children as good nutrition and adequate sleep."[58]

Climate change has a direct effect on mental health through extreme weather events and impacts on the underlying social, economic, and environmental determinants of mental health.[59] Disruptions driven by climate change can undermine mental health in a variety of ways: people may suffer post-traumatic stress disorder after a natural disaster, psychological consequences follow extreme heat and drought, and significant stress is associated with the need to relocate.[60] Mental health and well-being are negatively affected by the loss of a "sense of place" felt by flood victims.[61] The mere awareness of the threat of climate change can create distress and anxiety.[62]

One report estimated that millions of Americans will suffer serious psychological harm related to climate change in the coming years.[63]

All of the foregoing evidence underscores the fundamental importance for human health and well-being of protecting biodiversity, maintaining healthy ecosystems, and ensuring that everyone has access to green spaces.

Environmental Hazards

Canadians are exposed to environmental hazards through the pathways of inhalation, ingestion, and direct contact. Exposure also occurs in utero, when fetuses absorb toxic substances to which their mothers have been exposed. Many harmful substances – including heavy metals, flame retardants, and pesticides – can penetrate the protection offered by the placenta and enter the unborn child.[64] Billions of kilograms of toxic chemicals – including known carcinogens, endocrine disruptors, and chemicals that harm respiratory health, cardiovascular health, and neurological development – are discharged into Canadian air, water, and land by industry each and every year.[65] Industrial chemicals spewed into the Canadian environment in large quantities include arsenic, cadmium, formaldehyde, toluene, and xylene. Every Canadian has a chemical body burden that includes flame retardants, phthalates, heavy metals, pesticide residues, stain repellents, and hundreds of other toxic substances.

Environmental hazards can be grouped into four broad categories: chemical, biological, physical, and psychosocial.[66] Although these environmental hazards will be dealt with individually, it is imperative to understand that their impacts are cumulative and potentially synergistic or interactive. Adverse health effects can occur as a result of single or multiple exposures to toxic substances. A single exposure to food contaminated with pathogens may result in gastrointestinal illness. Children may be exposed to multiple sources of lead through various routes, including juice or drinking water, food, paint in older homes, consumer products, and air contaminated with lead dust, potentially resulting in harmful effects on development.[67] A recent study conducted in Ottawa found that indoor lead levels were far higher than soil concentrations and that indoor dust is a major source of lead exposure for children.[68]

Chemical hazards are generally categorized as organic or inorganic (a completely different meaning from organic in the agricultural context). Organic chemicals are hydrocarbons (combinations of carbon and hydrogen) and substituted hydrocarbons (carbon and hydrogen combined with other elements). Inorganic chemicals include both metallic (e.g., lead, cadmium) and nonmetallic elements (e.g., nitrogen, phosphorus). Chemical hazards include pesticides, heavy metals, the air pollutants that make up smog, and the vast number of toxic substances produced by industry.[69] Examples range from lead, recognized as a toxic substance for many centuries, to nanoparticles, a twenty-first-century development discussed later in this chapter. Of particular concern are toxic chemicals that are persistent and bioaccumulative. "Persistent" means that a substance breaks down slowly or not at all in the environment. "Bioaccumulative" means that a substance builds up in the environment and ultimately in the bodies of living organisms, including humans. Some industrial chemicals are deliberately engineered so that they cannot be broken down or metabolized. Persistent and bioaccumulative substances are problematic from a health perspective because they can become widely dispersed across ecosystems before working their way up the food chain and into humans. Examples include hexachlorobenzene, polychlorinated biphenyls (PCBs), perfluorochemicals (PFCs), and polybrominated diphenyl ethers (PBDEs). Other major concerns are chemicals that cause cancer or disrupt normal neurological development.[70]

Lead exposure can cause a range of chronic health impacts, affecting children, menopausal women, and the elderly. Among children, lead exposure, even in minuscule quantities, can cause developmental delays, hypertension, impaired hearing, ADHD, reduced intelligence, and learning disabilities.[71] Large decreases in children's IQ occur at low levels of lead exposure, with decreases levelling off at higher levels of exposure.[72] Evidence is accumulating about the dangers posed by lead to adults, particularly menopausal women and the elderly.[73] As bones become thinner with age, lead is released into the blood, contributing to an array of negative health effects, including cataracts, Alzheimer's and Parkinson's diseases and other forms of dementia, high blood pressure, cardiovascular disease, and impaired kidney function. Medical experts now recognize that harmful health effects may occur at blood lead levels so low that there is no safe level of exposure.[74] The health effects of lead may be exacerbated by exposure to other toxic substances and vice versa, although little is known about these interactive effects.

Consumer products can pose a wide variety of health hazards. Thousands of chemicals are used in a dizzying array of ordinary household items, including cleaning products, cosmetics, paints, plastics, furniture, building materials, computer equipment, and more. Examples include bisphenol A, used in water bottles, linings for tin cans, and myriad plastic products; di(2-ethylhexyl) phthalate (DEHP), used in perfumes and hair sprays;

and cyclotetrasiloxane, an ingredient used in lip balm. Ordinary consumer products – laundry soaps, nail polish, air fresheners, hair spray, perfumes, oral contraceptives, toilet cleaners, mothballs, paint strippers, and tile cleaners – may contain carcinogens.[75]

Nanotechnology involves the manipulation of matter at the atomic or molecular level, on a scale of less than 100 nanometres. To put this in perspective, there are a billion nanometres in a metre, and a single sheet of paper is 100,000 nanometres thick. Proponents of nanotechnology envision cameras flowing through your bloodstream to identify constrictions or blockages; supercomputers the size of a grain of salt with unprecedented speed, memory, and power; limitless, pollution-free energy; and bulletproof clothing the thickness of spandex. Engineered nanomaterials can be made from almost any substance and offer a range of useful properties, including conductivity, strength, durability, reactivity, and reliability. In terms of health implications, knowledge gaps – in toxicology, epidemiology, and occupational health and safety – dwarf current understanding. However, early warning signs exist and levels of exposure are increasing due to the proliferation of products. Nanoparticles can be inhaled, ingested, or absorbed through the skin. They can enter the bloodstream and be transported to the brain, spleen, liver, kidneys, and heart. Scientists have observed respiratory disease, cardiovascular disease, and cancer in laboratory animals exposed to nanoparticles.[76] Damage to DNA in other species raises concerns about genotoxicity and cancer in humans.[77] Researchers anticipate that engineered nanoparticles are likely to have effects similar to those resulting from exposure to ultrafine particles in air pollution, which can cause respiratory illness, lung cancer, heart disease, and premature mortality. Nanotechnology has already emerged from research laboratories around the world and is being used in hundreds of consumer products ranging from cell phones to sunscreen.

Another area of increasing health concern involves endocrine disruptors, a class of chemicals that imitate or block hormones. Exposure to endocrine disruptors can result in reproductive and neurodevelopmental problems such as infertility and reduced intelligence.[78] Hundreds of industrial chemicals have been associated with endocrine-disrupting effects, including some metals (cadmium, lead, mercury, aluminum), phenolic derivatives (phenol, bisphenol A, pentachlorophenol), phthalates, substituted benzenes (e.g., benzo[a]pyrene), styrenes, carbon disulphide, dioxin, and several organochlorine pesticides, fungicides, and herbicides.[79] One of the bedevilling attributes of endocrine-disrupting chemicals is that health impacts can occur at extremely low doses, previously assumed to be safe. For example, scientists have identified negative health impacts of bisphenol A, methoxychlor, and atrazine at exposures well below the levels previously regarded by regulators as the "no effect" levels.[80] A 2013 report by the World Health Organization and the United Nations Environment Programme identified a burgeoning body of evidence demonstrating that maternal, fetal, and childhood exposure to chemical pollutants plays a larger role than previously believed in causing many endocrine diseases and disorders of the thyroid gland and the immune, digestive, cardiovascular, reproductive, and metabolic systems (including childhood obesity and diabetes).[81]

New research suggests that exposure to toxic chemicals, particularly those that disrupt the endocrine system, can have profound effects not only on individuals but also on future generations. Instead of damaging or altering genes, these chemicals can change the way genes are expressed (translated into proteins). Epigenetics is the study of how chemical alterations to the DNA either facilitate or prevent the DNA's instructions from being read and implemented. Computers provide a useful analogy. Genes, or the human genome, are analogous to the computer's hardware, whereas the epigenome is like the software. In addition to affecting the DNA structure (hardware), environmental exposures can affect the software – how genes express themselves.[82] A concrete example uncovered by researchers involves transplacental exposure to traffic-related polycyclic aromatic hydrocarbons (PAHs). The children of mothers exposed to elevated levels of PAHs experienced aberrant DNA methylation patterns, leading to the silencing of specific genes potentially linked to asthma susceptibility.[83] Even more startling, experiments with mice show that once a protein called HOXA9, which plays a critical role in suppressing breast tumour growth and metastasis, is down-regulated in a mouse, it stays turned off in the offspring of those mice, making future generations of mice more vulnerable to breast cancer.[84]

Biological hazards are pathogenic organisms (e.g., bacteria, viruses, fungi, protozoa, prions) that, if introduced into the human body, may disrupt biochemical and physiological functions. Zoonoses, or diseases transmitted from other animals to humans, involve biological agents. Examples include anthrax, brucellosis, Ebola, Marburg, rabies, salmonellosis, trichinosis, bovine tuberculosis, tularemia, and ringworm. Many ecological factors contribute to the emergence of zoonotic diseases, such as mutation, natural selection, individual host determinants (e.g., acquired immunity and physiological factors), and host population factors (behavioural, societal, and transport). However, human influences are also a major factor, particularly the burgeoning human population, the explosive growth in livestock numbers, the resulting large numbers of people and animals living in close proximity, damage and disturbance of natural habitats, and the global transportation system. Vector-borne diseases are a subcategory of zoonotic diseases involving a biological disease agent that undergoes a transformation in an intermediary animal host, resulting in a pathogen capable of infecting humans (e.g., malaria). Another subcategory is arboviral diseases, viral diseases acquired when blood-feeding arthropod vectors infect a human host (e.g., West Nile virus).

Physical hazards include noise, vibration, extremes of heat, cold, and weather, and radiation (ionizing and non-ionizing). Ionizing radiation includes ultraviolet (UV) radiation and X-rays. Non-ionizing radiation includes infrared radiation, microwaves, radiowaves, and extremely low frequency electromagnetic fields. Psychosocial hazards are factors that cause stress (psychological and physiological), such as overcrowding, lack of sufficient green or recreational space, or close proximity to known or suspected environmental dangers. Although this chapter focuses on chemical, biological, physical, and psychosocial hazards, it also identifies the indirect causes of harm to human health arising from poor urban design, climate change, and the loss of biological diversity.

The remainder of this chapter provides an overview of the main environmental hazards posing a risk to Canadians, focusing on air pollution (outdoor and indoor), contaminants in water and food, and toxic substances in consumer products. There are brief references to several other environmental hazards, including noise, radiation, and asbestos.

Outdoor Air Pollution

Air pollution, primarily from burning fossil fuels in vehicles, power plants, and industrial facilities, involves many compounds that harm our health: small airborne particles, nitrogen oxides, sulphur oxides, ozone, carbon monoxide, lead, volatile organic compounds, mercury, and other hazardous substances. These pollutants can cause impaired lung function, asthma attacks, cardiovascular disease, cancer, and premature death.[85] Air pollution can also cause reduced lung growth and function in children, along with decreased immune system function and illness-related school absenteeism.[86] Long-term exposure to fine particulate matter or PM 2.5 (referring to small particles less than 2.5 microns in diameter) at levels found in many Canadian cities increases the risk of premature mortality from heart disease.[87] Long-term exposure to air pollution increases the risk of developing lung cancer.[88]

There is also evidence, including studies conducted in Vancouver, that prenatal exposure to air pollution plays a role in adverse birth outcomes such as early fetal loss, preterm delivery, and lower birth weight.[89] There is strong evidence indicating that both outdoor and indoor pollution can trigger and exacerbate asthma attacks and symptoms.[90] It also appears increasingly likely that air pollution can contribute to the onset of asthma in both children and adults.[91] Thus, reducing exposure to air pollution is one of the five key actions required to reduce the health impacts of asthma.[92] Recent evidence also demonstrates that air pollution can damage children's cognitive abilities, increase adults' risk of cognitive decline, and contribute to depression.[93]

The relationship between air pollution and cardiovascular disease illustrates the rapid evolution of knowledge in the field of environmental health. A comprehensive Canadian study published in 2000 described seventeen risk factors known to be associated with cardiovascular disease, including major contributors such as smoking, unhealthy diet, and lack of exercise.[94] Air pollution was not mentioned at all. Since then, however, there have been major breakthroughs in medical understanding of the adverse effects of air pollution upon cardiovascular health. Medical researchers and organizations such as the American Heart Association now agree that short- and long-term exposure to ambient particulate matter is a risk factor for cardiovascular disease.[95] Air pollution can contribute to angina (chest pain), myocardial infarction (heart attack), arrhythmias (abnormal heart rhythm), and congestive heart failure.[96] The specific pathways linking exposure to fine particulates and death include pulmonary and systemic inflammation, accelerated atherosclerosis (hardening of the arteries), and changes in cardiac function (as measured by changes in heart rate variability).[97]

Canadians who live, work, study, or play near busy roads or large industrial facilities face elevated exposures to air pollution and correspondingly higher health risks. Air pollution generated in Asia poses a growing health risk to western Canada, while air pollution from the United States comprises as much as half of the problem in eastern Canada.[98]

Particulate Matter

"Particulate matter" refers to airborne particles and includes both solids and liquid droplets suspended in the air (known as aerosols). Particles are classified according to size, and research indicates that fine particles less than 10 microns in size are more likely to cause adverse health effects. Fine particulate matter is created primarily by the combustion of fossil fuels, while coarse particulate matter originates from road dust, diesel engines, and crushing and grinding operations. Exposure to fine particulates causes premature mortality, increased hospital admissions for cardiovascular and respiratory diseases, increased prevalence of bronchitis, increased risk of lung cancer, aggravation of asthma, accelerated progression and exacerbation of chronic obstructive pulmonary disease (COPD), and decreased lung function.[99] Children in particular are likely to suffer from a range of respiratory ailments as a result of exposure to particulate matter. The elderly and individuals with heart ailments are also especially vulnerable.[100] It is important to note that there is no safe level of fine particulate matter – negative health effects will occur in some people even at very low levels. A study published in 2002 estimated that for every 10 micrograms per cubic metre ($\mu g/m^3$) increase in fine particulates, cardiopulmonary deaths rose by 6 percent.[101]

Sulphur Dioxide

Most sulphur dioxide emissions are produced by the combustion of fossil fuels, including coal, oil, gasoline, and diesel, as well as cement plants and metal smelters. Exposure to sulphur dioxide can cause severe problems for people with asthma and is also associated with increased risks of lung cancer and chronic bronchitis. Sulphur dioxide reacts with other air pollutants in the atmosphere to form particulate matter.[102]

Nitrogen Oxides

Nitrogen oxides are produced by the combustion of fossil fuels. Exposure to elevated levels of nitrogen oxides can contribute to respiratory illness, aggravation of asthma in children, and reduced lung growth. Nitrogen oxides react with other air pollutants to form smog.[103]

Ozone

Ground-level ozone is a key component of smog, and is formed by atmospheric reactions involving nitrogen oxides, volatile organic compounds, and sunlight. Sunlight intensity and higher temperatures exacerbate the formation of ozone, which is why smog is generally worse during summer months and is affected by the warmer temperatures caused by climate change. Ground-level ozone must be distinguished from stratospheric ozone, which provides the vital service of blocking ultraviolet radiation from the sun. Ozone exposure irritates the respiratory tract and is linked to both respiratory and cardiovascular mortality.[104] Exposure to ozone in sensitive people can cause chest tightness, coughing, and wheezing. Children who are active outdoors during the summer, when ozone levels are elevated, are particularly vulnerable. Other groups at risk include individuals with pre-existing respiratory disorders, such as asthma and COPD. Ozone contributes to reduced lung function, increased hospital admissions for acute respiratory diseases, and premature mortality.[105]

Smog

Smog is a combination of fine particulate matter and ground-level ozone and may also contain nitrogen oxides, volatile organic compounds, and sulphur dioxide. The majority of Canadians are exposed to smog at concentrations that pose a threat to their health. In southern Ontario and Quebec, levels of ground-level ozone and particulate matter exceed World Health Organization guidelines many days each summer.[106] As Rona Ambrose, Canada's former environment minister, observed, "it is unacceptable that such days happen, when children with asthma and elderly people with respiratory conditions can't even leave their homes."[107]

Hazardous Air Pollutants

There are hundreds of other air pollutants that are known or suspected to cause cancer, birth defects, or other serious illnesses. Hazardous air pollutants are released by motor vehicles, factories, power plants, and incinerators. Examples include mercury, which is associated with developmental deficits in children, and polycyclic aromatic hydrocarbons (PAHs), which cause cancer. Some of these pollutants, such as PCBs, mercury, and dioxins, may be released in other countries but eventually reach Canada. The US Environmental Protection Agency (EPA) reports that breathing hazardous air pollutants increases the lifetime cancer risk of many Americans.[108]

Indoor Air Pollution

Indoor air pollution is often overlooked as an environmental health issue, yet the US EPA ranks indoor air quality as one of the top five environmental health problems. Canadians spend approximately 90 percent of their time indoors, meaning that exposure to air pollutants in residential, occupational, institutional, and recreational settings may outweigh outdoor exposure. Hockey fans, partaking in Canada's national pastime at indoor arenas, may be exposed to unhealthy levels of air pollution when the Zamboni resurfaces the ice between periods.[109]

Indoor air pollution is caused by combustion, building materials, furnishings, human activities (e.g., smoking or painting), radon, and biological contaminants. Combustion from sources including gas ovens, furnaces, and wood stoves releases nitrogen oxides, carbon monoxide, and particulate matter. Exposure to elevated levels of carbon monoxide can adversely affect the functioning of the heart, resulting in cardiac ischemia, increased hospital admissions, and premature mortality. Furnishings, carpets, adhesives, construction materials, home office equipment, household cleaners, and consumer products can contaminate indoor air with benzene, formaldehyde, and other volatile organic compounds (VOCs) that cause cancer, birth defects, and brain damage. Biological contaminants, including moulds, bacteria, dust mites, cockroaches, and animal dander, are linked to asthma and allergies.[110]

Asbestos

Asbestos used to be described as a "miracle mineral" for its ability to withstand heat. It was used in thousands of products, including fireproofing and insulating material in ships, buildings, and consumer products, and in wallboard, flooring, cement, automobiles, clothing, home appliances, and even children's toys. However, exposure to asbestos causes a form of cancer called mesothelioma, increases the risk of lung cancer, and causes asbestosis, a lung disease. These diseases may take twenty to forty years to develop after exposure. The global authority on cancer-causing substances, the International Agency for Research on Cancer (IARC), classifies all types of asbestos fibres as human carcinogens. The World Health Organization recommends the elimination of all uses of asbestos.

Although widely perceived as an occupational health problem, exposure to asbestos could affect thousands of other Canadians. The spouses and children of individuals who worked with asbestos – in mining, manufacturing, or construction – are at risk because of exposure to asbestos fibres unwittingly brought home from the workplace (e.g., on clothing). Women living in asbestos mining communities in Quebec suffer from a sevenfold increase in mortality from cancer linked to asbestos exposure.[111] As well, between 200,000 and 300,000 Canadian homes contain vermiculite insulation that is contaminated by asbestos.

Mould

Exposure to some kinds of mould can cause acute and chronic health effects ranging from headaches and wheeze to nausea, fatigue, dizziness, sepsis, and even death. An estimated 30 percent of buildings in Canada and the United States have moisture problems that make them susceptible to mould. Exposure is largely through inhalation, although direct contact and ingestion of contaminated food are also possible.[112]

Environmental Tobacco Smoke

Although rates of smoking are declining in Canada, smoking and exposure to environmental tobacco smoke (also referred to as second-hand smoke) continue to be major public health concerns. Burning tobacco produces a complex array of gases, vapours, and particulate matter, including dozens of known or suspected carcinogens. Environmental tobacco smoke is implicated in asthma, bronchitis, heart disease, and sudden infant death syndrome (SIDS). Smoking continues to be the single greatest preventable contributor to premature death in Canada. Roughly 16 percent of Canadians are daily or occasional smokers, while 34 percent of Canadians are exposed to environmental tobacco smoke on a regular basis.[113]

Radon

Radon is a naturally occurring radioactive gas produced by the decay of uranium, which is distributed in varying concentrations throughout soil and rocks in Canada. Although radon receives little public attention, it is one of the most harmful indoor air pollutants. Radon is the second most important cause of lung cancer after smoking, accounting for 9–15 percent of lung cancer deaths in Europe and North America.[114] The carcinogenic properties of radon have been confirmed by cellular mutagenesis studies, research experiments with animals, and epidemiological studies of underground miners exposed to high concentrations of radon.[115] The IARC classifies radon as a known human carcinogen.[116] The World Health Organization states that "no safe level of exposure can be determined," a position confirmed by the US National Academies of Science.[117] There are synergistic effects between radon exposure and smoking, so that the risks of lung cancer due to radon exposure increase at a much higher rate for smokers and ex-smokers. However, radon is also the number one cause of lung cancer among non-smokers. Certain regions of Canada face far higher radon risks than other regions. For example, 29 percent of the homes in Prince George, BC, and 59 percent of the homes in Castlegar, BC, have elevated radon levels, threatening residents' health.[118]

Radon seeps into buildings through cracks and other weaknesses in foundations and floors. Radon can also enter homes when drinking water is obtained from aquifers in close proximity to rock containing natural uranium. However, the greatest cancer risks resulting from radon are from inhalation rather than ingestion. The good news is that radon concentrations in buildings can be measured inexpensively and mitigated effectively at a moderate cost, both in new construction and in retrofitting existing buildings.[119] Exposure to radon is the dominant source of an individual's exposure to ionizing radiation in most countries, including Canada.[120]

Volatile Organic Compounds

Volatile organic compounds are emitted as gases from certain solids and liquids, including paints, varnishes, paint strippers, cleaning supplies, hair spray, cosmetics, windshield washer fluid, liquid fuels, building materials, furnishings, office equipment (e.g., copiers and printers), craft materials (including glues and adhesives), permanent markers, and photographic solutions. VOC levels are generally higher indoors than outdoors, and can be up to a thousand times higher than normal during activities such as paint stripping. According to the US EPA, the adverse health effects of exposure to VOCs include eye, nose, and throat irritation; headaches, loss of coordination, and nausea; damage to the liver, kidneys, and central nervous system; and cancer. VOCs are particularly problematic for Canadians suffering from chemical sensitivities. Among the most hazardous VOCs are benzene, formaldehyde, toluene, methylene chloride, and perchloroethylene.[121]

Contaminated Water

Drinking water can be a source of exposure to pathogens and chemical and radioactive contaminants. Compared with many other countries, Canada is blessed with clean and abundant fresh water. For purposes of this book, safe drinking water means that the "level of risk is so small that a reasonable, well-informed individual need not be concerned about it, nor find any rational basis to change his/her behaviour to avoid a negligible but non-zero risk."[122] In general, municipally treated drinking water in Canada is safe for consumption.

However, it would be a mistake to take drinking water for granted despite a plethora of laws, policies, programs, and investments intended to protect public health from potential threats posed by drinking water. Affluent nations, including Canada, Japan, the United States, the United Kingdom, and Australia, have experienced serious outbreaks of waterborne disease in recent decades.[123] High-profile water contamination events in Canada include:

- Walkerton, Ontario, where seven people died, sixty-five were hospitalized, and thousands more became ill
- North Battleford, Saskatchewan, where thousands of people became ill
- the Aboriginal community of Kashechewan in Ontario, where many
  residents were evacuated.

While the severity of these public health disasters is uncommon in Canada,
water quality problems are not. Rural and Aboriginal populations experience both greater threats to drinking water quality and inferior treatment
(if any treatment at all).[124] Over a thousand boil-water advisories are in effect in Canada on any given day, predominantly in these smaller communities.[125] According to the Commissioner of the Environment and Sustainable
Development, as many as 75 percent of the water systems on Aboriginal
reserves face significant threats to the quality and safety of drinking water.[126]
Approximately 7 million Canadians depend on private, untreated sources,
mostly groundwater wells, for their drinking water.[127]

Microbiological Contaminants
There is a general consensus among health, medical, and scientific experts
that the most important threats to drinking water quality in Canada are
microbiological pathogens such as *Escherichia coli, Giardia, Cryptosporidium,* and *Toxoplasma.* [128] Waterborne pathogens pose a greater threat than
chemical contaminants because of the risk of immediate and severe health
effects, the fact that infected persons can transmit the illness to others who
may not have been exposed to the pathogen, and the fact that a single micro-
organism has the potential to cause harm.[129] The three main categories of
waterborne pathogens are bacteria, viruses, and protozoa. The individuals
at greatest risk of infection or most likely to suffer serious adverse health
effects caused by waterborne illness are infants, young children, people with
compromised immune systems, and the elderly. The adverse effects caused
by waterborne pathogens range from mild gastroenteritis (upset stomach)
to severe diarrhea and death.

Governments and agencies responsible for providing drinking water
must cope with both established and emerging waterborne pathogens.
Waterborne disease outbreaks in Canada have been caused by bacteria
(e.g., *E. coli* O157:H7, *Salmonella, Shigella,* and *Campylobacter jejuni*),
viruses (e.g., hepatitis A), and protozoa (e.g., *Giardia, Cryptosporidium,*
and *Toxoplasma gondii*). Scientists have identified hundreds of emerging

pathogens in recent years, including noroviruses, *Legionella*, *Mycobacterium avium* complex, and *Helicobacter pylori*.[130]

A recent concern in drinking water management involves cyanobacteria, a type of bacteria naturally found in fresh water. Cyanobacteria pose a risk when found in excessive numbers, known as blooms. They produce toxic substances that, when ingested through drinking water, can damage the liver, kidneys, nervous system, and gastrointestinal system. Exposure when swimming, showering, or bathing in water contaminated by cyanobacteria can also cause eye irritation and a skin rash. Blooms are due to factors such as high temperatures, direct sunshine, high levels of nutrients, and low flows. These risk factors are exacerbated by today's agricultural practices, urbanization, and climate change.

Chemical Contaminants
Chemical contamination of drinking water supplies can be caused by natural sources (e.g., arsenic), point sources of pollution (e.g., factories, sewage treatment plants, gas stations, drycleaners), and nonpoint or dispersed pollution sources (e.g., urban and agricultural runoff, airborne deposition). Potential health effects associated with exposure to chemicals in drinking water include cancer, neurological disorders, gastrointestinal illness, reproductive problems, developmental disorders, and disruption of the endocrine system. In contrast to the acute health effects caused by waterborne pathogens, health problems associated with chemical contaminants generally arise after prolonged periods of exposure. For most chemical contaminants, exposure through food and air is more important than exposure through drinking water. However, arsenic is an example of a chemical present in drinking water in some parts of Canada at levels that can pose public health risks. Concentrations of arsenic above the Guidelines for Canadian Drinking Water Quality are found in parts of every province except New Brunswick and Prince Edward Island.[131] Arsenic increases the risk of lung and bladder cancer and can adversely affect children's intellectual development.[132] Arsenic can be removed from drinking water by relatively expensive treatment methods. Carcinogenic solvents such as perchloroethylene and trichloroethylene have been detected in Canadian water supplies.[133]

There are also health concerns related to disinfection byproducts (chemicals created when substances used to disinfect drinking water interact with substances naturally occurring in the water supply). The most common disinfection byproducts – trihalomethanes and chlorinated acetic acids –

are created by reactions between chlorine and organic materials. Exposure to disinfection byproducts increases the risk of bladder cancer.[134] Other types of disinfectants produce different byproducts. For example, ozone disinfection can produce formaldehyde and other aldehydes. Most experts agree that the risks posed by disinfection byproducts are smaller than the risks posed by pathogenic microorganisms in untreated water; however, there are approaches to drinking water management (e.g., ultraviolet disinfection and limiting organic materials in the source water) that reduce or eliminate the risk posed by disinfection byproducts.

Radioactive Contaminants

Radioactive contaminants in drinking water include naturally occurring substances such as uranium and radon, as well as a wide range of radionuclides produced by mining, operation of nuclear reactors, and disposal of nuclear waste. Different forms of radiation are emitted by various radioactive species (alpha particles, beta particles and positrons, gamma rays and X-rays). Exposure to radiation at low doses over long periods of time is linked to an increased risk of both genetic damage and cancer. The acute health effects of radiation exposure – skin burns, vomiting, reduced blood cell counts, and death – occur at much higher exposures and are not caused by drinking water. Ingesting water contaminated with radionuclides causes internal radiation that can last for months or even years, potentially causing chronic health problems. The radiation dose resulting from ingestion depends on biological and chemical factors. Health effects depend on the type of radiation and the tissues or organs that are exposed. In general, a very low proportion of human exposure to radiation, generally less than 10 percent, comes from drinking water.[135]

Other Adverse Health Effects Caused by Water Pollution

Water pollution can also jeopardize the health of Canadians who participate in aquatic activities at beaches and eat shellfish or fish. Every year thousands of beaches are closed to recreational activities because of water pollution. Thousands of square kilometres along the coasts of British Columbia, Quebec, and Atlantic Canada are subject to shellfish closures due to bacterial contamination from municipal wastewater and other pollution sources.[136]

Food

Food is essential to human health yet can be an important source of exposure to bacteria, viruses, heavy metals, pesticides, and persistent organic pollutants such as dioxins. Meat is a major source of exposure to persistent organic pollutants, foodborne pathogens, heavy metals, antibiotics, and hormones. High levels of meat consumption increase the risk of a Pandora's box of chronic health problems, including heart disease, stroke, cancer, and gall bladder disease. Excessive use of antibiotics in the livestock industry is exacerbating the problem of antibiotic resistance. There are also continuing concerns about bird flu, swine flu, and bovine spongiform encephalopathy (mad cow disease), diseases linked to industrialized meat production. Overeating, urban design, and exposure to toxic chemicals are contributors to the obesity epidemic plaguing North America and other regions of the globe.[137] Obesity dramatically increases the risk of diabetes and associated problems, including blindness, amputation, kidney failure, and heart disease.

Foodborne Pathogens

The majority of foodborne illnesses can be traced to items of animal origin – meat, poultry, fish, dairy products, and eggs – although produce-related outbreaks are on the rise.[138] Young children, elderly people, pregnant women, and individuals with compromised immune systems are particularly vulnerable. Five pathogens account for 90 percent of food-related deaths and the majority of foodborne illnesses in the United States and Canada: *Salmonella, Listeria, Toxoplasma, Campylobacter,* and *E. coli.*[139] Consumption of food contaminated with these pathogens can lead to serious and life-threatening illnesses, such as the listeriosis outbreak in 2008 when twenty-three Canadians died after eating contaminated deli meat.[140] Symptoms include severe abdominal pain and bloody diarrhea. Some people may have seizures or strokes and some may need blood transfusions and kidney dialysis. Others may live with permanent kidney damage. Roughly half of skinless chicken breasts sold in Canada test positive for *Campylobacter,* while another 25–30 percent harbor *Salmonella.*[141] *Campylobacter* causes diarrhea, abdominal pain, fever, nausea, muscle pain, and headache. In rare cases, it can also lead to meningitis, arthritis, and Guillain-Barré syndrome, a severe neurological disorder. Salmonellosis may cause short-term symptoms such as high fever, severe headache, vomiting, nausea, abdominal pain, and diarrhea. Long-term complications may include severe arthritis. *Listeria* is detected in ground beef and ground pork, and also occurs in processed meat products such as cold cuts.[142] Listeriosis can cause high fever, severe headache, neck stiffness, and nausea. Infections during pregnancy can lead to premature delivery, infection of the newborn, or even stillbirth. Improper food handling is a major factor in foodborne illness. For example, undercooked hamburger meat and poorly washed lettuce are two common sources of *E. coli* O157:H7.

Persistent Organic Pollutants

Persistent organic pollutants found in the food supply include dioxins, PCBs, and several banned pesticides (e.g., chlordane, dieldrin, and DDT). A wide variety of foods contain small concentrations of these extremely toxic substances.[143] Tests conducted by the Canadian Food Inspection Agency found dioxins in almost all samples of beef fat and raw milk tested, and in the majority of samples of chicken fat, mutton fat, and pork fat. The World Health Organization estimated that meat, dairy, poultry, and fish products account for over 90 percent of human exposure to dioxins.[144] In Canada, over 95 percent of the general population's exposure to dioxins and many other chlorinated organic compounds comes through diet, yet our understanding of how these substances enter the food supply is relatively weak.[145] On a brighter note, exposure to dioxins has declined by over 90 percent over the past forty years.[146]

Pesticides

It is likely that every person living in Canada carries pesticide residues in their body, although the adverse health effects of these low-dose exposures are not well understood.[147] Multiple pesticides are found in the umbilical cord blood of newborn infants.[148] Residues from pesticides banned years ago continue to be detected in the meconium (the first stool) of newborn infants.[149] Pesticide exposures can produce two distinct types of adverse health effects: acute or short-term effects and chronic long-term effects. Acute pesticide poisoning occurs when an individual is directly exposed to a large dose of pesticides, resulting in the immediate development of adverse health effects.[150] Acute pesticide poisoning can harm the eyes, skin, gastrointestinal tract, nervous system, respiratory system, cardiovascular system, liver, kidneys, and blood.[151] In extreme cases, death may occur (a very rare occurrence in Canada, although not in developing countries). Acute pesticide poisoning can occur by various means, including accidental ingestion of pesticides in the home or garden, consumption of food containing pesticide residues, occupational exposure, and involuntary exposure to pesticides applied to homes, other buildings, lawns, gardens, forests, and farms. In Canada, acute pesticide poisoning linked to food consumption is rare.

Chronic effects develop in response to lower levels of exposure over long periods of time. There is a large body of scientific evidence linking pesticide exposures to chronic health effects, including increased risk of cancer (e.g., non-Hodgkin's lymphoma, childhood leukemia, and breast cancer), neurological impairment (e.g., Parkinson's disease and Alzheimer's disease), developmental effects (e.g., autism), reproductive effects (e.g., sperm abnormalities and birth defects), organ damage, and interference with the endocrine system.[152] A recent systematic review concluded that exposure to specific pesticides – even at low levels – increased the likelihood that an individual will suffer from Parkinson's disease by 60 percent compared with individuals not exposed to these pesticides.[153] Individuals exposed to substantial quantities of certain pesticides face triple the risk of non-Hodgkin's lymphoma compared with unexposed individuals.[154] A study published in the medical journal *Paediatrics and Child Health* concluded that "cancer, neurological impairment and reproductive problems are persuasively linked to phenoxy herbicide exposure."[155] Congenital disorders (i.e., birth defects) have been linked to pesticides.[156]

Exposure to pesticides does not necessarily cause health problems. A number of factors are involved, including the dose (magnitude and concentration of the exposure); route of exposure (inhalation, ingestion, dermal contact, or in utero); the toxicity of a particular product; an individual's genetic vulnerability, age at the time of exposure, and general health; the length of exposure (e.g., one time versus ongoing); environmental factors; and potential interactions with other chemicals. It is difficult to ascribe chronic health outcomes to specific pesticides because of multiple factors, including the long period between exposure and illness, the fact that an individual is exposed to thousands of chemicals over the course of a lifetime, the different genetic susceptibility of individuals, and the presence of other confounding factors such as occupation, geographic location, socioeconomic status, behaviour, and lifestyle. However, research is gradually unmasking some of the connections between pesticides and specific health effects, and experts agree that reducing exposure reduces health risks.[157]

Heavy Metals

Food can expose people to heavy metals, including arsenic, lead, and mercury. For example, recent studies revealed high concentrations of arsenic in rice products.[158] Although eating fish is generally considered to be part of a healthy diet, mercury contamination in some species (e.g., swordfish, shark, and marlin) and some regions represents a serious health risk. Mercury can harm the development of fetuses and young children at very low concentrations, causing brain damage and impairing the nervous system.[159] A study found that 95 percent of fish taken from Ontario lakes had mercury levels higher than the World Health Organization guideline.[160] As a result, the Ontario government warns citizens interested in eating fish that women of child-bearing age and children under fifteen years should restrict their consumption of most sport fish, and some fish species should not be consumed at all.[161] Most of the mercury pollution in Canada originates from coal-fired electricity-generating facilities, both in Canada and the United States, although this source is declining as coal plants in Ontario and other jurisdictions are shut down.[162]

Antibiotics

More than three-quarters of all antibiotics used in Canada are administered to livestock, and in most cases are used to accelerate growth, not treat infections.[163] The inappropriate use of antibiotics in livestock is contributing to the growth of multidrug-resistant strains of bacteria, including *E. coli* O157:H7, *Salmonella,* and *Campylobacter,* and the spread of antibiotic-resistant organisms. The US Food and Drug Administration (FDA) recently concluded that each year the use of fluoroquinolones in chickens compromises the treatment of almost ten thousand people who suffer from *Campylobacter* infections. When these people are treated with the fluoro-quinolones commonly prescribed for *Campylobacter,* the bacteria are found to be resistant. Antibiotic resistance leads to more deaths and long-term illness from untreatable disease, increases the risk of drug-resistant pathogens spreading globally, and raises health care costs.[164]

Genetically Modified Foods

There is an ongoing scientific debate about whether genetically modified (GM) products, particularly food crops, will harm human health or provide net benefits by increasing yields and addressing vitamin deficiencies and malnutrition.[165] Potential adverse effects include allergic responses, antibiotic resistance, genetic damage, the turning on or off of genes through epigenetic changes, damage to organs and the immune system, and cancer.[166] However, a review of research over the past decade concluded that "the scientific research conducted so far has not detected any significant hazard directly connected with the use of GM crops."[167] Similarly, a decade-long research program funded by the European Union spent over 200 million euros on more than eighty projects and concluded that the use of GM plants does not imply higher risks than classical breeding methods or production technologies.[168]

Depletion of the Ozone Layer

The Earth's protective ozone layer has been damaged by exposure to industrial chemicals, including chlorofluorocarbons (CFCs) and other ozone-depleting substances. Because of this damage, higher levels of ultraviolet B (UVB) radiation are reaching the Earth's surface and harming human health.[169] Adverse effects include sunburn, skin cancer, other skin disorders, cataracts, other forms of eye damage, and reduced immune system function. The impacts of ozone depletion vary according to geographic location. Canada is at greater risk because of increased thinning of the protective ozone layer in northern regions. The thickness of the ozone layer over the northern hemisphere has declined between 10 percent and 40 percent in winter and spring months. It has been estimated that "as a rule a 10% reduction in the ozone layer thickness causes a 20% increase in UV-radiation and a 40% increase in skin cancers."[170] The extent of the increase in skin cancer incidence experienced in Canada will depend on international compliance with the Montreal Protocol on Substances that Deplete the Ozone Layer, as well as the rate of regeneration of the ozone layer. Mid–twenty-first-century estimates for the United States suggested a range of excess skin cancer cases per million people ranging between 150 and 700, with a best estimate of 500 per million.[171] Canadian estimates could be even higher because of our northern location. The latest information indicates that the ozone layer is beginning to recover, with full recovery estimated by mid-century.[172]

Noise

Noise is widely overlooked in Canada as an environmental health hazard.[173] Health impacts associated with excessive noise include hearing loss, high blood pressure, heart disease, changes in hormone levels, sleep disturbance/deprivation, and circulatory problems.[174] Noise receives much more attention as an environmental health issue in Europe. The Supreme Court of Canada has concluded that noise pollution in Montreal violated residents' right to live in a healthy environment, perhaps indicating growing prominence for this issue in Canada.[175]

Electromagnetic Radiation

Exposure to radiation from radon and sunlight was addressed earlier in this chapter. However, there is also concern about the health impacts of exposure to extremely low frequency electromagnetic fields. Electromagnetic radiation is produced by power lines, electrical appliances, Wi-Fi, and products ranging from cell phones to microwave ovens. Evidence indicates that children exposed to high levels of extremely low frequency electromagnetic fields may face an elevated risk of childhood leukemia.[176] As well, a portion of the population seems to suffer from electro-hypersensitivity, akin to an allergic reaction to electromagnetic fields. Swedish studies suggested that exposure to electromagnetic radiation from heavy cell phone use may be associated with the development of brain tumours and non-Hodgkin's lymphoma.[177] The tumours were found on the side of the brain associated with the dominant hand of phone users. However, other studies, including a large Danish study and the Interphone research covering thirteen countries, contradict these results, finding no increased risk of cancer.[178] Faced with this uncertainty, European governments have urged parents to limit children's use of cell phones, as their thinner skulls increase their vulnerability. Additional research is ongoing in response to changing use patterns and technological evolution.

Urban Design
Poor urban design can influence a variety of outcomes that contribute to adverse health effects, including fragmented and sprawling communities, car dependency, inactivity, obesity, loneliness, accidents involving pedestrians, cyclists, and motorists, and wasteful fossil fuel and resource consumption. The phrase "built environment" refers to "aspects of a person's surroundings which are human-made or modified, as compared with naturally occurring aspects of the environment."[179] The built environment has significantly influenced Canadian lifestyles over the past fifty years, contributing to the increased prevalence of chronic diseases by reducing levels of physical activity, communities' strength and connections, and access to healthy food.[180] The US Centers for Disease Control and Prevention (CDC) point out that the ways in which the built environment affects human health are not only "direct pathological impacts of various chemical, physical, and biological agents, but also ... factors in the broad physical and social environments, which include housing, urban development, land use, transportation, industry, and agriculture."[181] Lack of access to natural or green spaces for urban residents is correlated with worse physical and mental health, including a higher risk of mortality from cardiovascular disease.[182]

Researchers have established strong links between the built environment and levels of physical activity. Urban design can either encourage or discourage active lifestyles. People who live in compact, mixed-use communities with safe infrastructure, such as wide sidewalks and traffic control devices, will walk and cycle. Urban sprawl, on the other hand, separates various land uses (places to live, shop, work, and recreate) and necessitates vehicle use to travel between them.[183] The built environment is a significant influence on both mode of transportation choices (walking, cycling, public transit, driving) and the amount of time available for healthy leisure activities.[184] People living in low-walkability neighbourhoods (longer distances, lack of infrastructure, and associated safety concerns) are more likely to be inactive and overweight than those living in high-walkability neighbourhoods.[185] North Americans on average walk for only about four minutes per day, and spend five times more time driving than exercising or playing sports.[186] For every thirty minutes of commuting spent in a car, one's chances of becoming obese increase by 3 percent compared with those who drive less.[187] As obesity rates increase, so do rates of heart disease, type II diabetes, hypertension, stroke, and cancer.[188] The CDC estimates that 200,000 to 300,000 people die every year in the United States because of physical inactivity.[189] Increased driving also leads to increased air pollution, greenhouse gas emissions, and traffic accidents.[190]

The built environment also affects residents' access to healthy food, and influences the availability of land for local agriculture. The number of fast food restaurants and convenience stores in a given area is positively correlated with obesity rates, even after adjusting for income.[191] Conversely, zoning can be used to create neighbourhoods with independent grocers, farmers' markets, and community gardens that may help provide affordable healthy foods.[192] Enforceable urban boundaries can protect farmland for local food production, reducing air pollution, greenhouse gas (GHG) emissions, and traffic accidents.[193]

The built environment influences health in many other ways, through noise, air pollution, proximity to major sources of industrial pollution and contaminated sites, lack of access to green space, and the heat island effect that increases the risk of heat-related illness.[194] A lower-quality built environment, characterized by indicators such as property damage, vacancy, and inadequate maintenance, is linked to increased stress levels, depression, and other adverse mental health effects.[195] Improved urban planning, design, and zoning have the ability to alleviate or eliminate these environmental risk factors.[196]

Climate Change

Medical experts believe that climate change will cause wide-ranging, mostly adverse health consequences in Canada.[197] Prominent health concerns include weather-related mortality, infectious diseases, decreased availability of water, and air pollution.[198] Health Canada identified six major categories of health-related impacts associated with climate change:

- illnesses and deaths caused by hotter and colder temperatures
- deaths, injuries, and illnesses caused by extreme weather events
- increased exposure to outdoor and indoor air pollutants
- waterborne and foodborne contamination
- increased exposure to ultraviolet radiation
- the spread of vector-borne diseases to previously unaffected areas.[199]

Climate change will have disproportionate impacts on vulnerable populations, including the elderly, young children, the homeless, the Inuit, other Aboriginal people, and individuals with pre-existing illnesses.[200]

Air quality in Canada will suffer due to climate change, largely because warmer temperatures exacerbate the formation of ground-level ozone and smog.[201] Climate change may also increase risks associated with respiratory illnesses because allergenic pollens grow more profusely in a warmer environment. A study by researchers at Harvard University showed that ragweed, a potent allergen producer, grew 61 percent faster under climatic conditions expected to prevail by 2050.[202] Storms are expected to increase in frequency and severity. For example, hurricanes increase in intensity when surface sea temperatures rise.[203] As Hurricane Katrina demonstrated, even the citizens of wealthy industrialized nations are not immune to these natural disasters. Among the vector-borne diseases that may spread to new regions because of climate change are West Nile virus, Lyme disease, and hantavirus.[204] The number of reported cases of West Nile virus in Canada between 2002 and 2012 was 5,097, ranging from a high of 2,215 in 2007 to a low of 5 in 2010.[205] The number of reported cases is only a fraction of the many people who have the virus but suffer only minor symptoms or are unaffected.

Conclusion

Environmental factors affect human health in myriad ways, both positive and negative, although the former are often overlooked. This chapter has attempted to provide a broad overview, inevitably sacrificing depth and detail in order to do so. The difficulties inherent in composing a summary are exacerbated by the rapid evolution of scientific knowledge in these fields. An example mentioned earlier is the importance of epigenetics and interactions between genes and environmental risk factors.

It is important to note that environmental degradation can also have substantial indirect impacts on human health. A classic Canadian example is the history of overfishing in the Maritimes that led to the collapse of Atlantic cod populations. This ecological catastrophe led to widespread unemployment, major social problems, and substantial adverse health effects.[206]

Finally, it is important to acknowledge that Canada has made substantial progress in reducing or even eliminating some environmental health hazards. Lead was banned from gasoline and dramatically reduced in paint. Regulations governing pulp and paper mills resulted in a 99 percent reduction in the release of dioxins and furans via effluent. The production, use, and release of CFCs and other ozone-depleting substances have been virtually eliminated. Consistent with the Stockholm Convention on Persistent Organic Pollutants, Canada has banned more than a dozen of these chemicals. New motor vehicles produce a fraction of the air pollution of earlier models. Sulphur levels in gasoline have been slashed, as well as sulphur dioxide emissions from industry. Levels of wastewater treatment are improving and some contaminated sites have been remediated. Despite this progress, problems persist, and environmental hazards continue to contribute to disease and death in Canada. The magnitude of that contribution is the subject of Chapter 3.

3

The Environmental Burden of Disease

Never forget that the numbers in your tables are human
destinies, although the tears have been wiped away.
– IRVING SELIKOFF, MD

How many Canadians die or become sick every year because of exposure to
environmental hazards? How many of these deaths or illnesses could be
prevented through healthier environments? How much could the health of
Canadians improve as a result of stronger laws, policies, and programs that
protect the environment? There are no definitive answers to these questions.
In fact, because of scientific uncertainties, it is a challenge to accurately determine the "environmental burden of disease" (EBD), a phrase used to refer
to the mortality and morbidity (the number of deaths, cases of illness, and
disabilities) caused by exposure to preventable environmental hazards.[1] In
particular, most chronic diseases are multifactorial, meaning they result from
the complex interactions of lifestyle, socio-economic, environmental, cultural, and genetic factors over the course of a person's lifetime. The potentially long lag time between environmental exposures and the onset of health
effects adds to the difficulty of proving causal links. According to British
scientist David Briggs:

The complexities involved in the link between environmental pollution and
health, and the uncertainties inherent in the available data on mortality and

morbidity, in existing knowledge about the aetiology of diseases, and in environmental information and estimates of exposure, all mean that any attempt to assess the environmental contribution to the global burden of disease is fraught with difficulties.[2]

Despite the challenges, striving to quantify the environmental burden of disease is important because it highlights the magnitude of environmental harm and helps identify specific risk factors that affect public health. This information can be used to support and direct research; inform public education efforts; assist physicians in providing advice to patients; guide priorities in health and environmental policymaking; and evaluate the effectiveness of laws, policies, programs, and other interventions. In 2006, Canadian experts identified research into the EBD as one of the most pressing national priorities in the field of environmental health.[3]

To estimate the EBD, the burden of disease is first calculated for a given affliction (e.g., lung cancer) or for a number of diseases of interest (e.g., all types of chronic disease). The EBD is then calculated as the percentage of the overall burden of disease attributable to a specific environmental risk factor or group of risk factors. There are two accepted approaches to estimating the EBD: the exposure-based approach and the outcome-based approach.[4] The exposure-based approach requires three kinds of data: identification of the increased risk of an adverse health outcome (e.g., lung cancer); the population's exposure to relevant risk factors (e.g., ambient air pollution and second-hand smoke); and the dose-response relationships. The outcome-based approach also requires three kinds of data: identification of outcomes associated with relevant environmental risk factors; statistics on morbidity and mortality; and the environmentally attributable fraction (experts' best estimate of the proportion of a given outcome caused by environmental factors).

The first EBD studies, published in the late 1990s, estimated that 25–33 percent of the global burden of disease was caused by environmental factors.[5] In 2001, the Organisation for Economic Co-operation and Development estimated the global EBD to be between 7.5 percent and 12 percent, with only 2–5 percent of the total disease burden in high-income OECD countries resulting from environmental hazards.[6] Using updated information and a broader definition of "environmental risk factor" that included occupational exposures, work-related stress, and injuries from environment-related motor vehicle accidents, the World Health Organization estimated that 23 percent of all deaths and 24 percent of all disability adjusted life years (DALYs) globally are attributable to environmental factors, with the EBD being higher in developing countries (25 percent) than in developed ones (17 percent).[7] The single largest environmental risk factor is air pollution (indoor and outdoor), which causes over 7 million people to die prematurely every year.[8] Developing countries suffer a higher burden of communicable disease associated with environmental factors, such as diarrheal diseases caused by contaminated water and inadequate sanitation. Industrialized nations, in contrast, have a higher burden of chronic illnesses, such as cardiovascular disease.

Estimates of the environmental burden of disease have also been conducted at the regional, national, and subnational levels. The WHO assessed the environmental burden of pediatric disease in Europe.[9] Researchers carried out national EBD studies in the United States and the United Kingdom.[10] As well, there have been EBD studies in Washington, Massachusetts, and Minnesota.[11] Collectively, these studies suggest that the total EBD for high-income, developed countries may range from as low as 1–5 percent to as high as 15–22 percent, depending on how EBD is defined and calculated.

The Canadian government has never conducted an EBD study, which is a telling indication of the lack of priority accorded to environmental health in Canada. However, several recent studies conducted by other organizations and experts provide, for the first time, preliminary estimates of the environmental burden of disease in Canada.

The World Health Organization's Estimate of the EBD in Canada

The first estimate, published by the World Health Organization, resulted from a global study that addressed the contribution of environmental hazards to eighty-five diseases and disabilities.[12] The WHO's approach to assessing the EBD relied on a combination of comparative risk assessment and expert judgment to estimate the environmentally attributable fraction (EAF) of mortality and morbidity.[13] The EAF is defined as "the percentage of a particular disease category that would be eliminated if environmental risk factors were reduced to their lowest feasible levels."[14] In other words, the EAF is the proportion of each health condition that can reasonably be attributed to exposure to environmental hazards, such as air pollution or contaminated water. For example, the WHO estimated that 5 percent of birth defects (range of 2–10 percent) are caused (in whole or in part) by maternal exposures to harmful chemicals.[15] To determine appropriate ranges of the EAF for eighty-five diseases, the WHO relied on the most recent comparative risk assessment data available and consulted more than a hundred leading environmental health, epidemiology, and toxicology experts.[16]

The WHO estimated that 36,800 deaths and 13 percent of the overall burden of disease in Canada are caused, in whole or in part, by exposure to environmental hazards.[17] It acknowledged that these are preliminary estimates and should be further refined.[18]

The Boyd and Genuis Study

The second study, published by D.R. Boyd and S.J. Genuis in the journal *Environmental Research* in 2008, provides a more detailed estimate of the EBD in Canada for four categories of adverse health outcomes: respiratory disease, cardiovascular illness, cancer, and congenital disorders.[19] These health outcomes were selected because of the strong evidence of an environmental connection and because reliable Canadian data on mortality and morbidity are available. As well, cancer, cardiovascular disease, and respiratory disease are among the most important causes of death and illness in Canada.[20]

In view of the inherent complexity and uncertainty associated with definitively quantifying the EBD, the goal of the Boyd and Genuis study was to identify the potential range of the environmental burden of disease, based on the best available current knowledge. Like the OECD in its EBD research, the purpose was "simply to come up with a rough estimate of the fraction of disease that will be avoided by feasible and conceivable reductions of environmental exposures."[21] The study was designed to illustrate the magnitude of the problem, the need for further research, and the potential health benefits of stronger laws, policies, programs, and actions.

Boyd and Genuis used the latest WHO estimates of EAFs as a starting point to estimate the EBD in Canada for respiratory disease, cardiovascular disease, cancer, and congenital disorders. The WHO's EAFs were compared with EAFs used in other EBD studies and evaluated in conjunction with available knowledge regarding the environmental contribution to disease in Canada. The study used a narrower definition of environmental risk factor than the WHO, limiting it to chemical, biological, and radiological hazards. For example, the WHO included occupational risk factors (e.g., work-related stress).[22] This difference resulted in slightly lower EAFs than used by the WHO for some categories of disease. In the following summary of the results of the Boyd and Genuis study, some mortality and morbidity figures have been updated with more recent data.

TABLE 3.1

The environmental burden of respiratory disease in Canada

	Number	EAF (%)	EBD range
COPD			
Hospitalizations	256,461	10–30	25,646–76,938
Days in hospital	1,706,106	10–30	170,611–511,832
Deaths	9,773	10–30	977–2,932
Asthma			
Restricted activity days	3,591,000	26–53	933,660–1,903,230
Hospitalizations	31,000	26–53	8,060–16,430
Days in hospital	109,414	26–53	28,448–57,989
Deaths	288	26–53	75–153

Respiratory Disease

In Canada, the burden of respiratory disease is enormous: more than 700,000 Canadians suffer from chronic obstructive pulmonary disease (COPD), while 3 million Canadians (one in twelve persons) have asthma. Rates of childhood asthma have risen dramatically. From 1978 to 1999, the percentage of children with asthma quadrupled to greater than 12 percent (one in eight children).[23] Poor air quality is linked to a significant proportion of respiratory illnesses, since "the two most important preventable risk factors for respiratory disease are smoking (both personal smoking and exposure to environmental tobacco smoke) and air quality (indoor and outdoor)."[24] The Boyd and Genuis study included the adverse effects of environmental tobacco smoke but not personal smoking, because the latter is a lifestyle choice instead of an environmental hazard.

The study estimated that the burden of respiratory disease caused by preventable environmental exposures in Canada includes approximately 34,000–93,000 hospitalizations; 200,000–570,000 patient-days in hospital; and between 1,000 and 3,100 deaths each year (Table 3.1). Exacerbations of asthma caused by air pollution also have a substantial impact on the day-to-day life of many Canadians, indicated by an estimated 1 million to 2 million restricted activity days annually.[25] The wide range of estimates results from uncertainty related to risks and exposures.

Cardiovascular Disease

Cardiovascular disease continues to be one of the leading causes of morbidity and mortality in Canada.[26] Major risk factors include smoking, high

TABLE 3.2

The environmental burden of cardiovascular disease in Canada

	Number	EAF (%)	EBD range
Hospitalizations	447,218	7.5–15	33,541–67,083
Days in hospital	3,885,588	7.5–15	291,419–582,838
Deaths	72,743	7.5–15	5,456–10,911

cholesterol, high blood pressure, obesity, and physical inactivity. Significant environmental risk factors include short- and long-term exposures to indoor and outdoor ambient particulate matter, while exposures to lead and noise are relatively minor risk factors.[27]

Use of a conservative range for the EAF (7.5–15 percent), lower than that used by the WHO but similar to that used by the OECD and other researchers, results in the following estimate of the burden of cardiovascular disease in Canada attributable to adverse environmental factors: 33,000–67,000 hospitalizations; 290,000–580,000 patient-days spent in hospital; and 5,500–11,000 deaths (Table 3.2).

Cancer

Cancer is a leading cause of sickness and death in Canada. Almost half of all Canadians will be diagnosed with cancer, while one in four will die from this disease.[28] In part this is because people are living longer and other diseases have been vanquished, and in part this is because we live in a society where carcinogens are ubiquitous. Cancer is a multifactorial disease with long latency periods, making it difficult to conclusively prove causation in many cases. However, a peer-reviewed report published by the Ontario Division of the Canadian Cancer Society found evidence correlating environmental exposure to arsenic with lung, skin, and bladder cancers; particulate air pollution and polycyclic aromatic hydrocarbons (PAHs) with lung cancer; asbestos with mesothelioma and lung cancer; ultraviolet (UV) radiation with skin cancer; drinking water disinfection byproducts with bladder cancer; and extremely low frequency electromagnetic fields with childhood leukemia.[29] There is also evidence linking environmental contaminants with cancer of many organs and tissues, including bladder, bone, brain, breast, esophagus, larynx, kidney, pancreas, liver, scrotum, skin, and salivary glands, as well as to leukemia, angiosarcoma, multiple myeloma, and Hodgkin's lymphoma.[30] For example, individuals exposed to substantial quantities of pesticides face triple the risk of non-Hodgkin's lymphoma compared with unexposed individuals.[31] In utero exposure to industrial chemicals, particularly those produced by the combustion of fossil fuels, is linked to the development of childhood cancer.[32]

The precise proportion of cancer cases attributable to environmental exposures remains the subject of ongoing research and discussion.[33] However, the Boyd and Genuis study summarized the best available evidence about the environmental burden of several specific types of cancer in Canada, including cancer caused by radon, environmental tobacco smoke, asbestos, air pollution, and UV radiation.

Radon

As a recognized determinant of lung cancer, exposure to radon is believed to be responsible for approximately 9–15 percent of lung cancer deaths worldwide.[34] Estimates suggest that 1,800–3,130 deaths per year in Canada are caused by lung cancer associated with exposure to radon.[35] This conclusion is consistent with the findings of studies on the health effects of radon by the US National Research Council and the World Health Organization.[36] In the United States, radon exposure is estimated to be responsible for about 15,000–22,000 lung cancer deaths every year.[37]

Environmental Tobacco Smoke

Exposure to environmental tobacco smoke (second-hand smoke) is associated with both cancer and cardiovascular disease. More than one thousand Canadians die annually because of lung cancer and heart disease caused by exposure to second-hand smoke.[38]

Asbestos

Besides increasing the risk of lung cancer, asbestos exposure causes a rare form of cancer called mesothelioma. There were approximately 515 new cases of mesothelioma in 2010 and 455 deaths from mesothelioma in Canada in 2010, numbers that are on the rise.[39]

Air Pollution

Air pollution causes cancer of the lungs, trachea, and bronchus.[40] The primary cause is believed to be fine particulate matter, although benzene and other chemicals may also be responsible. A comprehensive study of the EBD attributable to air pollution in Canada, published in 2012, estimated that it accounted for 7.4 percent of lung cancer deaths, resulting in an estimated 1,496 deaths in 2013.[41]

Skin Cancer (Melanoma and Non-melanoma)
Between 1969 and 1992, rates of melanoma (an aggressive form of skin cancer) in Canada tripled, partially due to ozone depletion.[42] Statistics from the Canadian Cancer Society estimate that 1,150 Canadians will die of melanoma in 2015. As well, an estimated 6,800 new cases of melanoma and 78,300 new cases of non-melanoma skin cancer were expected to be diagnosed in 2015.[43]

Drinking Water
Cancer may be caused by certain contaminants found in Canadian drinking water, including arsenic and disinfection byproducts (i.e., chemicals such as trihalomethanes and haloacetic acids created when chlorine added to water as a disinfectant combines with naturally occurring organic materials).[44] Disinfection byproducts are linked to bladder cancer and leukemia.[45]

Summary of Cancer EBD
A conservative range of 5–15 percent for the EAF of cancer was used by Boyd and Genuis. The evidence described above results in the following estimate of the mortality and morbidity in Canada caused by cancer attributable to adverse environmental factors: 8,500–25,500 new cases of cancer diagnosed; 11,000–32,000 hospitalizations; 100,000–310,000 patient-days spent in hospital; and 3,800–11,000 deaths (Table 3.3).

In Utero Exposure and Congenital Disorders
The annual burden of congenital morbidity and mortality in Canada includes 1,700 infant deaths, 25,000 cases of low birth weight infants, 1,900 stillbirths, and 6,400–9,600 serious congenital anomalies.[46] The most common birth defects in Canada are musculoskeletal anomalies, heart defects, and urinary system anomalies.[47]

The human fetus is routinely exposed to a myriad of chemical contaminants as a result of acute as well as accumulated maternal exposure.[48]

TABLE 3.3
The environmental burden of cancer in Canada

	Number	EAF (%)	EBD range
New cases	171,000	5–15	8,550–25,650
Hospitalizations	215,493	5–15	10,775–32,324
Days in hospital	2,078,966	5–15	103,948–311,845
Deaths	75,300	5–15	3,765–11,295

TABLE 3.4
The environmental burden of congenital disorders in Canada

	Number	EAF (%)	EBD range
Low birth weight babies	25,000	2–10	500–2,500
Serious congenital anomalies	6,400	2–10	128–640
Hospitalizations	15,580	2–10	312–1,558
Days in hospital	99,103	2–10	1,982–9,910
Deaths	3,600	2–10	72–360

Congenital disorders have been linked to exposure to a wide range of chemical contaminants, including:[49]

- lead[50]
- chlorination byproducts and nitrate in drinking water[51]
- environmental tobacco smoke[52]
- polycyclic aromatic hydrocarbons[53]
- solvents[54]
- phthalates[55]
- pesticides[56]
- ethanol[57]
- residential proximity to hazardous waste sites.[58]

More than 1,200 chemical and physical agents have been shown to cause developmental defects in tests using laboratory animals, while a much smaller number have been proven to affect humans (in part because of the impossibility of direct experiments).[59] Exposure to toxic substances in utero is associated with a wide range of adverse health effects that may manifest prior to birth, at birth, at later stages of development, or even in adulthood, including hyperactivity, attention deficit hyperactivity disorder (ADHD), learning disabilities, mental retardation, and autism spectrum disorder.[60] Table 3.4 provides estimates of the burden of congenital disorders in Canada attributable to environmental factors: 500–2,500 low birth weight babies; 100–600 serious congenital anomalies; 300–1,600 hospitalizations; 2,000–10,000 patient-days spent in hospital; and 70–360 deaths.

Summary of the EBD in Canada for Respiratory Illness, Cardiovascular Disease, Cancer, and Congenital Disorders
The environmentally attributable proportion of respiratory illness, cardiovascular disease, cancer, and congenital disorders in Canada is substantial:

TABLE 3.5

A summary of the environmental burden of disease in Canada for respiratory illness, cardiovascular disease, cancer, and congenital disorders

	Deaths	Hospitalizations	Days in hospital
COPD	977–2,932	25,646–76,938	170,611–511,832
Asthma	75–153	8,060–16,430	28,448–57,989
Cardiovascular disease	5,456–10,911	33,541–67,083	291,419–582,838
Cancer	3,765–11,295	10,775–32,324	103,948–311,845
Congenital disorders	72–360	312–1,558	1,982–9,910
Totals	10,345–25,651	78,334–194,333	596,408–1,474,414

10,000–25,000 deaths; 78,000–194,000 hospitalizations; and 600,000 to 1.5 million days spent in hospital (Table 3.5). In addition, there are 1 million to 2 million restricted activity days for asthma sufferers; 8,600–25,700 new cases of cancer; and 500–2,500 low birth weight babies.

The NCCEH Review of the Environmental Burden of Disease in Canada

In 2011, the National Collaborating Centre for Environmental Health (NCCEH), established by the Public Health Agency of Canada, published an overview of the evidence regarding the EBD in Canada. The NCCEH identified and reviewed all relevant studies and concluded that while there are many unanswered questions, the estimates provided by Boyd and Genuis "are likely to be the most relevant for Canada at this time."[61] The Boyd and Genuis study is cited in Canada's National Strategic Framework on Children's Environmental Health and referred to by Health Canada when responding to inquiries about the EBD.[62]

Other Canadian Evidence Regarding the EBD

The estimates of the WHO and the Boyd and Genuis study are consistent with other Canadian evidence about the adverse health effects of environmental hazards. For example, experts with Health Canada estimated that air pollution is linked to 5,900 premature deaths annually in parts of eight large cities with a population of 8.9 million.[63] The 5,900 deaths can be conservatively doubled to 11,800 deaths because including the full population of the eight cities in the original study (Windsor, Hamilton, Ottawa, Toronto, Montreal, Quebec City, Calgary, and Vancouver) as well as the populations of London, Winnipeg, and Edmonton (among the ten most populous cities in Canada) represents another 8.4 million Canadians.[64] In a 2005 study, the Ontario Medical Association estimated that air pollution caused 5,800 premature deaths, more than 16,000 hospitalizations, and more than 60,000 emergency room visits annually in Ontario alone.[65] In 2008, the Canadian Medical Association used a sophisticated computer model to estimate that air pollution causes 21,000 premature deaths, 11,000 hospitalizations, 92,000 emergency room visits, and 620,000 doctor's office visits annually in Canada.[66] In 2014, the OECD published a report on air pollution from traffic that estimated 7,469 premature deaths annually in Canada because of PM 2.5 and ozone pollution.[67] These striking health impacts are projected to grow significantly as the population ages, unless effective steps are taken to reduce air pollution.[68]

Other Elements of the Environmental Burden of Disease

Additional research is needed to determine the overall environmental burden of disease in Canada for all categories of illness. However, efforts in this field are hampered by gaps in surveillance and reporting as well as epidemiological and toxicological uncertainties. Attempting to estimate the EBD for acute pesticide poisonings, lead poisoning, and gastrointestinal illness will demonstrate the nature of these data gaps and evidentiary problems, while also illustrating that these obstacles can be overcome.

Acute Pesticide Poisonings

While Canadian governments do collect some information on pesticide poisonings, it is not done systematically, so the number of people suffering acute impacts is not known.[69] Deaths resulting from acute exposure to pesticides do occur in Canada but appear to be extremely rare.[70] Cases of illness caused by acute exposure to pesticides, on the other hand, appear to be surprisingly common. It is important to note that pesticide poisonings make up a small percentage of total poisonings in Canada. Based on comprehensive US data, the three leading causes of poisoning are probably cleaning products, cosmetics, and analgesics (painkillers), common household items that often contain toxic substances.[71]

Statistics compiled by provincial poison control centres indicate that at least six thousand Canadians are victims of unintentional pesticide poisoning annually (Table 3.6).[72] This figure includes more than 2,800 cases where the victim is a child under the age of six. Such children comprise only 6.8 percent of the total Canadian population but experienced 46.5 percent of the acute pesticide poisonings.[73] This disproportionate level of impact

TABLE 3.6
Annual acute pesticide poisonings in Canada

Province	Pesticide poisonings	Cases involving child <6 years	Pesticide poisonings per 100,000 residents
BC	436	190 (43.6%)	10
AB	1,021	461 (45.2%)	30
SK	322	138 (42.9%)	33
MB	211	98 (46.4%)	18
ON	1,629	821 (50.4%)	13
QC	2,096	966 (46.1%)	27
NB/NS/PEI	319	144 (45.2%)	18
NF	37	5 (13.5%)	7
YT/NWT/NU	19	8 (42.1%)	18
Totals	6,090	2,831 (46.5%)	18

Source: D.R. Boyd, *Northern Exposure: Acute Pesticide Poisonings in Canada* (Vancouver: David Suzuki Foundation, 2007).

reflects a number of factors, including the different behaviours of young children (e.g., the propensity to put things in their mouths) and their inability to read warning labels and respond appropriately. Parents and other adults bear some of the responsibility for protecting children from exposure to pesticides, but there is also an important role for governments in preventing and/or minimizing risks. Young children cannot protect themselves.

The number of acute pesticide poisonings listed in Table 3.6 almost certainly underestimates the true magnitude of the problem. In the United States, governments provide more resources to poison control centres and fund the management of a national poisonings database. The annual report from the American Association of Poison Control Centers recorded 88,694 pesticide poisonings in 2012.[74] Almost half of these cases (37,035, or 41.8 percent) involved children under six years old. The annual number of pesticide poisonings in the United States is fifteen times higher than the corresponding Canadian estimate. Given that the American population is only nine times larger, there is a discrepancy in reported pesticide poisonings that merits investigation.

Lead Poisoning
There is an overwhelming body of evidence proving that lead has extensive negative health effects, affecting children, menopausal women, and the elderly (see Chapter 2). The most critical concerns involve neurological effects in children, in whom lead exposure can cause developmental delays,

ADHD, reduced intelligence, aggressive behaviour, decreased coordination, and learning disabilities. Acute lead poisoning that causes death is extremely rare in Canada, as are clinical cases of lead poisoning (i.e., cases so severe that they result in a physician's diagnosis).[75] Growing evidence of the chronic, subclinical effects of exposure to lead has caused regulatory agencies, including Health Canada, to acknowledge that there is no safe level of exposure to lead.[76] Studies clearly document adverse health effects – including neuro-developmental, neurodegenerative, cardiovascular, renal, and reproductive effects – at blood lead levels below the current intervention level of 10 micrograms per decilitre (μg/dL). Research suggests that each incremental increase in blood lead levels of 1 μg/dL is associated with a deficit of approximately one IQ point.[77]

For three decades after the Canada Health Survey of 1978–79, Canada failed to monitor the blood lead levels of children or adults. Finally, the Canada Health Measures Survey began monitoring and publishing blood lead levels in 2009–10.[78] Because of the elimination of leaded gasoline, tighter regulations governing industrial lead emissions, and restrictions on the lead content of paint and other consumer products, average blood lead levels have declined dramatically. Although most Canadians still carry measurable levels of lead in their bodies, fewer than 1 percent of Canadians aged six to seventy-nine now have blood lead concentrations at or above the Health Canada blood lead intervention level of 10 μg/dL, compared with approximately 27 percent in the 1970s. Health Canada acknowledges that the current blood lead intervention level is too high, and is in the process of revising it. Given evidence of the impacts of lead exposure even at low levels, ongoing efforts to reduce population-wide exposures are warranted.

Of grave concern is the fact that there is still severe lead poisoning in certain communities, including people with lower household incomes, born outside Canada, living in older homes, or residing in areas where large industrial lead emitters are located. Children in northern Canada, heavily industrialized areas, or communities with lead smelters (e.g., Hamilton, Port Colborne, Flin Flon, and Belledune, NB) have blood lead levels that are significantly higher than the Canadian average.[79] A recent survey of blood lead levels in children under the age of three from Trail, BC, near a Cominco smelter showed that 16 percent of children had blood lead levels above 10 μg/dL.[80] In other words, one in six children growing up in this community risks an IQ deficit of at least ten points, with potentially devastating consequences for their future. For the Canadian population as a whole, it appears that roughly 1 percent of children under the age of six have blood lead levels above 10 µg/dL, indicating that they are at risk of neurodevelopmental damage (such as diminished IQ) and behavioural problems. Based on recent population figures, this means that approximately twenty-three thousand Canadian children face major developmental threats because of excessive lead exposure.[81]

Gastrointestinal Illness

Gastrointestinal illness is an underrated public health problem that is often linked to environmental hazards. Gastrointestinal illnesses are primarily caused by exposure to pathogens transmitted through the fecal matter of humans, livestock, and other animals. Exposure can occur through a variety of paths, including fecal-oral exposure, human-to-human contact, consumption of contaminated food, contact with animals, and exposure to contaminated water (through drinking or recreation). Food and water are the primary sources of exposure, although pathogens are also routinely detected in waters used for recreation in Canada.[82]

Gastrointestinal illnesses can cause a broad spectrum of effects, including mild upset stomach, cramps, vomiting, diarrhea, headache, muscle pain, and flu-like symptoms. In a minority of cases, gastrointestinal infections can cause severe dehydration, kidney damage, and death. The American Academy of Microbiology observed: "Every single resident of developed countries is expected to become ill from an enteric infection at least once in the next 18 to 24 months, and yet gastrointestinal illness hardly registers as a major public health problem."[83]

The statistics shown in Table 3.7 describe the annual number of reported cases of a variety of gastrointestinal illnesses reported to the National Enteric Surveillance Program in Canada (using a six-year average):[84]

TABLE 3.7
Average annual reported cases of gastrointestinal illness (2005–10)

Illness	N
Campylobacteriosis	1,755
Parasites	1,677
E. coli O157:H7	707
Viruses	3,681
Salmonellosis	6,321
Shigellosis	675
Total	14,816

Because of widespread underreporting, the actual number of cases is believed to be ten to one thousand times higher than the number of confirmed cases.[85] A survey in Hamilton revealed that only one out of every 313 cases of gastrointestinal illness is reported.[86] Canadian estimates suggest 10–47 cases for every reported case involving *E. coli*, 13–37 cases of *Salmonella* for every reported case, and 23–49 cases of *Campylobacter* for every reported case.[87] A 2004 study estimated that there are roughly 1.3 cases of enteric gastrointestinal illness per capita in Canada annually.[88] In the most recent and detailed study, the Public Health Agency of Canada estimated that 4 million Canadians – roughly one in nine – suffer episodes of domestically acquired foodborne illness in Canada every year.[89] This rate of illness is roughly consistent with numerous studies in other industrialized nations, including the United States, Australia, and Western European countries. The US Centers for Disease Control estimate that one in six Americans (48 million people) are afflicted with foodborne illness annually, resulting in 128,000 hospitalizations and 3,000 deaths.[90]

Food is a significant pathway for many of the pathogens that cause gastrointestinal illness, usually when raw or not cooked thoroughly. Canadian studies show that pathogens are found in a high proportion of chicken and turkey products (e.g., *Campylobacter* and *Salmonella* detected in 41 percent and 26 percent of chicken breasts, respectively), a substantial proportion of retail beef (e.g., *Listeria* detected in 22 percent of samples in Ontario and 12 percent in British Columbia), and a lower percentage of pork and fresh soft berries (e.g., *Giardia* detected in up to 10 percent of berry samples).[91] There were 6,908 recorded outbreaks of foodborne illness in Canada between 1976 and 2005.[92] A listeriosis outbreak caused by contaminated deli meat killed twenty-three Canadians in 2008.[93]

As mentioned earlier, drinking water is also a pathway for exposure to some of the pathogens responsible for gastrointestinal illness. There were an estimated 288 outbreaks of waterborne disease in Canada between 1974 and 2001, caused by pathogens including *Giardia, Campylobacter, Cryptosporidium,* Norwalk-like viruses, *Salmonella,* and hepatitis A.[94] The federal government estimates that contaminated drinking water in Canada causes roughly 90 deaths and 90,000 cases of gastrointestinal illness annually.[95] These estimates represent a rough extrapolation from American figures (900 deaths and 900,000 cases of illness) published by the US Centers for Disease Control and Prevention.[96] Estimates by independent health experts suggest that a much higher number of Canadians may suffer from gastrointestinal illness because of contaminated drinking water. Two studies in Montreal found that 35 percent and 14–40 percent, respectively, of cases of gastrointestinal illness in a given year were caused by contaminants in tap water.[97] A study examining the relationship between drinking water quality and enteric illness in Vancouver over a period of six years found that variations in drinking water quality explained approximately 1.6 percent of physician visits, 0.6 percent of hospital admissions, and 1.6 percent of pediatric hospital emergency room visits for gastrointestinal illness.[98] On a brighter note, a similar study in Edmonton, a city renowned for the high quality of its water treatment system, found no correlation between drinking water quality and gastrointestinal illness.[99]

The environmentally attributable proportion of gastrointestinal illness from waterborne pathogens appears to vary widely from city to city, ranging from 0 percent (Edmonton) to 1 percent (Vancouver) to 14–40 percent in Montreal. The low Edmonton rate and the high end of the Montreal range represent extreme ends of the spectrum. These are admittedly rough estimates, and represent only a subset of the overall burden of gastrointestinal illness caused by exposure to environmental hazards. Exposure to contaminated foods is also difficult to track accurately but probably contributes to the majority of the cases of gastrointestinal illness suffered by Canadians annually.

Conclusion

This chapter provides the best available estimates of the environmental burden of disease in Canada for a subset of illnesses. Much remains unknown, despite the efforts of researchers in Canada and around the world. Among the environment-related health impacts that have not been accurately quantified at this time are:

- the endocrine-disrupting consequences of exposure to industrial chemicals, pesticides, and heavy metals[100]
- the relationship between environmental exposures and multiple chemical sensitivities
- the consequences of unhealthy built environments, such as their influence on the rising rates of obesity[101]
- the implications of new scientific advances, such as nanotechnology, and recent developments in consumer products (such as cell phones and other wireless devices that emit electromagnetic radiation)[102]

- some impacts caused by climate change, including the extended range of vector-borne diseases and the spread of potentially hazardous fungi[103]
- the consequences of declines in native biodiversity.[104]

The official health statistics (deaths, illnesses, hospitalizations, and so on) used in EBD calculations represent only the tip of the iceberg of the actual environmental impact on human health. Many adverse health effects (e.g., neuropsychiatric disorders, fertility impairment, intellectual impairment, and so on) escape detection, are not reported, or are attributed to factors other than adverse environmental exposures. Of particular note is the recent finding, discussed in Chapter 2, that some toxic substances have the potential to alter gene regulation and expression by previously unrecognized epigenetic changes, alterations that may persist through successive generations.[105] Finally, in addition to single environmental exposures, multiple exposures may facilitate synergistic toxicity, where the combined impact is greater than the sum of the individual impacts.[106] According to Canada's National Collaborating Centre for Environmental Health, the foregoing factors "have led many researchers to conclude that the true burden of disease attributed to the environment has been severely underestimated."[107] The dramatic recent changes in the World Health Organization's estimates of the total number of premature deaths attributable to air pollution illustrate the potential for new scientific evidence to push estimates of the environmental burden of disease substantially higher. The latest WHO estimates doubled the number of deaths caused annually by indoor and outdoor air pollution, which now total more than 7 million.[108]

Despite large gaps in our knowledge and understanding, it is apparent that a significant proportion of premature deaths, illnesses, and disabilities in Canada are linked to environmental hazards. The involuntary and often population-wide nature of exposure to such hazards places a greater onus on governments to take the lead in reducing the health risks. As the NCCEH concluded, "while an understanding of and appreciation for existing data gaps is important, data uncertainties and limitations should not necessarily prevent potentially protective actions from being taken to try to reduce public exposures and health risks."[109] Most adverse environmental exposures could be prevented through stronger laws and policies that drive technological change and behaviour modification. As evidence for environmental influences on the health of Canadians continues to accumulate, ongoing EBD research and assessment should provide a foundation for strategic improvements in environmental legislation, health policy, and public health programs. Future work on the EBD in Canada could also benefit from both a regional approach (because of wide variations among regions in the distribution of environmental hazards) and a focus on vulnerable populations (e.g., children, Aboriginal people, and low-income Canadians). As the next chapter will emphasize, there is substantial unfairness in the distribution of environmental harms and benefits, both within Canada and around the world.

4

Environmental Injustices

Environmental justice advocates are not saying, "Take the
poisons out of our community and put them in a white
community." They are saying that no community should have to
live with these poisons.

– BENJAMIN CHAVIS, FIRST NATIONAL PEOPLE OF COLOR
ENVIRONMENTAL LEADERSHIP SUMMIT (1991)

Exacerbating the effects of the environmental burden of disease described
in Chapter 3 is the fact that the costs and benefits of the EBD are not equitably distributed among Canadians. Instead, vulnerable individuals and communities bear a disproportionate share of the burden of pollution and other
environmental hazards, and receive an inadequate share of access to environmental amenities, benefits, and resources (e.g., parks, community gardens, beaches, and farmers' markets). Environmental injustices also occur
when the voices of an identifiable group of people are excluded or silenced
in debates about pollution, development, and ecology. Environmental injustice based on race is described as environmental racism.[1] Some scholars
argue that future generations and Nature can also be the victims of environmental injustice.[2] Many environmental injustices are caused by structural
inequalities in society that result in discrimination against socially and economically marginalized groups. The converse, environmental justice, can be
defined as the meaningful involvement and fair treatment of all people and

communities – regardless of socio-economic status, ethnicity, gender, or age – in the development, implementation, and enforcement of environmental laws, regulations, and policies.[3]

Environmental injustices can take many forms, both substantive and procedural. A huge body of evidence demonstrates that major point sources of industrial pollution – chemical factories, landfill sites, pulp mills, contaminated sites, refineries, and so on – are more likely to be located in communities that are poor and/or populated by visible minorities. These neighbourhoods also suffer adverse effects related to noise, traffic, contaminated soil, odours, fewer amenities, and poorer-quality housing.[4] Nonpoint source pollution – from vehicles, urban runoff, and agricultural activities – is also inequitably distributed.[5] For example, low-income communities are more likely to be located beside highways and other busy roads. In urban settings, the proportion of green spaces and the tree canopy are consistently higher in wealthier communities.[6] Brownfield redevelopment (cleaning up and using contaminated industrial or commercial land) and other urban restoration efforts may have unintended consequences in displacing disadvantaged and marginalized populations.[7] There is also compelling evidence that environmental damage caused by the exploitation of natural resources has had, and continues to have, extensive negative health effects on Aboriginal people.[8]

An additional problem is that populations exposed to a greater proportion of environmental hazards may be more vulnerable to those hazards because their health status is already compromised. This double jeopardy could be due to poverty, poor diet, stress, or other social, psychological, and physical factors. Triple jeopardy may arise when these vulnerable populations, disproportionately exposed to environmental hazards or deprived of environmental amenities, lack access to or are underserved by the health care system. In this regard, it is also critical to understand the devastating magnitude of environmental impacts on health in developing nations. Canada has an important international role to play in addressing, not exacerbating, environmental health problems in these countries.

This chapter will briefly summarize the emergence and evolution of environmental justice in the United States before turning to Canada. The emphasis will be on assessing the extent to which Aboriginal people, visible minorities, low-income communities, and children are systematically subjected to an unfair share of environmental health risks or deprived of a fair share of environmental benefits. Canada's role in preventing environmental injustices at the international level will also be evaluated.

Environmental Injustice in the United States

Beginning in the late 1970s, American citizens, communities, and non-governmental organizations (NGOs) concerned about the unfair distribution of environmental hazards coalesced into a grassroots movement linking civil rights and environmental protection. In 1979, an African-American community in Houston, Texas, filed the first civil rights lawsuit challenging the location of a proposed landfill site.[9] In 1982, more than five hundred people were arrested in Warren County, a predominantly African-American community in North Carolina, for protesting the location of a proposed landfill for soil contaminated with PCBs. Two landmark studies during the 1980s galvanized the nascent American environmental justice movement. In 1983, prompted by the Warren County protests, the US General Accounting Office published a report looking at the racial and socio-economic characteristics of communities in southern states where hazardous waste sites were located. A disproportionate number of these environmental hazards were found in African-American communities.[10] In 1987, the United Church of Christ Commission for Racial Justice produced a report that reached the same conclusions but was national in scope. Among a suite of demographic variables, race was the most powerful predictor of where hazardous waste facilities were located. According to the report, "people of color were twice as likely as whites to live in a community with a commercial hazardous waste facility and three times as likely to have multiple facilities."[11]

In response to these reports and a growing series of local struggles, five basic principles of the environmental justice movement emerged:

- All individuals have the right to a healthy environment, free from excessive pollution or degradation, including the right to be fully involved in decision making that may affect their environment or health.
- Prevention (i.e., eliminating environmental hazards before harm occurs) is the preferred strategy (versus remediation and restoration).
- The burden of proof should be shifted to polluters who do harm.
- Discrimination is established by disparate impact and does not require proof of intent.
- Disproportionate risk burdens require immediate remediation through targeted action and resources.[12]

Hundreds of quantitative and qualitative environmental justice studies have been published in the United States in the past three decades, with most concluding that environmental hazards are disproportionately located in poor African-American and Hispanic-American neighbourhoods.[13] Among communities with one or more dangerous contaminated sites (known in the United States as Superfund sites), communities with higher proportions of African Americans and Hispanic Americans are less likely to be on the National Priority List for eventual cleanup.[14] Studies show "a strong likelihood that members of these same groups experience higher levels of environmentally generated disease and death as a result of this elevated risk."[15] Children are another vulnerable group, with studies showing that schools are often located in heavily polluted areas and that students at these schools perform more poorly than students at schools in cleaner locations.[16] There are multiple confounding factors, but the correlation between pollution and academic performance is consistent and strong. African-American children are more likely to live in close proximity to major sources of industrial air pollution.[17]

Some studies challenge the framing and methodology of the environmental justice paradigm, arguing that people are highly mobile and that poor and minority communities migrate to the cheaper land around industrial facilities. The dissenters also argue that there is no conclusive evidence that mere proximity to an environmental hazard results in health problems.[18] However, it is well established that African Americans and Latin Americans are exposed to higher levels of environmental hazards. Compared with Caucasians, African Americans suffer higher-than-average rates of infant mortality and diseases caused by environmental exposures, including asthma, other respiratory ailments, cancer, and lead poisoning.[19] Similarly, Latin Americans are more likely to suffer from asthma, lead poisoning, stomach, cervical, and uterine cancer, and some forms of leukemia.[20]

Because of the growing political power wielded by the environmental justice movement, some strides have been made at both the federal and state levels in addressing the problem.[21] In 1994, President Bill Clinton signed Executive Order 12898, mandating federal actions to address environmental justice in minority and low-income communities. The executive order required that: (1) federal agencies identify disproportionately high and adverse human health or environmental effects on minority and low-income populations that may result from federal government programs, policies, and activities; and (2) the government take action to address such disparities. More specifically, the executive order mandated improved methods of assessing and mitigating the impacts of proposed projects, incorporating health considerations into environmental assessment, collecting data from minority and low-income populations whose health may be disproportionately at risk, and taking into consideration communities that rely on subsistence hunting and fishing.[22] There is now an Office of Environmental Justice in the US Environmental Protection Agency and a National Environmental Justice Advisory Council. Environmental justice laws have been passed in many states, including Connecticut, Florida, Louisiana, Maryland, and California.[23] According to surveys published in 2007 and 2010, at least thirty-two states and the District of Columbia have adopted formal environmental justice laws, executive orders, or policies. At least ten additional states either employ full-time environmental justice officers or personnel, or have active environmental justice programs.[24]

Besides progress in the political and policy arenas, there have been victories on the ground. A proposed uranium enrichment facility in rural Louisiana was rejected on the basis of noncompliance with Executive Order 12898, as local citizens raised questions about the fairness of locating the facility in an African-American community. It was the first time that the Nuclear Regulatory Commission had ever denied a permit application.[25] American courts have begun to respond positively to lawsuits asserting both substantive and procedural environmental injustices.[26] Other local victories include shutting down major incinerators and landfills in Los Angeles and Chicago, preventing chemical factories and coal-fired power plants from being built or expanded, improving environmental sanitation services, reducing hazardous releases at major industrial facilities, and negotiating compensation packages for affected residents.[27]

Of course, the problems are far from resolved.[28] As noted by the EPA's inspector general, the federal government is still not doing an effective job of enforcing its environmental justice mandate.[29] The impacts of the National Environmental Justice Advisory Council and Executive Order 12898 have been positive in raising the profile of environmental justice issues but not as successful in terms of changing on-the-ground practices. Under President George W. Bush, less attention and fewer resources were dedicated to alleviating environmental injustices. According to the US Commission on Civil Rights, the Bush administration failed to develop a comprehensive strategic plan for realizing Executive Order 12898, failed to establish performance measures for assessing implementation, de-emphasized the disproportionate exposure of minority and low-income communities in its approach to addressing environmental hazards, and failed to increase the participation of affected minority and low-income communities in meaningful decision-making processes.[30] The Obama administration increased the profile of environmental justice and allocated more resources to this issue, but is regarded by critics as having a mixed record, with more promises than achievements.[31] However, when announcing new regulations limiting carbon pollution from coal plants in 2014, President Obama noted that "the health issues that we're talking about hit some communities particularly hard. African-American children are twice as likely to be hospitalized for asthma, four times as likely to die from asthma. Latinos are 30 percent more likely to be hospitalized for asthma. So these proposed standards will help us meet that challenge head on."[32]

Environmental Injustice in Canada

The environmental justice paradigm has now spread from the United States to other nations, including the United Kingdom, Australia, South Africa, and Sweden.[33] The World Health Organization published a comprehensive report on environmental health inequalities in Europe.[34] As recently as 2007, however, scholars stated that there was no discernible "environmental justice" movement in Canada, and environmental justice research was limited.[35] The mainstream environmental movement in Canada was accused of failing to address environmental injustices.[36] Even in 2014, researchers concluded that the role of sex/gender and race/ethnicity in influencing exposures to environmental contaminants has not been adequately addressed.[37] The slow emergence of the environmental justice paradigm in Canada may be due to the delayed availability of reliable data on environmental hazards and census data on race and ethnicity. The National Pollutant Release Inventory was first published in 1994. The federal Contaminated Sites Inventory was not published until 2002. Information on the racial and ethnic composition of the Canadian population was not compiled until the 1996 and 2001 censuses. These types of data were available much earlier in the United States. The delayed attention to environmental justice may be partly attributable to the fact that other labels have been applied to these issues in Canada. A thorough review of scholarly journals identified hundreds of articles dealing with Canadian subjects that could have been, but were not, described as environmental justice.[38] Canada must also overcome the cultural myth that our relatively small population and huge country combine to ensure a pristine environment. Another prevailing myth, that Canada is a bastion of multiculturalism where racism has been expunged, may also contribute to the delayed emergence of an environmental justice perspective.

Although the environmental justice movement was slow to emerge in Canada, it is now gaining momentum. Activists and scholars are using the language and framing of environmental justice with increasing frequency. In recent years, a national network was created, the Centre for Environmental Health Equity was established, several books were published, and dozens of academic articles addressing environmental justice in Canada were written.[39] In contrast to the United States, however, Canadian laws and policies have not yet been revised to take environmental justice considerations into account.

The Government of Canada admits that "we know that some segments of our population are exposed to unacceptably high levels of environmental pollutants."[40] Vulnerable groups of Canadians include children, Aboriginal people, African Canadians, recent immigrants, migrant workers, individuals with compromised immune systems or environmental sensitivities, and people experiencing social and economic disadvantages such as poverty and homelessness. Often these factors operate in combination. For example, authorities have known since the mid-1980s that Ontario children living in poverty are at greater risk of exposure to harmful levels of lead.[41] Aboriginal children in socio-economically disadvantaged communities are exposed to high levels of PCBs, mercury, lead, pesticides, and other harmful contaminants.

Individuals have different levels of susceptibility to environmental health impacts. For example, some individuals may have variations in the genes that are involved in metabolizing toxic substances, so that exposure to certain toxic substances may be harmless for some people while making other individuals sick.[42] An American study found that some individuals are ten thousand times more sensitive to certain types of particulate air pollution.[43]

Aboriginal People

In our region, Elders say that the weather is Uggianaqtuq –
meaning it behaves unexpectedly, or in an unfamiliar way ...
We depend on the bounty of the land for our survival. The
traditional Inuit diet is being eroded as animals are less plentiful,
less healthy and more difficult to harvest. Further, as the planet
warms more persistent organic pollutants, of which Inuit are
the net highest recipients on the planet, find their way to our

homeland through the additional run-off from watersheds that empty in the Arctic. We can no longer rely on the traditional practice of food caching as food rots and insects invade caches. Often our access to our traditional hunting is cut-off as sea-ice is depleted and permafrost slumps or melts. These changes undermine the realization of our rights to culture, life, health and means of subsistence ... For the first time in my history, my hometown had to start to use air conditioners. Imagine, air conditioners in the Arctic. It's almost unbelievable.

– SHEILA WATT-CLOUTIER (2007)

The closest Canadian analogy to the American experience of pollution and other environmental hazards being disproportionately targeted towards poor, minority communities lies in the mistreatment of Aboriginal people, including First Nations, Métis, and the Inuit. This mistreatment is part of a broader pattern that includes dispossession, colonial oppression, economic exploitation, social marginalization, and physical, sexual, and psychological abuse. As noted in a recent book on environmental injustices in Canada, ever "since European contact, Aboriginal peoples have been articulating environmental injustices in relation to loss of land, Aboriginal title, and devastation of their traditional territories and the life forms they support."[44] In many cases, these environmental injustices have taken an extreme form, such as the notorious exploitation of Aboriginal workers at the Eldorado uranium mine at Port Radium (near Great Bear Lake in the Northwest Territories) and the displacement of entire communities to make way for industrial development.[45] The original James Bay hydroelectric projects in Quebec and Alcan's Kemano Project in British Columbia displaced thousands of Cree and Cheslatta Carrier people. It is estimated that sixty Aboriginal communities in Canada were moved to make way for hydroelectric projects.[46] Hydroelectric projects being planned and developed today – in British Columbia, Manitoba, Quebec, and Newfoundland and Labrador – will result in flooding of traditional territories and additional relocations. Exploration for uranium on traditional Aboriginal lands continues in Canada today, with opponents sent to prison for attempting to defend their land and their people.[47] Displacement of Aboriginal people for resource development results not only in health problems but also in devastating social and cultural impacts.[48] On nearly every marker of social inclusion or equity, Aboriginals fare far worse than other Canadians, with higher poverty rates, poorer housing, lower levels of formal education, lower employment levels, lower retention and promotion in employment, higher suicide and incarceration rates, and poorer health.[49]

Aboriginal communities that rely on traditional diets are vulnerable to mercury and other contaminants in fish and wildlife. For example, the Aboriginal community of Fort Chipewyan, located near the tar sands projects in Alberta, appears to be experiencing disproportionate levels of cancer, and studies have identified high levels of contaminants in their traditional foods, including fish and moose.[50] Many Aboriginal communities situated in proximity to hydroelectric projects have experienced mercury contamination of fish species that were a dietary staple.[51] Mercury dumped into an Ontario river by a pulp and paper mill between 1962 and 1972 poisoned hundreds of members of the Grassy Narrows First Nation.[52] The Aboriginal community on Walpole Island in Ontario suffers the ongoing health consequences of toxic chemicals spilled or dumped into the St. Clair River, one of the most polluted water bodies in Canada.[53] Although Canada has reduced or eliminated the use of some harmful pollutants, including dioxins, mercury, and PCBs, new studies indicate that levels of these toxic substances are still rising in some locations. For example, burbot caught in the Northwest Territories' Mackenzie River in 2009 contained higher levels of PCBs, mercury, and DDT than fish caught in previous years.[54]

Northern Aboriginals, particularly Inuit eating a traditional diet, have body burdens of toxic chemicals that threaten both their health and the health of their children.[55] For example, 73 percent of Inuit mothers have PCBs in their blood at concentrations that exceed Health Canada's level of concern, as well as oxychlordane and trans-nonachlor concentrations (from pesticides) that are six to twelve times higher than other Canadian mothers.[56] Similar patterns were observed for other toxic chemicals, including PCBs, hexachlorobenzene (HCB), mirex, and toxaphene. Inuit women have significantly higher levels of mercury in their blood than other Canadian women.[57] Mercury levels in Inuit children, at ten to twenty times higher than the general Canadian population, are high enough to cause neurological damage.[58] A recent study demonstrated that exposure to lead, mercury, and PCBs is having adverse effects on Inuit children's behaviour and development, including increased risk of ADHD.[59]

One of Canada's most notorious pollution hotspots – Chemical Valley in Sarnia, Ontario – has disturbing health effects on the Aamjiwnaang

First Nation. There are more than sixty large petrochemical, polymer, and chemical facilities in close proximity to the Aamjiwnaang reserve.[60] This community has the worst air quality in Canada.[61] Both physical and psychological health problems are rampant, ranging from high rates of miscarriages and childhood asthma to cancer and premature deaths.[62] In the five years from 1999 to 2003, the proportion of male babies born on the Aamjiwnaang reserve fell from normal levels (slightly over half of all births) to less than 35 percent of births.[63] The sex ratio may be affected by exposure to environmental contaminants, including dioxins, PCBs, pesticides, and mercury.[64] The ongoing public health disaster at Aamjiwnaang has been described as "a particularly distressing example of the failure of our regulatory system to uphold environmental justice."[65]

Aboriginal people living on reserves face severe drinking water contamination and indoor air quality problems. Thousands of Aboriginal people live in communities without running water or indoor toilets, raising the risks of infectious diseases such as shigellosis and influenza.[66] The majority of the community of Kashechewan (in northern Ontario) was evacuated in 2006 because of unsafe drinking water. The problem was caused by the placement of the drinking water intake pipe downstream from the sewage outflow pipe. An audit by Canada's Commissioner of the Environment and Sustainable Development uncovered a long list of problems plaguing the provision of drinking water on reserves, including inadequate resources, lack of trained operators, inappropriate treatment systems, and the lack of legally binding standards for water quality.[67] Boil-water advisories in Aboriginal communities are much more common than in non-Aboriginal communities. At any given time, more than a hundred reserves (one in six) face boil-water advisories, many of which drag on for months and even years.[68] Shigellosis is an acute bacterial disease – characterized by bloody diarrhea, nausea, and fever – that is, fortunately, rare in Canada and thus unfamiliar to most Canadians. However, the incidence rate of shigellosis is twenty-six times higher for people living on Aboriginal reserves than for non-Aboriginals, and a hundred times higher for Aboriginal children than for non-Aboriginal children.[69] Susceptibility to shigellosis is related to water quality, sewage treatment practices, and housing conditions. Housing conditions on Aboriginal reserves are often terrible, with severe indoor air quality problems caused by mould, poor construction, and overcrowding.

Additional examples of environmental injustices facing Canada's Aboriginal people include abandoned mines that are now classified as contaminated sites, new mines in traditional territories, salmon farming (due to its ad-verse effects on native salmon species that sustain BC First Nations both physically and culturally), and oil and gas development.

Finally, it is likely that, of all the people in the world, the Inuit and First Nations in northern Canada are among those most severely affected by climate change.[70] Many Inuit continue to live a traditional lifestyle, relying directly on plants, animals, and healthy ecosystems for their mobility, nutrition, and cultural survival.[71] According to scientists, average Arctic temperatures have risen twice as fast as global temperatures, and this gap is expected to grow in the decades ahead. The impacts are already substantial:

> Warmer spring and autumn temperatures are associated with earlier ice thaw and later freeze-up. In some cases, these phenomena pose significant hazards for transportation in hunting as well as diminishing habitat for marine mammals and polar bears. Diminished shore-fast and sea ice has led to increased storm intensity causing severe coastal erosion and requiring the relocation of homes and communities. Lakes are drying up and water temperatures in lakes and rivers are increasing, affecting fish populations. Weather patterns that have for generations served as cues for hunters in accessing game and traveling safely are no longer familiar or predictable.[72]

Both the Inuit and Arctic Athabaskan people have filed complaints with the Inter-American Commission on Human Rights, asserting that climate change is violating their rights, including rights to health and to live in a healthy environment.[73] Professor Sophie Theriault argues persuasively that the Inuit need to be given a greater role in territorial, national, and global decision-making processes in order to achieve more just outcomes and to enhance the Inuit's ability to adapt to changing environmental conditions.[74]

Visible Minorities

> It's pretty intimidating to have three or four white people in your community and you don't know what the hell is going on and they're talking about cells and there is going to be 17 cells. Well I asked one of the elders of the community "do you know what cells mean?" All they could think of was a jail cell.
>
> – ANDREA, VOCAL OPPONENT OF LINCOLNVILLE,
> NOVA SCOTIA, LANDFILL (2012)

> There were a few meetings I think. I don't know how much input
> the people actually had. I think by the time those sessions were
> scheduled the dump was a done deal. It was just, what's the
> saying? Lip service.
>
> – GERALD, LONG-TERM LINCOLNVILLE, NOVA SCOTIA,
> RESIDENT (2012)

There is a modest amount of evidence indicating that environmental racism afflicts visible minorities in Canada, though the situation is less systemic than in the United States. A prime example was Africville, a community established just north of Halifax in the early 1800s. Africville's population, as the name suggests, was almost entirely black. Africville was eventually incorporated into the growing city of Halifax but never received municipal services such as treated drinking water. In the 1960s, the citizens of Africville were relocated and the community was bulldozed as part of an urban renewal program.[75] A second example, also from Nova Scotia, involved the Halifax Metropolitan Authority's 1992 decision to locate a solid waste landfill at East Lake, close to several communities with majority African-Canadian populations. This decision, made without consulting local residents, was typical of the situations that spawned the environmental justice movement in the United States. Halifax reversed its decision in 1993 as a result of vocal opposition to the proposed location.[76] In 2006, however, a new solid waste landfill was approved adjacent to Lincolnville, a predominantly African-Canadian community. Local residents believed that the public consultation process preceding the approval was grossly inadequate and failed to consider environmental justice issues.[77]

For the most part, urban settlement patterns in Canada are quite distinct from those in American cities. Canadian patterns of environmental injustice also differ significantly for reasons related to history, politics, and demographics. Research on the relationship between ethnicity and disproportionate exposure to environmental hazards in Canada has yielded mixed results.[78] Studies from Hamilton show that the Latino immigrant population lives in areas with poor ambient air quality, the Korean immigrant population (with the advantage of higher socio-economic status) lives in the cleanest neighbourhoods, and there is no clear connection between Black Canadians and levels of air pollution.[79] However, a recent study from Toronto suggests that both visible minorities and communities with low socio-economic status "are disproportionately located near facilities that release both large quantities

and the most harmful pollutants."[80] These findings were particularly clear
for South Asian and Filipino populations.

Low-Income Communities and Socio-Economically
Disadvantaged Canadians

> The number one problem for a homeless person right now,
> you got to realize that if your feet get wet and they stay wet you
> are going to get sick, people suffer with cracked feet, sores on
> their feet.
>
> – ECHO, HOMELESS PERSON IN WATERLOO, ONTARIO

Poor rural communities and poor neighbourhoods in Canadian cities suffer
from various forms of environmental injustice. A groundbreaking study by
the Canadian Population Health Initiative found that Canadians with lower
socio-economic status are much more likely to live near roads with high
traffic density and much more likely to live within one kilometre of a major
pollution-emitting facility. In total, more than 1 million low-income Canadians (one in four) live less than a kilometre from a major industrial polluter. Not surprisingly, rates of hospitalization for cardiovascular and
respiratory diseases are significantly higher for residents of those neighbourhoods. The closer Canadians live to major polluting facilities, the higher
their rates of hospitalization for cardiovascular and respiratory diseases.[81]
In a particularly egregious case, low-income residents of Ontario's Sarnia
region suffer the highest exposure to air pollution in Canada but have sub-
par access to family doctors.[82]

There are many notorious specific examples of the linkage between
poverty and elevated exposure to environmental hazards in Canada. The
steel- and coal-producing communities of Cape Breton County in Nova
Scotia are both socio-economically disadvantaged and among the most
polluted areas in North America. Cancer rates in the steel-producing communities, and respiratory diseases and lung cancers in the coal-producing
regions, are far above national averages.[83] The Sydney Tar Ponds, where over
a century of steel production occurred without adequate environmental
regulation, are often cited as an example of environmental injustice.[84] They
have been identified by the federal government as the worst contaminated
site in Canada, and nearby residents and their children continue to be
exposed to levels of lead, arsenic, and polycyclic aromatic hydrocarbons

(PAHs) that exceed Canadian guidelines.[85] There are now more than two hundred epidemiological studies related to the adverse health effects of the Tar Ponds, including the finding that the rate of cervical cancer among women in Sydney is 134 percent above the provincial average.[86]

Socio-economic status is a good predictor of pollution levels, as proven by studies from Hamilton, Toronto, Montreal, and Vancouver. It was first reported in 1977 that low-income neighbourhoods in Hamilton suffer a disproportionate amount of air pollution.[87] More recently, researchers using geographic information system technology confirmed that low income, low education (less than Grade 9), family status (single parents), dwelling value, and unemployment are significant predictors of exposure to particulate air pollution in Hamilton.[88]

Within Toronto, there are seventeen neighbourhoods where high levels of air pollution and poverty coincide, indicating that people in these communities face a double challenge when it comes to protecting their health.[89] Neighbourhoods marked by low education, single-parent families, and low incomes were more likely to have higher ambient nitrogen dioxide exposure.[90] In areas of Toronto where tall apartment towers are filled with a mixture of recent immigrants, food deserts exist due to zoning restrictions that limit mixed land uses and make food services and retailers inaccessible to pedestrians.[91]

In Montreal, pollution patterns do not consistently support the environmental justice hypothesis. Some neighbourhoods with higher proportions of visible minorities, low-income households, unemployed adults, and individuals living alone faced higher ambient levels of nitrogen dioxide.[92] However, higher levels of air pollution cross social and economic boundaries to afflict both low-income and affluent communities.[93]

A comparison of patterns of exposure to air pollution in Seattle and Vancouver found that while lower income was consistently correlated with poorer air quality, immigrant populations in Seattle but not Vancouver were exposed to higher levels of pollution.[94]

In contrast, wealthier communities are often able to use their political power to avoid the siting of industrial or waste management facilities. In 2010 and 2011, the Ontario government responded to pressure from the high-income residents of Oakville and Mississauga by violating contracts with a company that was planning to build natural gas–fired electricity plants in those cities. These cancellations helped the Liberals retain power in the subsequent election, but at a cost of hundreds of millions of dollars to Ontario taxpayers.

The flip side of excessive exposure to environmental hazards is inadequate access to environmental assets. Relatively little research addresses this issue. A pioneering study found that lower-income neighbourhoods in Toronto, Montreal, and Vancouver have less vegetation, which is an environmental amenity associated with better physical and mental health, improved developmental conditions for children, and better social conditions (e.g., less crime).[95]

Homeless People

Researchers and local governments have begun to investigate the effects of climate change upon homeless individuals, who are among Canada's most vulnerable people. Homeless individuals endure higher rates of underlying disease (including respiratory and cardiovascular diseases), social isolation, drug and alcohol addiction, and greater exposure to the elements, and are more likely to occupy high-risk urban areas.[96] Thus, homeless people will be disproportionately harmed by increased heat waves, increased air pollution, increased frequency and severity of floods and storms, and the changing distribution of vector-borne diseases such as West Nile virus.[97] Future increases in ambient ozone concentrations will also be particularly detrimental to those people who spend the majority of time outside and who may already have weakened respiratory and immune systems. In addition, many people experiencing homelessness experience compounding stresses such as psychiatric illnesses. Some psychotropic medications increase the risk of sunstroke, heat exhaustion, sunburn, and dehydration. While some health benefits may result from warmer winters, such as fewer deaths from freezing, the adverse impacts of climate change are expected to outweigh any benefits.

Children

Children are potential victims of environmental injustice because they may face disproportionate levels of exposure to toxic substances and are particularly sensitive to harm.[98] Children are uniquely vulnerable to environmental impacts on their health for five reasons. First, children are different from adults in terms of behaviour, diet, physiology, and metabolism. Relative to the size of adults, children breathe more air, drink larger volumes of fluids, and consume more food. Children are more active and engage in activities such as crawling and putting things in their mouths. Second, environmental exposures can cause developmental damage to children during what experts call "windows of vulnerability," when children and fetuses are particularly sensitive. Third, children will live longer than adults, so there is a longer time for exposure to environmental chemicals to result in adverse consequences. Fourth, the natural defences of children's bodies, such as their ability to metabolize toxic substances into less harmful substances, are less developed. Fifth, children have limited knowledge of potential environmental risks and limited ability to avoid risks to their health.[99] Serious afflictions, including diabetes, cardiovascular disease, Parkinson's disease, and cancer, are influenced by early environmental exposures.[100]

The most important environmental threats to the health of children are lead, air pollution (both indoor and outdoor air), water contaminants, environmental tobacco smoke, and pesticides.[101] Biomonitoring studies demonstrate that young children have higher body burdens than adults for some chemicals, including polybrominated diphenyl ethers (PBDEs). The dramatic increase in the prevalence of childhood asthma in Canada is linked to environmental factors. Although asthma is a complex disease, environmental threats, including air pollution, second-hand smoke, pesticides, plasticizers, volatile organic compounds, and dust, exacerbate asthma and may play a role in the development of the disease.[102] Cancer is the second leading killer of children in Canada, although cases are rare, the incidence rate is fairly stable, and mortality rates are declining due to improved treatments.[103] Breastfed infants younger than six months in the Great Lakes region are likely to be exposed to six times the tolerable daily intake of dioxins, a potent carcinogen.[104]

Children under the age of six years old comprise only 6.4 percent of the total Canadian population but experience almost half of the acute pesticide poisonings.[105] Canadian children who live near lead smelters continue to suffer from elevated blood lead levels, placing them at risk of substantial developmental effects. Striking new studies indicate that childhood lead exposure may be linked to violent behaviour in adults.[106] The US National Academy of Sciences estimates that 28 percent of learning disabilities and developmental disorders are caused by environmental factors and the interactions between genes and environmental hazards.[107] Children from low-income families and children in Aboriginal communities face a double risk, as the health effects of living in poverty are exacerbated by environmental hazards. For example, research from Saskatchewan indicates that levels of asthma in Canada are greater among school-aged children from low-income families, although other nonenvironmental factors are involved.[108]

These disturbing examples make it clear that much work remains to be done to adequately protect Canadian children from environmental hazards. Many Canadian NGOs are working to promote children's environmental health issues in Canada, led by the Canadian Partnership for Children's Health and Environment.[109] Some progress is being made, although the rate of change is slow. To the extent that they incorporate health considerations, most Canadian environmental standards are designed to protect adults, not children, for whom more stringent standards are often required.[110] The first phase of the federal government's national biomonitoring program excluded children under the age of six – the most vulnerable segment of the population. And yet, as the North American Commission for Environmental Cooperation concluded, "if we create an environment that is safe and healthful for children, possibly the most sensitive and vulnerable among us, we create an environment safe and healthful for all."[111]

Environmental Impacts on Health in Developing Countries

> I think the economic logic behind dumping a load of toxic waste in the lowest wage country is impeccable ... I've always thought that under-populated countries in Africa are vastly UNDER-polluted.
>
> – LAWRENCE SUMMERS, FORMER VICE-PRESIDENT
> OF THE WORLD BANK, 1991[112]

Another aspect of environmental injustice involves the environmental harms suffered by citizens of countries that are less economically wealthy than Canada. In developing nations, one-quarter of the total burden of disease is attributable to environmental factors.[113] Air pollution (indoor and outdoor), contaminated water, acute exposures to pesticides, and toxic waste are pervasive problems.[114] The environmental impacts on health experienced in developing nations may be caused, directly or indirectly, by wealthy citizens of rich nations. For example, scientific research has revealed that air pollution from the northern hemisphere (predominantly Europe and North America) has played a role in the crippling droughts that have afflicted sub-Saharan Africa in recent decades.[115]

The World Health Organization estimates that more than 1.6 million people die annually in poor countries because of unsafe drinking water and inadequate sanitation facilities, which result in diarrheal diseases.[116] Indoor air pollution, predominantly from burning fuels for cooking and heating, is estimated to kill more than 3.5 million people per year.[117] Outdoor air pollution, caused by motor vehicles, burning of fossil fuels to generate electricity, and industrial activity, causes more than 3 million deaths annually.[118] Exposure to lead causes thousands of deaths globally each year, besides damaging the development of a substantial proportion of the world's children.[119] Poisonings caused by exposure to pesticides and other toxic chemicals are estimated to kill thousands of people annually.[120] The impacts of climate change in the short term, including more extreme weather events, changing patterns of disease, and changing agricultural patterns, are estimated to cause 150,000–300,000 deaths per year, while adversely affecting the health of hundreds of millions of people.[121] A study in the British medical journal *The Lancet* estimates that 700,000 premature deaths will occur annually worldwide by 2020 if climate change policies are not implemented successfully.[122] Although climate change is primarily caused by the wealthy industrialized nations, the adverse health effects are predominantly suffered by developing nations. These countries bear little responsibility for the problem but are more vulnerable and less equipped to adapt. Malaria is already spreading to higher elevations in Africa, threatening new populations. Increased drought is projected to have the greatest impact on regions of Africa that are already experiencing significant levels of malnutrition. Even the shift towards biofuels in wealthy nations will cause a backlash in developing nations if fuel crops replace food crops or if commodity prices rise, making it more difficult to afford adequate levels of nutrition.

Unless preventive and remedial steps are taken immediately, these devastating environmental health outcomes may worsen in the decades ahead. Canada has a moral responsibility, as one of the wealthiest and healthiest nations in the world, to assist developing nations in moving towards a sustainable future. In the area of environmental impacts on health, to its credit, Canada led the creation of the Health and Environment Linkages Initiative, now run by the World Health Organization and the UN Environment Programme. The project is a small but well-intentioned global effort to reduce environmental threats to human health in developing nations. However, there is much more that Canada could and should be doing, as outlined in Part 3 of this book.

In several cases of international environmental injustice, Canada is behaving unconscionably, including the promotion of asbestos use and consistent opposition to listing asbestos pursuant to the Rotterdam Convention on hazardous substances. Canada has been criticized for the mining industry's substandard practices in developing nations. Canadian mining companies have been embroiled in health and environmental controversies in Papua New Guinea, Indonesia, Colombia, Mexico, Chile, Guatemala, Ecuador, Argentina, and El Salvador.[123] Mining companies are often accused of causing extensive environmental damage and human rights violations, ranging from air and water pollution to loss of forests and violence against local communities.

Canadian Asbestos: Exporting Death and Disease
Compelling evidence that every type of asbestos is carcinogenic has led more than fifty industrialized nations (including Australia and the European Union) to ban the import, sale, and use of asbestos.[124] Asbestos exposure causes over ninety thousand deaths annually worldwide, leading the WHO to conclude that "the most efficient way to eliminate asbestos-related diseases is to stop using all types of asbestos."[125] The International Labour Organization also supports a global ban on the use of asbestos.[126] Most uses of asbestos are banned in Canada.

Until recently, Canada ranked among the top asbestos-producing and exporting nations in the world. Over 95 percent of the asbestos mined in Canada in recent years was exported to developing countries such as India, Mexico, Thailand, and the Philippines, where adequate health and safety regulations either do not exist or are not enforced.[127] As a result, Canada knowingly exported a product that in coming decades will result in thousands of deaths from mesothelioma, asbestosis, and lung cancer in Asia, Africa, and Latin America.[128] Despite the well-established health hazards, until 2014 Canada opposed international efforts to restrict global trade in asbestos. In 2006, 2008, and 2011, Canada led efforts to block restrictions on international trade in chrysotile asbestos pursuant to the Rotterdam Convention, against the recommendations of scientific experts.[129] The Canadian government also subsidized an industry lobby group called the Chrysotile Institute, pouring in roughly $20 million over the past twenty-five years.[130] The Chrysotile Institute downplayed the health risks of chrysotile asbestos and promoted its use in developing countries. Although Canada stopped exporting asbestos in 2013, this change was the result of economic factors rather than government policy, and it is possible that exports could resume in the future. The export of Canadian asbestos, with its inevitable byproducts of death and disease, has tarnished our nation's good name with the stain of hypocrisy.

Conclusion

Environmental justice is becoming an increasingly prominent political issue, social movement, and media topic in Canada. As Chapter 6 will explore, policymakers have not yet responded. However, the growing evidence of inequality – from British Columbia to Nunavut to Nova Scotia – suggests that this situation could reach a tipping point in the near future. Even in rural Alberta, ranching and farming families are being described as environmental refugees, forced to leave their homes because of intolerable pollution from fracking and the extraction of bitumen.[131] Vulnerable people are underrepresented in environmental governance and treated unfairly, resulting in "compounded disadvantages" caused by the combined effects of environmental disadvantage, poverty, and poor health.[132] As several of this country's leading experts observed: "While there have been many examples of communities across Canada advocating for local environmental justice, the overall trend in this country is one of increasing prevalence and severity of environmental hazards, compounding social vulnerabilities, further marginalizing communities and exacerbating overall health inequity."[133] Anger is brewing at the grassroots level, and researchers are finally focusing attention on these previously neglected problems. A similar combination of fury and evidence helped spark the emergence of the American environmental justice movement, a movement that has become a prominent force in promoting the equal protection of all Americans from environmental hazards, regardless of economic status or the colour of their skin.

Canada trails other nations, from the United States to Scotland, in attempting to remedy environmental injustices. As two leading authorities on the distribution of environmental harms concluded, "[Canadian] policy on environmental justice remains in its infancy."[134] Ultimately, as explored in Part 3, Canada needs to go beyond addressing the unfair distribution of environmental hazards to eliminate these hazards, ensure equitable access to environmental amenities, and overcome the structural determinants of inequality.[135]

5

The Economic Costs of the Environmental Burden of Disease

Information on the costs of disease caused by environmental contamination can lead to major policy changes, save hundreds of billions of dollars and improve the lives of generations.
– PHILIP J. LANDRIGAN, MD (2012)

As noted in Chapter 1, health care expenditures in Canada have been locked in an upward spiral in recent decades, devouring resources previously allocated to education, social programs, and environmental protection. In the past decade alone, total health expenditures doubled from $100 billion per year to over $200 billion.[1] Spending by provincial and territorial governments ballooned from $8.7 billion in 1975 to $126 billion in 2012.[2] Health care now consumes approximately 40 percent of provincial and territorial budgets. Since 1996, the average annual increase has been 4.4 percent, well above the overall rate of inflation. Per capita health care expenditures surpassed $6,000 per year in 2013, compared with approximately $500 per person in 1975.[3] Health care spending as a proportion of GDP rose from 7 percent in 1975 to 12 percent today.[4] As Canada's population continues to grow older, health care spending is expected to continue its ascent, with hospitals, drugs, and doctors consuming the biggest slices of the spending pie.

As astounding as these statistics may seem, they mask even larger economic impacts, for they include only direct spending on health care. Not incorporated are the indirect costs of lost productivity due to illnesses, injuries, and premature deaths, or the intangible costs related to pain, suffering, decreased quality of life, and loss of life.

Remarkably, despite the extensive attention devoted to rising Canadian health care expenditures, "the question of whether societal investments in environmental protection lead to reduced health expenditures remains largely unaddressed."[5] For example, a 2011 report published by the Canadian Institute for Health Information on the drivers of health care spending contained zero references to environmental factors.[6] Similarly, a report by the Conference Board of Canada on the relationship between the sustainability of our health care system and the state of our economy ignored environmental factors.[7] A common theme in the scholarly literature about the health care costs associated with environmental hazards is that these costs are consistently overlooked or underestimated.[8] This is particularly true with respect to new or complex issues such as climate change, nanotechnology, epigenetics, and endocrine-disrupting chemicals.[9]

The surprising magnitude of the environmental burden of disease (EBD) in Canada, described in Chapter 3, carries with it immense economic costs. This chapter will examine the health care costs attributable to environmental pollution and degradation, including direct, indirect, and intangible costs. Then the perspective will be reversed. Most environmental harms and their associated health effects are preventable, meaning that these costs can be reimagined as potential benefits. The latter half of the chapter will investigate the extent to which, given today's health care costs inflicted by the environmental burden of disease, stronger environmental protection in Canada could produce substantial economic benefits by preventing morbidity and mortality. Economic studies measuring the health benefits of stronger environmental regulation – from Canada and around the world – illustrate the realistic possibility that Canadians could save not only thousands of lives but also billions of dollars annually. It is important to note that there are additional economic costs related to environmental degradation not addressed in this chapter, such as the diminished value of natural capital, ecosystem services, agricultural productivity, the cost of remediation and restoration, and decreases in utility (e.g., diminished visibility due to air pollution).

Estimating the Direct, Indirect, and Intangible Costs

The environmental burden of disease, examined in depth in Chapter 3, provides the basis for estimating the economic costs associated with preventable environmental hazards in Canada. There are three elements of the total

TABLE 5.1
The direct economic costs of the EBD in Canada

Disease category	Direct costs (2014)	EAF[a]	EBD (2014 dollars)
Respiratory	$5,413	10–30%	$541–1,624
Cardiovascular	$13,360	7.5–15%	$1,002–2,004
Cancer	$21,366	5–15%	$1,068–3,205
Congenital	$521	2–10%	$10–52
Total			$2,621–6,885

Note: All monetary amounts are in millions of Canadian dollars per year.
a   Environmentally attributable fraction.

health care costs to society: direct costs, indirect costs, and intangible costs. Direct health care costs represent the value of goods and services used in treatment, care, and rehabilitation related to illness or injury.[10] The three largest direct costs in Canada are hospital expenses, payments to physicians, and prescription drugs. Second, indirect costs represent "the value of economic output lost because of illness, injury-related work disability, or premature death."[11] These costs are often measured in terms of lost potential earnings. Other indirect costs, not often included in calculations because of poor data availability, include underperformance at work due to sickness, the value of lost nonmarket services (e.g., volunteering) due to illness or disability, and the value of time lost from work and leisure activities by family members or friends providing care to ill persons. The third category, intangible costs, reflects the economic value people attribute to better health or the avoidance of pain, stress, suffering, and premature death.

This economic analysis builds on the data in the Boyd and Genuis study described in Chapter 3, which covered only four categories of illness: respiratory, cardiovascular, cancer, and congenital disorders.[12] The analysis is inherently conservative, as environmental hazards contribute to a much broader range of adverse health outcomes than these four categories. Direct costs were determined by using the most recent publicly available data on health care expenditures and adjusting for inflation.[13] The direct health care costs caused by environmental hazards for these four categories range from $2.6 billion to $6.9 billion per year (see Table 5.1).

Indirect costs were also determined by using the most recent publicly available data on health care expenditures and adjusting for inflation.[14] The

TABLE 5.2
The indirect economic costs of the EBD in Canada

Disease category	Indirect costs (2014)	EAF[a]	EBD (2014 dollars)
Respiratory	$5,200	10–30%	$520–1,560
Cardiovascular	$20,805	7.5–15%	$1,560–3,121
Cancer	$24,729	5–15%	$1,237–3,709
Congenital	$895	2–10%	$18–90
Total			$3,335–8,480

Note: All monetary amounts are in millions of Canadian dollars per year.
a   Environmentally attributable fraction.

calculation results in a range of indirect health care costs from $3.3 billion to $8.5 billion (see Table 5.2). Adding the direct and indirect costs of the EBD in Canada results in a total range from $6.0 billion to $15.4 billion per year.

Intangible costs were estimated through a method widely used by Health Canada, Environment Canada, the Conference Board of Canada, the US Environmental Protection Agency, and other experts. Economists developed a concept called the "value of a statistical life" (VSL) to monetize the reduced risk of death. The VSL approach does not assign an economic value to any particular person's life. Instead, it uses data on individual willingness to pay for small reductions in the risk of death, and extrapolates from these data to determine society's cumulative willingness to pay for reductions in risk that, on a statistical basis, would be expected to result in the avoidance of a premature death. For example, on average, individuals might be willing to pay $75 to reduce the annual risk of dying from contaminated drinking water from 2 in 100,000 to 1 in 100,000. Adding the average willingness to pay of the 100,000 individuals provides the VSL, which in this example would be $75 times 100,000, or $7.5 million.[15] A law, policy, or program could be implemented to reduce the risk so that there would be one less death per 100,000 from contaminated water. Thus the VSL approach estimates the economic value of health or environmental regulations or actions that, on a statistical basis, are expected to save lives. In the preceding example, if a new drinking water regulation was expected to prevent 100 deaths, it would offer an economic benefit of $750 million (subject to a discount rate if the deaths would have occurred over a number of years), to be weighed against the costs of implementation. The VSL was used by Canadian and

TABLE 5.3
The value of a statistical life in Canada

Estimate	Value
Low estimate	$3.5 million
Central estimate	$6.5 million
High estimate	$9.5 million

American governments in the cost-benefit analyses described later in this chapter for air pollution laws, rules governing coal-fired electricity plants, and regulations restricting sulphur levels in gasoline.

The latest guidance from Health Canada recommends using a range of low, medium, and high values for the VSL, as set forth in Table 5.3.[16] This approach is consistent with a recent meta-analysis of VSLs used in wealthy industrialized countries that examined thirty-two studies and found that the average VSL was $8.4 million, while the median VSL was $5 million. The majority of the thirty-two studies were from the United States and Canada.[17]

These VSL figures were used in conjunction with estimates of premature deaths attributable to environmental factors in Canada provided by the World Health Organization, the Canadian Medical Association, and the Boyd and Genuis study.[18] The average of the three studies, using Health Canada's VSL figures, ranges from $87.6 billion to $237.8 billion, with a central estimate of $162.7 billion (see Table 5.4). The Boyd and Genuis study provides the most conservative approach, with a central estimate of $112.5 billion as the yearly cost of premature mortality in Canada due to the EBD.

Using the central estimate for the Boyd and Genuis approach to intangible costs and adding the direct and indirect costs, in 2014, of the EBD in Canada for just four categories of illness results in a total cost ranging from

TABLE 5.4
The intangible costs of premature deaths caused by environmental hazards in Canada

	Death estimate	Low VSL	Central VSL	High VSL
World Health Organization	36,800	$128,800	$239,200	$349,600
Canadian Medical Association	21,000	$73,500	$136,500	$199,500
Boyd and Genuis study	17,300	$60,550	$112,450	$164,350
Average		$87,617	$162,717	$237,817

Note: All figures are in millions of Canadian dollars per year.

TABLE 5.5
The total economic costs of the EBD in Canada

Disease category	Direct costs	Indirect costs	Intangible costs	EBD (2014 dollars)
Respiratory	$541–1,624	$520–1,560	$6,838–20,053	$7,899–23,237
Cardiovascular	$1,002–2,004	$1,560–3,121	$35,464–70,922	$38,026–76,047
Cancer	$1,068–3,205	$1,237–3,709	$22,204–66,612	$24,509–73,526
Congenital	$10–52	$18–90	$468–2,340	$496–2,482
Total	$2,621–6,885	$3,335–8,480	$64,974–159,927	$70,930–175,292

Note: All figures are in millions of Canadian dollars per year.

$70.9 billion to $175.3 billion annually (see Table 5.5). This includes $8–23 billion for respiratory disease, $38–76 billion for cardiovascular disease, and $25–74 billion for cancer. The midpoint of this range, $123 billion, provides a useful and conservative estimate of the annual health costs inflicted by environmental hazards in Canada. These figures, although substantial, are in line with other estimates. In 2001, the Organisation for Economic Cooperation and Development indicated that the economic costs of the EBD were between $35 billion and $40 billion annually in Canada.[19] A Canadian study in 2001 estimated that the cost of treating and caring for children affected by neurodevelopmental diseases linked to chemical exposures (including autism and autism spectrum disorders, speech and language disorders, learning disorders, and reduced IQ) was $32–37 billion annually.[20] In 2004, Health Canada estimated that the direct health care costs and lost productivity caused by environmental factors added up to between $46 billion and $52 billion annually.[21] These earlier estimates did not fully account for the costs of premature mortality.

In 2005, the Ontario government estimated the health and environmental costs of air pollution in that province alone at over $9 billion annually.[22] The Ontario Medical Association reached a similar conclusion, estimating that air pollution in 2015 would cause:

• $571 million in direct health care costs
• $403 million in lost productivity and work time
• $593 million in reduced quality of life caused by pain and suffering
• $8.3 billion due to premature deaths.[23]

The Canadian Medical Association estimated that the economic costs of air pollution in Canada would approach $10 billion in 2015, including:

- direct health care expenses of $485 million
- lost productivity costs of $721 million
- reduced quality of life costs of $410 million
- premature deaths valued at a cost of $7.9 billion.[24]

The CMA found that unless effective steps are taken to improve air quality, the cumulative health costs of air pollution in Canada would exceed $250 billion between 2008 and 2031.[25] In 2007, the costs of air pollution from just one sector in Canada – transportation – were estimated to be between $4 billion and $6 billion each year (with one-third of these costs in just two cities, Toronto and Montreal).[26] In 2014, the OECD estimated that the economic cost of premature deaths from traffic-related air pollution in Canada was $34.1 billion in 2010.[27]

An analysis of Ontario's decision to eliminate coal-fired electricity generation revealed the potential for preventing 660 premature deaths, more than 2,000 emergency room and hospital visits, and more than 330,000 minor illnesses every year. The study estimated that the annual health costs of coal-fired electricity exceeded $3 billion.[28] The majority of these costs have been eliminated now that Ontario has phased out all coal-fired plants. In Alberta, the health costs of coal-fired electricity generation are over $300 million annually.[29] This is smaller than the Ontario costs because of lower population densities in Alberta. In Toronto, the mortality-related costs imposed by air pollution from traffic are approximately $2.2 billion per year. Reducing vehicle emissions in Toronto by 30 percent would save almost 200 lives and $900 million annually.[30] Researchers at the University of Ottawa examined the health benefits of removing one average vehicle from the roads, thus reducing air pollution on a local level. The estimated health care savings for every vehicle removed varied from $450 per year in Vancouver to $770 per year in Montreal.[31] These are conservative estimates of the adverse health effects, as the researchers limited their study to acute mortality, excluding long-term effects. Professor Amir Hakami, a coauthor of the study, pointed out: "While reducing emissions from vehicles and power plants is costly, not reducing emissions also costs money. Our research suggests that ignoring pollution will cost much more in the long term."[32]

International Evidence on Economic Costs of Adverse Health Effects Caused by Environmental Hazards

Extensive work has been carried out in other countries to estimate the economic costs of the adverse health effects caused by pollution and other environmental hazards. In 2005, the European Environment Agency estimated that the total health costs of air pollution in the European Union were between 305 billion and 875 billion euros per year.[33] In 2013, a study using a different approach estimated the health costs of air pollution in Europe to be 803 billion euros in 2000, declining to 537 billion euros in 2020 if proposed pollution reduction programs are successfully implemented.[34] In 2015, the World Health Organization published a comprehensive assessment of the impacts of air pollution in fifty-three European countries, estimating 600,000 premature deaths annually and a cost of $1.6 trillion.[35] The European Union has responded to these striking studies by proposing a stronger law to tackle emissions from power plants, industry, and vehicles. The stricter standards would cost 3.4 billion euros annually but would produce an estimated 40 billion euros in health savings.[36] In 2015, a study estimated that exposure to endocrine-disrupting chemicals in the EU contributes to IQ loss, intellectual disability, autism, attention-deficit hyperactivity disorder, obesity, and other adverse health effects that cost more than 150 billion euros per year.[37] A German study of the economic costs of the environmental burden of disease in that country found costs ranging from 15 to 62 billion euros annually.[38] It is estimated that the costs of failing to take action to reduce nitrates in drinking water amount to 2.6 billion euros annually for the United Kingdom alone.[39]

Researchers at the Massachusetts Institute of Technology estimated that air pollution cost the United States approximately $200 billion in the year 2000.[40] An American study looked at four categories of pediatric illness with strong links to environmental factors and estimated that the annual cost of the environmental burden of disease from lead poisoning, asthma, cancer, and neurobehavioural disorders was US$54.9 billion.[41] This cost estimate was updated and expanded by researchers in 2011. The annual costs of lead poisoning, prenatal mercury exposure, childhood cancer, asthma, intellectual disability, autism, and ADHD were revised to between $60 billion and $106 billion, with a best estimate of $76.6 billion.[42] Recent American research suggests that early exposure to environmental chemicals (lead, organophosphate pesticides, and methyl mercury) causes a population-wide loss of IQ points that is "surprisingly large – in some cases larger than those estimated for major medical conditions and events."[43] The IQ reduction due to methyl mercury exposure and the consequent reduction in lifetime economic productivity has a nationwide impact of $8.7 billion per year (with a range of $2.2 billion to $43.8 billion).[44] In the state of Massachusetts, the direct costs (health care and special education) and indirect costs (school

days missed and future earnings lost) of environmentally attributable childhood illnesses are estimated to be between $1.1 billion and $1.6 billion annually.[45] An evaluation of the effects of traffic-related air pollution on new
and existing cases of childhood asthma in two California communities
found annual health care costs of $18 million.[46] As gaps in the knowledge of
environmental exposures and their role in chronic childhood disease are
filled, future cost estimates of environmentally mediated diseases in children may continue to increase.[47] Overall, Michigan law professor David
Uhlmann concluded, "environmental protection laws have saved hundreds
of thousands of lives in the United States and saved billions of dollars in
health care costs."[48] It is also important to appreciate that the costs of compliance with environmental regulations are almost always less than anticipated by governments and industry.[49]

Climate change is expected to have substantial impacts on human health
in the coming years, due to more frequent and intense floods, droughts,
heat waves, hurricanes, storms, and forest fires, the spread of vector-borne
diseases, increased production of allergens, and higher levels of ground-
level ozone. At this time, however, only preliminary estimates of the increased health costs caused by climate change are available. An investigation
of six climate-related events that occurred in the United States between
2000 and 2009 revealed 1,700 premature deaths, 9,000 hospitalizations,
21,100 emergency department visits, 730,000 outpatient visits, and $14 bil-
lion in health costs.[50] The health costs of a single Alberta forest fire linked
to climate change were found to be $9–12 million and included premature
mortality, respiratory and cardiac hospital admissions, asthma symptoms,
and emergency department visits.[51]

As noted in Chapter 2, built environments are contributing to diminish-
ing levels of physical activity, with adverse health consequences in the form
of obesity and elevated risks of chronic diseases. Although we do not yet
know the proportion of these adverse health effects that can be attributed
to environmental factors, a recent study indicated that the total health costs
of physical inactivity in Canada for adults are almost $7 billion per year.[52]

Another challenging area for economists involves placing a value on the
cost of ecosystem services lost or degraded as a result of damages inflicted
by human activity. Economists have estimated the total value of these services to be in the tens of trillions of dollars, yet the free market system assigns
them no value at all. The UN's ambitious Millennium Ecosystem Assessment
examined twenty-four global ecosystem services – from enriching the soil
to protecting against floods – and concluded that 60 percent were being

degraded or exploited unsustainably.[53] A Dutch expert on ecosystem services provocatively suggested that "every year we lose three to five trillion dollars' worth of natural capital, roughly equivalent to the amount of money we lost in the financial crisis of 2008–2009."[54] Unfortunately, when looking specifically at health costs associated with declines in ecosystem services, there is a complete lack of data. As two leading experts wrote in 2009, "there is a big gap between the research showing associations between changes in natural systems and health outcomes, and actually being able to quantify the specific health benefits or costs of incremental changes in the system."[55] Although efforts are being made to fill in this gap, the challenges are daunting.[56]

Cost-Benefit Analysis

Thus far, the discussion has focused on the economic costs of pollution and other environmental hazards. The fact that these are preventable risks means that today's costs can be reconceptualized as tomorrow's benefits. Health care costs – direct, indirect, and intangible – can be dramatically reduced through stronger environmental laws, policies, programs, and enforcement. Given the strong connections between human health and the environment, resources allocated to stronger environmental protection should be considered as investments with potentially positive economic returns rather than mere costs. According to the OECD, "it is essential to understand that under an economic perspective the 'costs of inaction' are simply analogous to the benefits that can be obtained with proper controls."[57] Cost-benefit analyses by academics and governments provide ample evidence of the capacity for environmental regulations to generate health benefits that dwarf the economic costs of implementing those rules. It is also worth noting that the *ex ante* or anticipated costs of environmental regulation tend to be overstated.[58]

Economic Benefits of Improved Environmental Health in Canada

The experiences of Canada and other countries demonstrate that strong regulations to protect health and the environment can have huge health benefits. When the federal government enacted a regulation in 2002 dramatically reducing the legal limit of sulphur in gasoline, experts predicted that the regulation would prevent the following over the next twenty years: 11 million new cases of croup and pneumonia; 5 million restricted activity days associated with asthma; 100,000 new cases of bronchitis; 9,000 emergency or hospital admissions; and 2,000 premature deaths.[59] These health benefits were estimated to exceed the total costs of implementing the regulation (costs borne by industry and, to a much lesser extent, government) by several billion dollars.[60] New federal regulations governing coal-fired electricity stations are expected to provide substantial health benefits over the period 2015–35 by reducing Canadians' exposure to smog and mercury. The cumulative totals of avoided impacts include 900 premature deaths, 120,000 asthma episodes, and 2.7 million days of breathing difficulty and reduced activity. These health benefits have a total value of over $4.2 billion.[61] The total benefits of the new regulations are $23 billion, including $5.6 billion in avoided climate change costs and $7.2 billion in avoided generating costs. The total costs are $16 billion, resulting in a net benefit of $7 billion. Environment Canada estimated that achieving a 10 percent reduction in national levels of fine particulates and ground-level ozone would result in economic benefits of over $4 billion per year, including $500 million in reduced health care expenses and $3.5 billion for the value of avoiding premature deaths, illnesses, pain, and suffering.[62] Most recently, a proposed federal regulation to reduce air pollution from several specific industrial sectors estimated that the benefits would exceed costs by ratios of 15:1 for engines, 24:1 for boilers and heaters, and 34:1 for cement manufacturing facilities.[63] The lion's share of the benefits would result from premature deaths and emergency room visits avoided.

These cost-benefit studies are not limited to the field of air pollution, although this gathers the lion's share of attention as the environmental risk that causes the largest health impacts in Canada. According to a 2013 report from Health Canada, early childhood exposure to lead in Canada causes a decrease in future earnings due to reduced intellectual development that comes to between $1.5 billion and $9.4 billion annually. Health Canada also turns this cost around, stating that from a social welfare perspective, "an economic benefit valued at over $9 billion per year could be gained if the exposure of Canadian children to lead could be eliminated."[64] A cost-benefit analysis of the federal regulation requiring all municipalities to employ a minimum of secondary sewage treatment found net benefits for all provinces. In part this conclusion was due to the economic benefits of reduced human health risks associated with safer drinking water; safer water for recreational activities, including swimming, fishing, and shellfish harvesting; increased biodiversity; and improved ecosystem functioning.[65]

Evidence from the United States and Europe
There is an even richer body of evidence from the United States and Europe

demonstrating the enormous health and economic benefits of strengthening environmental regulations. For example, the net economic benefits of removing lead from gasoline in the United States for the past two decades were estimated at over $3 trillion, largely due to reduced adverse impacts on children's brains.[66] A comprehensive study of the costs and benefits of the US *Clean Air Act* from 1970 to 1990 found that the act imposed $523 billion in costs on businesses, consumers, and governments, but resulted in between $5.6 trillion and $48.9 trillion in benefits, with a central estimate of $22.2 trillion. Even these enormous benefit totals are believed to be underestimates since some factors, such as the economic value of improvements in ecosystem health, were not included in the analysis.[67] A peer-reviewed study of the US Acid Rain Program identified annual benefits of $122 billion and annual costs of just $3 billion.[68] The same study suggested that Canada would gain $6 billion in health and environmental benefits annually by 2010, including one thousand avoided premature deaths every year, as a result of decreased transboundary air pollution.

Federal regulations introduced in 2005 requiring American power plants to substantially reduce air pollution (nitrogen oxides, sulphur dioxide, and particulate matter) are projected to provide between $85 billion and $100 billion in annual health benefits in the United States by 2015, an amount roughly equal to twenty-five times the cost of implementation.[69] New vehicle emission standards proposed by the US Environmental Protection Agency in 2013 are expected to cost industry and consumers $2 billion in 2017, rising to $3.4 billion per year by 2030. However, estimates of the economic value of the anticipated health benefits produced by cleaner air range from $8 billion to $23 billion annually by 2030.[70] The EPA estimates that the full implementation of the *Clean Air Act* and various amendments to that law will prevent 230,000 deaths per year by 2020, with all health and environmental benefits producing an economic value that will exceed $2 trillion annually. The costs of achieving these benefits are $65 billion annually. The EPA notes that under every scenario, the economic benefits of air quality regulation exceed the costs, with the most conservative estimate of benefits exceeding costs by a factor of 3 to 1, the central estimate of benefits exceeding costs by 30 to 1, and the high estimate of benefits exceeding costs by 90 to 1.[71]

The return on investment for some types of environmental regulation is extraordinarily high. Studies indicate that every dollar invested in reducing pollution from diesel engines saves between $12 and $28 in health costs.[72] Every dollar spent to reduce lead hazards in housing (paint, plumbing, soil) is expected to produce between $17 and $221 in benefits by reducing expenditures on screening and treatment for lead exposure, treating ADHD, and special education; increasing income and tax revenue; and reducing crime.[73]

A 2013 report by the White House Office of Management and Budget (OMB) analyzed the costs and benefits of thirty-two major rules promulgated by the EPA between 2002 and 2012 and found total annual benefits of $112 billion to $638 billion, compared with total annual costs of $30.4 billion to $36.5 billion.[74] In other words, despite some degree of uncertainty, the benefits are three to twenty-one times greater than the costs. The OMB noted that the highest levels of both costs and benefits were related to rules reducing air pollution, particularly the reduction of fine particulates.[75]

European evidence is consistent with the North American experience. A European study published in 2013 looked at the economic benefits of reducing mercury exposure and thus preventing adverse neurodevelopmental outcomes. By examining levels of mercury in the hair of women of reproductive ages in twenty-five countries, researchers were able to calculate the loss in IQ that could be avoided by reducing exposure. The economic benefits of prevention within the European Union were estimated to be between 8 and 9 billion euros annually.[76] The annual health benefits in twenty major European cities flowing from EU rules on sulphur in liquid fuels were approximately 200 million euros.[77] As well, it is estimated that if Europe reduced greenhouse gas emissions 20 percent by 2020, the continent would enjoy a reduction in health care costs of 52 billion euros (as a result of cleaner air from reduced burning of fossil fuels).[78]

Prevention Is the Key to Unlocking Economic Benefits

The scientific community has reached the conclusion that taking action to prevent environmental pollution and damages will benefit ecosystems and is also one of the most cost-effective means of reducing health care costs. A study published in the *New England Journal of Medicine* in 2012 compared the cost-effectiveness of various approaches to disease prevention and concluded that "environmental interventions were generally more cost-effective than clinical interventions or nonclinical, person-directed interventions."[79] It is often less expensive to modify an environmental hazard that poses a risk to many people than to interact with each person individually. The authors concluded that "environmental prevention is key to addressing the growing disease burden and cost of chronic illnesses."[80]

Another recent American study forecast the success of three different strategies for reducing avoidable deaths and lowering health care costs:

extending the coverage of health insurance, delivering better preventive and chronic care, and improving behavioural and environmental conditions (e.g., reducing tobacco use and reducing air pollution).[81] The authors concluded that environmental protection would save more lives over a twenty-five-year period than the other approaches. While extending and improving health care would also save lives, these approaches would cost hundreds of billions of dollars, whereas the protection strategy would actually save money. Not only would increasing spending on environmental protection prevent illnesses, injuries, and premature deaths but "by reducing demand on the health care delivery system, protection also helps alleviate the shortage of clinical capacity to care for people with existing health problems. In this indirect way it can also ultimately lead to more people getting better care."[82]

An innovative Canadian study offers further evidence of the potential health care savings that could be achieved through stronger environmental protection. Researchers at McMaster University discovered strong correlations between levels of pollution, municipal expenditures on environmental protection, and health care costs after controlling for other factors that influence spending.[83] The higher the level of pollution in an area (using data from Canada's National Pollutant Release Inventory), the higher the health care costs, by $355 per capita annually. The higher the level of municipal expenditures on protecting the environment, the lower the health care costs, by $200 per capita annually.[84] The authors warned that failing to invest adequately in environmental protection would lead to higher health care expenditures, which would then place downward pressure on spending for environmental protection, creating a vicious cycle. A similar study in the United States found that states with stronger environmental programs enjoyed lower levels of pollution and better health outcomes.[85] A study of the links between environmental quality and health care spending in eight OECD nations also warned that failing to address the environmental drivers of health costs would lead to more pollution, more adverse health effects, and higher health care costs.[86]

Additional proof that prevention can lower health care costs comes from Sweden and the United Kingdom. Health care economists with the Conference Board of Canada concluded that Sweden's relatively slow growth in health care expenditures is partially due to strong environmental laws and policies.[87] A British study estimated that improving public access to green spaces could generate roughly $4 billion in annual health care savings.[88] It should also be noted that there is a growing body of evidence supporting the hypothesis of Harvard economist Michael Porter that stronger environmental regulations, if well designed, can spur innovation, improve environmental performance, and bolster productivity.[89]

Conclusion

This chapter provides a clear and compelling indication of the magnitude of economic costs inflicted by the environmental burden of disease in Canada. The economic costs of illness, injury, and premature death caused by environmental hazards are enormous, inflicting over $100 billion in annual costs by a conservative estimate. Of critical importance, these costs are preventable. Yet Canada spent only $19.7 billion on environmental protection in 2010 (including expenditures by business and all three levels of government), demonstrating the need for increased investments in this area to reduce the excessive costs.[90] This information should motivate the public, politicians, and policymakers to strengthen environmental laws and increase environmental budgets. The fact that the health and economic benefits of environmental protection outweigh the costs means that improvements in ecosystem health, which are difficult to monetize, are akin to icing on the cake. Economic data on the costs of disease can help counter one-sided arguments put forward by business interests that focus exclusively on the costs of preventing pollution. As the European Environment Agency notes, "the costs of preventive actions are usually tangible, clearly allocated and often short term, whereas the costs of failing to act are less tangible, less clearly distributed and usually longer term."[91]

PART 2

DIAGNOSIS

Inadequate Environmental Health
Laws and Policies

Canada's environmental performance is, by most measures, the worst in the developed world. We've got big problems.

– PRIME MINISTER STEPHEN HARPER (2006)

6

Environmental Health Law and Policy: The Big Picture

When it comes to Canada's record of environmental stewardship, our Government has a remarkable record of achievement. There is absolutely nothing for which we need to apologize to anyone, anywhere.

— PETER KENT, CANADIAN MINISTER OF THE ENVIRONMENT (2013)

Contrary to the claims of political leaders, Canada lags behind other wealthy industrialized nations in terms of the big picture related to reducing or eliminating environmental impacts on health. Unlike other countries, Canada stands out for:

- refusing to recognize that its citizens have a legal right to breathe clean air, drink safe water, and live in a healthy environment
- lacking a national strategy or action plan to address adverse environmental effects on human health
- having no laws, regulations, or policies intended to ameliorate or prevent environmental injustices
- lacking a comprehensive environmental health monitoring and surveillance system

- refusing to make adequate investments in environmental health research and education
- exacerbating international environmental injustices (e.g., promoting asbestos exports and open-pit mining while withdrawing from international agreements addressing climate change and desertification).

Each of these failures will be addressed in detail in this chapter. Comparisons will be drawn with the United States, the European Union, and Australia, where federal or multilevel governance systems create political challenges similar to those facing Canada. Although provincial and territorial governments play a major role in environmental protection in Canada, this is generally within a federal framework (e.g., air quality, drinking water safety). As well, from health and equity perspectives, there are strong arguments to be made that all Canadians should enjoy an equal level of protection from environmental hazards. Both the United States and Australia are ahead of Canada in terms of laws, policies, and programs intended to protect human health from environmental hazards and ensure fair access to environmental amenities. Even further ahead are European nations, particularly those with strong reputations for environmental leadership (e.g., Sweden, Finland, Norway, France, Germany, and the Netherlands). These countries place health and environment linkages at the forefront of their national sustainable development strategies.[1] For example, Sweden's ambitious strategy for achieving sustainability within a generation is based on five fundamental principles, the first of which is "promotion of human health."[2] Sweden exemplifies the health and economic benefits of integrating health and environmental issues and enacting strong environmental laws and policies.

The only advantage of being a laggard is that Canada can learn from the experiences of other nations in belatedly developing a comprehensive response to environmental threats to health. Canada's poor environmental health performance compared with our peers underscores the urgency of dedicating substantial time, energy, and resources to these issues.

The Right to Live in a Healthy Environment

Constitutional recognition of the right to a healthy environment is fundamentally important for five reasons. First, a constitution is the supreme law of a nation, requiring all other laws and policies to be consistent with its provisions. Second, a constitution is a mirror of a nation's soul, both reflecting and reinforcing the most fundamental and cherished values of a people.

It is clear from extensive research that environmental protection has evolved into a fundamental value held by the vast majority of Canadians. Third, there is an urgent need to improve Canada's poor environmental record and preserve this country's extraordinary natural beauty. Research on the experiences of nations whose constitutions recognize the right to a healthy environment indicates that these legal provisions are positively correlated with superior environmental performance, meaning that people are breathing cleaner air, drinking safer water, and living healthier, more ecologically sustainable lifestyles. For example, in a comparison of seventeen wealthy industrialized nations, the nations whose constitutions include environmental protection reduced emissions of sulphur oxides, nitrogen oxides, and greenhouse gases more rapidly than nations without such provisions.[3] Fourth, for more than a century uncertainty about constitutional responsibility for environmental protection has undermined Canada's efforts to become more sustainable. Prime Minister Wilfrid Laurier's Commission of Conservation identified this problem in a report on water pollution in 1912.[4] Corporations use this uncertainty to delay, defeat, and dismantle environmental policies. Fifth, environmental rights and responsibilities are cornerstones of Indigenous law, and thus need to be incorporated into the Canadian legal system.[5]

Despite this array of compelling reasons, the Canadian government refuses to recognize or acknowledge that Canadians have the right to live in a healthy environment.[6] Canada's Constitution, including the *Charter of Rights and Freedoms,* is silent on the matter of environmental protection. This is a stark contrast to the 90 percent of Canadians who believe that the right to a healthy environment should enjoy constitutional protection. Incredibly, a majority of Canadians believe that this right is already entrenched in the *Charter.* In terms of recognizing the right to live in a healthy environment, Canada trails many other nations. Since 1972, when the human right to live in a healthy environment was first formally recognized in the Stockholm Declaration on the human environment, this right has gained remarkably widespread recognition in legal systems around the world. The right to a healthy environment is explicitly recognized in 100 national constitutions.[7] It is acknowledged as an implicit but essential aspect of the constitutional right to life in another 12 countries (due to decisions of Supreme or Constitutional courts).[8] As well, at least 120 nations in Europe, the Americas, Africa, and the Middle East have ratified the following international treaties that recognize the right to a healthy environment:

- African Charter on Human and Peoples' Rights (1981)
- San Salvador Protocol to the American Convention on Human Rights (1988)
- Aarhus Convention on Access to Information, Public Participation, and Access to Justice in Environmental Matters (1998)
- Arab Charter on Human Rights (2004).[9]

In 2012, 10 Asian nations signed the ASEAN Declaration on Human Rights, a political agreement that included recognition of the right to a healthy environment. Fifteen Caribbean nations have signed the Charter of Civil Society for the Caribbean Community, expressing their support for the right to a healthy environment.

In total, 181 of the United Nations' 193 member nations have agreed that the right to a healthy environment is a human right, deserving of the same legal protection as the right to life or the right to vote. Canada is among the dozen holdouts, with Afghanistan, Lebanon, North Korea, Oman, Kuwait, China, Japan, Australia, New Zealand, the United Kingdom, and the United States. Canada and the United States appear to be the only countries that actively oppose recognition of the right to a healthy environment. During the 1990s, Canada participated in negotiations for the Aarhus Convention, but argued against inclusion of the right to a healthy environment and then refused to sign the treaty when this right was included.[10] In a case before the Inter-American Commission on Human Rights, the US government took the position that the right to a healthy environment has no legal status, or, alternatively, that it did not apply to American citizens.[11]

Constitutional recognition of the right to a healthy environment leads to stronger environmental laws, improved implementation and enforcement of those laws, increased public participation in environmental decision making, greater access to justice, and improved environmental performance.[12] More than a hundred countries have written the right to a healthy environment into their national environmental laws. In some of these countries, including Argentina, Brazil, Colombia, Costa Rica, France, the Philippines, Portugal, and South Africa, the right to a healthy environment has systematically transformed the environmental legal system, providing a unifying goal that all laws and policies are restructured to achieve. For example, in Argentina all major environmental laws at the national and provincial level have been strengthened since the right to a healthy environment was added to the constitution in 1994, and many new laws and standards have been enacted. A landmark decision from Argentina's Supreme Court in

2008, based on the right to a healthy environment, has led to remarkable efforts to clean up the Matanza-Riachuelo watershed, resulting in cleaner air, water, and ecosystems for millions of people in and around Buenos Aires.[13] Sophisticated quantitative analysis confirms that constitutional environmental rights are a causal factor in superior environmental performance, including more rapid reductions in air pollution and greenhouse gas emissions, as well as ranking on the well-known Environmental Performance Index.[14]

National Health and Environment Strategies

Canada is the only wealthy industrialized nation that lacks a comprehensive national strategy or action plan to protect human health by improving environmental quality. According to the World Health Organization, national environmental health action plans "represent a comprehensive, holistic and intersectoral way of planning and implementing environmental health action at the national level."[15] These national approaches provide a focal point, drive the improvement of environmental laws and policies, identify priorities, guide research and monitoring, and establish targets and timelines to ensure accountability for evaluating results. The United States, Australia, and every nation in Europe have a health and environment strategy or action plan.

United States

In 1988, a committee of health experts appointed by the US Institute of Medicine published a report criticizing the lack of attention paid to the health dimensions of environmental problems.[16] In 1993, the National Research Council published a landmark book called *Pesticides in the Diets of Infants and Children,* which focused national attention on children's environmental health.[17] In 2000, a report called *Healthy People 2010,* by the US Department of Health and Human Services, identified environmental factors as one of the three top threats to the health of Americans.[18] The United States responded to these developments and the public pressure they generated by creating a national environmental health strategy, formulating environmental health indicators, initiating the long-term National Children's Study and other vital research initiatives, and becoming a world leader in assessing the public's exposure to environmental chemicals.[19] Research and public outreach efforts in the United States are led by two organizations, the National Institute of Environmental Health Sciences and the National Center for Environmental Health.

In 2000, the Department of Health and Human Services and the Environmental Protection Agency established a variety of short- and long-term environmental health goals, such as:

- Reduce the risk to human health and the environment by protecting and improving air quality so that air throughout the country meets national clean air standards by 2012 for ozone and by 2018 for particulate matter.
- By 2005, reduce pollutant loadings from key point and nonpoint sources by at least 11 percent from 1992 levels.
- By 2010, reduce exposure to pesticides as measured by urine concentrations of metabolites.
- By 2010, reduce hospitalizations for asthma for children under five.
- By 2020, eliminate unacceptable risks of cancer and other significant health problems from air toxic emissions for at least 95 percent of the population, with particular attention to children and other sensitive subpopulations.[20]

Substantial progress has been made towards some of these targets, while others remain unfulfilled. In 2010, the Department of Health and Human Services updated its strategy, setting a revised set of goals for 2020.[21] Six priority areas were identified, including outdoor air quality, surface and ground water quality, toxic substances and hazardous wastes, homes and communities (the built environment), surveillance, and global environmental health.

Healthy People 2020 set forth a comprehensive array of twenty-four environmental objectives to be achieved by 2020, the majority of which meet the SMART criteria (specific, measurable, attainable, relevant, and time-limited):

- 10 percent increase in the proportion of people walking and cycling to work or taking public transit
- 10 percent decrease in poor air quality days
- 44 percent decrease in toxic air emissions from mobile sources
- provision of water that meets health-based drinking water standards to 95 percent of the population served by community water systems
- reduction, by 200,000 annually, in the number of deaths globally that are caused by poor water quality and inadequate sanitation
- elimination of elevated blood lead levels in children.[22]

A progress report published in 2014 indicated that reductions in the number of days when the air quality index exceeds 100 (indicating health risks to vulnerable groups) met and exceeded the original target, as did the decline in the number of children exposed to second-hand smoke.[23] Although the United States has a long way to go to achieve all of these goals, its rigorous monitoring and reporting system provides a substantial incentive to improve and puts it well ahead of Canada.

Australia

Australia has a comprehensive national environmental health strategy that recognizes that "all Australians are entitled to live in safe and healthy environments."[24] Key elements of the Australian strategy include creating a Charter for Environmental Health that establishes both rights and responsibilities; appointing a National Environmental Health Council; developing an environmental health information system; reporting on environmental health indicators; focusing on vulnerable populations (socially and economically disadvantaged groups, children, and Aboriginal Australians); investing in environmental health research; and conducting health impact assessments of proposed developments. Perhaps most importantly, Australia acknowledges that a preventive approach is more effective, more efficient, and more equitable than a "pollute now and pay later" approach. Scholars describe the Australian environmental health strategy as an important benchmark in policy development, pointing the way to a cleaner, greener, healthier future for Australians.[25]

Europe

The European Union has a comprehensive health and environment action plan and all individual EU nations also have national strategies.[26] Health is also a central element of the pan-European Sustainable Development Strategy.[27] The European Health and Environment Action Plan 2004–2010 focused on addressing knowledge gaps, strengthening existing policies, and improving communication so that citizens can make better health choices. The overarching goals were to reduce the environmental burden of disease and to prevent the emergence of new health threats caused by environmental factors. Specific actions underway include development of environmental health indicators; biomonitoring programs to assess human exposure to environmental hazards; and targeted research on priority hazards, exposures, and diseases. Importantly, the EU's health strategy identifies environmental health as a crucial issue, ensuring that there is a multifaceted but coordinated approach to issues ranging from air and water pollution to nanotechnology and climate change.[28] The EU has continued to enact and implement stronger laws governing air pollution, pesticides, toxic chemicals, and climate change, each with a central focus on reducing health as well as environmental impacts. A review of progress under the Health and Environment Action Plan concluded that "the strengthened cooperation between the environment, health and research fields at Community and Member States level is a true achievement."[29]

Canada

Despite repeated promises over a period of years, Canada has no environmental health strategy. In 1999, the federal cabinet gave approval in principle for a health and environment strategy to be developed and implemented by Health Canada and Environment Canada, with a promised budget of $600 million over a period of five years.[30] The strategy was never developed, and funds were never allocated. The Federal Sustainable Development Strategy (FSDS), updated in 2013, contains many references to the health effects of environmental pollution and degradation, but is neither systemic nor comprehensive. Unlike national environmental health action plans, Canada's FSDS does not address environmental rights, environmental health research, monitoring and surveillance, education, or international environmental health. As a result, the federal government's approach to environmental health has been ad hoc and piecemeal. For example, the Conservatives rebranded a Liberal program on protecting Canadians from toxic substances as the Chemicals Management Plan, carrying out long-overdue assessments of the health effects of more than twenty thousand chemicals used, produced, or imported by industry in Canada. The use of bisphenol A (BPA) in baby bottles was banned in 2009, making Canada the first country in the world to take this step. In 2006, Prime Minister Stephen Harper promised a tough new *Clean Air Act* that would reduce industrial pollution 50 percent. This legislation has never been enacted, however. After many years of dragging its heels, Canada finally developed a Children's Environmental Health Strategy (discussed in the next section).

No Environmental Justice Laws, Policies, or Programs in Canada

There is no mention of environmental justice, environmental injustice, environmental equity, or environmental racism in any Canadian law, regulation, or policy at the federal, provincial, or territorial level. No Canadian court or tribunal has ever directly addressed environmental justice. Searches of the Canadian Legal Information Institute's encyclopedic database of legislation, regulations, court decisions, and tribunal decisions reveal no substantive references to environmental justice. In a 2007 case where Alberta residents sought to challenge a decision of the Energy and Utilities Board related to the construction of a new transmission line between Calgary and Edmonton, the Alberta Court of Appeal stated that environmental justice "is an issue that has not been addressed by the courts."[31] In comparison to the state of the law in other countries, this is a glaring legislative and judicial omission. In 2015, a private member's bill called the End Environmental Racism Act was introduced in the Nova Scotia legislature which, if enacted, would set a Canadian precedent.[32]

A promising sign in Canada involves children's environmental health. The 2001 Speech from the Throne included a promise to safeguard children from environmental threats to their health. The federal cabinet subsequently approved a strategy designed to protect children's health from environmental threats, with a promised budget of $90 million over four years. In 2003, the Canadian Council of Ministers of the Environment also called for the development of a coordinated national approach to protecting children's health from environmental harms. After years of sustained pressure from the Canadian Partnership for Children's Health and Environment, a national strategic framework on children's environmental health was finally released in 2010.[33] This national framework was intended to provide the vision, principles, and goals to guide the development of action plans with concrete initiatives to protect children. Despite the stated intent of the framework, however, there is still no Canadian jurisdiction with an action plan in place.

Canada lags behind the United States in implementing effective policies to reduce environmental risks to children.[34] Beginning in the 1990s, at the behest of public health advocates and environmental groups, the American government took many steps to protect children's environmental health. Key actions included passage of the *Food Quality Protection Act of 1996*, mandating enhanced protection for children from the risks posed by pesticides, and the issuance of an executive order requiring all federal agencies to consider health impacts on children when formulating policies and programs. According to Vice President Al Gore: "This executive order says to every federal agency and department: put our children first. We Americans owe our largest responsibility to our smallest citizens."[35]

Environmental Health Monitoring and Surveillance Systems

The challenge of effectively addressing environmental health problems in Canada is magnified by significant gaps in our knowledge. While this problem plagues public health in Canada generally, it is particularly acute in the environmental health field.[36] In the field of public health, "surveillance" refers to the systematic collection, assessment, integration, analysis, interpretation, and dissemination of data in order to prevent or control disease. Timely and accurate information generated by surveillance systems may enable public health authorities to "determine disease impacts and trends, recognize clusters and outbreaks, identify populations and geographic areas most affected, and assess the effectiveness of public health interventions."[37] The data can also facilitate planning, spur new research, inform medical practitioners, and alter the behaviour of the general public. Unlike other jurisdictions, such as the United States and Europe, Canada has no comprehensive national health and environment surveillance system.[38]

United States

The Centers for Disease Control and Prevention are implementing a National Environmental Public Health Tracking Program that is gathering and integrating data on hazards, exposures, and health effects.[39] The CDC's vision is to accomplish five goals:

- build a national surveillance network
- enhance the capacity of the environmental health workforce and infrastructure
- disseminate useful information to guide policies and practices
- advance science and research on health-environment linkages
- foster broad collaboration among health and environmental sectors.[40]

An important element is the creation of a national network, comprising stakeholders from federal, state, and local health and environmental agencies; nongovernmental organizations (NGOs); state public health and environmental laboratories; and schools of public health. This national network performs the following functions:

- compile and provide access to a core set of nationally consistent data and measures
- describe, discover, and exchange data

• provide data management, analysis, and visualization tools
• inform and interact with the public.[41]

The nascent American system, built on approximately $25 million per year in federal funding, has already contributed to some significant advances in public health, such as connecting student asthma problems with mould in schools, reducing residential pesticide exposure in New York City, and reducing trichloroethylene exposures in Wisconsin.[42]

Europe

In the EU, a project called the European Environment and Health Information System has developed a consistent and comparable set of data that combines environmental and health indicators to enable evaluation of policies, programs, and practices.[43] The EU evaluated potential indicators on the basis of data availability, quality, comparability, and policy relevance. After a pilot period that tested forty-eight potential indicators, the EU decided to focus on twenty-four indicators in four priority areas (access to safe water and sanitation, addressing obesity, improved air quality, and preventing disease caused by chemical, biological, and physical factors). The EU's indicators include levels of radon in buildings, levels of lead in children's blood, incidence of melanoma, and policies to reduce exposure to second-hand smoke.

Canada

Four broad categories of surveillance information are needed in order to formulate effective policies and programs to protect the health of Canadians from environmental threats: (1) data on environmental hazards – what harmful chemical, biological, and physical agents, in what quantities or concentrations, in what locations, and at what times, are present in our environment? (2) data on human exposures to environmental hazards – what harmful substances are entering or affecting our bodies, in what concentrations, at what stages in our lives, and via which pathways? (3) an understanding of the relationships between human exposures to environmental hazards and the ensuing adverse health outcomes; and (4) an ability to evaluate, both *ex ante* and *ex post*, the effectiveness of interventions intended to reduce the environmental burden of disease.

In each of these categories, Canada faces substantial knowledge gaps that undermine efforts to formulate effective environmental health policies.

Health Canada admits that "environmental health surveillance lags behind other health domains."[44] A report on children's health and the environment in North America demonstrated the extent of the problem, as Canada was unable to report on half of the indicators chosen by experts to measure environmental impacts on children's health.[45] For example, Canada was unable to provide information on the percentage of children living in areas where air pollution levels exceed air quality standards, or the percentage of children living in areas where drinking water violates local standards. The lack of information may reflect the fact that for some governments and industries, "it is preferable not to know" because public awareness of the facts could cause a media uproar and spur demands for action.[46]

Since the establishment of the Public Health Agency of Canada in 2004, a substantial amount of effort and resources has been dedicated to improving public health surveillance in Canada. New programs have been created, with hundreds of millions of dollars allocated to improving Canada's capacity for public health surveillance.[47] The field of environmental health has seen some positive developments, described below, but continues to suffer from the lack of a comprehensive, integrated national approach.

Missing Information, Part 1: Environmental Hazards

> We do not have consistent national databases that track trends in contaminants in drinking water, foods, or the indoor environment.
>
> – DR. RAY COPES, FORMER DIRECTOR, NATIONAL
> COLLABORATING CENTRE FOR ENVIRONMENTAL
> HEALTH (2006)

Hazard data provide information regarding releases or concentrations of an environmental agent in air, water, soil, plants, and animals. Canada's information systems for environmental hazards are an uneven patchwork quilt. For example, although there is an extensive national network that monitors outdoor air quality, there is little monitoring of indoor air quality. Drinking water is monitored at all public drinking water systems, but hazard monitoring is limited in smaller communities, in rural areas, and on Aboriginal reserves, where water quality problems are more likely to arise. Food surveillance in Canada lagged behind that in other industrialized nations until very recently.[48] Surveillance for emerging infectious disease ranges from impressive, as in the case of West Nile virus, to incompetent, as was the case for mad cow disease.[49] Canada monitors some industrial pollutants from large facilities while largely ignoring small and medium-sized businesses and urban and agricultural runoff.

Canada has an extensive outdoor air quality monitoring network, called the National Air Pollution Surveillance (NAPS) Network. Established in 1969, the NAPS Network measures concentrations of sulphur dioxide, carbon monoxide, nitrogen dioxide, ozone, PM 10, PM 2.5, volatile organic compounds (VOCs, such as aromatics, aldehydes, and ketones), and semi-volatile organic compounds (polycyclic aromatic hydrocarbons [PAHs], dioxins, and furans). The network consists of 286 monitoring stations in 203 communities measuring up to 340 chemicals.[50] Some provinces and municipalities operate additional outdoor air quality monitoring programs.

In contrast, there is no national program to monitor indoor air quality despite the fact that most Canadians spend about 90 percent of their time inside buildings of one kind or another. Indoor air and house dust in a typical North American home may contain dozens of toxic substances, including radon, lead, combustion byproducts, VOCs, pesticides, and biological contaminants (e.g., mould or dust mites). Indoor air may be an important source of exposure to known carcinogens, including benzene, formaldehyde, chloroform, and naphthalene.[51]

Water quality monitoring is a complex issue because all levels of government in Canada have overlapping responsibility for protecting water quality. A national survey of water monitoring activities identified major gaps, particularly with respect to key threats to water quality, a lack of common terminology among databases intended for linkage, and weaknesses in the linkage between monitoring results and policy/decision making.[52] With respect to drinking water, there are four stages at which monitoring is important: at the source (whether surface water or groundwater), at the treatment plant, in the distribution system, and at the tap. The Water Quality Index employs 172 monitoring stations to rank water bodies based on a range of parameters, including nutrients, metals, and other chemicals.[53] The Walkerton Inquiry recommended that all municipal water providers

> should have, as a minimum, continuous inline monitoring of turbidity, disinfectant residual, and pressure at the treatment plant, together with alarms that signal immediately when any regulatory parameters are exceeded. The disinfectant residual should be continuously or frequently measured in the distribution system. Where needed, alarms should be accompanied by automatic shut-off mechanisms.[54]

The federal, provincial, and territorial governments reached agreement on a national framework to improve water quality monitoring in 2006.[55] Since then, additional monitoring programs have been established, although national integration remains a challenge.[56]

The federal government, through Health Canada and the Canadian Food Inspection Agency, conducts total diet studies (based on food purchases), monitors pesticide residues, and does ad hoc surveillance on other contaminants. However, there is no systematic or comprehensive national surveillance of environmental contaminants, exposures, and risks, which limits our ability to understand the relationships between food intake, nutritional status, environmental exposures, and health status. Canada lacks adequate information about chemical and microbiological contaminants in food and water; hormones and antibiotics in meat, eggs, and dairy products; the declining nutritional value of industrially produced foods; and the risks of genetically modified foods. It also lacks longitudinal data about the actual food intake of Canadians, especially vulnerable populations. Experts interviewed for an assessment of Canada's food surveillance system "were emphatic that the gaps in Canada's food and nutrition surveillance capacity are extremely serious and must be remedied to protect and promote public health. All agreed that a systematic approach that improves and links existing data sources, and develops new data sources to fill the gaps, is urgently needed."[57] A report prepared for the government of Ontario by Justice R.J. Haines also recommended improvements to foodborne disease surveillance, primarily through coordinated investigation of agriculture, retail food, and the human population.[58]

On a positive note, in 2004 the Canadian Community Health Survey provided the first major national survey of food intake and nutritional status since the Canada Nutrition Survey in 1972.[59] Another bright note is the First Nations Environmental Contaminants Program, operated by Health Canada, which carries out on-reserve risk assessment, dietary surveys, and epidemiological studies to evaluate effects of environmental contaminants such as persistent organic pollutants (POPs), heavy metals, and biological contaminants in the food supply.[60] The Northern Contaminants Program also has a significant food surveillance component.[61] These programs targeting Aboriginal people are vital but would benefit from additional resources.

An important, but flawed, source of information on environmental hazards in Canada is the National Pollutant Release Inventory (NPRI), established in the 1990s to track releases of toxic chemicals by major polluters. Although the NPRI is a step in the right direction, it is far from comprehensive, covering only a fraction of the total pollution produced in Canada annually. As Robert Smith, the director of Environment Accounts and Statistics for Statistics Canada, told the Standing Committee on the Environment and Sustainable Development, "the NPRI, unfortunately, does not provide a comprehensive estimate of any pollutant emission in the country."[62] The NPRI is limited in that it:

- covers only 363 of the tens of thousands of chemicals used or released by major polluters in Canada
- covers only the largest polluting facilities in Canada
- does not include pollution from sources such as oil, gas, and coalbed methane exploration, maintenance and repair of vehicles (including cars, trucks, ships, trains, and planes), dry cleaners, gas stations, and small or medium-sized manufacturing facilities
- does not include pollution from nonpoint sources such as agricultural operations and urban runoff.

There are high thresholds for reporting releases to the NPRI. Facilities are required to report to Environment Canada only if they release at least ten thousand kilograms of a substance (at a concentration of 1 percent or more), and if they exceed twenty thousand employee hours per year. For a limited number of highly toxic substances, including mercury, arsenic, dioxins, and polycyclic aromatic hydrocarbons, lower thresholds have been established.[63] The NPRI's focus on the volume of toxic releases, rather than toxicity, may create perverse incentives for industry. Some companies attempt to improve perceptions of their performance by replacing less toxic, higher-volume chemicals with more toxic but lower-volume chemicals.[64] Another concern is that "in light of the disproportionate reliance on storage options of underground injection and landfilling in managing wastes off-site, one might ask to what degree we are engaged in a shell game, with the apparent progress in reducing releases to date merely reflecting transfer of risks to other communities and future generations."[65] Finally, NPRI data are self-reported by polluters, with no independent audits carried out to ensure accuracy. Reported figures can be gross underestimates. For example, benzene emissions reported to the NPRI by oil and gas companies were 60 percent lower than actual emissions measured by independent researchers.[66]

Canada has a poor track record when it comes to monitoring many environmental hazards not covered by the NPRI, including agricultural runoff, hazardous waste, contaminated sites, and toxic substances in consumer products. For example, for many years Canada and the Slovak Republic were the only members of the Organisation for Economic Co-operation and Development that failed to require public reporting of pesticide sales.[67] This situation finally changed in 2006.[68] While Ottawa maintains a fairly comprehensive inventory of contaminated sites on federal lands, there is no comparable inventory for lands that fall under provincial or territorial jurisdiction. A commendable example of the potential for cooperation in monitoring environmental hazards is the joint federal/provincial surveillance program for West Nile virus.[69] In contrast, the federal government is unable to provide reliable data on hazardous waste generation and disposal because provincial and territorial governments are unable or unwilling to share data.[70]

Missing Information, Part 2: Environmental Exposures

> Nowhere is the information gap more evident than with respect to the quantities and trends in body-burden of synthetic chemicals.
>
> – STANDING COMMITTEE ON ENVIRONMENT AND SUSTAINABLE DEVELOPMENT (2007)

Biological monitoring, or biomonitoring, is the direct measurement, through testing of blood, urine, hair, breast milk, or other human material, of environmental chemicals and their metabolites. As the CDC notes, biomonitoring measurements are the most health-relevant exposure assessments because they indicate the amount of the chemical that actually gets into people from all environmental pathways combined.[71] Biomonitoring studies have produced some surprising discoveries, including the fact that people continue to be exposed to industrial chemicals that are no longer used or produced, and the fact that toxic chemicals can be passed from the mother to the fetus. Biomonitoring decreases the uncertainty of assessing human exposure and improves our ability to make timely and appropriate public health decisions. The purposes of biomonitoring include:

- establishing a baseline of chemical exposures in a population
- determining the prevalence of people with levels above safe levels (where safe levels are known)

- tracking trends in levels of exposure of the population
- determining whether exposure levels are higher among minorities, children, women of childbearing age, or other potentially vulnerable groups or in particular geographic regions
- establishing reference ranges that can be used by physicians and scientists to determine whether a person or group has an unusually high exposure
- assessing the effectiveness of public health efforts to reduce exposure of populations to specific chemicals
- examining the relationship between the amount of exposure (i.e., the dose) and health effects
- identifying substances that were not thought to accumulate in people
- setting priorities for research on human health effects.

The United States has conducted an extensive national biomonitoring program through the National Health and Nutrition Examination Survey since the late 1990s, with comprehensive reports produced regularly by the CDC.[72] The *Fourth National Report on Human Exposure to Environmental Chemicals,* published in 2009, covered 212 chemicals. Individual exposure measurements on priority substances have also been published, including BPA, perfluorochemicals (PFCs), and perchlorate. BPA turned up in 93 percent of Americans, with higher concentrations in children and women.[73] PFCs were found in 98 percent of Americans.[74] Perchlorate (used in rocket fuel) is present in 100 percent of Americans sampled.[75] Germany, Sweden, and other European nations also have national biomonitoring programs.[76]

Canada lagged behind other countries, beginning a national biomonitoring program only in 2009, after the NGO Environmental Defence Canada published several studies indicating that the bodies of Canadians are contaminated by industrial chemicals, pesticides, heavy metals, phthalates, and flame retardants.[77] In 2010, as part of the Canadian Health Measures Survey (CHMS), Canada published the results of its first national biomonitoring program to measure the actual exposure of Canadians to environmental pollutants.[78] The first cycle of the CHMS looked at eighty-one toxic substances, including metals, phthalates, PCBs, pesticides, PFCs, and BPA. For example, small but measurable levels of BPA were found in the urine of 91 percent of Canadians. The second national biomonitoring report was published in 2013, reporting on ninety-one chemicals, forty-two of which were included in the first report.[79]

Health Canada also funds a project called Maternal-Infant Research on Environmental Chemicals (MIREC) that is studying exposure to environmental chemicals and the health effects in pregnant women and their babies.[80] Initially focused on infants, MIREC was extended to follow children from prior to birth up to five years of age. The province of Alberta also conducted biomonitoring studies on pregnant women, babies, and young children for a variety of contaminants.[81]

While biomonitoring programs are important, the science is still in its early stages and daunting challenges remain. For example, atrazine is the second most heavily used pesticide in the United States and has been linked to extensive adverse health effects ranging from cancer to endocrine disruption.[82] The CDC reported on the body burden of atrazine by testing Americans for just one of this chemical's metabolites (atrazine mercapturate). According to the CDC, less than 5 percent of Americans are exposed to atrazine. However, recent independent studies looking for a wider range of atrazine metabolites suggest that the CDC's approach significantly underestimated human exposures, both in terms of the proportion of population exposed and the levels of exposure.[83] Another problem related to biomonitoring is that our technological capacity to measure environmental contaminants in humans is far ahead of our ability to understand the health implications of chronic, low-level environmental exposures.

Missing Information, Part 3: Environmental Impacts on Health

> Given the level of scientific activity, societal interest, and
> government response to environmental issues with implications
> for human health, it is surprising how little is known about the
> health outcomes in the Canadian population that can be attributed
> to environmental factors, both in absolute and relative terms.
>
> – DR. RAY COPES, FORMER DIRECTOR, NATIONAL
> COORDINATING CENTRE FOR ENVIRONMENTAL
> HEALTH (2006)

There are significant gaps and inconsistencies in Canadian surveillance of adverse health outcomes linked to environmental hazards. Canada lacks up-to-date, consistent, and accessible data on key environmental health endpoints, including birth defects; developmental disabilities; asthma and other chronic respiratory diseases; and neurologic diseases, including

Parkinson's disease, autism, multiple sclerosis, and Alzheimer's disease.[84] Another important example is the lack of a nationally standardized surveillance system for waterborne illness. Although laboratory-confirmed cases of most waterborne diseases are notifiable nationally, provincially, and territorially, reporting on the source of the infection is not required. A review of waterborne infectious disease in Canada described existing data as "erratic, not easily accessible, and kept in diverse locations and formats."[85] As a result of this gap, policymakers lack important information on risks and the effectiveness of different drinking water policies and programs.[86] As an article in the *Canadian Medical Association Journal* concluded, "without better data, we cannot accurately identify health risks from drinking water or track our progress (or lack thereof) in reducing these risks."[87]

With respect to acute gastrointestinal illness, which is largely caused by exposure to pathogens in food and water, "there currently is no national outbreak reporting system that systematically and routinely collates outbreak summary data from provincial health authorities."[88] It is challenging (but possible) to identify the source of enteric infectious diseases. Source attribution involves determining what proportion of cases of a particular enteric disease (e.g., campylobacteriosis) is acquired from a given source (e.g., chickens) via a particular transmission pathway (e.g., food, direct contact with animals, and so on). Source attribution would help focus resources to improve food safety, water safety, and disease prevention with the greatest and most cost-effective impact on public health. The Public Health Agency of Canada acknowledges that efforts to monitor enteric pathogens capture only the "tip of the iceberg."[89] Health Canada also admits that "current available knowledge does not allow estimation of yearly illnesses or deaths from exposure to foodborne environmental chemical hazards."[90]

Another problem involves identifying the number of Canadians poisoned by exposure to pesticides, cleaning products, and other toxic substances.[91] Poisonings are generally not considered a reportable or notifiable disease or event.[92] As a recent article on poisonings in British Columbia observed, "data are unavailable on poisonings that present to physicians, medical clinics, or emergency rooms and are discharged without hospital admission or BCPCC [BC Poison Control Centre] contact."[93] The Canadian Association of Poison Control Centres, unlike the American Association of Poison Control Centers, does not have the resources to compile and publish national data on poisonings. Health Canada concluded that "the very limited and heterogeneous data sets collected by Canadian poison control centres do not allow for surveillance of acute poisonings in Canada. This severely impairs the development and implementation of effective prevention, regulatory, and information/education programs."[94]

When Canada has invested in environmental surveillance initiatives, valuable information has been gleaned. Examples include the National Enhanced Cancer Surveillance System, Canadian Childhood Cancer Surveillance and Control Program, Canadian Perinatal Surveillance System, National Enteric Surveillance Program, and FoodNet Canada. During the 1990s, federal and provincial governments cooperated on the National Enhanced Cancer Surveillance System, a project that illuminated connections between cancer and exposure to environmental tobacco smoke, drinking water disinfection byproducts, pesticides, and other environmental hazards.[95] The Canadian Childhood Cancer Surveillance and Control Program is a multistakeholder partnership that aims to decrease mortality, improve the prognosis, and reduce the suffering and burden of childhood cancer by filling knowledge gaps.[96] The Canadian Perinatal Surveillance System monitors dozens of indicators of both the determinants of maternal, fetal, and infant health and the associated health outcomes (e.g., maternal mortality, preterm birth rate, and prevalence of congenital disorders).[97]

The National Enteric Surveillance Program (NESP) is designed to provide timely analysis and reporting of laboratory-confirmed enteric disease cases in Canada. It debuted in 1997 and attempts to provide an up-to-date picture of the current status of major enteric infectious diseases in the human population, such as those caused by *Salmonella, Campylobacter,* verotoxigenic *E. coli,* intestinal parasitic organisms such as *Giardia* and *Cryptosporidium,* and enteric viruses such as noroviruses and rotavirus. FoodNet Canada focuses on surveillance of human cases of gastrointestinal illness, and also monitors possible sources of illness in food, animals, and water at three sentinel sites across Canada.[98] Systematic data collection and analysis includes active sampling of people with infectious enteric disease, and sampling of water, agricultural operations, and retail food. The development of these programs suggests that Canada is attempting to close some of the long-standing gaps in environmental health surveillance.

A related problem is the lack of environmental health education provided to medical professionals in Canada. American research indicates that the average medical student receives six hours of environmental health training, and the Canadian figure is likely to be similar or lower.[99] As a result, "it is likely that many diseases of environmental origin are undiagnosed, that proper treatments are not provided, and that opportunities for prevention are lost."[100]

Missing Information, Part 4: The Effectiveness of Interventions

Because of the knowledge gaps described in this chapter, it is difficult to evaluate the degree to which previous interventions (laws, policies, programs, projects, and so on) have been effective in reducing the impacts and risks associated with environmental hazards. For example, "Canada lacks the national food and nutrition surveillance information required to support policy and program development, to measure the impact and outcomes of policies and programs, and to anticipate emerging issues to allow a proactive response. This lack places Canada alone among western industrial countries to which we usually compare ourselves on health matters."[101] There are only a handful of instances in Canada where the effectiveness of environmental health interventions has been evaluated following their implementation. For example, programs aimed at reducing children's exposure to lead in areas with heavily contaminated soil appear to be effective, based on declines in blood lead levels following implementation.[102] The elimination of leaded gasoline had a tremendous positive effect on the blood lead levels of Canadian children. Canadian studies confirm that regular inspections of restaurants and other food purveyors are an effective tool in preventing foodborne illness.[103] A recent study assessed the effectiveness of municipal programs intended to reduce pesticide use.[104] More effort is now being spent to evaluate the effectiveness of interventions, but further resources are required.

Inadequate Investment in Environmental Health Research and Monitoring

One of the main reasons for the gaps and weaknesses outlined in this chapter is that resources for environmental health research in Canada are relatively meagre compared with other wealthy industrialized nations. The National Collaborating Centre for Environmental Health (NCCEH) was created in 2004 by the Public Health Agency of Canada to examine how changes in the environment, climate, shelter, and water, food, and air quality affect the health of Canadians, with a focus on knowledge synthesis and exchange, gap analysis, and capacity building.[105] For a decade, the NCCEH's budget has been a measly $1.5 million per year. The Canadian Institutes of Health Research (CIHR), the primary source of health research funds in Canada, has thirteen institutes but lacks an institute focused on environmental health, despite the fact that its governing legislation explicitly instructs the CIHR to examine "environmental influences on health."[106] The federal government's explanation for the lack of a dedicated national institute for environmental health is that "all Institutes address environmental health issues, which are multidisciplinary in nature and cut across disease specific boundaries."[107] This is tantamount to suggesting that Environment Canada is superfluous because sustainability concerns are part of every federal department's business.

Eleven of the thirteen institutes at the CIHR have participated in environmental health research activities. A search of the CIHR funding database found that the total dollar amount spent on projects that included "environmental influences on health" was $17.6 million over a period of six years (2000/01–2005/06). During the same period, a total of $24,487,995 was awarded to projects that included "environmental influences on health."[108] This represents less than 1 percent of the total amount ($3.2 billion) spent on grants and awards by the CIHR from 2000 to 2006. A major effort to develop national research priorities for environmental influences on health stalled due to an inability to convince key decision makers of the importance of environmental determinants of health.[109] In understated fashion, the CIHR acknowledges that environmental health in Canada is "relatively underdeveloped."[110] A recent positive sign was the CIHR's role in funding the Canadian Epigenetics, Environment and Health Research Consortium in 2012 to study the role of DNA/environment interactions in human health and disease. Another important study funded by the CIHR and Allergen (the Allergy, Genes and Environment Network) is the Canadian Healthy Infant Longitudinal Development (CHILD) study, investigating the genetic and environmental triggers of allergy and asthma, and the ways these triggers interact. Unlike major national children's studies in other countries, the CHILD study is narrowly focused on allergic disorders, including asthma, rather than a full range of health outcomes. Although the study may produce interesting results, the researchers could recruit only 3,500 infants instead of the goal of 5,000 because of insufficient funding. This will reduce the study's ability to reach statistically valid conclusions. Comparable but broader studies are already underway in the United Kingdom, France, the Philippines, Denmark, Spain, the Netherlands, Germany, Finland, Japan, and Norway.[111] For example, Norway is studying 100,000 children from before birth to the age of six, with goals that include understanding environmental influences on children's health and gene/environment interactions.[112]

The expected benefits from health care savings, increased productivity, and improved quality of life are expected to exceed the costs of these studies. This has been the experience with other large longitudinal health studies, notably the Framingham Heart Study and the US Nurses' Health Study.[113] The Framingham Heart Study, which has been running for over fifty years and has involved more than 10,000 participants, contributed to breakthrough insights about risk factors for cardiovascular disease (cigarette smoking, obesity, elevated cholesterol and blood pressure levels, and lack of exercise), which led to behavioural and policy changes that have saved hundreds of billions of dollars in the United States alone.[114]

Policymakers in Canada have a pressing and often unfulfilled need for relevant environmental health research evidence.[115] They need to know, usually within strict time limits, what is known, what is unknown, and the costs, benefits, and risks of alternative courses of action.[116] Their decisions often have not only substantial health consequences but also environmental, political, economic, and ethical ramifications.[117] Because of extensive and systemic knowledge gaps, it can be difficult for Canadian governments to establish environmental health priorities or make the informed policy and regulatory decisions necessary to protect Canadians from environmental threats. A gap analysis based on interviews with ninety environmental health practitioners and policymakers concluded that conducting surveillance of environmental hazards, estimating the environmental burden of disease, and evaluating the effectiveness of environmental health programs and interventions should be top priorities for governments in Canada.[118] Another expert study, commissioned by the CIHR, concluded that "there is an urgent need to increase research on the environmental influences on health by increasing levels of funding and other support."[119] The need for Canada to strengthen and coordinate its environmental health research and surveillance has been recognized by many organizations, including the Public Health Agency of Canada, the National Round Table on the Environment and the Economy, the Commissioner of the Environment and Sustainable Development, the Canadian Institute for Health Information, the Canadian Public Health Association, the International Joint Commission, and the Royal Society of Canada.[120]

In comparison, spending on environmental health research in the United States is dramatically higher than in Canada. The National Institute of Environmental Health Sciences (NIEHS), established in 1969, is one of twenty institutes under the auspices of the US National Institutes of Health, which is analogous to the Canadian Institutes of Health Research. The mission of the NIEHS is to reduce the burden of human illness and disability by understanding how the environment influences the development and progression of human disease.[121] The NIEHS budget for 2015 was US$665,080,000.[122]

Additional spending on environmental health–related research occurs at other institutes separately funded by the US National Institutes of Health (including the National Cancer Institute, the National Heart, Lung, and Blood Institute, and the National Institute of Child Health and Human Development). The National Center for Environmental Health (NCEH) is part of the US Centers for Disease Control and Prevention, an agency similar to the Public Health Agency of Canada. The mission of the NCEH is to plan, direct, and coordinate a national program to maintain and improve the health of the American people by promoting a healthy environment and by preventing premature death and avoidable illness and disability caused by noninfectious, nonoccupational, environmental, and related factors. The 2012 budget for the NCEH was US$140 million.[123] The combined total for these two American institutions, exceeding US$800 million per year, is roughly a hundred times the annual Canadian investment in environmental health research through the NCCEH and the CIHR (while the US population is only nine times larger).

Undermining International Environmental Health

Canada has no coherent policy regarding the international environmental consequences of our actions. The Federal Sustainable Development Strategy 2013–16 makes no mention of the Millennium Development Goals, the need to ensure that Canadian aid and trade policies and programs promote rather than impede sustainable outcomes, or the impact of Canadian production and consumption on the citizens and ecosystems of other nations. In this regard, Canada has failed to learn from the pioneering leadership of Sweden, whose legislated national goal of solving environmental problems within a generation was amended in 2010 to add that "this should be done without increasing environmental and health problems outside Sweden's borders."[124] Sweden is striving to ensure that neither the production of goods it imports nor the use of products it exports causes or exacerbates health and environmental problems in other countries. As the Swedish government observed, "policy instruments and measures must be designed in such a way that Sweden does not export environmental problems" but rather solves them through changing patterns of production and consumption.[125] Similarly, Norway's sustainable development strategy places major emphasis on Norway's role in reducing environmental health problems in other nations, particularly through its generous foreign aid programs and through aggressive action to address climate change.[126] Norway (along with Sweden, the Netherlands, and Denmark) currently allocates official development assistance or foreign aid at a level that is three times higher than Canada (measured as a percentage of GDP).[127] Norway met its original Kyoto commitment and pledged to reduce emissions of greenhouse gases to 20 percent below 1990 levels by 2020.

Canada, for the most part, has turned a blind eye to these fundamentally important international environmental health considerations. Canada trails other nations in allocating foreign aid funding to safe drinking water and sanitation infrastructure. Out of an annual average of $5 billion in foreign aid spending from 2008 through 2013, Canada allocated only $50 million per year to water and sanitation, or approximately 1 percent, compared with 5 percent for the OECD as a whole.[128] Canada has limited most uses of asbestos and spent many millions removing asbestos from the Parliament Buildings in Ottawa but continued exporting this cancer-causing product to developing countries, including India, Thailand, and the Philippines, until 2013. As a party to the Rotterdam Convention, Canada played a leading role in blocking the addition of asbestos to the list of substances governed by that treaty, contrary to recommendations by scientific experts. Canada's foreign policy has recently shifted away from alleviating poverty in Africa towards supporting Canadian mining and oil and gas corporations operating in Latin America. As a result, the beneficiaries of Canada's official development assistance budget are no longer the most impoverished people in the world, but rather large corporations like Barrick Gold and Rio Tinto Alcan. These two corporations are part of corporate social responsibility projects that received over $50 million in funding from the Canadian International Development Agency as part of Canada's Corporate Social Responsibility Strategy for the International Extractive Sector.[129]

In 2012, Canada announced that it was withdrawing from the Kyoto Protocol. Canada had promised to reduce greenhouse gas emissions to 6 percent below 1990 levels by 2012, but came nowhere near to fulfilling this obligation, as emissions actually rose by 20 percent. Canada effectively banned the construction of new coal-fired electricity plants but continues to export coal, which will not only generate huge volumes of greenhouse gas emissions but also harm the health of millions of people in countries such as India and China. Canada's energy regulator, the National Energy Board, refuses to admit or consider any evidence related to climate change or downstream impacts of burning fossil fuels when considering applications to export oil and gas or build new pipelines to facilitate exports.[130] In 2013,

Canada became the first country in the world to turn its back on the UN Convention to Combat Desertification, formally withdrawing from the agreement.

On a brighter note, Canada recently reversed its long-standing opposition to international recognition of the right to water.[131] For many years, Canada was the only country to vote against UN resolutions seeking to recognize this right.[132] Canada also deserves credit for being one of the original sponsors of a World Health Organization project called the Health and Environment Linkages Initiative, which promotes action to reduce the environmental burden of disease in developing countries.[133] Canada fulfilled its commitment under the Copenhagen Accord to fast-track $1.2 billion in assistance to developing countries to help address climate change between 2010 and 2012.[134] However, 74 percent of Canada's assistance came in the form of loans, which must be repaid, rather than grants, one of the highest proportions of loans among OECD donor countries. As well, overall levels of development assistance fell from 2012 to 2014, raising concerns that the climate funding came at the expense of other aid programs.[135]

Conclusion

This chapter compared Canada and other wealthy nations on a number of critical, overarching issues related to protecting human health from environmental hazards. The unsettling results indicate that Canada lags behind most wealthy industrialized countries in its refusal to recognize citizens' right to live in a healthy environment, its failure to have a national environmental health action plan, the absence of a national environmental health monitoring or surveillance system, a total lack of laws and policies to prevent or ameliorate environmental injustices, inadequate funding for environmental health research, and international policies that undermine the environmental health of citizens in poor countries. These systemic failures contribute to the magnitude of the environmental burden of disease, as measured by thousands of preventable premature deaths, millions of illnesses, and billions of dollars in health costs annually.

7

A Comparative Analysis of Environmental Health Laws and Policies

Canadian environmental quality and environmental policy are worse than one might expect in a relatively wealthy country.

– PROFESSOR INGER WEIBUST, CARLETON UNIVERSITY (2009)

Canada's disappointing environmental record was described in Chapter 1. Given the compelling evidence connecting environmental quality to human health, a fundamental question is whether existing Canadian laws, regulations, and standards provide an adequate degree of protection for air, water, food, and biodiversity. To answer that question, this chapter provides a comprehensive examination of rules governing air quality (outdoor and indoor), drinking water safety, pesticides, toxic substances, climate change, and endangered species protection. Canadian laws, regulations, standards, and guidelines are compared with the relevant legal provisions in the United States, Australia, and Europe. The results are striking, demonstrating that Canada's laws and policies are consistently and substantially weaker than those of our industrialized peers. This indicates that governments and industry treat Canadians as second-class citizens, causing unnecessary and unjustifiable risks for human health and the environment.

Outdoor Air Quality

The first analysis compares Canada's air quality guidelines with the standards in the United States, Australia, and Europe, as well as the guidelines recommended by the World Health Organization. The comparison focuses on six criteria air pollutants: ozone, particulate matter, sulphur dioxide, nitrogen oxides, carbon monoxide, and lead. Humans are exposed to many other harmful pollutants through the air, such as mercury, benzene, and hundreds of additional airborne toxic substances. While these air pollutants are certainly important, ambient air quality standards are less common for these substances. Instead, governments rely on regulations that address these emissions on a source-by-source basis. For example, in addressing the health and environmental threats posed by mercury, some jurisdictions established regulations governing mercury emissions from coal-fired electricity plants, hazardous waste incinerators, consumer products containing mercury (from cars to thermometers), and dental amalgam. Focusing on the six criteria air pollutants facilitates international comparison.

When assessing the results of this comparison, it is critical to understand that Canada, in contrast to the vast majority of other wealthy industrialized countries, does not employ legally enforceable national standards for air quality. The United States and Australia both have legally binding and enforceable national air quality standards, even with the federal form of government that they share with Canada. The European Union establishes regional air quality standards that must be transposed into national law by all member countries and achieved by specific dates. The guidelines from the WHO are merely recommendations because the WHO lacks the authority to enact enforceable standards.

National air quality standards set a benchmark that all levels of government must strive to achieve, thus influencing a wide range of laws, policies, and investments. These decisions range from licensing individual industrial facilities to improving public transit systems. If set too low, air quality standards will lower the bar for all of these essential activities, resulting in deaths and illnesses from unnecessary air pollution.

The Canadian Ambient Air Quality Standards (CAAQS) for ozone and particulate matter are not "standards" in the ordinary legal sense, but are more accurately described as voluntary guidelines, because they are nonbinding on any level of government and have no legal consequences if they are not met. This is a vitally important distinction. As Environment Canada acknowledged in 2013, "under the American *Clean Air Act*, penalties can be levied on states where the NAAQS [National Ambient Air

Quality Standards] are not being met. Under the *Canadian Environmental Protection Act, 1999,* the CAAQS are voluntary objectives," meaning that no penalties flow from noncompliance.[1] Canada also has voluntary National Ambient Air Quality Objectives (NAAQO) for sulphur dioxide, nitrogen dioxide, and carbon monoxide. Some provinces have used the national objectives to formulate legally binding air quality standards but the majority have not. An extensive body of research demonstrates that voluntary approaches to environmental protection are generally ineffective.[2]

Comparative Analysis of Results

It is surprising to learn that despite being voluntary, Canada's current air quality guidelines lag behind the legally enforceable standards found in other western industrialized nations (see Table 7.1). For each of the six criteria air

TABLE 7.1
International comparison of ambient air quality standards and guidelines

Pollutant	Canada	EU	US	Australia	WHO
Ozone[1]	63	60	75	80	50
Fine particulate[2]	28	–	35	25	25
Sulphur dioxide[3]	115	48	–	80	8
Sulphur dioxide[4]	334	132	75	200	–
Nitrogen dioxide[5]	53	21	53	30	21
Nitrogen dioxide[1]	213	105	100	120	105
Carbon monoxide[6]	13	9	9	9	9
Lead[7]	–	0.5	1.5	0.15	0.5

Note: A dash (–) indicates that no standard or guideline has been established.
1   8 hours, parts per billion
2   24 hours, micrograms per cubic metre
3   24 hours, parts per billion
4   1 hour, parts per billion
5   Annual, parts per billion
6   8 hours, parts per million
7   Micrograms per cubic metre, averaged over one year (the United States is more stringent, using a three-month average)

Sources: Canada – Canadian Ambient Air Quality Standards are established by the Canadian Council of Ministers of the Environment (http://www.ccme.ca); National Ambient Air Quality Objectives are jointly set by Health Canada and Environment Canada (http://www.hc-sc.gc.ca and http://www.ec.gc.ca).
European Union – *Directive 2008/50/EC of the European Parliament and of the Council of 21 May 2008, on Ambient Air Quality and Cleaner Air for Europe.*
United States – National Ambient Air Quality Standards are established by the Environmental Protection Agency pursuant to the *Clean Air Act of 1963,* P.L. 88-206 (http://www.epa.gov/air/criteria.html).
Australia – National Ambient Air Quality Standards are established by the National Environment Protection Council (http://www.environment.gov.au/atmosphere/airquality/standards.html).
World Health Organization – "WHO Air Quality Guidelines Global Update 2005" (2005), http://www.who.int.

pollutants, there is at least one jurisdiction, and as many as all three other jurisdictions, that have more stringent outdoor air quality standards than Canada. Canada does not have the highest level of health protection for any of the air pollutants. Finally, Canada is the only jurisdiction that has no guideline at all for ambient levels of lead despite the fact that lead is one of the most universally acknowledged environmental threats. There seems to be a pattern of Canadian foot-dragging in response to the threat of lead to children's health. Canada was slow to prohibit the use of lead as a gasoline additive, slow to restrict the use of lead in paint, and slow to restrict lead content in children's jewellery.[3]

Canada's air quality guidelines are weaker than the EU and Australian standards on five out of six air pollutants, and weaker than the WHO recommendations for all six pollutants. Only in comparison with the United States does Canada fare slightly better, with Canada having more stringent numerical values than the United States for two air pollutants, whereas the United States has more stringent numerical targets for three pollutants. All of the US standards are inherently stronger, however, because they are legally binding and enforceable. The US standard for sulphur dioxide is almost five times more stringent than the Canadian guideline (75 ppb versus 334 ppb). As well, the US Environmental Protection Agency is in the process of strengthening its national ozone standards.[4]

Discussion

Given that air pollution represents the single greatest environmental threat to the health of Canadians, it is disturbing to learn that Canada lags behind other wealthy industrialized nations in regulating air quality. Canada's CAAQS and NAAQO provide a very weak form of protection. Comparisons of Organisation for Economic Co-operation and Development nations show that Canada consistently ranks among the three worst industrialized nations for per capita emissions of sulphur dioxide, nitrogen dioxide, volatile organic compounds (VOCs), carbon monoxide, and greenhouse gases.[5] This dismal performance reflects the weakness of the existing air pollution rules in Canada, and confirms that provincial regulations do not fill the void left by lax federal guidelines. In 2006, the Conservative government promised a *Clean Air Act* and strong regulations to reduce industrial air pollution 50 percent by 2015.[6] As of 2015, there is no *Clean Air Act* and no new regulations, although a draft regulation addressing a subset of industrial sectors was published in 2014.[7] In addition to uncertainty about whether the draft regulation will become law, Environment Canada admits that "in subsequent phases, requirements for oil sands, petroleum refining, chemicals, fertilizers, upstream oil and gas, and volatile organic compound emissions from hydrocarbon sources *may be proposed* for addition to the proposed Regulations" (emphasis added).[8]

Weak laws and guidelines are a major reason why the ongoing impacts of air pollution in Canada are so high. Unless laws and regulations are strengthened and additional actions are taken, pressures from population and economic growth could exacerbate the problem. It is therefore imperative that the substandard legal protection for air quality be strengthened. This will require a greater commitment to honesty from the federal government. When announcing revised air quality objectives for ozone and fine particulates in 2013, Environment Canada published a backgrounder describing the new objectives as "stringent," "comprehensive," and "health-based."[9] All three of these claims are demonstrably false. Voluntary objectives are inherently the opposite of stringent. The new objectives address only two pollutants and are thus not comprehensive. And finally, if the objectives were really health-based, then they would meet the WHO's recommendations and be at least as protective as the standards in other wealthy industrialized countries. As the preceding analysis demonstrates, even Canada's newest air quality objectives lag behind.

In recognition of the importance of other toxic air pollutants, the European Union has now established air quality standards for arsenic, benzene, cadmium, nickel, and polycyclic aromatic hydrocarbons (PAHs).[10] Canada has not set national air quality objectives for any of these pollutants. Canada does regulate benzene through gasoline regulations, but these regulations permit benzene concentrations in gasoline at twice the level of US standards.[11] The US EPA has identified sixteen priority PAHs, based on concerns about cancer, cardiovascular and respiratory problems, and negative impacts on birth outcomes. Unlike the United States, Canada does not regulate PAH emissions from fuels.[12]

Indoor Air Quality

In wealthy industrialized nations, most people spend the overwhelming majority of their time indoors. Regulating indoor air quality is widely understood to be impractical, so governments limit themselves to setting guidelines and regulating products that have adverse health effects in the indoor environment. Apart from tobacco smoke, the single greatest environmental health threat encountered indoors is radon. The following analysis compares radon guidelines in Canada, the United States, the European Union, and Australia.

Radon

As recently as 2006, the Canadian guideline for taking action to reduce residential radon levels was the weakest in the industrialized world.[13] It was over five times weaker than the American standard and four times weaker than the European standard.[14] In 2007, Health Canada succumbed to public pressure and revised the Canadian radon guideline downward from 800 Bq/m^3 (becquerels per cubic metre) to 200 Bq/m^3. However, the new guideline is still 33 percent weaker than the American guideline of 150 Bq/m^3 and twice as high as the level recommended by the WHO.[15] It still exposes Canadians to a significantly increased risk of developing lung cancer. By setting the guideline at a level that leads citizens to believe they are safe when they are not, Canadian governments create a false sense of security.

Radon concentrations as low as 100 Bq/m^3 cause a significant increase in the risk of lung cancer. According to leading British experts, "around 90 per cent of radon-induced deaths in the United Kingdom probably occur as a result of exposures to radon concentrations below the currently recommended action level of 200 Bq/m^3."[16]

Radon has a much higher profile in the United States than in Canada, due largely to a variety of government policies and programs. The EPA offers extensive programs to assist homeowners who are facing radon problems.[17] The agency has a long-standing national public information campaign, maintains a comprehensive map of areas where radon is most likely to be found in high concentrations, and offers a useful citizen's guide about radon. January is National Radon Action Month in the United States, and the EPA runs public service announcements on television, warning of the health risk posed by radon and explaining that solutions are readily available. The EPA recommends that all Americans test their residences for radon. In 2013, Canada finally established a radon awareness month and dedicated resources to public information about radon risks.[18]

According to the WHO, the recommended level for remedial action in European buildings should be an annual average radon concentration greater than 100 Bq/m^3. This would be the most stringent radon protection level in the world, although the WHO acknowledges that even this level of protection will still result in some excess deaths from cancer.[19] Germany,

Denmark, and other EU nations have adopted the WHO recommendation.[20] In Australia, the recommended intervention level is 200 Bq/m^3, equal to the Canadian guideline.[21]

In addition to radon, the current Canadian guideline for formaldehyde (a human carcinogen) also is weaker than the WHO's recommended guideline. Following the pattern established for outdoor air, Canada has weaker indoor air quality guidelines than other jurisdictions.[22] According to Pollution Probe, Canada's indoor air quality guidelines are not adequate to protect vulnerable populations such as children and seniors, and have not kept pace with standards in other countries.[23] A wide range of stakeholders has called for a complete overhaul of Canada's Exposure Guidelines for Residential Indoor Air Quality.[24]

Drinking Water Quality

There is no silver bullet for ensuring safe drinking water quality. Experts generally agree that a multiple-barrier approach – comprehensively addressing threats to water quality all the way from sources to tap – is necessary. The key elements of a comprehensive approach include protection of water sources (to keep raw water as clean as possible); adequate treatment (including disinfection and additional processes to remove or inactivate contaminants); a well-maintained distribution system; strong water quality standards; regular inspection, testing, and monitoring; operator training and certification; public notice, reporting, and involvement; contingency planning; research; adequate funding; and rigorous enforcement.[25]

While each component in the multiple-barrier approach is important, the focus of the following comparative analysis is on the standards (or in Canada's case guidelines) employed to ensure safe drinking water. Strong water quality standards are at the heart of effective drinking water protection systems. Standards are the key driver for other elements of the system, providing clear, specific, and measurable benchmarks that all of the various elements must be coordinated to achieve. Water quality standards address treatment techniques and establish maximum acceptable concentrations (MACs) for biological, chemical, and radioactive contaminants in drinking water post-treatment.

As discussed in the context of air quality, standards provide better protection for human health than guidelines because they are legally binding and enforceable. Failure to meet standards generally results in actions being taken to ensure future compliance, whereas failure to meet guidelines may not result in remedial action. Because of this subtle but crucial distinction, the WHO states that there should be legally binding national standards for drinking water quality in all countries.[26] Similarly, Justice Dennis O'Connor, in his extensive report on the causes of the Walkerton water disaster, concluded that drinking water quality standards "should have the force of law."[27] O'Connor added that "conservative and enforceable water quality standards are an important basis for a multi-barrier approach to water safety."[28] However, standards can be ineffective if they are poorly designed, not enforced, or fail to prioritize the most important environmental hazards and pathways of exposure.

In Canada, all levels of government share responsibility for the provision of safe drinking water, although most aspects of drinking water management fall under provincial jurisdiction. In the United States, Australia, and many European nations, subnational governments also bear extensive responsibility for drinking water safety. The federal government plays a vital role in the establishment of the Guidelines for Canadian Drinking Water Quality, which provide recommendations for treatment techniques and MACs for contaminants. Although a federal/provincial/territorial committee develops these guidelines, it is the federal government's responsibility to ensure that the health of Canadians is protected, as it does through standards for food, drugs, and bottled water under the *Food and Drugs Act*. The Guidelines for Canadian Drinking Water Quality were originally called standards, but the name was changed in the 1970s to clarify that they are not legally enforceable.[29]

The United States and Europe provide their citizens with mandatory, legally binding national standards for drinking water quality. Lower levels of government in the United States and Europe are bound to comply with the national or, in the EU's case, supranational standards. Although there are differences in the approaches employed by European nations, all must meet the minimum standards prescribed by the EU's Drinking Water Directive.[30] In contrast, Canada is the only G8 country, and one of only two OECD countries (with Australia) lacking legally enforceable drinking water quality standards at the national level.[31]

Canadian drinking water guidelines are not legally binding unless incorporated into provincial or territorial laws, regulations, or operating permits for drinking water purveyors. These rules vary widely in the level of legal protection provided.[32] Canada has national drinking water guidelines for ninety-four microbiological, chemical, physical, and radiological parameters. Adoption of these guidelines is inconsistent among provinces and territories, ranging from twenty-seven to ninety-four, which are enforceable in some provinces or territories and not in others.[33] The Canadian guidelines are legally binding in some municipalities because they have been incorporated into operating permits for water treatment facilities.

International Comparison of Drinking Water Standards and Guidelines

The following analysis compares the Guidelines for Canadian Drinking Water Quality with corresponding frameworks in the United States, the European Union, and Australia. Guidelines for drinking water quality recommended by the WHO and intended to assist nations in establishing their own legal standards are also included. The analysis addresses treatment methods and MACs for microbiological, chemical, and radioactive contaminants in drinking water. Most jurisdictions also establish drinking water guidelines for physical characteristics of water, including turbidity, colour, hardness, total dissolved solids, pH, temperature, taste, odour, and dissolved oxygen. These guidelines are primarily related to aesthetic considerations, although they can influence matters such as the corrosion of pipes (thus requiring corrosion control programs). Turbidity is important because it can have indirect implications for public health and can serve as a surrogate for pathogens that are difficult to monitor. Because they are not directly connected to public health, no comparison of the physical water quality guidelines is undertaken. Other standards and guidelines, such as requirements for operator certification and public reporting, are also important but are not suited to international comparison.

Microbiological Contaminants

One of the objectives of drinking water treatment is to reduce concentrations of pathogens to levels too low to cause infection, while maintaining the water's aesthetic qualities. In general, it is important to focus on outcomes rather than specific processes. For example, because of the small physical size of viruses, conventional water filtration has limited effectiveness. Advanced forms of filtration (e.g., membrane filtration) or a different disinfection method such as UV or ozonation is required to minimize health risks posed by viruses and protozoa because many of these pathogens, such as *Cryptosporidium*, are resistant to chlorination. It is also important to note that treatment technologies are effective only when used by trained and experienced operators.[34]

All nations in this comparison have set standards or guidelines for coliform bacteria and turbidity. In all nations, the MAC for *E. coli* and fecal coliforms is none detectable per 100 mL. The Canadian guideline for total coliforms is also zero if only one sample is taken monthly, but 10 percent of multiple samples can contain coliforms as long as there are fewer than ten organisms per 100 mL. The United States, Australia, and Europe have slightly more stringent limits for total coliforms than Canada, placing a maximum limit of 5 percent of multiple samples testing positive for coliforms.[35]

For technical reasons, none of the nations studied have set MACs for most bacterial, viral, and protozoan waterborne pathogens. Instead, the United States and Canada employ outcome-based standards for effective treatment. In the United States, these standards require filtration (or an equally effective alternative form of treatment such as UV or ozonation) in all public water systems that rely on either surface water or groundwater directly influenced by surface water. The treatment process must remove or inactivate 99.9 percent of *Giardia*, 99.99 percent of viruses, and 99 percent of *Cryptosporidium*.[36] The Guidelines for Canadian Drinking Water Quality were recently amended to emulate the American approach. The Canadian guideline for *Cryptosporidium* is slightly stronger, recommending 99.9 percent reduction. The EU Drinking Water Directive includes a general requirement that water be free from microorganisms and parasites that "constitute a potential danger to human health." The European Union requires monitoring for a bacterium called *Clostridium perfringens*, which serves as a warning sign for the presence of harmful microorganisms. Australia does not have guidelines for *Giardia*, viruses, or *Cryptosporidium*, choosing instead to emphasize protecting source water from contamination. Although the Guidelines for Canadian Drinking Water Quality recognize that microbiological contaminants are the greatest threat to public health and recommend filtration, only Nova Scotia, Quebec, Ontario, Alberta, and the Yukon require the filtration of surface water.[37] Some individual communities in provinces and territories without mandatory filtration provide filtration, but these communities are exceptions to the rule. Filtration is recommended but not legally required by the European Union and Australia.

Scientists are concerned about toxic substances produced by cyanobacteria, particularly a toxin called microcystin. The WHO recommends a limit of 0.001 mg/L. Canada's guideline for microcystin (0.0015 mg/L) is slightly less stringent than the WHO recommendation or the Australian guideline (0.0013 mg/L), but the difference is modest. The US EPA has placed cyanobacterial toxins on its contaminant candidate list, a step that presages a future drinking water standard. The European Union does not have a microcystin standard but individual countries, including France, Spain, and the Czech Republic, have adopted legal limits incorporating the WHO's recommendation.

Overall, the United States has the most rigorous standards for protecting public health from microbiological contaminants because of mandatory filtration and outcome-based treatment standards that require a high level of effectiveness in addressing bacteria, viruses, and protozoa. Canada employs weaker guidelines, but recommends achieving similar levels of protection from waterborne pathogens.

Chemical Contaminants

Of sixty-five chemical contaminants assessed in this study, Canada has established a weaker MAC than at least one of the other jurisdictions or the WHO for fifty-three contaminants (see Table 7.2). In other words, over 80 percent of the Guidelines for Canadian Drinking Water Quality relating to chemical contaminants provide less protection for public health than the standards or guidelines in other industrialized nations. In some cases, the difference may seem relatively minor, as in the case of 1,2-dichloroethane, where Canada's guideline of 0.005 mg/L is only slightly weaker than the standard of 0.003 mg/L used by the European Union and Australia. Yet even in this case, it is important to recognize that 1,2-dichloroethane is recognized by the International Agency for Research on Cancer (IARC) as a possible human carcinogen, indicating that any level of exposure should be avoided.

In other cases, however, there is a wide gap between Canada's guidelines for acceptable drinking water quality and the standards applied in another jurisdiction. European standards range from 50 to 1,000 times stronger than Canadian guidelines. For example, the European Union's MAC for 2,3,4,6-tetrachlorophenol is 1,000 times stronger than the Canadian guideline. For the pesticide trifluralin, its MAC is 450 times stronger than the Canadian guideline. The European Union does not establish specific guidelines for individual pesticides but uses a generic guideline of 0.0001 mg/L, well below all of the Canadian guidelines for acceptable concentrations of pesticides in drinking water. It also sets an overall limit of 0.0005 mg/L for the total amount of all pesticides that can be in drinking water. This approach recognizes that cumulative exposure to a number of different pesticides, each of which may be below the individual level of concern, may cause negative health effects. Canada does not have any comparable cumulative limit, meaning that Canadians can be exposed to combinations of various pesticides in drinking water at levels that would be unlawful in Europe. In

TABLE 7.2

International comparison of drinking water quality standards and guidelines

Parameter	Canada	US	EU	Australia	WHO
2,4-D	0.1	0.07	0.0001	0.03	0.03
Antimony	0.006	0.006	0.005	0.003	0.02
Arsenic	0.01	0.01	0.01	0.01	0.01
Atrazine	0.005	0.003	0.0001	0.02	0.002
Azinphos-methyl	0.02	–	0.0001	0.03	–
Barium	1.0	2.0	–	2.0	0.7
Benzene	0.005	0.005	0.001	0.001	0.01
Benzo[a]pyrene	0.00001	0.0002	0.00001	0.00001	0.0007
Boron	5.0	–	1.0	5.0	0.5
Bromate	0.01	0.01	0.01	0.02	0.01
Bromoxynil	0.005	–	0.0001	0.01	–
Cadmium	0.005	0.005	0.005	0.002	0.003
Carbaryl	0.09	–	0.0001	0.03	–
Carbofuran	0.09	0.04	0.0001	0.01	0.007
Carbon tetrachloride	0.002	0.005	0.0001	0.003	0.004
Chloramines – total	3.0	4.0	–	3.0	3.0
Chlorate	1.0	–	0.0001	–	0.7
Chlorite	1.0	1.0	0.0001	–	0.7
Chlorpyrifos	0.09	–	0.0001	0.01	0.03
Chromium	0.05	0.1	0.05	0.05	0.05
Cyanide	0.2	0.2	0.05	0.08	0.07
Diazinon	0.02	–	0.0001	0.004	–
Dicamba	0.12	–	0.0001	0.1	–
1,2-Dichlorobenzene	0.2	0.6	0.0001	1.5	1.0
1,4-Dichlorobenzene	0.005	0.075	0.0001	0.04	0.3
1,2-Dichloroethane	0.005	0.005	0.003	0.003	0.03
1,1-Dichloroethylene	0.014	0.007	–	0.03	–
Dichloromethane	0.05	0.005	–	0.004	0.02
2,4-Dichlorophenol	0.9	–	0.0001	0.2	–
Diclofop-methyl	0.009	–	0.0001	0.005	–
Dimethoate	0.02	–	0.0001	0.007	0.006
Diquat	0.07	0.02	0.0001	0.007	–
Diuron	0.15	–	0.0001	0.02	–
Ethylbenzene	0.14	0.7	–	0.3	0.3
Fluoride	1.5	4.0	1.5	1.5	1.5
Glyphosate	0.28	0.7	0.0001	1.0	–

Parameter	Canada	US	EU	Australia	WHO
Haloacetic acids	0.06	0.08	–	–	0.05
Lead	0.01	0.015	0.01	0.01	0.01
Malathion	0.19	–	0.0001	0.07	–
MCPA	0.1	–	0.0001	0.04	0.002
Mercury	0.001	0.002	0.001	0.001	0.006
Metolachlor	0.05	–	0.0001	0.3	0.01
Metribuzin	0.08	–	0.0001	0.07	–
Monochlorobenzene	0.08	–	–	–	–
Nitrate	45.0	10.0	50.0	50.0	50.0
Nitrite	10.0	1.0	0.5	3.0	3.0
Nitrilotriacetic acid	0.4	–	–	0.2	0.2
Paraquat	0.01	–	0.0001	0.001	–
Parathion	0.05	–	0.0001	0.02	–
Pentachlorophenol	0.06	0.001	0.0001	0.01	0.009
Phorate	0.002	–	0.0001	–	–
Picloram	0.19	0.5	0.0001	0.3	–
Selenium	0.01	0.05	–	0.01	0.01
Simazine	0.01	0.004	0.0001	0.02	0.002
Terbufos	0.001	–	0.0001	0.0009	–
Tetrachloroethylene	0.03	0.005	0.01	0.05	0.04
2,4,6-Trichlorophenol	0.005	–	0.0001	0.2	0.02
2,3,4,6-Tetrachlorophenol	0.1	–	0.0001	0.02	–
Toluene	0.06	1.0	–	0.8	0.7
Trichloroethylene	0.005	0.005	0.01	–	0.02
Trifluralin	0.045	–	0.0001	0.09	0.02
Trihalomethanes	0.1	0.08	0.1	0.25	–
Uranium	0.02	0.03	–	0.017	0.015
Vinyl chloride	0.002	0.002	0.0005	0.0003	0.0003
Xylenes – total	0.09	10.0	–	0.6	0.5

Note: A dash (–) indicates that no standard or guideline has been established for a given parameter. All guidelines and standards are in mg/L.

Sources: Health Canada, *Guidelines for Canadian Drinking Water Quality: Summary Table* (Ottawa: Health Canada, 2014); US Environmental Protection Agency, "Primary Drinking Water Standards, enacted pursuant to the Safe Drinking Water Act" (n.d.), http://water.epa.gov/drink/contaminants/index.cfm#List; *EU Council Directive 1998/93/EC of 3 November 1998, on the Quality of Water Intended for Human Consumption;* National Health and Medical Research Council and National Resource Management Ministerial Council, *Australian Drinking Water Guidelines* (Canberra: NHMRC/NRMMC, 2011); World Health Organization, *Guidelines for Drinking-Water Quality,* 3rd ed. (Geneva: WHO, 2004).

the past, Canada established a guideline for the maximum level of total pesticides in drinking water, but it was discontinued.[38]

It is not only Europe that is ahead of Canada in establishing more conservative MACs for chemical contaminants. For example, Canada's guidelines for the pesticides diazinon, diuron, and diquat are 5, 7.5, and 10 times weaker, respectively, than Australia's guidelines.

Radioactive Contaminants

Standards and guidelines for radioactive contaminants are difficult to compare across nations, due to different approaches to measurement and standard setting. Canada and the European Union both set 0.1 milliseverts per year (mSv/year) as the maximum acceptable level of exposure to radioactivity in water. Europe's value is a legally binding standard whereas Canada's guideline is voluntary. The European standard specifically excludes tritium, potassium −40, and radon and radon decay products, which are subject to separate individual standards. Canada also has gross alpha and gross beta guidelines (0.5 Bq/L and 1 Bq/L, respectively), plus a series of radioisotope-specific guidelines that are to be applied if gross alpha or beta guidelines are exceeded. Australia sets the guideline for annual exposure to radioactivity in water at 1.0 mSv/year (ten times higher than Canada), with screening levels for both gross alpha and gross beta activity set at 0.5 Bq/L. The United States sets slightly higher maximum contaminant levels for alpha and beta particles (0.56–1.85 Bq/L).

Although comparing rules for radioactive contaminants is difficult, the Canadian guideline for tritium in drinking water is seventy times higher (i.e., weaker) than the corresponding European standard. Tritium is a radioactive isotope that occurs naturally but is also produced and discharged by nuclear reactors. The Canadian guideline for tritium is 7,000 Bq/L, whereas the European standard is 100 Bq/L. The American standard for tritium lies between these, at 740 Bq/L.

Discussion

Although Canada is envied around the world for its natural wealth of fresh water, this is not the case for Canadian drinking water guidelines. The first problem is the lack of enforceable national standards, which puts us behind the United States and the European Union and at odds with the recommendations of both the WHO and the Walkerton Inquiry. In terms of setting MACs for chemical and radiological contaminants, the Guidelines for Canadian Drinking Water Quality are substantially weaker than the standards set by the United States and the European Union, the Australian guidelines, and the WHO recommendations. There are fifty-six contaminants (fifty-three chemicals plus coliform bacteria, cyanobacteria, and tritium) for which Canada has weaker drinking water quality guidelines than at least one other jurisdiction or the WHO recommendation. In some cases, the Canadian guideline is 50, 100, or even 1,000 times weaker than the corresponding European standard.

The difference between the Canadian MAC guidelines and the European standards is striking. Canada's voluntary MAC guidelines are weaker than the mandatory EU standards for forty-two chemical drinking water contaminants and one radioactive contaminant; stronger for only two contaminants; and the same for nine contaminants. There are twelve contaminants included in this study for which either Canada or the European Union has not established a maximum acceptable concentration.

Australia's MAC guidelines are also superior to the Canadian guidelines. Canada's MAC guidelines are weaker than the Australian guidelines for thirty drinking water contaminants, stronger for twenty-one contaminants, and the same for eight contaminants. There are six contaminants included in this study for which either Canada or Australia has not established a maximum acceptable concentration.

Canada's MAC guidelines are weaker than the WHO recommendations for twenty-two drinking water contaminants, stronger for fifteen contaminants, and the same for seven contaminants. There are twenty-one contaminants included in this study for which either Canada or the WHO has not established a maximum acceptable concentration.

Only in comparison with the United States does Canada fare better, as Canada's MAC guidelines are more conservative than the American standards for eighteen drinking water contaminants, weaker for twelve contaminants, and the same for ten contaminants. There are twenty-five contaminants included in this study for which either Canada or the United States has not established a maximum acceptable concentration.

In contrast to the fifty-six substances for which the Guidelines for Canadian Drinking Water Quality are weaker than the standards or guidelines applied in other industrialized nations or the recommendations of the World Health Organization, the only contaminants for which Canada has the most stringent guideline are *Cryptosporidium* and three hydrocarbons added in 2014 – ethylbenzene, toluene, and xylenes.[39]

Finally, other jurisdictions have set guidelines or standards for contaminants that Canada has not yet addressed. For example, Australia, the United

States, and the WHO all have a standard or a guideline for di(2-ethylhexyl) phthalate (DEHP), an industrial substance used to soften plastic. There is evidence suggesting that DEHP is carcinogenic and capable of disrupting the human endocrine system, leading to a potentially broad array of adverse health effects.[40] Canada has no guideline for DEHP in drinking water. The WHO recommends limits for some plastics, solvents, and water disinfection byproducts for which Canada has no guidelines.[41] Asbestos, beryllium, and thalium have legal limits under the US *Safe Drinking Water Act*, but these substances are not included in the Guidelines for Canadian Drinking Water Quality.[42] Australia has drinking water quality guidelines for dozens of pesticides that Canada has not addressed.[43] Although it is beyond the scope of the present review, it appears that regulations for bottled water in Canada also fare poorly in international comparisons. To provide just one example, the Canadian regulation for arsenic in bottled water allows ten times more arsenic than the corresponding American standard.[44]

Pesticide Regulations

The following assessment compares three areas of government activity related to protecting health from the adverse effects of pesticides: authorizing pesticides for specific uses; setting maximum residue limits (MRLs) for pesticides on food; and monitoring the food supply for pesticide residues.

Registration data provide information on pesticides that are approved for use in a given jurisdiction. If the government does not register a pesticide, it cannot be used legally. Registration data from Canada, the United States, and Europe were analyzed to determine how many pesticides registered for use in Canada are not permitted in other nations for health and environmental reasons.

MRLs regulate the amounts of specific pesticides that are allowed to contaminate particular foods. Canadian MRLs are compared with MRLs established by the United States, the European Union, and Australia, as well as recommendations made by Codex, an international organization established by the WHO and the UN Food and Agriculture Organization (FAO).

Finally, Canadian data on levels of pesticide residues found on food products, particularly fresh fruit and vegetables, are compared with data from the United States, Australia, and the European Union.

Pesticide Registration

Registration involves an application by a corporation seeking to manufacture, import, or sell a pesticide product. In theory, the registration of a pesticide should indicate that the product in question will not have significant adverse effects on human health or the environment if used properly. A long history of mistakes proves that this theory is false. Many pesticides that were once approved and widely used, from DDT to carbofuran, are no longer legal in Canada because negative health or environmental effects were discovered after many years of use. Inadequate testing for health effects continues to be a problem, as studies focus on acute toxicity rather than chronic effects, address a narrow range of adverse health outcomes, and ignore the interactive effects of exposure to multiple pesticide ingredients. As medical experts noted in a recent article, "potentially toxic chemicals should not be approved for use when more benign solutions exist, when risks are not clearly quantifiable, or when the potential risk outweighs the benefit."[45]

The comparative analysis of registration data in this study focuses on pesticides that have been banned, prohibited, or withdrawn, or have had their registration cancelled because of health and environmental concerns. As of 2015, there are at least forty-six active ingredients, used in more than one thousand pesticide products, that continue to be registered for sale and use in Canada despite being prohibited in other western industrialized nations because of health and environmental concerns (see Table 7.3). The

TABLE 7.3
Pesticides registered in Canada but prohibited in European nations

Active ingredient	Not permitted by	Number of registered products containing the ingredient in Canada
2,4-D	Norway	150
Acephate	European Union	5
Aminopyralid	European Union	10
Amitraz	European Union	3
Atrazine	European Union	15
Bifenthrin	European Union	1
Brodifacoum	European Union	20
Bromacil	European Union	6
Bromethalin	European Union	13
Bromoxynil	Norway	48
Carbaryl	European Union	41
Chlorophacinone	European Union	32
Chloropicrin	European Union	6
Chlorthal-dimethyl	European Union	3

Active ingredient	Not permitted by	Number of registered products containing the ingredient in Canada
Diazinon	European Union	15
Dichlobenil	European Union	12
Dichlorprop	European Union	20
Dichlorvos	European Union	11
Difenoconazole	Norway	13
Difethialone	European Union	18
Dinocap	European Union	1
Diphacinone	European Union	44
Diphenylamine	European Union	5
Endosulfan	European Union	4 (scheduled to be phased out in Canada by 2016)
Ethylene oxide	European Union	1
Ferbam	European Union	3
Fluazifop-p-butyl	Norway	3
Fluazinam	Norway	2
Hexazinone	European Union	8
Imazapyr	Norway	5
Linuron	Norway	8
Pentachlorophenol	European Union	4
Paradichlorobenzene	European Union	7
Paraquat	European Union	3
Permethrin	European Union	332
Petroleum oil	European Union	8
Phorate	European Union	2
Propoxur	European Union	67
Quintozene/PCBB	European Union	5
Simazine	European Union	6
Sodium chlorate	European Union	6
Terbacil	European Union	3
Thiabendazole	Norway	14
Tributyltin oxide	European Union	4
Trichlorfon	European Union	3
Trifluralin	European Union	17
Total		1,007

Sources: European Union, "EU Pesticides Database" (2014), http://ec.europa.eu/sanco_pesticides/public/?event= homepage; Health Canada, "Pesticide Product Information Database" (2014), http://pr-rp.hc-sc.gc.ca/pi-ip/index-eng. php; US Environmental Protection Agency, "Pesticide Re-registration Database" (2014), http://www.epa.gov/pesticides/ reregistration/status.htm; Pesticide Action Network, "PAN Pesticide Database" (2014), http://www.pesticideinfo.org.

majority of these pesticides have been prohibited throughout the European Union.

Discussion

Three of the top ten herbicide active ingredients sold in Canada in 2010 cannot be used in European nations, including 2,4-D (over 1 million kg sold in Canada), bromoxynil (over 1 million kg), and atrazine (over 500,000 kg).[46] Additional insight can be gleaned through published surveys of pesticide use in Ontario and British Columbia.[47] For example, one of the most heavily used pesticides in Ontario, atrazine, is not registered for use in the European Union. Three of the most heavily used active ingredients in British Columbia – carbaryl, diazinon, and pentachlorophenol – are also not permitted for use in the European Union.

Quebec's *Pesticide Code,* which came into force in 2006, prohibits the use of hundreds of pesticide products registered for use in the rest of Canada, including pesticides containing the active ingredients 2,4-D, carbaryl, and quintozene. Quebec appears to be moving towards the European approach of providing greater protection for the health and well-being of its citizens. Ontario, Manitoba, Nova Scotia, New Brunswick, and Prince Edward Island have also restricted the sale and/or use of cosmetic pesticides.[48] In the absence of national standards, Canadians in the remaining provinces face elevated health risks.

Another cause for concern when considering Canadian pesticide registrations in an international context stems from the WHO's ranking of pesticides in terms of acute toxicity, from extremely hazardous to relatively safe. The WHO rates seven active ingredients still registered for use in Canada in more than 200 commercial pesticide products as "extremely hazardous" (number of registered products in Canada in parentheses): brodifacoum (20), bromadialone (75), bromethalin (13), chlorphacinone (32), difethialone (18), diphacinone (44), and phorate (2).[49] The WHO rates a number of other pesticides still registered for use in Canada – including dichlorvos, methamidophos, and oxamyl – as "highly hazardous." Many other countries, including some developing countries, no longer permit the use of these dangerous pesticides. For example, methamidophos is registered for use in Canada but banned in Indonesia. Methamidophos is an acutely toxic organophosphate pesticide, causing nausea, dizziness, confusion, and, at very high exposures (e.g., accidents or major spills), respiratory paralysis and death.

Maximum Residue Limits for Pesticides on Food

An essential element of ensuring food safety is monitoring food products to ensure that they are not excessively contaminated by pesticides or other toxic substances used in growing, handling, preservation, transportation, and distribution. All industrialized nations have established maximum residue limits and conduct random sampling to ensure that both domestic and imported food products comply with these limits. Although there is an international program established by the WHO and the FAO that recommends MRLs, called the Codex program, nations retain the sovereign right to determine their own MRLs, resulting in widely divergent levels of health protection.[50]

This analysis examines legally binding, enforceable MRLs in Canada, the United States, the European Union, and Australia. The nonbinding recommendations provided by Codex are also included. MRLs are established not only for hundreds of different pesticides but also for hundreds of different food products potentially contaminated by a specific pesticide, so there are literally thousands of MRLs in each nation. For example, for carbaryl there are different MRLs for sixty-seven different crops and meat products in Canada. This study compares MRLs for a small subset of the overall number of pesticide/crop combinations. Many of the MRLs selected for this study involve pesticides that are still registered in Canada but have been prohibited in at least one OECD nation because of health and environmental concerns.

Maximum residue limits are set at levels that theoretically prevent harm to human health, based on toxicology data and human exposure assessments. Unfortunately, for some substances, such as chemicals that disrupt the endocrine system, seemingly tiny concentrations can produce adverse health effects. Atrazine, widely found in Canadian drinking water supplies, causes sexual deformities and reproductive problems in frogs at concentrations measured in just a few parts per billion – concentrations that have been found in drinking water in Canada.[51]

Comparative Analysis of Maximum Residue Limits

Comparing MRLs for forty pesticide/food combinations (see Table 7.4) demonstrates that the European Union has the strongest standards.[52] For twenty-seven of the pesticide/food combinations in this study, it had the most stringent MRL, in many cases by a substantial margin. Australia has the second-strongest record, with the most stringent MRL for five of the pesticide/food combinations. The United States had the most stringent

TABLE 7.4

International comparison of maximum residue limits for pesticides on food products

Pesticide	Food	Canada	EU	US	Australia	Codex
Aldicarb	Potatoes	0.5	0.02	1.0	–	–
Atrazine	Corn	0.2	0.1	0.2	0.1	–
Azinphos-methyl	Grapes	5.0	0.05	–	2.0	1.0
Bromoxynil	Eggs	0.1	–	0.05	0.02	–
	Milk	0.1	0.01	0.4	0.1	–
	Meat	0.1	0.05	0.5	0.02	–
Captan	Cranberries	5.0	0.02	–	30.0	–
Carbaryl	Citrus fruit	10.0	0.01	10.0	7.0	15.0
Carbofuran	Strawberries	0.4	0.01	0.5	–	–
Chlorothalonil	Celery	15.0	20.0	15.0	10.0	20.0
Chlorpyrifos	Lemons	1.0	0.2	1.0	0.5	1.0
Diazinon	Apples	0.75	0.01	0.5	0.5	0.3
	Strawberries	0.75	0.01	0.5	0.5	0.1
Dichlorvos	Tomatoes	0.25	0.01	0.5	0.5	–
Dicofol	Cucumber	3.0	0.02	2.0	2.0	0.5
	Strawberries	3.0	0.02	10.0	1.0	0.5
Diquat	Lentils, dry	0.2	0.2	0.05	1.0	0.2
Diuron	Asparagus	7.0	2.0	7.0	2.0	–
Endoşulfan	Pears	2.0	0.05	2.0	1.0	–
Ferbam	Peaches	7.0	–	4.0	–	–
Glyphosate	Soybeans	20.0	20.0	20.0	10.0	20.0
Heptachlor	Dairy products	0.1	0.004	–	0.15	0.006
Imidacloprid	Cherries	3.0	0.5	3.0	0.5	0.5
Iprodione	Lettuce	25.0	10.0	25.0	5.0	25.0
Malathion	Blueberries	8.0	0.02	8.0	2.0	10.0
Maleic hydrazide	Onion	15.0	15.0	15.0	15.0	15.0
Methamidophos	Broccoli	1.0	0.01	1.0	1.0	–
Metribuzin	Potatoes	0.5	0.1	0.6	0.05	–
Nicosulfuron	Corn	0.1	0.05	0.1	–	–
Paraquat	Onions	0.1	0.02	0.1	0.05	0.05
Permethrin	Leaf lettuce, spinach	20.0	0.05	20.0	5.0	2.0
Phosmet	Grapes	10.0	0.05	10.0	–	10.0
Propiconazole	Plums	1.0	0.05	0.6	2.0	–
Quinclorac	Barley	2.0	0.01	2.0	–	–
Spinosad	Kale	7.0	2.0	8.0	5.0	10.0
Thiabendazole	Apples, pears	10.0	5.0	5.0	10.0	3.0
Thiram	Tomatoes	7.0	0.1	7.0	2.0	–

Pesticide	Food	Canada	EU	US	Australia	Codex
Trifluralin	Carrots	0.5	0.01	1.0	0.5	–
Vinclozolin	Apricots	5.0	0.05	–	–	–
Ziram	Tomatoes	7.0	0.1	7.0	3.0	2.0

Notes: A dash (–) indicates that no specific MRL has been established for that particular pesticide-food combination. All MRLs are measured in parts per million (ppm).

Sources: Canada, *Food and Drug Regulations,* C.R.C. c. 870, as amended: "Division 15: Adulteration of Food"; European Union, Council Directives 76/895/EEC, 86/362/EEC, 86/363/EEC, and 90/642/EEC, as amended; United States, *Code of Federal Regulations,* Title 40, Part 180, "Tolerances and Exemptions from Tolerances for Pesticide Chemicals in Food," http://www.access.gpo.gov/nara/cfr/waisidx_05/40cfr180_05.html; Commonwealth of Australia, *Australia New Zealand Food Standards Code,* http://www.foodstandards.gov.au/code/Pages/default.aspx; Food and Agriculture Organization and World Health Organization, "Codex Pesticide Residues in Food Online Database," http://www.codexalimentarius.net/pestres/data/pesticides/index.html.

MRL for three pesticide/food combinations, Codex for one, and Canada for none. At the other end of the spectrum, Canada and the United States have the lowest standards of any of the jurisdictions examined in this study, each with the weakest MRL for twenty-three of the pesticide/food combinations in the study.

In a head-to-head comparison with the European Union, Canada has a weaker MRL in thirty-four out of thirty-eight cases, a stronger MRL in one case, and the same MRL in three cases. In some cases, the difference between the Canadian and European MRLs is enormous. For example, for diazinon on apples and strawberries, the Canadian limit is seventy-five times higher than the European limit. For both permethrin on leaf lettuce or spinach and malathion on blueberries, the Canadian limit is four hundred times higher. For carbaryl on citrus fruit, the Canadian limit is one thousand times higher.

Canada also has significantly weaker protection standards for pesticide residues than Australia, with a weaker MRL in twenty-three cases, a stronger MRL in only five cases, and the same MRL in five cases. However, the gap between individual Canadian and Australian MRLs is not as large as the chasm between Canadian and European MRLs. The biggest gap involves the Canadian limit for metribuzin on potatoes, which is ten times higher than the Australian limit.

Canada's MRLs for pesticide residues are closest to American MRLs. Despite ongoing trade harmonization efforts, there are still many significant differences between the standards set by the two countries. Canada has the same MRL in fourteen cases, a stronger MRL in nine cases, and a weaker MRL in eight cases.

TABLE 7.5

International comparison of detectable pesticide residues in domestic and imported food products

	Canada	US		EU
		USDA	FDA	
Percentage with detectable pesticide residues	46.2	59.5	36.2	49.3
Percentage with pesticide residues in excess of MRLs	2.5	3.23	6.1	1.6

Compared with the recommendations of the international Codex, Canada also fares poorly. The Canadian MRLs are weaker than the Codex recommendation in eleven cases, stronger than the Codex recommendation in only four cases, and the same as the Codex recommendation in six cases.

Monitoring for Pesticide Residues

Government agencies in all industrialized nations sample food products – both domestic and imported – for pesticide residues, heavy metals, and other pollutants. The purpose of these sampling programs is to ensure compliance with MRLs and to prevent severely contaminated food products from reaching consumers. This study compares the level of pesticide residues detected by monitoring programs, based on government reports from Canada, the United States, and the European Union (see Table 7.5).

Canada

In 2009–10, the Canadian Food Inspection Agency (CFIA) sampled 9,062 plant products, predominantly fresh fruits and vegetables. Pesticide residues were detected on 46.2 percent of the samples, and 2.5 percent of samples had pesticide concentrations that violated (i.e., exceeded) the relevant MRLs.[53] The violation rate was significantly lower for domestic produce (0.86 percent) than for imported produce (3.1 percent). Imported produce was also more likely to be contaminated by multiple pesticide residues (23.5 percent) than was domestic produce (16.1 percent). China had a particularly low compliance rate, with over 13 percent of samples violating Canadian MRLs. According to the CFIA, when a violation is identified, the result is examined to determine potential follow-up actions, which may include notifying the importer or producer, additional inspections, or a recall of the products if a health risk is involved. However, the CFIA provides no details regarding what, if any, follow-up actions were undertaken, and makes no mention of any enforcement actions or penalties. When CBC News found pesticide residues that violated the MRL on over half the tea brands they tested, including one product with twenty-two different residues, the CFIA declined to take any enforcement action.[54]

United States
There are two different sources of information on monitoring of pesticide residues in the United States: the Department of Agriculture (USDA) and the Food and Drug Administration (FDA). In 2013, the USDA tested 10,104 samples of fruit, vegetables, soybeans, wheat flour, and milk for pesticide residues.[55] Overall, 59.5 percent of samples showed detectable residues (23.5 percent contained one pesticide and 36 percent contained multiple pesticides). Testing found residues exceeding the MRL in 0.23 percent of the samples. In another 3.0 percent of samples, residues were detected for which no MRL had been established, which is also regarded as a violation in the United States.[56]

The FDA found that 7.1 percent of imported foods and 1.6 percent of domestic samples violated rules regarding pesticide residues in 2011.[57] Annual violation rates in recent years have ranged from 2.6 to 6.2 percent for imports and from 0.7 to 2.4 percent for domestic products. The higher rate of violations is because FDA's sampling program targets products or countries with a history of pesticide residue problems. China, Guatemala, India, Mexico, and Vietnam were identified as countries worthy of particular focus due to higher than average violation rates. Spinach and ginseng were among 24 foods singled out as products with high violation rates. No residues were detected on 60.5 percent of 1,080 domestic samples and 64.5 percent of 4,897 imported samples.[58]

European Union
In the European Union, a study published in 2013 by the European Food Safety Authority (EFSA) examined 77,075 samples taken in twenty-nine countries. The EFSA found that 49.3 percent of food products sampled were contaminated by pesticides, and that 1.6 percent of the food products sampled had pesticide residues exceeding the legal limit.[59] The percentage of violations in Europe has varied from 1.2 to 2.3 percent for the past five years.

These results show a degree of consistency across nations. Pesticide residues are detected on roughly half of the food products that are sampled. The majority of MRL violations in Canada, the United States, and Europe involve imported foods. Given the stricter standards in place in the European Union, it is possible that exporters take greater precautions in applying pesticides to foods destined for the European market. This would explain the lower rate of violations compared with Canada and the United States, where residue rules are weaker and fewer violations would therefore be anticipated.

Toxic Substances
There are approximately 100,000 chemicals in use in society today, presenting an immense challenge to both the scientific community, in terms of understanding the potential health and environmental effects of exposure to these chemicals, and to government regulators, tasked with determining which of these chemicals should be permitted, for what uses, in what concentrations, and with what safeguards in place. Neither scientists nor regulators have been able to adequately address this problem. The failures in some cases are well known. Entire classes of substances – organochlorine pesticides, chlorofluorocarbons, polybrominated flame retardants – have been or are being phased out globally because of serious yet unanticipated health and environmental consequences. The overwhelming majority of substances in commerce today have never been comprehensively tested for adverse effects upon humans or ecosystems.[60] Many chemicals in use today were already being manufactured, sold, and used before legislation was introduced to address the health and environmental hazards caused by manmade chemicals. Tens of thousands of chemicals already in use were grandfathered, meaning their use was allowed to continue without any new restrictions or even testing to assess their potential effects. Regulators are still struggling to cope with this enormous backlog.[61]

The following comparison looks at the regulatory frameworks in Canada, the United States, the European Union, and Australia through the lens of rules governing a handful of toxic substances. The five substances selected for this analysis include known carcinogens (asbestos and formaldehyde), endocrine-disrupting chemicals (polybrominated diphenyl ethers [PBDEs] and DEHP), and perfluorochemicals (PFCs).

Asbestos
Asbestos used to be described as a "miracle mineral" for its ability to withstand heat. It was used in a myriad of products, including fireproofing and insulating material in ships, buildings, and consumer products, and in

wallboard, flooring, cement, automobiles, clothing, home appliances, and children's toys. There are six different asbestos fibres with distinctive properties, but exposure to all types of asbestos can cause lung cancer, mesothelioma, and asbestosis.

Canada

In Canada, asbestos was mined and exported until 2013, when the last operating mine went bankrupt. Yet asbestos continues to be used in many applications. In 2015, new data indicated that Canadian imports of products containing asbestos were steadily increasing, particularly brake pads and linings, which hit a seven-year high in 2014.[62] The *Canada Consumer Product Safety Act* bans the import, sale, or advertising of pure asbestos products, or products from which a reasonably foreseeable use could result in asbestos fibres becoming airborne.[63] The Asbestos Products Regulations allow asbestos products that do not contain crocidolite asbestos to be sold, advertised, and imported into Canada, if the asbestos cannot become separated from the product as a result of a reasonably foreseeable use. Permitted products include:

• clothing that provides protection from fire or heat
• products used by children in play or learning
• brake pads and linings for vehicles
• certain drywall products
• spraying products.

The *Hazardous Products Act*'s Ingredient Disclosure List requires that any product containing over 0.1 percent of dry weight asbestos must disclose this information.[64] Federal and provincial occupational safety regulations provide some protection for workers, although experts believe there is no safe level of exposure. Under the *Canadian Environmental Protection Act, 1999*, asbestos is on the List of Toxic Substances, and a regulation limits releases of asbestos from mines and mills.[65]

European Union

In the European Union, all uses of all types of asbestos are prohibited as a result of a law passed in 1999 that came into effect in 2005.[66] A handful of states were granted exemptions for a limited number of products, but only on a temporary basis. Most of these have expired.

United States

Asbestos was first regulated in American schools and public buildings in 1986. The EPA introduced a comprehensive ban on asbestos-containing products in 1989. Unfortunately, a federal court overturned this regulation in 1991, concluding that the EPA had not, as required by the *Toxic Substances Control Act*, proven that asbestos posed an "unreasonable risk." As a result, the only restrictions on asbestos in the United States involve flooring felt, rollboard, several specialty papers, and new uses. More than 600,000 individuals have filed lawsuits against more than 6,000 defendants, related to asbestos exposure and the ensuing adverse health effects. Defendants and insurers have so far spent an estimated US$54 billion on resolving claims. Estimates of the total number of people who will eventually file claims range from 1.1 million to 3 million, while the eventual cost of asbestos litigation is estimated at $200 billion to $265 billion.[67] Despite this huge volume of costly litigation, asbestos is still used in the United States, and the EPA admits: "Currently, the manufacture, importation, processing and distribution of most asbestos-containing products is still legal."[68] There are limits on asbestos imposed under the *Clean Air Act* through a National Emission Standard for Hazardous Air Pollutants, which is intended to minimize the release of asbestos fibres when the substance is being handled.[69]

Australia

Crocidolite asbestos was banned in Australia in 1967, and other types of asbestos were phased out after 1980. Asbestos was banned from building products in 1989, although it continued to be used in gaskets and brake linings. All forms of asbestos were completely prohibited after 2003, and asbestos cannot be imported, used, or recycled.[70]

Di(2-ethylhexyl) Phthalate (DEHP)

Worldwide, phthalates are the most common group of chemicals used as plasticizers (plastic softeners). Consumer products such as soft plastic articles and cosmetics are potentially significant sources of long-term exposure to phthalates through migration and leaching. The adverse effects caused by exposure to phthalates include reproductive and developmental health effects, asthma, and organ damage. Some phthalates are also suspected of being carcinogenic. For example, di(2-ethylhexyl) phthalate (DEHP) is classified by the US EPA as a probable human carcinogen.[71] DEHP is used in the production of vinyl chloride, in medical tubing, toys, food containers, food packaging, and other consumer products. Medical experts believe that the potential health effects of phthalates should be assessed on the basis of cumulative exposure rather than on a substance-by-substance basis, as has traditionally been the case. People are exposed to multiple phthalates at all stages of life, beginning in the womb.[72]

Canada

In 1998, there was an international furor about the presence of phthalates in products used by infants and toddlers. Canada's response was not to regulate these products but rather to issue an advisory requesting parents and caregivers to stop using polyvinyl chloride (PVC) teethers and rattles containing diisononyl phthalate (DINP). The advisory did not include pacifiers and feeding bottle nipples, although these may also contain phthalates. Health Canada also asked manufacturers of small, soft vinyl toys to find a safe substitute for vinyl containing DINP over the next six months.[73] Regulatory action was not taken until 2010, however.

DEHP was placed on the List of Toxic Substances under the *Canadian Environmental Protection Act, 1999*.[74] The addition of a substance to the list gives the federal government the authority to take steps to limit or eliminate its use or release, but does not in and of itself create any restrictions. In 2002, an expert panel appointed by Health Canada to investigate the potential health effects of exposure to DEHP recommended extensive restrictions on its use in medical settings.[75] It was not until 2010, however, that Canada finally enacted regulations limiting the use of DEHP in toys and childcare articles (to 1,000 mg/kg).[76] The regulation also limits the levels of five other phthalates – butylbenzyl phthalate (BBP), dibutyl phthalate (DBP), DINP, diisodecyl phthalate (DIDP), and di-n-octyl phthalate (DNOP) – in articles used by children.

European Union

In the European Union, four common phthalates (DEHP, DBP, diisobutyl phthalate or DIBP, and BBP) have been added to the list of substances that are subject to a total ban in all products under the REACH (Registration, Evaluation, Authorisation and Restriction of Chemicals) legislation.[77] Other phthalates (DINP, DIDP, and DNOP) are subject to a near-total ban from use in toys and childcare articles intended for children under three years of age that can be placed in the mouth. Earlier regulations had banned phthalates with known carcinogenic, mutagenic, or reproductive toxicity potential (such as DEHP, DBP, and BBP) from use in cosmetics.[78]

United States

The United States has a variety of regulations dealing with phthalates, although its approach is not as comprehensive or strict as the European regulations. The FDA limits the types of food packaging materials that may contain certain phthalates. In 1996, the US Consumer Product Safety Commission urged toy manufacturers to voluntarily remove DINP from mouthing toys intended for children under three because of its potential health effects. The *Consumer Product Safety Improvement Act of 2008* banned the use of six phthalates, including DEHP, from toys and other products intended for use by children. There are no legal restrictions on DEHP in cosmetics. The EPA's limit for DEHP in drinking water is 6 ppb. In California, DEHP is regulated as a carcinogen (since 1988) and a developmental toxicant (since 2003). California requires businesses to provide a "clear and reasonable" warning before knowingly and intentionally exposing anyone to DEHP.

Australia

In February 2011, the Australian Competition and Consumer Commission introduced a permanent ban on children's plastic products with over 1 percent DEHP.[79] The use of DEHP in cosmetics is prohibited.[80]

Perfluorinated chemicals

Perfluorinated chemicals (PFCs) are a class of manmade chemicals that includes perfluorooctane sulphonate (PFOS), perfluorooctanoic acid (PFOA), and other related compounds. PFCs are used in many industrial processes as well as in consumer products, including firefighting foams, household cleaners, cosmetics, electronics, food packaging, nonstick coatings on pots and pans, and stain repellents on furniture and clothing.[81] They are linked to cancer, birth defects, and damage to organs, including the liver and pancreas, the immune system, and the reproductive system.[82] Scientists are particularly concerned because of the persistent nature of these chemicals and the fact that they bioaccumulate in living organisms. Studies have found PFOS in the blood of humans from all over the world, including Canada, the United States, Colombia, Brazil, Belgium, Italy, Poland, India, Malaysia, and Korea.[83] PFOS was added to the Stockholm Convention on Persistent Organic Pollutants in 2009, subject to several exemptions. Due to increasing regulatory restrictions on PFOS, levels of this chemical in human blood samples have been declining, whereas concentrations of PFOA, the regulation of which has been slower, continue to rise.[84]

Canada

The manufacturing, import, and use of four perfluorinated chemicals, including those that break down into PFOA, were temporarily prohibited by the Canadian government in 2004 and 2005, a restriction that was subsequently made permanent.[85] In 2008, Canada passed a law called the *Perfluorooctane Sulfonate Virtual Elimination Act*, effectively prohibiting the manufacture, import, use, sale, or release of PFOS in Canada.[86] Canada is proposing additional regulations to comprehensively address PFOA, long-chain perfluorocarboxylic acids (PFCAs), and their precursors.[87] These actions positioned Canada as a world leader, along with the European Union, in regulating PFCs. One weakness in the Canadian approach is that it has allowed the continued import of products containing PFOS and PFOA.[88]

United States

The EPA has used a combination of voluntary agreements and regulations to address PFCs. In 2001, manufacturer 3M announced that it was ending the production and use of PFOS. In 2006, after an expert panel determined that PFOA was a probable human carcinogen, the EPA asked eight manufacturers to voluntarily reduce PFOA production by 95 percent by 2010 and to eliminate production by 2015. The eight companies, including DuPont, agreed.[89] In 2005, DuPont agreed to pay US$16.5 million to the US government for failing to report the results of studies showing serious threats to human health from exposure to PFOA. In the settlement of a civil class action lawsuit alleging PFOA contamination of drinking water, DuPont agreed to pay US$100 million to residents living in the vicinity of its manufacturing plant in West Virginia. According to the settlement agreement, DuPont could be liable for another US$235 million if studies reveal health problems.[90]

The EPA published two "significant new use rules" (SNURs) under the *Toxic Substances Control Act* in 2002 to limit any future manufacture or importation of 88 PFOS-related substances. These SNURs allowed the continuation of a few limited, highly technical uses of these chemicals for which no alternatives were available, and which were characterized by low volume, low exposure, and low releases. Another SNUR, affecting a further 183 chemicals, was published in 2007. Seven of the chemicals affected by this SNUR are exempted for specific uses. In 2012, the EPA proposed another SNUR under the *Toxic Substances Control Act* to add 7 PFOS-related substances to the existing SNUR and include "processing" in the definition of "significant new use" for these substances.[91]

European Union

The European Union banned most uses of PFOS and its derivatives in 2006, with limited exemptions, such as in hydraulic fluids for aviation.[92] It is in the process of designating PFOA as a very high concern substance under the REACH legislation, which is likely to result in the prohibition of this chemical in the future. Some individual European nations are already taking regulatory action to eliminate PFOA. For example, Norway's Pollution Control Authority banned PFOA in all consumer products beginning in 2013.[93]

Australia

Australia has not taken any regulatory steps to limit the use of PFOS or PFOA. The National Industrial Chemicals Notification and Assessment Scheme (NICNAS) began calling for a voluntary phaseout agreement for PFOS in 2000 and has since issued four alerts concerning the use of PFCs. For example, NICNAS has warned Australian industry to be aware of the growing scientific evidence that both PFOS and PFOA pose a threat to human health and the environment.[94]

Formaldehyde

Formaldehyde is widely used as an adhesive in wood products such as plywood, in textiles such as carpets, in producing plastics, and as a disinfectant or preservative. It is classified as carcinogenic to humans by the IARC, causing leukemia and nasopharyngeal cancer. Formaldehyde can exacerbate asthma symptoms and also cause irritation of the eyes, nose, and throat. Indoor air is the primary source of exposure to formaldehyde because it is present in products including particleboard and similar materials, permanent press fabrics, carpets, paints and varnishes, toilet bowl cleaners, and tobacco smoke. Canadian cancer researchers recently identified formaldehyde in indoor air as one of the most significant sources of excess cancer risk caused by environmental factors (after radon).[95] Similarly, European studies have identified formaldehyde as a top priority in addressing indoor air quality problems.[96]

Canada

In Canada, formaldehyde is on the List of Toxic Substances but there are only limited rules governing it. Regulations limit emissions of formaldehyde from motor vehicles.[97] The use of formaldehyde in cosmetic products is limited to concentrations of 0.2 percent in most products, although up to 5 percent in nail polish and nail hardeners.[98] In 2011, Health Canada issued a warning about excessive levels of formaldehyde in hair smoothing products used in salons, but did not take any enforcement action or require manufacturers to recall these products. Urea formaldehyde foam insulation was banned in Canada in 1980 because of off-gassing of high levels of formaldehyde.[99] Canada does not regulate any other sources of formaldehyde. Indoor air quality guidelines, which are not binding, are set by Health Canada. The short-term exposure limit is 0.1 ppm while the long-term exposure limit is 0.04 ppm. The WHO recommends a stronger short-term limit of 0.08 ppm.[100]

European Union

The European Union takes a more stringent approach than Canada to protecting people from the risks posed by formaldehyde.[101] A number of products are prohibited from containing formaldehyde (e.g., preservatives for liquid-cooling and processing systems, slimicides, metalworking-fluid preservatives, and antifouling products).[102] The limit on formaldehyde in cosmetics is four times stricter than in Canada, with a maximum concentration of 0.05 percent. The European Union also limits levels of formaldehyde in composite wood products.[103] By law, products sold in the European Union that contain formaldehyde must carry a warning label. Some countries, such as Denmark, Sweden, and Germany, impose even stricter restrictions.[104]

United States

The American guideline for formaldehyde in indoor air includes a short-term limit of 0.1 ppm and a long-term limit of 0.016 ppm (two and a half times as strict as the Canadian guideline). The United States regulates formaldehyde in composite wood products such as plywood, fibreboard, and particleboard.[105] This legislation was spurred by media reports indicating that the United States was becoming a dumping ground for wood products with high levels of formaldehyde because of higher standards enacted in Europe and Japan. The Consumer Product Safety Commission banned the sale of urea formaldehyde foam insulation (UFFI) in 1982, and shortly thereafter a law prohibiting its sale was enacted. In 1983, the US Court of Appeals struck down the law because there was no substantial evidence clearly linking UFFI to health complaints. UFFI is not widely used in the United States today. American legislation regulating toxic substances in cosmetics was enacted in 1938 and is badly out of date.[106] There is a general provision that cosmetics must be free of poisonous or deleterious substances that might injure users when used as labelled or under the normal use. There is no specific regulation of formaldehyde in cosmetics, but an advisory panel recommended limiting concentrations of formaldehyde to 0.2 percent except in nail hardeners (same as Canada).

Australia

Like Canada, Australia has few legal restrictions on formaldehyde. The occupational exposure standards are weaker, there are voluntary guidelines governing formaldehyde in wood products, and the restrictions governing cosmetics are similar to Canadian rules.[107] Australia has ordered recalls of several products violating the limits on formaldehyde in cosmetics, including hair straighteners, conditioners, and eyelash glue.[108]

Polybrominated Diphenyl Ethers

Polybrominated diphenyl ethers have been used extensively as fire retardants in products including clothing, computers, electronic equipment, motor vehicles, construction products, carpets, and furniture. However, scientists discovered that PBDEs were rapidly accumulating in women's breast milk, adipose tissue (body fat), human blood, wildlife, and the environment. In coastal British Columbia, the Great Lakes, and even remote Arctic regions, concentrations of PBDEs in species such as killer whales, ringed seals, and grizzly bears rapidly increased. PBDEs have been found in house dust, meat, fish, dairy products, sewage sludge (which is often applied to agricultural land as a fertilizer), and soil. Although the human health impacts of exposure to PBDEs are not well understood, tests on animals indicate impaired brain development, negative impacts on the hormonal and reproductive systems, and possibly cancer.[109] Evidence indicates that exposure to PBDEs damages human brain development, as levels of these chemicals in babies' cord blood are associated with developmental delays in children aged one to six.[110]

There are three commercial mixtures of PBDEs (referred to as pentaBDE, octaBDE, and decaBDE). As of 2001, decaBDE made up over 80 percent of global PBDE use. PBDEs are persistent, bioaccumulative, and toxic. PentaBDE and octaBDE were added to lists of prohibited substances under two major international environmental agreements, including the Stockholm Convention on Persistent Organic Pollutants and the United Nations Economic Commission for Europe's 1998 Aarhus Protocol on Persistent Organic Pollutants.

Canada

Canadians have the second-highest level of PBDE concentrations in women's breast milk in the world, behind Americans.[111] In Vancouver, PBDE levels measured in breast milk samples increased approximately fifteen-fold from 1992 to 2002. Some Canadian children have higher body burdens of PBDEs than their parents.[112] Canadian foods – including salmon, ground beef, cheese, and butter – are contaminated with PBDEs at levels up to a thousand times higher than levels found in similar food products in Europe.[113]

Canadian regulations enacted in 2008:

- banned the import of commercial PBDE mixtures that were already being phased out by manufacturers
- banned PBDE manufacturing facilities in Canada (where such facilities have never existed or been proposed)
- failed to regulate the most widely used PBDE (decaBDE), which breaks down into the very same toxic chemicals (pentaBDE and octaBDE) that were being banned for health and environmental reasons.[114]

In 2015, Canada published a draft regulation that belatedly promised to impose the same prohibitions on decaBDE that had been applied to other PBDEs in 2008, while maintaining the loophole for manufactured products containing PBDEs.[115]

European Union

In 2003, the European Union led the way in limiting the use of some PBDEs (pentaBDE and octaBDE) because of concerns about the health impacts of these chemicals.[116] It also prohibited the use of pentaBDE and octaBDE in the manufacturing of electronic and electrical equipment (at concentrations greater than 0.1 percent).[117] This prohibition was extended to include decaBDE in 2008. Additional restrictions on decaBDE are anticipated in the near future. Norway banned the use of decaBDE in electrical and electronic equipment in 2006, and in 2008 became the first country in the world to restrict the use of decaBDE in all manufactured products (at concentrations greater than 0.1 percent).[118] Norway has also proposed that decaBDE be added to the Stockholm Convention on Persistent Organic Pollutants.

United States

The world's highest levels of PBDEs in human breast milk are found in American women.[119] Five percent of American women have body burdens of PBDEs at levels that cause reproductive damage in laboratory animals.[120] As in Canada, American children sometimes have PBDE levels that exceed those of their parents.[121]

The EPA phased out the manufacture and import of pentaBDE and octaBDE in 2004. However, products containing these substances continued to be imported and there were no restrictions on decaBDE. In 2006, the EPA created a significant new use rule pursuant to the *Toxic Substances Control Act*, requiring any company or individual seeking to import or manufacture PBDEs to notify the agency.[122] This rule, which requires testing for health and environmental effects and reporting to the EPA, was broadened in 2012 to include decaBDE. The EPA received commitments from the principal manufacturers and importers of decaBDE to end sales by December 31, 2013.[123] Again, this does not include imported products containing decaBDE. As a result of federal inaction, a dozen American states enacted laws limiting the use of PBDEs, including four states (Maine, Washington, Vermont, and Oregon) that restrict the use of decaBDE in certain products.

Australia
Levels of PBDEs in women's breast milk in Australia are five times higher than those observed in Europe and Japan.[124] Australia banned the manufacture and import of pentaBDE and octaBDE in 2007, although the prohibition did not extend to products containing these chemicals (unlike the European Union). DecaBDE is not regulated in Australia, although assessment of its health and environmental effects has been underway since 2001.[125]

Discussion
In regulating the toxic substances examined in this comparison, Canada generally lags behind the European Union but is closer to being on par with the United States and Australia. The European Union has the strongest laws and regulations governing asbestos (along with Australia), PBDEs, PFCs (along with Canada), phthalates, and formaldehyde. A petition filed with the federal Commissioner of the Environment and Sustainable Development in 2014 by Ecojustice and the Canadian Environmental Law Association identified twenty-two toxic substances that were banned in the European Union under the REACH legislation but are still used in Canada, including musk xylene, 4,4'-diaminodiphenylmethane (MDA), three phthalates (BBP, DBP,

and DIBP), and 2,4-dinitrotoluene (2,4-DNT), reinforcing the evidence that Canada is failing to keep pace with the world leaders in regulating health threats from toxic substances.[126]

Asbestos is completely banned in the twenty-eight nations comprising the European Union and in Australia, as well as in Japan, Singapore, Turkey, South Korea, and New Zealand. Canada and the United States restrict asbestos use to some degree, but allow it in a surprising number of products, based on the untenable belief that it can be used safely. The export of asbestos from Canada is still permitted, although no asbestos mines are operating at present.

Europe is a world leader in regulating PBDEs, demonstrating a willingness to apply the precautionary principle and lead the push for international action. Norway's proposal to add decaBDE to the Stockholm Convention is, in light of the scientific evidence, likely to succeed, which will result in a global ban, albeit many years after adverse health effects were identified. In the United States, foot-dragging on PBDEs led states to introduce their own prohibitions, patterned after the European legislation. Canada has taken a disingenuous approach to PBDEs, passing regulations to prohibit non-existent manufacturing operations and banning the chemicals only after they have been phased out elsewhere. Australia, to date, relies on voluntary approaches to reducing the use of PBDEs.

While the gradual elimination of PBDEs is an environmental success story, there is a caveat. The chemicals used as substitutes for PBDEs are now raising similar health and environmental concerns. Other brominated flame retardants and organophosphate esters are turning up in the environment in surprising places and concentrations, while there are many unknowns about the potential impact of these chemicals.[127] As the Australian chemical safety regulator acknowledged in an assessment of hexabromocyclododecane (HBCD), "calculating 'safe' concentrations for compounds such as HBCD that are persistent in the environment, are bioaccumulative and also biomagnify in the food chain is difficult because potential adverse effects may not become evident for very long periods of time – much longer than can be captured by standard toxicity testing."[128]

Europe leads the world in regulating the health threats posed by phthalates, particularly DEHP, and in prohibiting the use of DEHP in toys and other children's articles, cosmetics, packaging, and most consumer products. Canada prohibits the use of DEHP in a narrower range of products, including cosmetics, toys, and other children's articles. Australia's rules are similar to Canada's regulations on DEHP, while the United States lags behind.

The European Union is also a leader in regulating formaldehyde, ranging from cosmetics to composite wood products. Canada regulates formaldehyde from vehicle emissions and in cosmetics but not in wood products. The United States regulates formaldehyde from vehicle emissions and in wood products but not in cosmetics. Australia has the weakest approach on paper, although the government has been active in identifying and recalling consumer products containing unsafe levels of formaldehyde.

Canada can legitimately claim to be a world leader in addressing one emerging environmental threat to human health. The initial Canadian prohibitions on the manufacture, import, or use of four PFCs that break down into PFOA were the first of their kind in the world. Europe's regulations governing PFCs are on par with Canadian rules. The US EPA successfully negotiated timelines for the phaseout of PFOS and PFOA with domestic manufacturers of these products. However, the United States has been slower to address the import of products containing PFCs. Australia is again relying on voluntary measures to address the various kinds of PFCs.

Climate Change

Climate change is a complex problem that requires laws, policies, and actions at all levels of government to protect health and the environment through mitigation (reducing emissions of greenhouse gases and protecting forests) and adaptation (preparing for the inevitable effects). The following comparison focuses on legislation and policy at the national level. National governments, often driven by international commitments, set overarching goals and enact laws that are intended to ensure that those goals are met. The following comparison examines the extent of international commitments to reduce emissions, flagship climate legislation, a national price on carbon (through a tax or an emissions trading program), motor vehicle fuel efficiency regulations, and support for the expansion of renewable energy.

International Commitment

International commitments can be viewed as a yardstick by which a country's intentions can be measured. In theory, once a legally binding international commitment has been made, a country will take the steps necessary to fulfill that obligation. All nations included in this comparison ratified the UN Framework Convention on Climate Change following the 1992 Earth Summit, making a pledge to collectively avoid dangerous anthropogenic interference with the Earth's climate system. That is where the similarities end in terms of international commitments.

Canada

Canada ratified the Kyoto Protocol in 2002, agreeing to reduce greenhouse gas (GHG) emissions 6 percent below 1990 levels by 2012. With emissions soaring more than 20 percent above the pledged level, Canada took the unprecedented step of withdrawing from the Kyoto Protocol in 2012. Having abandoned Kyoto, Canada substituted a nonbinding promise pursuant to the voluntary Copenhagen Accord to reduce GHG emissions 17 percent below 2005 levels by 2020. The latest reports indicate that Canada will fail to meet this modest emission reduction commitment.[129]

United States

The United States signed the Kyoto Protocol in 1997, promising to reduce emissions 7 percent below 1990 levels by 2012. However, Congress refused to ratify the agreement, meaning that the United States was never formally a party to Kyoto. In 2009, the United States signed the Copenhagen Accord, promising to reduce emissions 17 percent below 2005 levels by 2020. Unlike Canada, reports indicate that the United States is on track to meet its Copenhagen target.[130] In 2014, it signed an agreement with China committing to even deeper reductions by 2025 (26–28 percent below 2005 levels).

European Union

The European Union ratified the Kyoto Protocol, setting a collective target of reducing emissions 5.2 percent below 1990 levels by 2012. Led by the United Kingdom, Germany, and Sweden, the European Union actually cut GHG emissions more quickly and deeply than legally obligated. For the second round of commitments under the Kyoto Protocol, it has pledged to reduce emissions by 20 percent compared with the 1990 baseline.

Australia

Despite a new federal government elected in 2013 on an anti-climate change platform, Australia remains a party to the Kyoto Protocol. Its initial target was to limit growth in emissions to 8 percent above 1990 levels by 2012, although this commitment was not fulfilled. For the second Kyoto commitment period, Australia's commitment is to reduce emissions 0.5 percent below 1990 levels.

National Framework Law

A national framework law is intended to provide a strategic, coordinated approach to climate change that maximizes the likelihood of fulfilling a nation's commitments.

Canada

Canada responded to the challenge of climate change with a seemingly endless series of strategies and action plans that relied primarily on voluntary initiatives, education, and incentives, while promising future regulations to reduce industrial emissions. These initiatives were clearly inadequate, as between 1992 and 2007 Canadian emissions continued to rise.[131] Finally, in 2007, Canada enacted the *Kyoto Protocol Implementation Act.* In an unusual turn of events, the law was initiated by a private member's bill that garnered the support of all opposition parties in a minority Parliament. The law was passed despite being opposed by the Conservative government, which subsequently refused to comply with the law. An attempt to use the courts to force the government to comply with the act was unsuccessful, as the Federal Court ruled that climate change policy raised political questions inappropriate for judicial resolution.[132]

Once the Conservatives secured a majority government in 2011, they repealed the *Kyoto Protocol Implementation Act.* To the extent that Canada regulates greenhouse gas emissions, it will be done under the auspices of the *Canadian Environmental Protection Act, 1999,* the country's main pollution law. Carbon dioxide and other greenhouse gases have been declared toxic to human health and the environment under this act, thereby authorizing federal action. Thus far, regulations have been passed requiring improved fuel efficiency for motor vehicles and reduced GHG emissions from coal-fired electricity plants built after 2015. There is extensive climate change legislation at the provincial level, particularly in British Columbia, Alberta, Ontario, and Quebec, but a coordinated, coherent, and effective national approach is lacking.

United States

Numerous attempts have been made to enact flagship climate legislation in the United States, but none of the proposed laws has made it through an ideologically divided Congress. As a result, the United States, like Canada, is attempting to regulate greenhouse gas emissions pursuant to a pre-existing law. The EPA is relying upon the authority granted by the *Clean Air Act* to toughen standards for motor vehicle fuel efficiency and address industrial GHG emissions. The *Clean Air Act* is a venerable federal law designed to control air pollution. Like Environment Canada, the EPA determined that greenhouse gases posed a threat to the health of Americans and the environment. Having reached this conclusion (called an endangerment finding) in 2009, the EPA has proposed tough new regulations for new and existing coal-fired electricity plants. It is unclear whether these regulations will be enacted and/or survive legal challenges from industry. It should be noted that, as in Canada, there are a myriad of policies and legislation on climate change at the state level. For example, California is a leading state in this area, with the *Global Warming Solutions Act*, the *Pavley Law* and its stringent air quality targets for motor vehicles, and the *California Environmental Quality Act*, with its GHG emissions provisions.

European Union

The European Union's flagship climate change legislation is the Climate and Energy Package, which entered into force in 2009 and aims to transform Europe into a competitive low-carbon economy by 2050. The package focuses on achieving what the European Union refers to as its 20-20-20 targets: 20 percent emission reduction, 20 percent of energy produced by renewable sources, and 20 percent reduction in energy use through improvements in energy efficiency. New or amended EU directives address the extension of the Emissions Trading System, country-by-county allocation of responsibility, the energy performance of buildings, the energy efficiency of products, and promotion of renewable energy.[133]

Australia

In 2011, Australia passed its *Clean Energy Act* as the centrepiece of eighteen new pieces of legislation designed to comprehensively address the problem of climate change through various means, including placing a price on carbon emissions. The long-term objective is to reduce GHG emissions 80 percent by 2050. The legislative package created new regulatory bodies, including the Clean Energy Regulator (to oversee putting a price on carbon emissions), the Climate Change Authority (to provide independent advice on Australian emissions reduction policies), and the Land Sector Carbon and Biodiversity Board (to advise government on managing land to sequester carbon). In 2013, however, the Australian government changed hands and the new prime minister repealed the carbon tax, reversed several other initiatives, and took a generally counterproductive approach to climate change and renewable energy.

National Price on Carbon Emissions

The overwhelming majority of economists and environmentalists agree that one of the most effective ways to reduce GHG emissions is to put a price on carbon. Most economists are indifferent as to whether a carbon tax or a permit trading system is employed. Carbon taxes offer the advantages of administrative simplicity, low transaction costs, price certainty (critical for investment decisions), and transparency to consumers (critical for influencing behaviour). Permit trading systems may be preferable because they offer assurance that the government-imposed limit on emissions will be met and there may be less political opposition.

Canada

Canada does not have a national price on carbon dioxide emissions. A national carbon tax was proposed by former Liberal leader Stéphane Dion but the Conservatives triumphed in the 2008 election. Prime Minister Stephen Harper claimed that a carbon tax would "wreak havoc on Canada's economy, destroy jobs, [and] weaken business."[134] Harper endorsed a permit trading system to regulate emissions, but later reversed himself and disavowed any law or policy that would put a price on carbon, on the basis that such action would be economically destructive. Several Canadian provinces, led by British Columbia, put a price on carbon, which will be discussed in Chapter 8.

United States

The United States does not put a national price on carbon. Attempts to establish a permit trading system modelled after the successful sulphur dioxide permit trading program used to tackle acid rain have run into roadblocks in Congress. California's "cap-and-trade" scheme came into effect in 2012 with enforceable compliance obligations that began in 2013. It aims to help fulfill California's targets of reducing GHG emissions to 1990 levels by 2020 and to 80 percent below 1990 levels by 2050.

European Union

The European Union's Emissions Trading System (ETS) entered into force in 2005 in order to help reach the European Union's Kyoto targets.[135] Covering more than ten thousand factories, power plants, and other industrial facilities, the ETS sets a cap on overall emissions and requires participants to monitor and report their emissions. If an individual exceeds its allowances for GHG emissions, it must purchase additional allowances, whereas if a facility has leftover allowances (due to reducing its emissions), it can sell these credits. The ETS has been extended to include new sectors (e.g., aviation) and additional greenhouse gases (e.g., nitrous oxide and perfluorocarbons).[136] The European Union also enacted a framework law governing the taxation of energy products and electricity.[137] A number of EU member states have imposed carbon taxes, including the United Kingdom, Denmark, Ireland, Italy, the Netherlands, Finland, and Sweden. Norway and Switzerland, while not EU members, also have long-standing carbon taxes. The rate of carbon taxes in the European Union goes as high as $160 per tonne for certain sources of greenhouse gas emissions in Sweden.

Australia

Australia instituted a carbon tax in 2011, with a price of $23 per tonne. The tax applies to roughly five hundred large emitters responsible for 60 percent of Australian emissions. Transport fuels like gasoline and diesel were exempted for political reasons. The Australian system was intended to evolve into a permit trading system beginning in 2015, but the federal government elected in 2013 eliminated the carbon tax.

Fuel Efficiency Regulations

In all industrialized countries, the transportation sector is a major source of greenhouse gas emissions, often causing from one-quarter to one-third of all carbon emissions. A study published in 2012 identified the fuel efficiency requirements being legislated in different jurisdictions (Table 7.6).[138]

TABLE 7.6
Legal standards for motor vehicle fuel efficiency

Jurisdiction	Litres per 100 km
EU	3.9 (2021)
Japan	4.3 (2020)
China	4.7 (2020)
South Korea	4.8 (2020)
US	4.8 (2025)
Canada	4.8 (2025)
Mexico	6.7 (2016)

Notes: Figures shown are fleet averages. Deadlines are in parentheses.

It is clear from Table 7.6 that Europe has the most aggressive short-term targets for improving the fuel efficiency of motor vehicles. To put the numbers in perspective, the European Union is requiring that by 2021, the average fuel efficiency of all new light-duty vehicles will be substantially better than current versions of Toyota's Prius, a gas-electric hybrid that is one of the most fuel-efficient vehicles for sale in Canada today. Canada has fuel efficiency regulations that match American standards but trail those of the European Union, Japan, and China.

Renewable Energy

A vital part of the transition from today's fossil fuel–dependent society to a low-carbon future is increased reliance on renewable sources of energy, including solar, wind, geothermal, biomass, tidal, and wave energy. The development of renewable energy has been delayed by price advantages enjoyed by fossil fuels and nuclear energy, prices that fail to incorporate the substantial health and environmental externalities associated with exploiting these resources and dealing with the wastes they produce. In recent years, the costs of renewable energy have fallen dramatically, to the point where wind and solar are cost-competitive in some jurisdictions.

Canada

Canada has little in the way of federal legislation or financial support for renewable energy. Previous federal programs (e.g., eco-Energy) provided subsidies to encourage the generation of electricity from renewable energy sources. These programs invested over a billion dollars in projects producing 4,500 megawatts of renewable electricity capacity. The Conservative government terminated funding for new renewable energy projects in 2011.[139] On the transport side, the Renewable Fuels Regulations that came into effect in 2010 requires an average renewable fuel content of 5 percent in gasoline and 2 percent for diesel and heating oil. Some provinces continue to provide substantial support for renewable energy. Ontario passed a comprehensive *Green Energy Act* in 2009 to expand renewable energy generation, encourage energy conservation, and promote the creation of clean energy jobs. The act includes a feed-in tariff that provides higher prices to producers of renewable energy, extensive energy conservation measures, and a requirement that all coal-fired power plants close by 2014. Feed-in tariffs have been highly successful in building the renewable energy sectors in world-leading countries, including Germany and Japan.

United States

The United States is investing significant resources in renewable energy. The *American Recovery and Reinvestment Act of 2009* allocated US$94 billion to renewable energy technologies, energy efficiency, low-carbon vehicles, smart grids, and mass transit. Renewable energy also received a boost in other legislation.[140] The *Duncan Hunter National Defense Authorization Act of 2009* includes several provisions aimed at increasing renewable energy use by the military. For example, the act requires the Department of Defense to consider the use of wind and solar energy for expeditionary forces to reduce the need to deliver fuel to combat regions, where pollution-intensive diesel generators typically produce electricity. However, the United States is continuously revising and extending renewable energy legislation, creating uncertainty that adversely affects investment in this sector.

European Union

The European Union set legally mandated targets requiring 20 percent of all energy in the region to be produced from renewable sources by 2020.[141] National targets range from 10 percent in Malta to 49 percent in Sweden. The European Union has also put in place certification schemes, subsidies, and other incentive mechanisms at the community level to support the use of renewable energy.[142] Germany, a world leader in the production of solar energy, achieved this position largely through the imposition of a feed-in tariff that guaranteed high prices (declining over time) to producers of solar electricity. Spain and Portugal have also become leaders in solar electricity, while Denmark is a world leader in generating power from wind.

Australia

Australia enacted legislation providing targets and incentives for renewable energy in the *Renewable Energy (Electricity) Act 2000*. The act requires that 20 percent of Australia's electricity supply be generated from renewable sources by 2020. As of 2011, 7 percent of Australia's electricity was supplied by renewable sources. Hydroelectricity, bagasse (a byproduct of sugar cane), wood, and wood waste together account for 85 percent of renewable energy production in Australia. Wind energy and solar energy are rapidly growing sectors within the renewable energy market.

Discussion

The preceding assessment of international commitments, national targets for GHG reduction, carbon pricing, vehicle fuel regulations, and policies promoting renewable energy shows that Canada trails its peers in every category. Canada is the only country to withdraw from the Kyoto Protocol, shares a weak target for emissions reduction with the United States but unlike the Americans is not on track to meet that target, scorns the use of carbon pricing despite evidence of its effectiveness and absence of impact on economic competitiveness, has weak regulations for vehicle fuel efficiency, and has withdrawn the financial support previously available for new renewable energy projects.

At the other end of the spectrum is the European Union, which not only met but also exceeded the emissions reduction target it set for the first Kyoto commitment period. The European Union has the most ambitious emissions reduction commitment for 2020, the most comprehensive climate change legislation, the broadest carbon pricing mechanisms, the most aggressive fuel efficiency regulations, and the strongest support for renewable energy.

Other studies confirm that Canada lags behind other industrialized nations in terms of federal laws to address climate change. A 2013 report by Globe International compared climate legislation in the European Union and thirty-two other countries. Overall, the report was encouraging, observing that the European Union and seventeen countries achieved substantial legislative progress, while fourteen countries made modest legislative progress. Canada was singled out as the only country that made "negative progress." As Globe International concluded, "for the first time, one country – Canada – has regressed following its decision to withdraw from the Kyoto Protocol and the subsequent repealing of its 'flagship' climate legislation, the Kyoto Protocol Implementation Act."[143] Another report published in 2013 by European NGOs ranked Canada fifty-fifth out of fifty-eight countries for climate change performance, based on very poor policies and very high emissions. The only countries performing worse than Canada were Kazakhstan, Iran, and Saudi Arabia. The authors concluded that "Canada still shows no intentions to move forward on climate policy and thereby [maintains] its place as the worst performer of all western countries."[144]

These bleak assessments demonstrate that current Canadian laws and regulations are inadequate to prevent the adverse effects of climate change upon human health and environmental integrity. The federal government appears to be willfully blind to the fact that addressing climate change is expected to have modest economic impacts over the long term. In fact, a new study estimates that shifting from fossil fuels to renewable sources of energy would actually provide net benefits to society, based largely on the potential health gains.[145]

Endangered Species Legislation

Biological diversity is essential to human health but can be adversely affected by a myriad of human activities, including habitat destruction, over-exploitation, pollution, global change (e.g., ozone depletion and climate change), and the introduction of invasive species. Because of this diversity of threats, many different types of environmental laws and policies contribute to protecting biodiversity, including those governing protected areas, natural resources, agriculture, environmental assessment, hunting, fishing, and pollution. Because of widespread failures in these legal regimes, endangered species legislation is vitally important for preventing extinctions and promoting the recovery of species in decline. Laws to protect endangered species are comparable to emergency wards in hospitals, recognizing that while the emphasis ought to be on prevention, treating those in dire need is a necessary part of the system.

The following comparison evaluates five key elements of endangered species legislation: (1) strictly scientific criteria for listing a species or ecosystem as endangered; (2) the geographic scope of the legislation; (3) the strength of legal prohibitions on killing or harming an endangered species; (4) the extent of protection for critical habitat; and (5) mandatory implementation of recovery plans.

Scientific Listing

The first step towards protecting any species at risk through endangered species legislation involves adding the species to a list of species protected by law. In general, an expert group of scientists prepares a status report that determines the appropriate category for a given species (e.g., extinct, endangered, threatened, special concern, or not at risk). To give the recommendation the force of law requires government action. A key difference among endangered species laws is whether the government must adopt the experts' recommendation (the preferred approach) or whether the government has the discretion to reject that advice.

Under the *Species at Risk Act*, the Committee on the Status of Endangered Wildlife in Canada (COSEWIC) makes recommendations about the status of a species to the minister of the environment, who forwards the recommendations to cabinet. Cabinet has nine months to decide whether or not to list the species as proposed. If cabinet has not decided after nine months, the proposed species are automatically listed. If cabinet decides not to follow COSEWIC's recommendation, it must publish reasons.[146] This listing process has created two significant problems. First, there is a loophole in the law that allows COSEWIC recommendations to sit on the environment minister's desk indefinitely without being forwarded to cabinet. As of 2015, there are species that COSEWIC recommended be added to the List of Species at Risk as long ago as 2005 but that were not forwarded to cabinet, meaning that the nine-month clock never started ticking. From 2010 to 2013, 92 of 141 COSEWIC assessments – covering species such as loggerhead sea turtles and bobolink blackbirds – were not transmitted by the environment minister to cabinet. Canadian legal and biodiversity experts refer to this flaw in the law as "highly regrettable."[147] Second, despite COSEWIC recommendations, cabinet has refused to add dozens of species to the list, including polar bears, Atlantic cod, and populations of sockeye salmon, coho salmon, sturgeon, and beluga whales.[148]

In contrast, in the United States, listing pursuant to the *Endangered Species Act* must be based solely on the best available scientific information. Political, economic, and social factors are not allowed to interfere. If these improper considerations do intervene, concerned citizens can turn to the courts to hold governments accountable and ensure that species are listed as the law intended. The European Union, Australia, and Mexico also employ a strictly scientific process for the listing of species at risk.[149] Australia's legislation also authorizes the listing of endangered ecological communities and key threatening processes.

Scope of Legislation
In order to provide maximum protection for endangered species, the law should apply to all land and water, whether public or private, federal or provincial/state. In fact, this is the approach taken by endangered species laws in the United States, European Union, and Mexico. Canada and Australia, in contrast, have taken a narrow, ecologically indefensible, and cumbersome approach, protecting endangered species only on federal lands and water. The difference is striking. In the United States, European Union, and Mexico, a designated endangered species is protected from being killed or harmed wherever it lives or travels. In Canada, a species is protected by the *Species at Risk Act* only if it is on federal land (comprising just 5 percent of the country), or if it is an aquatic species or migratory bird. There is endangered species legislation in eight of the ten provinces, with British Columbia and Alberta being the exceptions. Among the eight provinces with legislation, the extent of protection provided by law varies considerably,

from a relatively strong law in Nova Scotia to a weak law in Saskatchewan.[150] Australia's endangered species law is similar to Canada's in protecting species only when they are on Commonwealth lands or water.[151]

Protection of Critical Habitat

Of central importance in conserving species at risk is protecting habitat that is critical to their survival and recovery. The US *Endangered Species Act* provides mandatory protection for critical habitat, as does European and Mexican legislation. The European Union puts the onus on individual nations to identify critical habitat but reserves the authority to order countries to protect this habitat. Despite the mandatory nature of critical habitat provisions in the US *Endangered Species Act,* critical habitat has been designated for only about half of all listed species.[152] For the other half of species, government agencies claim that identifying critical habitat is either "not prudent" (because it could further jeopardize the species) or "undeterminable."

Canada and Australia employ a narrower and less effective approach. In Australia, critical habitat is protected from damage or destruction only if found on Commonwealth land or in Commonwealth waters. Otherwise, species at risk are subject to a patchwork quilt of protection at the state or territorial level. Canada's approach is even less effective. The *Species at Risk Act* offers a novel approach to protecting the "residence" of endangered species. Under the Canadian law, the nest of an endangered bird found on federal land would be protected, but not the surrounding forest. If the nest is found on provincial, territorial, or private land, the *Species at Risk Act* would not apply unless it is a migratory bird.

Some critical habitat can be protected by Canada's *Species at Risk Act* through the development and implementation of recovery strategies and action plans. Mandatory protection for critical habitat is afforded only to land in national parks (excluding national park reserves), marine protected areas under the *Oceans Act* (but not under the *Canada National Marine Conservation Areas Act*), national wildlife areas, and migratory bird sanctuaries. Discretionary protection for critical habitat on provincial or territorial land is available in theory, but in over a decade since the *Species at Risk Act* was enacted, the federal cabinet has exercised this discretion for only one species (greater sage-grouse), and this decision faces a constitutional challenge from an oil and gas company.[153] As Professor Stewart Elgie of the University of Ottawa concluded, "it would be difficult to design a more cumbersome, discretion-laden, and delay prone process for protecting habitat."[154] To make matters worse, Canada has protected only 8.8 percent of its land area in parks and other legally protected areas, a smaller proportion than over 125 countries, including Australia, the United States, Japan, and almost every country in Europe.[155] Canada is also a laggard in protecting marine habitat, with only 1 percent of its marine area legally designated as protected, far behind 100 countries such as Australia at 36 percent.[156]

Mandatory Recovery Planning

Recovery plans are intended to ensure that a coordinated effort is made to halt the decline of populations of species at risk and undertake the actions required to rebuild their populations to healthy levels. The US *Endangered Species Act* requires recovery plans to be established for all listed species and biannual recovery reporting to Congress. The European Union also requires recovery plans for all listed species.

Canada and Australia trail other countries in terms of recovery plans. In Australia, the minister of environment has the discretion to direct the preparation of recovery plans and threat abatement plans for endangered species or ecological communities.[157] Canada's *Species at Risk Act* mandates that recovery strategies be prepared within one year after a species is listed as endangered or two years after it is listed as threatened. Unfortunately, these legal requirements are routinely violated.[158] In a 2014 court decision in a lawsuit based on delayed recovery plans affecting four species, the Federal Court concluded that "the delays encountered in these four cases are just the tip of the iceberg. There is clearly an enormous systemic problem within the relevant Ministries, given the respondents' acknowledgement that there remain some 167 species at risk for which recovery strategies have not yet been developed."[159] To make matters worse, the *Species at Risk Act* establishes a two-step process: the recovery strategy and the action plan. The recovery strategy identifies the steps required to promote the recovery of a species. The action plan identifies the actual actions and measures to be taken to achieve recovery. Another legal loophole means that there is no mandatory timeline for completing an action plan. As a result, only a dozen action plans had been completed by the end of 2014.[160]

Discussion

It is clear that Canada and Australia have considerably weaker species-at-risk legislation than other industrialized nations. Canada's *Species at Risk Act* is undermined by excessive political discretion and an extremely narrow scope, meaning that many endangered species are not being effectively protected.[161] The act was weakened further by an amendment in 2012 specifically reducing requirements for pipeline corporations to avoid damaging the habitat of listed wildlife species.[162]

In contrast, the United States and the European Union have robust legal regimes for protecting endangered species and their habitat. Published reports on the effectiveness of species at risk legislation in these two jurisdictions indicate that not only have likely extinctions been prevented but also hundreds of species have recovered or are on their way to recovery as a result of actions taken pursuant to these laws.[163]

Conclusion

Canadians should enjoy a level of protection from environmental threats to their health that is equal to or better than the highest standard enjoyed by citizens of other wealthy industrialized nations. Yet the voluntary national guidelines in Canada for air and drinking water quality are weaker than comparable but legally enforceable standards in other industrialized nations. More than forty toxic pesticide active ingredients whose use is prohibited in other industrialized countries are available in more than one thousand pesticide products sold in Canada. Canada allows higher levels of pesticide residues on food than other nations. Toxic substances banned or strictly regulated in other nations, from asbestos to formaldehyde, continue to be used with less stringent restrictions in Canada. Canada sits at the very back of the pack in terms of national laws and policies to address climate change. Canada's legislation governing endangered species is substantially weaker than comparable laws in the United States, the European Union, and Mexico. Canadian rules governing other important environmental health threats are also substandard. An expert in the field of infectious disease recently observed that "Canada is an international embarrassment" for failing to adequately regulate the use of antibiotics in livestock, contributing to antibiotic resistance.[164] The bottom line is that current Canadian environmental laws and standards fail to adequately protect either human health or the health of the environment in which we live, leading to thousands of premature deaths, millions of preventable illnesses, and billions of dollars in unnecessary health care expenses every year.

8

Canada's Failure to Make Polluters Pay

Price signals are powerful. Industry and consumers will not change their behaviour as long as it's cheap to pollute. Charging fees to those who actually pollute creates a strong incentive to change behaviour.

– DON DRUMMOND, FORMER CHIEF ECONOMIST, TD BANK (2014)

It is widely understood that the free market, a dominant institution in today's world, often treats environmental damage as an externality. As a result, health and environmental costs are borne by society rather than the corporations, governments, and individuals that cause the harm. Despite fifty years of recommendations from economists that putting a price on environmental harms such as pollution would be the most efficient means of addressing this fundamental market failure, Canada has refused to act on their advice. This failure will be contrasted with the situation in nations that have made substantial gains both environmentally and economically through ecological fiscal reform – using taxes and other market-based instruments to internalize externalities.[1] This chapter will compare environmental taxes levied on new motor vehicles, transportation fuels, carbon emissions, pesticides, industrial air pollution, and water pollution. Costs can also be internalized by imposing fines and penalties on individuals or businesses that violate environmental laws, although this approach is more reactive than proactive. Therefore, this chapter will also use international comparisons to evaluate the enforcement of Canadian environmental laws and regulations.

The polluter-pays principle means simply that the party responsible for generating pollution should be responsible for the costs imposed by that pollution, rather than imposing the costs on the government or the public.[2] The basic tenet of the principle is that the prices of goods and services should fully reflect their total costs, including all health and ecological damages. Comprehensive application of the polluter-pays principle will not only decrease health and environmental harms but also increase economic efficiency, promote justice through more equitable distribution of the costs of pollution, create a level playing field among competitors, and improve the fiscal balance of governments.[3]

Putting a price on pollution through emission and effluent taxes or fees offers the following advantages:

- It can be relatively simple to design and implement.
- It can generate revenues for governments, which can support further reductions in pollution, or alleviate the cost burden on emitters (through revenue recycling, as is done with Sweden's nitrogen oxide fees).[4]
- It provides a continuous incentive to reduce emissions.
- It can stimulate technological and process innovations.
- It provides flexibility for regulated entities in choosing their means of compliance.
- It can offer clarity, certainty, and transparency about the price of compliance.
- It allow a consistent price to be applied across individual facilities and sectors.
- When paired with emissions monitoring technologies, it can ensure efficient and effective compliance monitoring.[5]

The following are potential disadvantages of emission and effluent taxes or fees:

- There is no guarantee that a specific emissions goal will be met.
- Setting the price can be challenging for regulatory agencies if they lack information about the abatement costs of regulated entities.
- Setting taxes too low will undermine the environmental effectiveness of the system.

+ Setting fees too high could lead to significant output changes and negative economic impacts.
+ Emissions fees can be perceived as a government "tax grab."[6]

The polluter-pays principle is widely incorporated as a guiding principle of Canadian environmental legislation at both the federal and provincial/ territorial levels.[7] The Supreme Court of Canada has repeatedly endorsed the principle, observing that it is "found in almost all federal and provincial environmental legislation."[8] It is acknowledged as a general principle of international law.[9] However, while the concept is widely accepted as a legal principle, there has been little progress in terms of implementation.

Across the entire Organisation for Economic Co-operation and Development, nations generate an average of 7 percent of their total tax revenue from environmental taxes.[10] The leaders are the Netherlands at 12 percent and Japan at 10 percent, with Denmark close behind at 9 percent. Canada is among the laggards, with less than 4 percent of tax revenue coming from environmental taxes. Somewhat surprisingly, the proportion of tax revenue from environmental sources in Canada has been declining since the 1990s. A 2013 study published by KPMG reported that Canada ranked dead last among industrialized countries in using green taxes to make polluters pay, even trailing newly industrializing nations such as China and South Africa.[11] European nations have used pollution taxes with great success in reducing the release of toxic chemicals into air and water, reducing pesticide use, and reducing emissions of carbon dioxide, sulphur dioxide, and nitrogen oxides.[12] For example, the Netherlands used pollution taxes to achieve a 72–99 percent reduction in various water pollutants.[13] Sweden used a tax on sulphur to reduce sulphur dioxide emissions by over 80 percent, to per capita levels that are one-eighth of the level of emissions in Canada.[14] As Canada's Ecofiscal Commission recently observed, Canada "is behind the curve in shifting to policies that can more closely align its economic and environmental objectives."[15]

The following comparative case studies demonstrate the extent to which wealthy industrialized nations have implemented the polluter-pays principle through environmental taxation.

Motor Vehicle Taxes

While regular sales taxes generally apply to the purchase of new vehicles, the following analysis is restricted to taxes that are differentiated on the basis of fuel efficiency or carbon dioxide emissions. Twenty-one OECD member countries impose this specific type of one-off motor vehicle tax at the time of purchase.[16] The intent is to give prospective purchasers an incentive to buy more fuel-efficient vehicles and avoid buying gas guzzlers.

Canada's Green Levy is an excise tax on fuel-inefficient vehicles that came into effect in 2007.[17] It applies to new vehicles, including cars, station wagons, minivans, and sport utility vehicles (SUVs), but does not apply to pickup trucks or vans that carry ten or more people. The Green Levy is based on vehicles' average fuel consumption. Vehicles that consume more than 13 litres per 100 kilometres (L/100 km) are subject to a $1,000 tax, which rises to $4,000 for vehicles that consume more than 16 L/100 km. Only a very small minority of vehicles for sale in Canada today – primarily high-performance sports cars, large SUVs, and large luxury vehicles – trigger the Green Levy.[18]

In 1978, the US government created a Gas Guzzler Tax intended to discourage the production and purchase of fuel-inefficient vehicles. However, the law is undermined by two large loopholes. First, it does not apply to pickup trucks, minivans, or SUVs. Second, although the level of tax imposed depends on a car's fuel efficiency rating, the criteria have not been amended since 1991. Cars with a fuel efficiency rating of 22.5 miles per gallon (mpg) (10.5 L/100 km) or better are not subject to the tax. Cars that average 21.5–22.5 mpg are subject to a tax of US$1,000, rising to a maximum of US$7,700 for cars that get less than 12.5 mpg (18.8 L/100 km). Because cars have generally become more fuel-efficient over the past twenty-four years, the Gas Guzzler Tax now applies to a very small proportion of vehicle sales in the United States.[19]

Australia imposes a Luxury Car Tax of 33 percent of a vehicle's value above Aus$57,180. Exempt from this tax are fuel-efficient vehicles priced below Aus$75,000.[20]

Compared with Canada, the United States, and Australia, motor vehicle taxes in Europe cover a much broader spectrum of vehicles and are far higher. Most European motor vehicle taxes begin to apply to vehicles at 6 L/100 km; apply to cars, SUVs, vans, and small trucks; and increase steadily on vehicles with higher levels of fuel consumption. In Norway, the Netherlands, Portugal, and Finland, vehicles with fuel efficiency ratings of 8.2 L/100 km or higher are subject to a tax of at least 10,000 euros ($14,000).[21] These vehicles would not be taxed in Canada or the United States. Finland's purchase tax increases at a constant rate as emissions increase, whereas other nations, such as Portugal and Austria, have tax rates that jump sharply upward for highly polluting vehicles.[22] For example, consider a new car with a fuel efficiency rating of 12 L/100 km. In Norway and the Netherlands, the purchaser of this vehicle would pay a tax of at least 40,000 euros ($56,000). In Finland and Portugal, the tax on such a vehicle would be at least 15,000 euros ($21,000). In Austria and Ireland, the tax would be at least 5,000 euros ($7,000). A purchaser of this car in the United States would pay US$1,700 under the Gas Guzzler Tax, while Canada's Green Levy would not apply.

The Canadian and American taxes apply only to gas guzzlers at the extreme end of the fuel consumption scale, and are financially insignificant compared with European motor vehicle taxes. The US Gas Guzzler Tax applies to passenger cars that consume more than 10.5 L/100 km. Canada's Green Levy applies only to vehicles consuming more than 13 L/100 km. Of the motor vehicle purchase taxes in the twenty-one countries studied by the OECD, Canada's Green Levy is the weakest in terms of the magnitude of the tax, the proportion of vehicles subject to the tax, and the level of fuel efficiency at which it begins to apply.

At least eight OECD nations also impose an annual vehicle registration charge based on carbon dioxide emissions, including Denmark, France, Germany, the United Kingdom, Finland, Ireland, Portugal, and Sweden. These annual vehicle taxes average roughly 500 euros per year but go as high as 3,500 euros in France. Neither Canada nor the United States imposes a comparable tax.

Transportation Fuel Taxes

Burning fossil fuels contributes to air pollution, water pollution, and climate change, causing substantial negative impacts on human health and ecosystems. For the most part, businesses, individuals, and governments do not pay for these externalized costs, effectively creating a subsidy. As leading economists Jack Mintz and Nancy Olewiler note, this subsidy "is detrimental to the environment, human health, and economic efficiency."[23]

Transportation fuel taxes in Canada are significantly lower than in twenty-seven OECD nations and higher than two (see Table 8.1). The fuel tax in Canada consists of a federal excise tax of $0.10 per litre of gasoline or $0.04 for diesel, plus provincial and, in some cases, municipal fuel taxes (see Table 8.2). The total fuel tax in Canada (excluding sales tax) ranges from a low of $0.16 per litre in the Yukon to a high of $0.36 in Vancouver (not including the carbon tax).[24]

TABLE 8.1

Gasoline taxes in OECD nations in 2014, per litre (converted to Canadian dollars)

Country	Amount of tax	Country	Amount of tax
Turkey	$1.21	Switzerland	$0.68
Netherlands	$0.92	Czech Republic	$0.66
Germany	$0.90	Luxembourg	$0.63
United Kingdom	$0.86	Austria	$0.61
Finland	$0.86	Hungary	$0.59
Norway	$0.85	Spain	$0.58
Greece	$0.84	Korea	$0.58
France	$0.83	Japan	$0.57
Portugal	$0.80	Poland	$0.52
Denmark	$0.78	Iceland	$0.50
Belgium	$0.78	Australia	$0.29
Italy	$0.77	New Zealand	$0.26
Ireland	$0.74	Canada	$0.10
Sweden	$0.71	United States	$0.05
Slovak Republic	$0.70	Mexico	($0.09)

Source: OECD, "Database on Instruments Used for Environmental Policy: Taxes, Fees, Charges" (2014), http://www2.oecd.org/ecoinst/queries/.

In Australia and New Zealand, gas taxes are more than twice as high as in Canada. In Iceland, Poland, Japan, Korea, Spain, and Hungary, gas taxes are over five times as high as Canadian taxes; in Austria, Luxembourg, the Czech Republic, and Switzerland, over six times as high; in Sweden, the Slovak Republic, Ireland, Italy, Belgium, and Denmark, at least seven times as high; in Portugal, France, Norway, Finland, and the United Kingdom, over eight times as high; in Germany and the Netherlands, at least nine times as high; and in Turkey, over twelve times as high. Among all the OECD nations, only the United States and Mexico have lower gas taxes than Canada. The US federal excise tax on gasoline is US$0.05 per litre (US$0.186 per gallon). Unlike in Canada, the US excise tax is higher on diesel than on gasoline, at US$0.065 per litre (US$0.244 per gallon). In an assessment of fuel taxes, the OECD compared countries with high fuel taxes (the United Kingdom, Germany, Sweden, Norway, and Turkey) against countries with low fuel taxes (the United States, Canada) and concluded that "price mechanisms work – both in the short and in the longer term."[25] Higher taxes lead to lower fuel use and more efficient economies.

TABLE 8.2
Provincial gas taxes in 2015, per litre

Province	Amount of tax
British Columbia	$0.145
Alberta	$0.13
Saskatchewan	$0.15
Manitoba	$0.14
Ontario	$0.147
Quebec	$0.192
New Brunswick	$0.136
Nova Scotia	$0.155
Prince Edward Island	$0.131
Newfoundland	$0.165

Source: PetroCanada, "Gasoline Taxes Across Canada" (2015), http://retail.
petro-canada.ca/en/fuelsavings/2139.aspx.

Canada's federal excise tax was introduced in 1975 to curb reliance on imported oil and to raise revenue. It has been the subject of criticism for many years because it is neither economically nor environmentally rational. In 1998, Parliament's Technical Committee on Business Taxation concluded that "the current federal excise tax on fuels is inefficient and unfair."[26] The tax applies to only one category of environmentally damaging products, exempting coal, natural gas, and other fossil fuels whose combustion causes substantial negative impacts. Setting a lower rate for diesel is also irrational, since diesel causes more health and environmental damage per litre than regular gasoline (18 percent more greenhouse gas emissions per litre and more local air pollution).[27] The OECD recommends eliminating the disparity between gas and diesel and raising the tax on both to better reflect the health and environmental damage caused by these fuels.[28] Mintz and Olewiler recommended that Canada's federal fuel excise tax be replaced with a broadly based environmental tax covering all fuels that emit greenhouse gases and air contaminants. They point out that "such a tax would be more fair, in that it would apply to all fuels, not just motive fuels, and more effective in that the tax rate would be tied to the polluting impacts of a given fuel type."[29]

It is also important to note that if gas taxes are imposed as a flat rate per litre, as is the case in Canada, then they should be adjusted periodically to keep pace with inflation.[30] This has not happened in Canada, with the result that, in real terms, the tax rate on gas and diesel actually decreased almost 20 percent between 2000 and 2015.

Carbon Taxes

Carbon taxes were described briefly in Chapter 7 as one of the key policies available to address climate change. As the OECD concluded, "without a clear policy signal that there is a rising cost of CO_2 emissions over time, there will be little incentive for societies to undertake the needed shift away from fossil fuels."[31] A growing number of countries are imposing carbon taxes. A study by Australia's Climate Commission determined that as of 2013, there were at least thirty-three countries and eighteen subnational jurisdictions that employed carbon pricing rules (either through taxes or permit trading).[32] The following analysis focuses exclusively on nations with carbon taxes, including Finland, Norway, Sweden, the United Kingdom, Ireland, Switzerland, Iceland, Costa Rica, and Australia. Canada has no national carbon tax, and prospects in the short term are dim due to the vehement opposition of Prime Minister Stephen Harper and his Conservative government. Canada even took the unusual step of praising the efforts of Australian Prime Minister Tony Abbott to repeal that country's carbon tax, with Harper's parliamentary secretary, Paul Calandra, stating: "The Australian prime minister's decision will be noticed around the world and sends an important message."[33]

Nordic countries were pioneers in taxing carbon dioxide emissions. Finland introduced the world's first carbon tax in 1990, and it is currently set at 60 euros ($82) per tonne of CO_2 for transportation fuels, and 30 euros ($41) per tonne for coal, natural gas, and other heating fuels.[34] In Norway, "the polluter pays principle is a cornerstone in the policy framework on climate change."[35] The Norwegian government charges a carbon tax on petroleum, mineral oils, gasoline, natural gas, and liquefied petroleum gas.[36] In 2012, the government doubled the carbon tax on petroleum to 0.96 Norwegian kroner ($0.16) per litre,[37] which is equivalent to $70 per tonne. Sweden's carbon tax was introduced in 1991 and has increased over time to its current level of 114 euros ($156) per tonne of CO_2 emitted by households and the service sector.[38] The tax is set at 8 euros ($11) per tonne for combined heat and power systems run by businesses in sectors that face competition within the EU Emissions Trading System (ETS), is waived for other businesses in sectors that face competition within the EU ETS, and is 34 euros ($47) for sectors facing competition outside the EU ETS.[39]

Britain has a "climate change levy" that applies to various fuels. In 2013, the levy was increased to £0.00541 ($0.01) per kilowatt-hour (kWh) of electricity, and £0.0121 ($0.02) per litre of gasoline.[40] In 2014, the British tax on fossil fuels used to generate electricity was increased to approximately $20 per tonne of CO_2.[41] In 2010, Ireland imposed a carbon tax of 15 euros ($21) per tonne of CO_2 on coal, peat, natural gas, and petroleum oils.[42] The amount of carbon tax charged at the pump is approximately 0.03 euros ($0.05) per litre.

Switzerland implemented a carbon tax in 2008. Set initially at 12 Swiss francs ($13) per tonne, it is tied to Switzerland's greenhouse gas reduction obligations such that failure to meet reduction targets triggers an increase in the tax.[43] By 2012, it had risen to 36 Swiss francs ($40). Because Switzerland failed in 2012 to meet its reduction target of 21 percent below 1990 levels (emissions were down 17.5 percent), the carbon tax increased to 60 Swiss francs ($67) in 2014.[44]

In 2009, Iceland instituted a carbon tax on liquid fossil fuels, electricity, and hot water.[45] The carbon tax is $0.04 per litre of gas and diesel fuel, and $0.05 per kilogram of fuel oil. The carbon tax on electricity is $1.02 per 1,000 kilowatt-hours of electricity sold and 2 percent of the retail price for hot water.[46] In 2009, France established a carbon tax but that country's Constitutional Council blocked it because the tax granted excessive exemptions for industry.[47] In 2013, the French government introduced a more equitable carbon tax, beginning at 7.5 euros per tonne in 2014, rising to 14.5 euros in 2015 and 22 euros in 2016.[48] The Netherlands established a carbon tax in 1990 but later converted it to a broader energy tax. Slovenia relabelled its existing energy tax as a carbon tax in 1997.[49]

Australia implemented a carbon tax of $23 per tonne in 2012, which increased to $24 per tonne in 2013.[50] Newly elected prime minister Tony Abbott scrapped the tax in 2014, making Australia the first nation to abolish a carbon tax.[51] While the carbon price covered approximately 60 percent of Australian emissions, it did not apply to household transportation fuels, light-duty business vehicle fuels, or fuels used in the agricultural, logging, or fishing sectors.[52] A reduced rate applied to emission-intensive, export-oriented industries. New Zealand's government set up an emissions trading scheme in 2008.[53] The scheme covered forestry initially, and was expanded in 2010 to cover stationary energy, transport, liquid fossil fuels, and industrial processes. Japan passed legislation in 2012 authorizing a small carbon tax ($3 per tonne).[54] South Korea passed legislation in 2012 that authorizes a carbon tax as well as an emissions trading scheme to start in 2015.[55]

Costa Rica's carbon tax is levied at 3.5 percent of the price of all fossil fuels. Introduced in 1997, a portion of the revenue supports sustainable development and forest conservation initiatives, including payments to farmers for protecting ecosystem services.[56] Carbon taxes came into effect in 2014 in both Chile ($5 per tonne of CO_2, covering 55 percent of emissions) and Mexico ($3.50 per tonne).[57]

Even some of the world's poorest countries are beginning to impose carbon taxes. In 2010, India imposed a modest carbon tax on coal ($1 per tonne), with tax increases in 2014 and 2015 effectively tripling the levy. South Africa authorized a carbon tax in its 2012–13 budget, with an implementation date of 2016.

Despite extensive international experience with carbon taxes, Canada refuses to consider such a tax at the national level. The only carbon taxes in Canada exist at the provincial level, with British Columbia's tax by far the most substantial. This carbon tax took effect in 2008, starting at $10 per tonne and rising to $30 per tonne by 2012. The tax applies to the combustion of gasoline, diesel, propane, natural gas, and coal, thus covering roughly 80 percent of provincial GHG emissions.[58] In 2007, Quebec imposed a small tax of roughly $3.50 per tonne on energy producers. Alberta requires large companies that emit over 100,000 tonnes of CO_2 annually to reduce their emissions intensity, purchase offsets within the province, or pay $15 per tonne into a technology fund. British Columbia's carbon tax generates approximately $1 billion in annual revenue, whereas Alberta's system produces only $55–75 million despite far higher emissions.

Many studies conclude that carbon taxes can be effective in reducing GHG emissions.[59] British Columbia's carbon tax is producing both environmental and economic benefits. Since it took effect in 2008, per capita consumption of vehicle fuels in British Columbia has declined by 17.4 percent, while increasing slightly in the rest of Canada.[60] Since 2008, GHG emissions in the province have dropped more quickly (10 percent) than in the rest of Canada (1 percent). Over the same period, British Columbia's economy outperformed the rest of Canada (measured by changes in GDP per capita), contrary to the fears expressed by some critics that the tax would have adverse economic effects. The BC government has gone beyond its promise that the carbon tax would be revenue-neutral, instituting income tax cuts for individuals and businesses that exceeded carbon tax revenues by over $500 million over the first five years.[61] By 2013, British Columbia was tied with Alberta and New Brunswick for the lowest corporate income tax rate and had the lowest personal income tax rate for individuals earning less than $119,000.

In addition to carbon taxes, energy taxes are an essential part of internalizing the health and environmental costs from all sources of energy, not only fossil fuels. A 2013 OECD study looked at the "effective" tax rate on energy use, which includes all the "specific taxes and related tax expenditures that apply to energy use."[62] The effective tax on energy use includes carbon taxes as well as fuel taxes and other taxes directed at energy, and includes all sectors to give an overall picture of energy taxes. Although there is a carbon tax of $30 per tonne in British Columbia, the overall tax on energy use across Canada is only $11 per tonne. Converting energy taxes into effective carbon taxes reveals that out of thirty-four OECD countries, only Mexico and the United States have lower effective carbon tax rates than Canada. The OECD country in fourth place from the bottom, Chile, has an effective tax rate double that of Canada. It should be noted that both Chile and Mexico have established carbon taxes since the OECD conducted its comparison.[63] At the other end of the spectrum, Canada's $11 per tonne effective carbon tax rate is minuscule compared to the 33 percent of OECD countries with effective carbon tax rates that exceed $100 per tonne.[64] The net effect is that Canada provides relatively little financial incentive for the transition from polluting fossil fuels towards clean energy.

Pesticide Taxes

The world leaders in pesticide reduction are the Scandinavian nations, where pesticide use has fallen by over 50 percent over the past thirty years.[65] During the mid-1980s, Norway, Sweden, and Denmark pioneered the use of pesticide taxes as a means of applying the polluter-pays principle to these toxic substances, thus internalizing at least some of the previously externalized impacts upon the health of humans and ecosystems. Sweden's pesticide tax is the simplest, currently set at 30 Swedish kroner per kilogram of active ingredient (roughly $4.40). To maximize administrative simplicity, the tax is imposed on pesticide manufacturers and importers. Sweden also imposes a suite of registration charges on pesticides, which are used to offset the government's administrative costs. In 2013, annual pesticide charges were increased to 2.6 percent of annual sales revenue for chemical products and 1.3 percent of sales for biological products, with further fee increases scheduled for chemical products in 2014 and 2015. There are also substantial fees associated with applying for new or amended pesticide authorizations.[66]

Norway's pesticide tax begins with a basic tax (currently 25 Norwegian kroner, or about $4.30) that is multiplied by a factor reflecting health and environmental risks to determine the tax per hectare. The tax per hectare is converted into a tax per unit (kilogram or litre) based on the volume applied. Health risks are determined by factors related to toxicity and exposure, while environmental risks are evaluated by impacts on soil, wildlife, persistence, and ability to bioaccumulate. The multiplication factors range from 0.5 for pesticides with low health and environmental risks to 9.0 for pesticides with high risks. Pesticides intended for use by consumers face higher multiplication factors of 50 and 150. Taxes are imposed on manufacturers and importers, and the tax raises $11 million annually.[67] Norway's pesticide tax was applauded for being one of the first to apply higher rates to products of higher toxicity.[68]

In Denmark, pesticides used in agriculture were subject to a tax equal to 54 percent of the retail price for insecticides and 33 percent for herbicides, growth regulators, and fungicides. Following an extensive review of the effectiveness of this tax, it was restructured in 2013.[69] The new Danish pesticide tax is similar to Norway's, as it varies based on the health and environmental impacts of specific active ingredients. The health risks are based on effects such as "potentially carcinogenic" or "endocrine disrupting" and levels of workers' exposures. Environmental risks are determined by assessing how fast a pesticide degrades in the soil, the risk of accumulation in the food chain, the risk of leaching into groundwater, and toxicity to animals (including insects) and plants. The previous pesticide tax treated all insecticides and herbicides as equal. The new tax made some pesticides much more expensive, reflecting their greater environmental risks. For example, Cyperb is an insecticide with high environmental impacts. With the revised Danish tax, the cost is 1,577 Danish kroner per litre ($297), increasing the cost per hectare by a factor of ten.[70]

Other European nations, including Finland, France, and Italy, recently introduced pesticide taxes. Italy's tax is 2 percent of the price of pesticides, while Finland's tax is 3.5 percent of the price. The French tax is determined according to seven categories of pesticides with varying levels of risk, and ranges from 0.38 euros per kilogram up to 1.68 euros per kilogram.[71]

In Canada, there are no federal or provincial pesticide taxes. Even worse, any pesticide used in agriculture, regardless of its toxicity, is exempt from the federal Goods and Services Tax (GST).[72] Rather than discourage the use of pesticides or reflect their substantial negative effects on human health and ecosystems, this subsidy encourages farmers to use pesticides instead of alternative methods of pest control.

Industrial Air and Water Pollution Taxes

Canada does not have any national pollution taxes. British Columbia and Nova Scotia are the only Canadian provinces that currently impose pollution fees on air emissions and effluent discharges.[73] The fees are volume-based and vary according to the toxicity of the substances being released. British Columbia's air emission fees range from $0.45 per tonne of carbon monoxide to $673.60 per tonne for metals and fluorides, with fees for most contaminants ranging from $11 to $16 per tonne. British Columbia's water effluent fees range from $4.01 per tonne for sulphates to $273.24 per tonne for more toxic contaminants, such as arsenic, chlorine, cyanide, and phenols. Nova Scotia's industrial air emission fees are much lower than British Columbia's fees, with a flat rate of $7.15 per tonne charged on total emissions over thirty tonnes and no tax on emissions below this threshold. Nova Scotia does not currently charge water effluent fees.

Many nations tax nitrogen oxide emissions, in part because Sweden has enjoyed such success through its pioneering tax on this form of air pollution. The Swedish tax is imposed on electricity producers and then distributed back to power plants based on their portion of the total electricity produced, providing a major incentive for reducing emissions and increasing efficiency. Relatively clean energy facilities receive rebates in excess of payments while relatively dirty facilities pay more in charges than they receive in rebates. Renewable energy sources, which do not produce nitrogen oxides, pay no fees at all. The European Commission found that Sweden's tax on nitrogen oxides (NOx), which was set at 40 Swedish kroner per kilogram ($5.83 per kilogram), was effective in reducing NOx emissions by 37 percent during the first six years of its implementation.[74] These emissions reductions were achieved at little or no cost to the companies involved due to innovation and technological progress.[75] In addition to Sweden, NOx emissions are taxed at varying levels in France, Norway, Estonia, Denmark, Hungary, Italy, Poland France, the Czech Republic, and the Slovak Republic. France's tax rate on NOx is 167.30 euros per tonne ($237.57 per tonne). There are also NOx taxes at the subnational level in the United States, Australia, and Spain.

In Canada, there is no national tax on NOx but British Columbia and Nova Scotia do tax these emissions. British Columbia's tax is the highest in

Canada, at $11.29 per tonne. France's NOx tax is twenty times higher, while the Swedish tax is over five hundred times higher. Not surprisingly, France and Sweden release far lower volumes of NOx than Canada, both in total and on a per capita basis.

Pollution fees are widely used in the United States, on both air emissions and water effluents.[76] Pursuant to the *Clean Water Act*, all point sources of water pollution must obtain National Pollution Discharge Elimination System permits in order to discharge effluent. States impose effluent fees based on these permits, and do so using three different approaches. The simplest but least effective either environmentally or economically is a flat annual fee, used by eleven states.[77] A better approach, charging fees based on the volume of effluent, is used by eighteen states.[78] The strongest approach, charging fees according to both discharge volume and toxicity, is used in ten states.[79] For example, effluent fees in Louisiana are based on facility complexity, flow volume, type of pollutants released, heat load, and potential public health threat. However, the fees are capped at a maximum of US$90,000 per year for individual facilities. The Environmental Protection Agency acknowledges that these fees are not high enough to cause significant reductions in pollution.[80]

Similarly, the 1990 *Clean Air Act* amendments require states to impose fees to recover administrative costs.[81] The amendments set the minimum level for such fees at US$25 per ton of emissions of air toxics and criteria air pollutants (excluding carbon monoxide) adjusted for inflation (at present, about US$35 per ton). Although states can meet this requirement through flat fees, most have chosen incremental per-ton fees. Some states base their fees on a combination of volume and toxicity. New Mexico, for example, levies fees of US$150 per ton for air toxics and US$10 per ton for criteria air pollutants. New Mexico also imposes fees on volatile organic compound (VOC) emissions in areas that fall short of attaining national ambient air quality standards for ozone. The South Coast Air Quality Management District (located in Southern California, where there are severe air quality problems) levies the highest fees for air emissions in the United States. The fees for large emitters of criteria air pollutants such as nitrogen oxides, sulphur dioxide, and particulate matter are US$795.08, US$956.32, and US$1,053.91 per ton, respectively.[82] The fee for hazardous air pollutants ranges from US$0.03 per pound for ammonia to US$9.90 per pound for dioxins and furans.[83]

The *Comprehensive Environmental Response, Compensation, and Liability Act of 1980* created the Superfund program to clean up the worst hazardous waste sites in the United States.[84] Several new taxes were imposed pursuant to this law, including an excise tax of US$0.097 per barrel on crude oil or refined oil products; excise taxes of US$0.22 to US$4.87 per ton on certain hazardous chemicals; an excise tax on imported substances that use one or more of the hazardous chemicals subject to excise tax in their production or manufacture; and an environmental income tax of 0.12 percent on the amount of corporations' taxable income in excess of US$2 million. From 1991 to 1995, these taxes generated US$1.5 billion in revenue annually, which was dedicated to the cleanup and restoration of contaminated sites. Authority for these taxes expired in 1995 and despite several attempts, they have not been reinstituted.[85]

Pollution fees are widely used in the European Union and in other countries around the world.[86] Examples of nations imposing water effluent charges include Germany, France (where levies now total over 1 billion euros annually), the Netherlands, the Philippines, and Malaysia. Studies have shown that these water pollution taxes lead to a significant decline in pollution levels.[87] Air emission charges are used in many nations, including Sweden, Japan, France, Norway, Finland, Germany, and the Netherlands. The European Union also imposes comprehensive requirements for environmental liability, including not only contaminated sites but also damage to natural resources.[88]

Perhaps the most comprehensive example of implementation of the polluter-pays principle is France's General Tax on Polluting Activities, which was established in 1999. France imposes taxes on a wide range of pollutants, including benzene, arsenic, selenium, mercury, NOx, sulphur oxides (SOx), VOCs, polycyclic aromatic hydrocarbons (PAHs), and particulate matter, as well as pesticides and garbage.[89] The French pollution tax rates increased in 2013 in an effort to accelerate progress in reducing air pollution, with a tripling of the tax rate for particulate matter, VOCs, and sulphur dioxide.[90] For example, the rate of tax on particulate matter went from $121.43 per tonne to $364.29 per tonne. By contrast, British Columbia's tax on particulate matter, despite being the highest in Canada, is $16.78 per tonne, or twenty-two times lower.

Natural Resource Valuation
Although it is beyond the scope of the analysis in this chapter, it is worth noting that Canada is also notorious for "giving away" its natural wealth at bargain basement prices. Rates for municipally treated drinking water are the cheapest in the OECD.[91] Industrial water users, such as bottled water

companies, often get water for free or at minimal costs. Ontario began charging industrial users for water in 2007 at the rock-bottom rate of $3.71 per million litres, a price still in effect in 2015.[92] British Columbia's industrial water prices are even lower, ranging from $0.065 to $1.10 per million litres.[93] Stumpage fees for lumber from British Columbia's old-growth forests are as low as $0.25 per cubic metre (approximately a telephone pole worth of wood). Royalties for oil, natural gas, coal, and other minerals are also lower than those found in other countries. According to the OECD, Canada continues to provide over $2 billion in direct subsidies to fossil fuels, including coal, oil, and natural gas.[94] According to the International Monetary Fund, when air pollution and climate change impacts are considered, the annual Canadian subsidy is approximately $34 billion.[95] Electricity prices (for both households and industry) in Canada are the second-lowest in the OECD, with only South Korea offering cheaper electricity.[96] The net effect of underpricing valuable natural assets is that they are overused, used inefficiently, and wasted.

Liability Limits

A variety of legal mechanisms are employed in an effort to protect taxpayers from bearing the costs of environmental cleanup and restoration when damage is done in the course of private activity. Examples include contaminated sites, oil spills, and nuclear accidents. However, these mechanisms are undermined by liability limits that cap the maximum amount payable by corporations in certain circumstances. A 2012 audit by the Commissioner of the Environment and Sustainable Development found that in Canada's nuclear and offshore oil and gas industries, liability limits "are outdated and generally much lower than those in other countries ... As a result, taxpayers may have to cover shortfalls and pay for environmental remediation."[97] The liability limit for operators of nuclear facilities is a paltry $75 million, less than all seventeen countries in the Commissioner's comparison. Similarly, absolute liability for companies engaged in offshore oil and gas activities is capped at $30 million on the East coast and $40 million on the West coast and Arctic. In contrast, Norway has no cap on absolute liability, meaning that corporations in that country are responsible for the full costs of cleanup associated with any kind of spill or accident. The maximum liability that can be imposed on a corporation in the event of a major oil spill in Canadian waters is a total of $1.3 billion, while disasters such as the *Exxon Valdez* and BP Deepwater Horizon have cost tens of billions of dollars to clean up.[98] The *Energy Safety and Security Act* enacted in 2015 responded to the Commissioner's recommendations by substantially raising Canada's outdated environmental liability limits for the nuclear energy and oil and gas industries, although oil spill liability limits are still grossly inadequate.[99]

Environmental Law Enforcement

Another means of applying the polluter-pays principle is to impose fines or penalties upon individuals and businesses that violate environmental laws. There are various levels of environmental enforcement, including monitoring, inspections, warning letters, administrative penalties, and prosecutions. Prosecutions can be time-consuming and expensive but offer the potential for substantial fines, court-ordered environmental restoration or compensation, and even jail sentences that could serve as deterrents to future lawbreakers. Enforcement is an essential element of protecting the environment, whether a jurisdiction relies primarily on regulation or economic instruments or both. According to economic theory, "a potential polluter will make a rational calculus of costs and benefits of complying with environmental regulation and will only comply when the expected costs of a violation are higher than the potential gains [of non-compliance]."[100]

It is challenging to compare environmental enforcement records across countries because of difficulties in obtaining data and constructing comparable indicators.[101] Evidence from Europe, which has both stronger regulations and more extensive environmental taxes than Canada, is not encouraging. A Belgian study found that there was only a 1 percent chance of being prosecuted for violating environmental laws because of the low rate of inspections and the low rate of prosecutions even when violations are discovered.[102] In the United Kingdom, the prosecution rate in pollution incidents is less than 5 percent.[103] Average fines in successful criminal prosecutions for environmental offences are also generally very low in Europe.[104] Administrative fines, which are much easier to impose because no expensive and time-consuming judicial process is involved, may well be more important in achieving compliance and deterrence.

Enforcement of environmental laws in Canada ranges from lackadaisical to nonexistent.[105] When the *Canadian Environmental Protection Act (CEPA)* was introduced in 1987, Environment Minister Tom McMillan touted it as "the toughest environmental legislation in the western world."[106] One must ask, however, what good a tough environmental law is if it is rarely enforced. The total amount of fines imposed under the *CEPA* in the twenty-three years from 1988 and 2010 was $2,466,352.[107] By comparison, the Toronto

Public Library collected more in overdue book fines during a single year ($3,653,199 in 2012).[108] Violations of environmental laws occur every day in Canada. From coast to coast, air is being polluted, water and soil contaminated, and natural habitat destroyed. Yet prosecutions and even administrative penalties are rare. A report published in 2013 revealed that although Alberta Environment recorded more than four thousand violations arising from oil sands pollution between 1996 and 2012, enforcement action was taken in only 0.9 percent of these situations.[109] Spills of millions of litres of industrial wastewater into the Athabasca River resulted in investigations but no charges. Even where action was taken, the median penalty was $4,500, which provides little incentive for a large company to clean up its act. Data obtained through freedom of information requests by the environmental law organization Ecojustice (after long battles to gain access), also document how governments turn a blind eye to thousands of breaches of federal and provincial environmental laws every year.[110] Although the federal government has hired additional environmental enforcement personnel since 2007, the amount of enforcement has declined further from levels that were already abysmally low.[111]

By comparison, federal enforcement of environmental laws in the United States is much more aggressive and dwarfs enforcement in Canada. In 2012, the EPA hammered lawbreakers with over US$204 million in civil penalties (administrative and judicial), and secured court judgments requiring defendants to pay US$44 million in criminal fines.[112] The agency also sent executives or managers from corporate polluters and despoilers to prison for a total of ninety years and forced lawbreaking corporations to invest over US$19 billion to comply with their legal obligations.[113] In 2013, BP agreed to pay US$4 billion to settle criminal charges stemming from the Deepwater Horizon disaster.[114] According to the EPA, *Clean Air Act* enforcement actions in 2011 caused lower emissions of particulate matter, sulphur dioxide, nitrogen oxides, and VOCs, resulting in the following health benefits: avoidance of 1,800–4,500 premature deaths, 1,100 emergency room visits or hospital admissions, 1,200 cases of chronic bronchitis, 2,800 nonfatal heart attacks, 30,000 asthma attacks, 230,000 days of missed work, and 1.3 million restricted activity days. The EPA pegged the economic value of the health and environmental benefits of its enforcement action at US$15–36 billion.[115]

Another remarkable revelation about weak environmental law enforcement in Canada was unearthed by lawyers at West Coast Environmental Law, who used the province's *Freedom of Information and Protection of*

Privacy Act to acquire an internal document from the BC Ministry of the Environment on unpaid fines. It turned out that 66 percent of fines levied for *Water Act* violations and 40 percent of fines levied for other environmental violations had not been paid. The government was owed over $700,000 in outstanding fines from court-imposed penalties for environmental offences, mostly arising from convictions involving a few large corporations.[116]

One of the likely reasons for Canada's dismal record of environmental enforcement is a lack of human and financial resources. While federal spending on environmental protection has increased since 1983, it has failed to keep pace with inflation. Spending in 2012 was 13 percent below inflation-adjusted spending in 1983.[117] Provincial spending on environmental protection peaked in 1993 at $1.76 billion and fell to $1.27 billion in 2012, a 28 percent decline.[118] If 1993 spending is adjusted for inflation, provincial spending on environmental protection is barely half of what it was twenty years ago. The warning voiced by experts in Chapter 5, that provincial health care spending could cannibalize environmental protection spending, appears to have been prophetic. Further research is needed to determine whether and to what extent the cuts in environmental spending have created additional health costs that outweigh the apparent savings.

Conclusion

The polluter-pays principle is one of the most widely accepted tenets of environmental policy, at least in theory. Yet the foregoing analysis shows that in terms of motor vehicle levies, fuel taxes, carbon taxes, energy taxes, pesticide taxes, air pollution taxes, water effluent taxes, and general pollution taxes, Canada lags far behind European nations and, in some significant cases, the United States. The OECD has repeatedly criticized Canada for failing to use pricing mechanisms to internalize environmental externalities.[119] The OECD published five specific recommendations regarding environmental taxes for all of its members, but these apply with particular force to Canada as one of the laggards in this field:

1. Overall energy taxes should rise.
2. Taxes on diesel, relative to other transport fuels, are too low and should be increased.
3. Carbon taxes should be increased.
4. Taxes on coal – both for heating and electricity generation – should be increased.

5. Fuels used in agriculture, forestry, and fishing should be taxed, not subsidized.[120]

Policymakers in Europe understand that putting a price on pollution while lowering other taxes will lead to a competitive, prosperous, and low-pollution economy.[121] In contrast, Canadian policymakers apparently still subscribe to the outdated notion that putting a price on pollution will kill jobs in key resource and industrial sectors and drive away foreign investment. The available empirical evidence strongly supports the European perspective. In a promising development, a group of high-profile Canadian politicians, business leaders, and academics have formed the Ecofiscal Commission to develop policy recommendations that will shift taxes onto harmful activities, including pollution and waste, instead of beneficial activities such as employment and investment.[122]

9

Why Does Canada Lag Behind?

The field of environmental law embodies a deep contradiction
– it is a product of the state, yet the state is the primary agent of
development.

– MICHAEL M'GONIGLE AND LOUISE TAKEDA,
THE LIBERAL LIMITS OF ENVIRONMENTAL LAW (2013)

It is clear from Chapters 6, 7, and 8 that Canadian laws, regulations, and
policies intended to protect human health from environmental hazards are
consistently and significantly weaker than comparable rules in other wealthy
western industrialized countries. This conclusion holds true across the
entire spectrum of environmental issues, including air quality, drinking
water, food safety, toxic substances, climate change, and biodiversity. The
consequences of these weak environmental laws and policies include thousands of premature deaths, millions of preventable illnesses, billions of
wasted dollars, and troubling injustices in the distribution of negative health
outcomes. These facts raise a fundamental question: why does Canada lag
behind in protecting the health of its citizens from environmental hazards?
What are the economic, political, legal, and cultural factors that may explain
this systematic failure? Finally, what are the countervailing forces that have
led to occasional successes in Canadian environmental law and policy?

Answering these questions is a fundamental prerequisite to the final section of this book, which outlines potential solutions to Canada's environmental health problems.

Global Factors

Environmental law, not only in Canada but everywhere, is limited by three fundamental constraints. First, environmental law and policy fails to recognize the laws of nature (e.g., laws of thermodynamics) and the fact that the Earth is finite. As far back as the sixth century AD, the Roman Code of Justinian stated: "The laws of nature, which are observed by all nations alike, are established, as it were, by divine providence, and remain ever fixed and immutable."[1] Albert Einstein observed: "Everything that takes place is determined by laws of nature." More recently, the World Commission on Environment and Development (the Brundtland Commission) concluded: "Today, legal regimes are being rapidly outdistanced by the accelerating pace and expanding scale of impacts on the environmental base of development. Human laws must be reformulated to keep human activities in harmony with the unchanging and universal laws of nature."[2]

Despite the wishful thinking of industry, politicians, and some economists, the laws and limits of nature cannot be overturned by Parliament, provincial legislatures, or the free market. Extensive studies indicate that humanity has already surpassed the healthy limits of damage to vital natural systems, including the climate, the nitrogen cycle, and biodiversity.[3] Although limits to growth have been discussed since the pioneering Club of Rome report in 1972 and are garnering increasing academic attention, only a handful of nations have genuinely acknowledged the reality of ecological limits and responded in a meaningful way.[4] According to three Canadian environmental law professors: "The function of environmental law, therefore, remains limited to mitigating the worst effects of the dominant model of economic development rather than fundamentally challenging or transforming it."[5]

Second, environmental law suffers from a glaring internal contradiction.[6] The roles of lawmaker and policeman are both allocated to the state, but the state is dependent on revenue generated by the ecologically destructive activities that it is ostensibly supposed to regulate. The oil and gas industry and the agriculture, mining, chemicals, forestry, fishing, manufacturing, and construction sectors all provide governments with personal and corporate income taxes, payroll taxes, royalties, sales taxes, and other revenues. In societies where continued economic growth is viewed as essential, maintaining or improving the competitiveness of these sectors is regarded as the highest priority.

Third, an array of factors related to political economy also constrain the effectiveness of environmental law. These factors include globalization, trade liberalization, the primacy of private property rights over the public interest, the dominant role of transnational corporations, laissez-faire capitalism seeking limitless growth, the cultural emphasis on consumerism, and the linear economic model, in which the natural world is treated as a mere inventory of "natural resources" intended for human use and a garbage can for our pollution and waste.

While these three problems are daunting impediments to the successful enactment, implementation, and enforcement of environmental law, they apply to all western industrialized nations. As such, they cannot explain the exceptional weakness of Canadian environmental law. To probe Canada's particularly poor laws, regulations, standards, policies, and approach to enforcement requires an examination of factors that are specific to the Canadian context.

Economic Factors

The dominant reasons for Canada's relatively weak environmental laws are rooted in economics. There is a widespread misperception that Canada's economy is dependent on the extraction and export of natural resources. Agriculture, forestry, mining, fishing, and the oil and gas industry do provide substantial employment, tax revenue, and export earnings. However, these sectors contribute only about 15 percent of Canada's GDP. Of the more than 17 million Canadians in the labour market, 800,000 are directly employed in the natural resources sector, while approximately 800,000 jobs are indirectly dependent on natural resources.[7] In total, the natural resources sector accounts for less than 10 percent of all jobs in Canada.

It is in the field of exports that natural resources do dominate, accounting for slightly over half of all Canadian exports. Resource exports are defined as energy, forestry, agricultural products, and industrial materials (which include metals and chemicals such as potash and petroleum-based chemicals). In 2011, Canada was the largest producer of potash in the world, the second-largest producer of uranium, the third-largest producer of natural gas, hydroelectricity, and primary aluminum, the sixth-largest oil producer, and among the top ten producers for many metals and minerals, ranging from gold and diamonds to nickel and zinc.[8]

Decades of concerted effort to diversify Canada's economy and overcome our reputation as hewers of wood and drawers of water bore fruit in
the latter half of the twentieth century, as demonstrated by the emergence
and growth of the aerospace, telecommunication, and automotive industries. The share of Canadian exports represented by value-added products
peaked at nearly 60 percent in 1999.[9] However, since the election of Prime
Minister Stephen Harper, Canada has re-emphasized natural resources,
while simultaneously losing hundreds of thousands of jobs in manufacturing. The share of value-added exports from Canada fell to less than 40 percent
in 2011.[10]

Canadian industry, particularly the natural resources sector, has a disproportionately large impact on Canadian environmental law and policy.
Over the past four decades, Canadian business leaders have repeatedly
delayed, weakened, and reversed progress in laws and policies intended to
protect the environment. Canada's perceived economic dependence on the
resource sector leads to "rapid, opportunistic extraction" and constrains
the development of systemic, long-term approaches to sustainable environmental management.[11] Industry opposes national air quality standards, restrictions on logging in old-growth forests, constraints on fishing (even in
marine protected areas), requirements to clean up contaminated sites, laws
to reduce greenhouse gas emissions, and the phasing out of pesticides prohibited in other countries. While it may be common in many countries for
industry to oppose environmental regulation, Canada stands out in terms of
governments' willingness to respond to this opposition by consistently placing private interests ahead of the public good.

There are countless examples of industry's negative effect on environmental law and policy. In the 1990s, the chemical industry used its influence on the prime minister to block changes that would have substantially
improved the *Canadian Environmental Protection Act.*[12] The recent weakening of many major Canadian environmental laws came as a response to
industry requests. Between 2008 and 2012, thirty-five petroleum corporations and associated industry organizations reported over 2,700 communications between their lobbyists and cabinet ministers, deputy ministers,
and other senior federal officials.[13] In 2011, the Canadian Council of Chief
Executives (CCCE) reiterated a long-standing complaint that Canadian
environmental law caused "overlap and duplication in regulatory requirements, and unnecessary delay in getting final approval."[14] Independent analysis consistently rejects these assertions.[15] According to *Forbes Magazine*,
Canada is already one of the world's top-ranked nations for investing and

doing business, in large part due to the lack of regulatory red tape.[16] Nevertheless, in 2012, an industry coalition composed of the Canadian Association of Petroleum Producers, the Canadian Energy Pipeline Association, the Canadian Petroleum Products Institute (now the Canadian Fuels Association), and the Canadian Gas Association proposed sweeping changes to federal environmental laws. Writing to Environment Minister Peter Kent and Natural Resources Minister Joe Oliver, the coalition stated: "The purpose of our letter is to express our shared views on the near-term opportunities before the government to address regulatory reform for major energy industries in Canada."[17] Six pieces of legislation were mentioned as "outdated" or providing barriers to "shovel ready projects," including the *Canadian Environmental Assessment Act, Species at Risk Act, National Energy Board Act, Fisheries Act, Migratory Birds Convention Act,* and *Navigable Waters Protection Act.* Mere months later, the federal government introduced two controversial omnibus budget implementation bills that granted industry's wishes. During the period between the introduction of these laws and their eventual enactment, oil industry lobbyists met with federal cabinet ministers fifty-three times while environmentalists managed only one such meeting.[18] Bills C-38 and C-45 dramatically weakened the *Canadian Environmental Assessment Act, Fisheries Act,* and *Navigable Waters Protection Act;* inserted a provision in the *Species at Risk Act* explicitly allowing pipeline companies to damage or destroy the critical habitat of endangered species; repealed the *Kyoto Protocol Implementation Act;* and disbanded the National Round Table on the Environment and the Economy. The rollbacks were described by Professor Robert Gibson as "a particularly extreme set of regressive changes."[19]

Whenever stronger environmental laws are proposed in Canada, industry reacts with exaggerated rhetoric that sways politicians despite the absence of a factual basis. A good example was industry's response to the Canadian Environmental Bill of Rights (Bill C-469), a private member's bill proposed in 2009 by New Democratic Party MP Linda Duncan that would have recognized citizens' right to live in a healthy environment and created procedural tools for defending this right. Representatives from the Canadian Chamber of Commerce, the Canadian Association of Petroleum Producers (CAPP), and other industry groups warned that Bill C-469 would freeze capital investment in Canada and inflict economic chaos while serving the interests of a small number of "special interest" groups.[20] Tom Huffaker, vice-president of CAPP, claimed that the legislation would "significantly increase the risks and costs of doing business in Canada. The result will be a loss of competitiveness for Canada, with reduced investment in economic opportunities and fewer jobs."[21] Warren Everson, senior vice president of the Canadian Chamber of Commerce, warned that Bill C-469 would result in "an endless litigation process brought by private parties."[22] Echoing the concerns voiced by industry, Conservative MP Mark Warawa described the Canadian Environmental Bill of Rights as a "kill the Alberta oil sands bill" and a "shut down Hydro-Québec bill." In reality, Bill C-469 was far weaker than the constitutional protection for the right to a healthy environment enjoyed in over one hundred countries (including wealthy western nations such as Norway and France).[23] There is no evidence that these powerful constitutional provisions have adversely affected national economies. The Canadian Environmental Bill of Rights was reintroduced as a private member's bill in 2014 by the NDP's Linda Duncan but currently has no chance of being enacted as it is opposed by the Conservative majority government.[24]

A similar example was the opposition of Canadian business to the Kyoto Protocol and its aversion to a national carbon tax. The CCCE vehemently opposed Canadian participation in the Kyoto Protocol, warning that ratifying the agreement would be economically disastrous for Canada. Although Prime Minister Jean Chrétien did ratify Kyoto in 2002, it turned out to be a symbolic gesture, unaccompanied by any strong regulations or fiscal policies that would have required emissions reductions. As noted in Chapter 8, despite widespread support from economists for a carbon tax and positive experiences with this tax in other countries, Prime Minister Harper adopted the oil and gas industry's position that such a tax would devastate the economy and cause widespread job losses, a position for which there is no evidence. Indeed, despite constitutional recognition of the right to a healthy environment and a long-standing carbon tax, Norway continues to be one of the world's major oil and gas exporters. Unlike Canada, however, Norway is a world leader in reducing water pollution, air pollution, and greenhouse gas emissions from the oil and gas industry.[25] Since 1997, Norway has successfully implemented zero-discharge targets for releases of environmentally hazardous substances to the sea from petroleum activities, reducing toxic discharges by thousands of tonnes.[26] Carbon dioxide emissions per unit of oil produced in Norway are only one-third of the international average.[27] Norway's carbon tax is regarded as the driving force that led to the technological innovation of sequestering carbon dioxide from oil and gas development in underground saline aquifers. Norway also captures a larger share of the revenue from these publicly owned natural resources, collecting a special 78 percent tax on the income of oil and gas companies. These policies have enabled the country to be debt-free and build up a publicly owned sovereign wealth fund with a value in early 2015 of over Cdn$1 trillion.[28] Canada on the other hand, with tremendous natural wealth but weak environmental laws, low taxes, and low royalties, has a national debt of over $500 billion (over $1 trillion if provincial debts are included) and no sovereign wealth fund. Canada also lags behind in terms of innovation (ranked thirteenth out of sixteen large wealthy nations by the Conference Board of Canada) and private sector investment in research and development (fifteenth out of sixteen), problems that could be at least partially addressed by stronger environmental policies.[29]

For over a decade, since Canada ratified Kyoto in 2002, successive federal governments have pledged to implement regulations to limit greenhouse gas emissions from the booming and immensely profitable oil and gas industry. It was later revealed that Prime Minister Chrétien made a backroom deal with CAPP, promising that new rules would be limited to intensity-based targets that allow total emissions to continue increasing, and that industry's costs of meeting these targets would be capped at a very modest level.[30] In 2013, the oil and gas industry used bogus arguments to water down and further delay provincial and federal regulation of greenhouse gas emissions. CAPP warned that Alberta's proposed regulations could result in a ninefold increase in the cost of meeting environmental standards – from $0.09 per barrel of oil to $0.90. According to CAPP, this "dramatic step" would make the industry less competitive and threaten future investment in the oil sands, absurd assertions in light of maximum costs of less than a dollar per barrel.[31] As of 2015, Alberta has not yet moved forward with the modest strengthening of its regulations. As of 2015, no federal regulations governing emissions from the oil and gas sector have been enacted despite a decade of promises, with Prime Minister Harper claiming that it would be "crazy economic policy" to do so at a time when oil prices were falling.[32] In 2013, the federal government caved in to another oil and gas industry demand by reducing regulatory requirements for offshore oil and gas exploration. The previous rules required all new offshore wells to undergo an environmental assessment, while the new rules require an assessment only for the first well in a region, with assessments for subsequent wells subject to the minister's discretion. This creates a situation where industry will be able to influence the minister to forgo additional assessments.[33]

The influence of Canadian industry extends to battling against environmental laws in other jurisdictions, often with support from Canadian governments. In some cases, the oil and gas industry has dictated Canadian foreign policy, collaborating with the federal government to lobby against stronger environmental laws in the United States (e.g., California's low-carbon fuel standard) and Europe (e.g., the European Union's Fuel Quality Directive) and to lobby for approval of pipeline infrastructure (e.g., the Keystone XL Pipeline).[34] As noted earlier, at the behest of the asbestos industry, Canada spent tens of millions of dollars promoting the use of asbestos in developing nations and repeatedly scuttled efforts to restrict international trade in asbestos pursuant to the Rotterdam Convention.[35]

Beginning in the 1980s, both federal and provincial governments embraced a neoliberal agenda that prioritized debt and deficit reduction, deregulation, privatization, downsizing of government, and free trade, at the expense of social programs and environmental protection. Prime Ministers Brian Mulroney and Jean Chrétien ushered in the North American Free Trade Agreement, which has enabled American corporations to challenge and overturn Canadian environmental laws, forced Canada to pay hundreds of millions of dollars in compensation, and discouraged both federal and provincial governments from passing stronger environmental laws. The Liberal government under Chrétien slashed hundreds of millions of dollars from Environment Canada's budget in an effort to balance the budget, turning the seventh-largest federal department into the smallest. Conservative governments in Alberta and Ontario made even deeper cuts to provincial environment budgets during the 1990s. Environmental regulations were cut as part of "red tape reduction" programs, and there was a shift to voluntary programs and industry self-regulation.[36]

Another factor that hampers Canadian environmental law is the concentrated ownership of the media in Canada.[37] Privately owned media conglomerates are dependent on advertising revenue and are understandably reluctant to bite the hands that feed them by providing extensive or critical coverage of environmental issues. Five major conglomerates control over two-thirds of the media in Canada, based on share of revenues. Four companies control almost three-quarters of the newspaper industry. Canada's major broadcasters refused to air advertisements that challenged Canada's addictions to cars and economic growth, resulting in a lawsuit based on freedom of expression.[38] A notorious example of the media's negative influence is the practice of providing equal air time to a handful of scientists who deny that humans are changing the climate, despite a high level of consensus on the issue among scientists in this field.[39] Canadian broadcasters have repeat- edly refused to allow the Green Party leader to participate in leaders' debates during federal election campaigns. Although the Canadian Broadcasting Corporation is a public broadcaster, it has been subject to substantial budget cuts and increased political interference. The fear of further cuts appears to have influenced its journalistic behaviour, as it has become more small-c conservative.[40] In 2011, 95 percent of the Canadian newspapers that en- dorsed a candidate for prime minister chose Stephen Harper.[41] The bottom line, as summarized by Professor Donald Gutstein, is that "corporate power is in the driver's seat. It has the money, organization, and access to the media."[42]

It is also worth emphasizing that many major industries and corpora- tions have a long history of lying about the health and environmental conse- quences of their products, processes, and emissions.[43] As historians Gerald Markowitz and David Rosner concluded in their book *Deceit and Denial: The Deadly Politics of Industrial Pollution,* numerous industries have "re- sponded to potent evidence of the dangers of their products by hiding information, controlling research, continuing to market their products as safe when they knew they were dangerous, enlisting industry-wide groups to participate in denying that there was a problem, and attempting to influence the political process to avoid regulation."[44] The lead, asbestos, tobacco, chemical, and fossil fuel industries have manipulated and mis- represented science in efforts to delay, avoid, or overturn stronger environ- mental laws.[45] Unfortunately, this history of consistent dishonesty is rarely, if ever, taken into account by regulators in formulating, implementing, or enforcing environmental laws and policies in Canada.

Political Factors
The economic factors described in the preceding section also extend their tentacles into the discussion of political factors. The opponents of stronger environmental regulation are powerful, wealthy, and organized, whereas supporters and prospective beneficiaries of such laws tend to be relatively weak, poor, and diffuse. The political system is generally conservative, defending the status quo and favouring those with education, money, and power, rather than the poor and marginalized communities who bear the disproportionate burden of environmental harm.[46] Specific aspects of Canada's political system exacerbate the problem, resulting in industry's tremendous influence on governments at all levels.

Canada is one of a shrinking minority of nations that employs a first- past-the-post (FPTP) electoral system, which allows a party to form a powerful majority government despite receiving a minority of the vote.[47] Canada has had more than a dozen false majority governments since 1920, an outcome possible only in an FPTP electoral system. For example, all three of Prime Minister Chrétien's Liberal majority governments won only a minority (40 percent) of the popular vote. Similarly, Stephen Harper's Conservatives earned less than 40 percent of the popular vote in the 2011 federal election but formed a majority government with 54 percent of the seats. Professor Peter Russell describes such outcomes as "false majorities" that pose a serious threat to democracy. There are no effective checks and balances to prevent a prime minister with a false majority from implementing an agenda opposed by the majority of Canadians.[48] This is precisely what has occurred with Prime Minister Harper's repeated attacks on Canadian environmental law and policy, which a strong majority of Canadians opposed.

Smaller parties such as the Green Party are at a substantial disadvantage in FPTP systems because public support does not translate into elected representatives. In British Columbia's 2001 provincial election, the Green Party earned 12 percent of the popular vote but got zero seats. In 2008, the federal NDP received over 1 million more votes than the Bloc Quebecois, yet won thirteen fewer seats (thirty-seven versus fifty), while the Green Party received nearly as many votes as the Bloc but won no seats at all. The Green Party earned 4 percent of the vote in the 2011 federal election but elected only one MP.

The dominant electoral system worldwide is proportional representation, which does a much better job of fairly representing the voting intentions of the public. A party earns seats based on its proportion of the popular vote. For example, in Germany's 2013 election, the Green Party earned 9 percent of the vote and won 63 seats, approximately 10 percent of the Bundestag. In New Zealand's 2011 election, the Greens secured 11 percent of the vote and 14 of 120 seats in parliament. The Green Party has been part of national coalition governments in countries such as Germany, New Zealand, Belgium, Finland, the Netherlands, Ireland, and France. As a result, Green parties in Europe and New Zealand have exerted a positive influence on environmental law in these countries over the course of the past three decades.[49] Proportional representation also facilitates pluralism, encouraging a greater diversity of approaches to sustainability, as demonstrated in Europe. Countries with proportional representation systems also enjoy much higher rates of voter turnout and elect a higher proportion of women and minorities.

Another major problem for Canadian environmental law is the extreme and increasing concentration of political power in the offices of the prime minister and premiers. According to experts, Canada's prime minister wields much more power than the leaders of other western democracies.[50] This unparalleled concentration of power has resulted in Canada's federal government being described as a "court government" (in the medieval sense of courtiers) and even a "friendly dictatorship."[51] The prime minister appoints cabinet ministers and deputy ministers; signs nomination papers for all prospective MPs; appoints judges to the Supreme Court, Federal Court, and provincial courts; selects the members of agencies, boards, and tribunals; and chooses the heads of Crown corporations. Thus, the prime minister has a substantial influence over all three branches of government – legislative, executive, and judicial. By 2015, Prime Minister Harper had appointed seven of the nine judges of the Supreme Court, with one of his appointees rejected as unconstitutional. Harper's appointments at the provincial level include law professors with a history of criticizing the *Canadian Charter of Rights and Freedoms*. Cabinet ministers serve at the prime minister's pleasure, meaning that if they do not follow instructions, they can be demoted to the backbenches. Canadian legislators allow themselves to be whipped or coerced into voting in accordance with their leader's directions, rather than acting in the best interests of their constituents, their province, or the country. In a majority government, the prime minister has complete control of the making (or unmaking) of environmental legislation, as well as the implementation and enforcement of environmental laws, policies, and programs. Green Party MP Elizabeth May observed in her book *Losing Confidence:* "Although the trend toward increasing prime ministerial powers began under Prime Minister Trudeau, the exercise of total control under Stephen Harper is unlike anything in Canadian tradition."[52]

Unlike the United States, Canada's parliamentary system does not separate the legislative and executive powers of government. In the American system, Congress enacts detailed environmental laws that mandate the executive branch to act in accordance with the spirit and intent of the legislation. Congress also serves as an essential counterweight to the president's power. In Canada, when there is a majority government, environmental laws are deliberately crafted in general terms with a maximum of discretion and few if any mandatory duties, giving the executive branch wide leeway in the implementation and enforcement of the laws. For example, legislation in the United States mandates federal environmental assessment in a detailed array of circumstances. In Canada, changes made to the *Canadian*

Environmental Assessment Act in 2012 reduced the number of mandatory federal environmental assessments from several thousand annually to less than two dozen, while giving the environment minister the discretion to require additional assessments. Canada's *Species at Risk Act* gives cabinet the discretion to follow or ignore the recommendations of expert scientists about adding species to the list of endangered species. In contrast, the US *Endangered Species Act* requires the government to follow scientists' decisions in listing species. In the United States, governments that fail to follow their own laws can be held accountable through the courts, while in Canada the judiciary is reluctant to overturn government's exercise of discretion except in the most extreme cases.

Regulatory capture is a problem in which the agencies intended to oversee a particular industry begin to put that industry's private interests ahead of the public interest. This is a frequent problem in Canada, demonstrated by governments' support of and advocacy for the oil sands, asbestos, and pesticides prohibited in other nations.[53] A related concern is the revolving door between powerful corporations and the highest levels of political appointees. Ian Brodie, Prime Minister Harper's first chief of staff, subsequently became a lobbyist for Hill and Knowlton, a firm whose clients include Enbridge, Shell Canada, CNOOC International, and many other large corporations. Nigel Wright, Harper's chief of staff who lost his position in the Senate expenses scandal, returned to the private sector with Onex Corporation, where he is well-placed for future lobbying efforts. Peter Kent worked at Hill and Knowlton prior to his appointment as environment minister by Harper. In his first two years as environment minister, Kent met forty-eight times with lobbyists for the oil and gas industry and only seven times with representatives of environmental groups.[54] Thus it comes as no surprise that Kent belittled environmentalists and sang the praises of "ethical oil."[55]

Canada's parliamentary system is being further degraded by the increasing use of omnibus bills covering huge numbers of different issues. The major assaults on Canadian environmental law in 2012 were made through omnibus budget implementation bills, shielding them from the regular process of parliamentary scrutiny by the House of Commons Standing Committee on Environment and Sustainable Development. Despite pleas from experts and scientists, not a single change was made to these radical environmental law rollbacks from the time of their introduction to when they were signed into law by the Governor General, illustrating the declining influence of Parliament and parliamentary committees. In 2014, another omnibus budget implementation bill amended the *Canada Marine Act* in ways that undermine environmental protection.[56]

In attempting to support Canadian industry, politicians routinely misrepresent Canada's environmental record. Despite the overwhelming evidence that Canada is an environmental laggard, Environment Minister Peter Kent stated in 2012 that Environment Canada is a world-class leader in "developing, implementing and enforcing national, science-based environmental regulations and standards."[57] Also in 2012, Natural Resources Minister Joe Oliver claimed that despite his government's focus on speeding up resource extraction, Canada will maintain "the highest possible standards for protecting the environment."[58] Former Alberta premier Alison Redford repeatedly claimed that "the truth is that Alberta is home to some of the most environmentally friendly legislation in the world."[59] Despite the absurdity of these assertions, they are printed by the media with only occasional criticism.[60]

Legal Factors

A critically important legal factor contributing to the weakness of Canadian environmental law is the Canadian Constitution. A constitution is the supreme or highest law of a nation, meaning that all other laws must be consistent with it. It establishes the rules that guide and constrain government powers, defines the relationships between institutions, protects human rights, and reflects a society's most cherished values. Because the environment is not mentioned in Canada's constitution, there is much uncertainty about the allocation of responsibilities in this field. This uncertainty sabotages both federal and provincial governments' willingness and ability to enact and enforce environmental laws and regulations.[61] Governments either pass the buck (including downloading responsibilities onto underresourced municipalities) or resist intervention by other levels of government.[62] Provinces, with jurisdiction over natural resources, are generally opposed to federal environmental regulation. Constitutional ambiguity also results in a lack of transparency and accountability. Climate change, smog, and endangered species are examples of issues where constitutional squabbling has impeded Canada's progress towards the implementation of effective solutions.

It has been understood for over a hundred years that Canada's constitutional arrangements are inadequate for tackling environmental problems. In 1912, a paper on water pollution published by Prime Minister Wilfrid Laurier's Commission of Conservation identified the problems associated with jurisdictional uncertainty.[63] In 1969, Prime Minister Pierre Trudeau said: "This challenge of pollution of our rivers, and lakes, of our farmlands and forests, and of the very air we breathe, cannot be met effectively in our federal state without some constitutional reforms or clarification."[64] In 1970, Dale Gibson, one of Canada's leading constitutional law experts, concluded that amendments were required to dispel doubts about the environmental powers of both levels of government and to provide for improved environmental management.[65] In 1991, lawyer Paul Muldoon asserted that the federal government's constitutional powers were inadequate to support a strong role in environmental protection.[66] In 1992, the Supreme Court ruled that the environment "is a constitutionally abstruse matter which does not comfortably fit within the existing division of powers without considerable overlap and uncertainty."[67] In 1996, Kathryn Harrison criticized Ottawa's tendency to defer to the provinces on environmental policy.[68] In 2007, Stewart Elgie concluded that the ongoing uncertainty about the scope of jurisdiction sabotaged the federal government's ability to address modern environmental challenges, such as climate change.[69] Similarly, in 2011, Alastair Lucas and Jenette Yearsley questioned the federal government's constitutional ability to enact detailed laws governing greenhouse gas emissions.[70]

Another major problem caused by constitutional uncertainty is that corporations often challenge Canadian environmental laws – both provincial and federal – as being beyond the jurisdiction of the government that passed them. For example, the Supreme Court of Canada struck down a Manitoba law that imposed liability upon industrial polluters whose mercury discharges harmed fisheries.[71] Provisions of the federal *Fisheries Act* have been struck down in cases involving environmental damage inflicted by logging companies.[72] The *Ocean Dumping Control Act* was attacked by logging company Crown Zellerbach and was narrowly upheld by the Supreme Court in 1988.[73] In a case involving the Oldman Dam, the constitutionality of the federal environmental assessment process was challenged by the Government of Alberta but upheld by the Supreme Court.[74] The ability of municipal governments to protect the environment was also the subject of a constitutional challenge. When the town of Hudson, Quebec, banned the use of pesticides for cosmetic and nonessential purposes, lawn-care companies sued, arguing that municipalities had no jurisdiction to regulate pesticides. The Supreme Court ruled that all levels of government have a part to play in environmental protection, although it did not clarify the boundaries between those roles.[75]

In the 1990s, Ottawa almost lost its ability to regulate toxic pollution because of a constitutional challenge. The case arose when Hydro-Québec was charged with dumping PCBs into the St. Maurice River, in violation of the *Canadian Environmental Protection Act.* Hydro-Québec's defence was that the Act was unconstitutional – that the federal government lacked the requisite authority to regulate toxic substances. According to Hydro-Québec, pollution was a local matter falling within the provincial government's exclusive jurisdiction. Although most Canadians would reject such a defence as nonsense, Hydro-Québec was successful before the Quebec trial court, Quebec Superior Court, and Quebec Court of Appeal. Fortunately, a narrow majority of the Supreme Court upheld the constitutionality of Canada's most important environmental law, relying on the federal government's criminal law power.[76]

The most recent constitutional challenges to Canadian environmental laws involve the *Canadian Environmental Assessment Act, 2012* and the *Species at Risk Act.* Taseko Limited's proposed Prosperity gold mine in British Columbia has been repeatedly rejected by the federal government because of an array of significant environmental impacts, including the destruction of Fish Lake and adverse impacts on Aboriginal rights. In 2014, Taseko filed a lawsuit arguing that portions of the *Canadian Environmental Assessment Act, 2012* were unconstitutional.[77] Also in 2014, LGX Oil and Gas and the city of Medicine Hat sued the federal government for establishing an emergency order to protect the critical habitat of the greater sage-grouse.[78] The argument was that key parts of the *Species at Risk Act* lacked a valid constitutional basis.

Canada's constitutional gap is also used to delay, block, or water down proposed environmental legislation and regulations. A classic example is federal endangered species legislation. The United States passed a strong *Endangered Species Act* in 1973, yet three decades of prolonged effort from environmentalists and scientists were required in Canada before the weak *Species at Risk Act* was passed in 2002.[79] In part by playing the constitutional card, provinces and industries opposed to the act delayed the law and eventually secured "federal legislation that would help to cement a more decentralized vision of Canadian environmental responsibilities."[80] Another example was the *Nuclear Control and Administration Act,* introduced in 1977 to replace a badly outdated law governing the use of nuclear energy. Provinces objected that the proposed legislation invaded their jurisdiction and delayed its passage for twenty years.[81]

In addition to constitutional problems, Canadian environmental law is plagued by a number of systemic weaknesses, including:

- absence of laws that are commonplace in other industrialized nations
- excessive discretion in existing laws and regulations
- inadequate resources for implementation and enforcement
- failure to reflect contemporary scientific knowledge
- judicial conservatism
- insufficient opportunities for public participation
- undue reliance on a narrow range of law and policy options.[82]

Unlike the United States and Europe, Canada has no legally binding national standards for air quality and safe drinking water. Unlike the United States, Canada lacks federal laws governing the cleanup of contaminated sites, the disposal of hazardous waste, and citizens' right to know about toxic pollution in their communities. The chronic problems of excessive discretion and inadequate resources were discussed earlier in this chapter and in Chapter 8.

Environmental law in Canada is plagued by a failure to reflect contemporary scientific knowledge and understanding, reflected in a reductionist approach that underestimates the complexity, uncertainty, and unpredictability of biological and physical systems.[83] For example, endangered species legislation and laws governing protected areas are oblivious to key principles of conservation biology, such as the importance of biodiversity hotspots, endemic species, large reserves, buffer zones, and maintaining or restoring connectivity.[84] Canada's *Species at Risk Act* protects only the "residences" of endangered species found on federal lands or in federal waters, instead of protecting the habitat critical to their survival regardless of where it occurs.[85] In some provinces, including Alberta, Manitoba, and Ontario, industrial activities continue to be allowed in parks and protected areas.[86] Fisheries are permitted despite the total absence of data on some targeted species and evidence of compelling declines in other species.[87] Prime Minister Harper eliminated the Science Advisor to the Prime Minister, disbanded the National Round Table on the Environment and the Economy, and issued controversial edicts prohibiting government scientists from speaking publicly. One of the world's leading scientific journals, *Nature*, criticized the federal government's policy of muzzling environmental scientists, stating that "Canada's generally positive foreign reputation as a progressive, scientific nation masks some startlingly poor behaviour."[88] In 2012, Harper appointed a new deputy minister, Bob Hamilton, to lead Environment Canada. When asked, at a hearing held by the Standing Committee on Environment and Sustainable Development, to explain the causes of climate change, Hamilton responded, "Wow. They didn't tell me I'd have to answer questions like that when I took this job. I think that it's – I don't know the answer to that."[89]

On numerous vital environmental issues ranging from chemicals management and drinking water safety to air quality and climate change, Canada has relied heavily on voluntary initiatives, information, and subsidies. Unfortunately, voluntary initiatives are largely ineffective in achieving environmental objectives.[90] Information-based policies enjoy limited success because only a small percentage of people or businesses alter their behaviour.[91] There is disagreement about whether subsidies are effective or efficient.[92] Feed-in tariffs that pay high prices for solar and wind have been widely praised, whereas rebates for the purchase of fuel-efficient vehicles have been panned.[93]

Chapter 8 demonstrated Canada's reluctance to use fiscal policies to address environmental problems. A growing body of evidence indicates that price changes can spur technological progress, resulting in environmental gains.[94] Economic instruments or market-based approaches are increasingly popular because they are efficient and offer "dynamic incentives for technology innovation and diffusion."[95] For example, the United States achieved environmental benefits at reduced cost (compared with traditional regulatory approaches) by implementing tradable permit systems to reduce sulphur dioxide emissions, eliminate chlorofluorocarbons (CFCs), and decrease air pollution from stationary sources in Los Angeles.[96] Some experts believe that market-based regulations, such as renewable portfolio standards (imposing quotas for renewable energy production) or low-emission vehicle quotas (e.g., California's zero-emission vehicle regulation) offer the best of both worlds by combining the strengths of regulations and the market.[97] In Europe, there has been a shift towards combining policy instruments in more sophisticated mixes (capturing the strengths of different tools).[98]

Canadian courts sometimes play an important role in fostering accountability by holding governments and corporations responsible for failing to obey environmental laws. For example, Syncrude was fined $3 million following the death of more than 1,600 ducks in a tar sands tailings pond.[99] In 2014, a Quebec-based mining company, Bloom Lake, was ordered to pay $7.5 million after pleading guilty to 45 violations of the *Fisheries Act*, reportedly the highest fine ever levied in Canada for an environmental offence.[100]

However, the judicial system's ability to ensure accountability is undermined by several factors, including the courts' historical bias towards private rights rather than the public interest, the absence of effective environmental rights, limited access to the courts in some jurisdictions (e.g., Alberta), the high costs of litigation, judicial deference towards government decision makers, unfamiliarity with environmental cases, and precedents imposing low penalties for environmental offences. Corporations are aware of the low probability of being caught breaking environmental laws, the even lower likelihood of being prosecuted and convicted, and the high probability that any sentence imposed will be a slap on the wrist. Far more Canadians have gone to jail for attempting to protect the environment than for damaging it. A recent decision of the Federal Court in a lawsuit challenging the use of lakes as tailings ponds for mining waste illustrates the political naivete of the judiciary. The court ruled that the *Fisheries Act* authorizes regulations permitting destruction of fish habitat, and concluded that for opponents of this interpretation, "the will of the people, with respect to legislation, can be expressed at the ballot box."[101]

Another weakness is that people in various regions of Canada "do not have an equal ability to access information about, and participate in, environmental decision-making," because mechanisms are lacking or are too expensive, time-consuming, or ineffective.[102] Canada finished last in a 2010 study comparing the effectiveness of freedom of information laws in parliamentary democracies.[103] A 2013 report from the Centre for Law and Democracy ranked Canada fifty-seventh out of eighty-nine countries in providing access to information.[104] Worse yet, Prime Minister Harper's government has made it more difficult for Canadians to participate in public processes such as environmental assessments and hearings for proposed pipelines.[105]

Cultural Factors

Canadians consistently express strong environmental values in public opinion polls, but there is a large gulf between their words and their actions. We are among the world's most prolific consumers of oil, natural gas, electricity, and water. Canadians are world leaders in the unenviable categories of household garbage production and per capita emissions of greenhouse gases, sulphur dioxide, nitrogen oxides, carbon monoxide, and volatile organic compounds. Our ecological footprint, which provides a rough yardstick of resource consumption and pollution, is among the world's largest. What accounts for this contradiction? One possible explanation is that

Canadians are ecologically illiterate, meaning that we do not comprehend the environmental consequences of our actions. A report prepared for Environment Canada analyzed dozens of existing studies and concluded that "Canadians consistently showed little genuine understanding, or knowledge, of environmental issues."[106] One in four Canadians has no idea where their tap water comes from, and six in ten have no idea how much their water costs.[107] On average, Canadians use five times more water than they estimate.[108] Many Canadians are "clearly deficient in overall energy literacy," such as being unable to correctly identify the source of the majority of electricity produced in their province.[109] A 2013 survey found that six in ten Canadians were unaware that Canada withdrew from the Kyoto Protocol.[110] Recent research indicates that the less Canadians know about complex environmental issues, the more they avoid learning about them, preferring to seek solace in the (mistaken) belief that governments will solve the problems.[111]

Another potential explanation for the chasm between values and actions is that Canadians' pride in this country's striking natural beauty, bounty, and immensity creates a blind spot about environmental impacts. Canada is a vast country whose small population is increasingly concentrated in a handful of cities. Relatively few people have witnessed the tar sands, open pit mines, industrial feedlots, or clearcuts that stretch as far as the eye can see. The most visible and prominent forms of air and water pollution have been dramatically reduced. Thus there may be an enduring cultural myth of a great green Canada, comparable to the notion that the United States is a land of unparalleled opportunity, when in fact upward income mobility in America lags behind many other countries.

Environmental literacy is higher in Europe than in Canada, contributing to a consensus on environmental issues that often crosses political lines.[112] For example, French parliamentarians from across the political spectrum voted by an overwhelming margin (531 in favour versus 23 opposed) to approve adding a Charter for the Environment to their constitution in 2005. In Germany, all major political parties support the *Energiewende*, the transition away from fossil fuels and nuclear energy to renewable energy. In Sweden, all parties embrace the national goal of achieving sustainability within a generation, which is entrenched in legislation.

The Canadian environmental movement is surprisingly weak in terms of both members and financial resources, hampering its ability to influence policymakers. Less than 1 percent of Canadians who volunteer do so for environmental organizations. Although 85 percent of Canadians make charitable donations, only 2 percent of the money is given to environmental organizations. The Sierra Club of Canada has between 5,000 and 10,000 members, whereas the US Sierra Club has approximately 1.4 million members. Most Canadian environmental groups are also hamstrung by their charitable status, which limits their ability to engage in political activities such as lobbying and participating in public discussions during elections. The Conservative government set aside $8 million in the 2012 budget to increase the Canada Revenue Agency's capacity for auditing environmental groups. After nine hundred audits, only one organization, Physicians for Global Survival, had its charitable status revoked for excessive political activity.[113]

Reasons for Optimism

Although the foregoing analysis may suggest that the prospects for stronger environmental laws, regulations, and policies in Canada are bleak, countervailing forces could tilt the balance in a greener direction. Canada has made progress in reducing some types of industrial air and water pollution, banning some toxic chemicals, phasing out the production, use, and release of ozone-depleting substances, upgrading municipal wastewater treatment, decreasing cosmetic pesticide use, and improving the safety of drinking water. Reasons for optimism include pressure upon Canada to honour international commitments and live up to its potential for leadership, waves of public pressure, the influence of the United States, the growing role of local governments, occasional instances of federal/provincial cooperation, and the strong track record of the Supreme Court of Canada.

Sources of international pressure vary. The Organisation for Economic Co-operation and Development has urged Canada to adopt a national carbon tax and use economic instruments to make polluters pay. The North American Commission for Environmental Cooperation has repeatedly concluded that Canada is not adequately enforcing its environmental laws. Nongovernmental organizations portray Canada as an environmental laggard in international forums, attempting to embarrass Canada into improving its record. Using markets to create pressure on industry rather than governments has resulted in some positive actions, such as modest improvements in forest practices.

Because of our close economic and cultural ties, the United States has always had a substantial influence on Canadian environmental law. This is a double-edged sword because on some issues the United States has higher standards, whereas on other issues American foot-dragging gives Canada an excuse for inaction. Positive examples include Canadian adoption of American rules for motor vehicle fuel efficiency, air pollution from transportation fuels, and, despite the long lag time before adoption, endangered species legislation. Negative examples include American delays in regulating industrial greenhouse gas emissions and updating legislation covering toxic substances. Although the European Union has surpassed the United States as a global environmental leader, Canada rarely emulates European environmental laws, standards, or policies. The proposed Canada-EU Free Trade Agreement could potentially force Canada to raise environmental standards to European levels.

In the past thirty-five years, the Supreme Court of Canada has issued consistently progressive decisions in environmental cases.[114] In 1978, in a case dealing with garbage dumped in a creek, the court stated that the prevention of pollution "is a matter of great public concern."[115] In the *Sparrow* case involving Aboriginal fishing rights, the court ruled that legitimate conservation concerns must always be the overriding priority in fisheries management, even where constitutionally protected Aboriginal rights are involved.[116] In *Friends of the Oldman River,* the Supreme Court found that Ottawa had failed to follow its own rules governing environmental assessment and stated that "the protection of the environment has become one of the major challenges of our time."[117] In *Hydro-Québec,* the court upheld the constitutionality of the *Canadian Environmental Protection Act,* and described protecting the environment as a matter of "super-ordinate public importance."[118] In *Hudson,* the court upheld a municipal pesticide bylaw, endorsed the precautionary principle as a key element of environmental management, and concluded: "Our common future, that of every Canadian community, depends on a healthy environment."[119] In a case involving Imperial Oil's liability for cleaning up a contaminated site in Quebec, the court strongly endorsed the polluter-pays principle.[120] In a 2004 case involving damage to forests, the court repeatedly referred to the fundamental value of environmental protection and suggested that the law must evolve to assist in realizing this value.[121] In 2008, the Supreme Court endorsed the awarding of damages in an environmental class action lawsuit based on dust and foul odours from a cement plant.[122] Most recently, it reiterated the importance of broadly interpreting environmental laws and applying the precautionary principle.[123] The Supreme Court has also made repeated references to the right of Canadians to live in a safe or healthy environment.[124]

Local governments in Canada are playing a more prominent role in environmental protection, due to public pressure, the downloading of responsibilities from provincial governments, and the Supreme Court decision in the *Hudson* case, which expanded the jurisdiction of municipalities in environmental governance. Canadian cities have gone further than senior levels of government in regulating pesticide use, investing in public transit, reducing greenhouse gas emissions, and preparing to adapt to climate change. Vancouver is internationally renowned for its excellent environmental record and ambitious plan to become the greenest city in the world.[125] Oakville, Ontario, recently enacted a bylaw requiring polluters who release more than 300 kilograms of fine particulate matter annually to obtain a municipal permit, in addition to any provincial approvals.[126] In response to a campaign led by the David Suzuki Foundation and Ecojustice, cities are passing resolutions recognizing the environmental rights of their residents.[127] Richmond (BC), Montreal, Yellowknife, Victoria, Vancouver, and Hamilton were among the more than fifty early adopters.

The salience of environmental issues in terms of public opinion waxes and wanes. Canadian environmental policy is largely reactive. Major initiatives have coincided with periods of elevated public concern triggered by high-profile environmental disasters, from the Mississauga train derailment that led to enactment of the *Transportation of Dangerous Goods Act, 1992* to the extensive improvements to provincial drinking water rules after the Walkerton disaster. These events open policy windows at unpredictable times. Advocates of stronger environmental health laws and policies need to have well-crafted policy ideas and proposals prepared before appropriate policy windows open.[128] It is foreseeable that in the wake of a major public health disaster involving industrial chemicals or a large oil spill, a government could be persuaded to bring in comprehensive environmental law reforms.[129] Occasionally, concerted public pressure convinces Canadian governments to demonstrate leadership, as in the successful campaign to ban the use of bisphenol A in baby bottles.

It is noteworthy that in the majority of the cases where Canada has made substantial environmental progress (e.g., acid rain, ozone depletion, lead emissions from gasoline), strong regulations were the policy instrument used by governments to compel changes. The key characteristics of effective environmental laws include:

- clear jurisdiction or cooperation between different levels of government
- clear, measurable, and enforceable standards
- mandatory language instead of discretion

- effective compliance and enforcement mechanisms
- adequate resources for implementation and enforcement.

The success stories chronicled above indicate that there is the potential for making Canadian environmental law more effective in protecting human health and the environment if economic, political, and cultural barriers can be overcome.

Conclusion

Economic factors dominate the enactment, implementation, and enforcement of environmental law and policy in Canada to a greater extent than in many other nations. Canada's renewed dependence on natural resource industries, particularly for exports, has already led to the weakening of key environmental laws. Canada's unique parliamentary system, with a powerful prime minister, an unelected and unaccountable Senate, and a lack of separation of powers results in an absence of effective checks and balances. The first-past-the-post electoral system and the Canadian Constitution's failure to mention environmental rights and responsibilities exacerbate these political problems. Another factor is the surprising ecological illiteracy of many Canadians and the cultural perception of Canada as a vast and unpolluted land.

Altering the status quo is never easy, and is particularly difficult in the face of powerful entrenched interests. Political scientists describe a phenomenon called "path dependence," referring to the way in which past decisions limit future alternatives. After several decades of environmental budget cuts and watering down of environmental laws, it may be challenging to envision a new and more progressive direction for Canadian environmental law. Yet the staggering statistics set forth earlier in this book about the environmental burden of disease in Canada, as measured in premature deaths and unnecessary illnesses, combined with evidence of the associated economic and social costs, surely demand an extensive and coordinated response from governments. Since these adverse health impacts and costs are preventable, it behooves Canadian political leaders to explore the suite of policy responses that could be marshalled to save thousands of lives and billions of dollars.

PART 3

PRESCRIPTION

Catching Up with Environmental
Health Leaders

Most top-performing countries have achieved better health outcomes through actions on the broader determinants of health such as environmental stewardship and health-promotion programs.

– CONFERENCE BOARD OF CANADA (2013)

10

A Preventive and Precautionary Approach

It is environmental public health – the melding of environmental protection and public health concerns – which will provide the most effective path forward.

– PROFESSOR DAVID UHLMANN, UNIVERSITY OF MICHIGAN (2014)

This chapter sets forth a series of recommendations involving research, investment, education, and law reform intended to save lives, reduce costs, and transform Canada from a laggard to a leader in protecting the health of humans and ecosystems. To reflect the values of the overwhelming majority of its citizens, Canada must catch up to the level of protection for environmental health already provided by other wealthy industrialized countries. The following recommendations fall into five categories: (1) the development of a national environmental health action plan; (2) the integration of existing surveillance programs into a national environmental health surveillance system; (3) the strengthening of environmental laws, regulations, standards, and policies; (4) the implementation of measures to ensure effective enforcement of environmental laws; and (5) the recalibration of foreign policy to ensure consistent promotion of environmental health.

The majority of the following recommendations have been endorsed by doctors, scientists, and other health and environmental experts as well as

organizations such as the Canadian Cancer Society, the Learning Disabilities Association of Canada, the Canadian Public Health Association, the
Canadian Partnership for Child Health and the Environment, the Commission on the Future of Health Care in Canada, the American Academy of
Pediatrics, and the Canadian Lung Association.[1] These are actions that can
be taken immediately or within the short term, while the more challenging
changes required to overcome the systemic and institutional problems
facing Canada are addressed in Chapter 11.

National Environmental Health Action Plan

In the past, efforts to protect the health of Canadians from environmental
hazards have been ad hoc, reactive, fragmented, narrow, ineffective, inefficient, and inequitable. As noted in Chapter 6, Canada lacks a comprehensive
environmental health strategy or action plan. Most wealthy industrialized
nations, including the United States, Australia, and all western European
countries have already taken this vital first step. As scholars studying the
Australian experience in implementing a national environmental health
strategy concluded, "it is clear that the 21st century social and environmental challenges will require concerted national action if they are to be
faced effectively."[2]

To ensure that future efforts are systemic, proactive, results-oriented,
adaptive, effective, efficient, and equitable, Canada needs a national environmental health action plan. It must be national in scope in order to ensure
that the same level of protection is enjoyed by all Canadians, and because
everyone – governments, communities, businesses, and individuals – has a
role to play in developing and implementing solutions. A well-designed and
well-executed plan will save thousands of lives; prevent millions of illnesses
and disabilities; strengthen Canada's economy by stimulating innovation,
increasing productivity, and enabling people to reach their full potential;
and improve the quality of life for all Canadians, particularly the most vulnerable and marginalized individuals in our society.

Such a plan could be produced by an independent group of citizens in
consultation with Health Canada and Environment Canada, including health
professionals, toxicologists, epidemiologists, ecologists, policy experts, and
Aboriginal elders. Broad and inclusive public engagement would also be
essential. A potential model is the Greenest City Action Team appointed
by the City of Vancouver in its quest to become one of the greenest cities
in the world. The experts who comprised this team published two reports,

including a set of immediate short-term action items and a more comprehensive suite of long-term targets and timelines.[3] There was a broad outreach program using both in-person and online forums and tools. Vancouver has made substantial progress towards its goal, winning numerous national and international awards for municipal environmental leadership. A Canadian plan could also build on the David Suzuki Foundation's report *Prescription for a Healthy Canada: Towards a National Environmental Health Strategy*, which garnered widespread support from organizations such as the Canadian Cancer Society, the Canadian Public Health Association, and the Canadian Partnership for Child Health and the Environment.[4] The foundation's report inspired research by the Conference Board of Canada, which published environmental health policy lessons from other jurisdictions, including Sweden, Australia, and California.[5] The Canadian Public Health Association's report on the ecological determinants of health contains a suite of thoughtful recommendations.[6] Canada also has an opportunity to learn from innovations, success stories, failures, and best practices from other nations.

Targets and Timelines

As part of the national environmental health action plan, Canada should establish a comprehensive set of short-, medium-, and long-term environmental objectives, including specific targets and timelines for environmental health outcomes. Useful targets must be SMART:

- Specific – clearly articulated, well-defined and focused
- Measurable – able to determine extent of success or failure
- Achievable – realistic given constraints on resources and knowledge
- Relevant – related to a desired environmental outcome
- Time-bound – include a clear deadline for achieving results.

In 2004, the David Suzuki Foundation (DSF) worked with a group of environmental experts to produce *Sustainability within a Generation: A New Vision for Canada*, setting out a series of short-, medium-, and long-term targets for climate change, air pollution, water pollution, and the release of toxic substances. The targets were based on the best available scientific evidence as well as the objectives set (and in some cases already achieved) by nations leading the race towards a sustainable future. For example, DSF proposed long-term goals of reducing emissions of criteria air pollutants by 80 percent and reducing the release of toxic substances into the environment by 60 percent, both by 2030.[7]

Inspired by the work of the foundation, former prime minister Paul Martin's Liberal government began developing aggressive national environmental objectives. The draft objective for air pollution aimed to reduce concentrations of particulate matter and ground-level ozone "to levels where there is no discernible impact on health or ecosystems."[8] The draft targets sought to reduce emissions of smog-forming air pollutants – sulphur dioxide, nitrogen oxides, particulate matter, volatile organic compounds, and ammonia – by at least 75 percent from 2005 levels by 2030. Similarly, the draft objective for harmful chemicals was to eliminate industrial releases of persistent, bioaccumulative, and toxic substances by 2030 and prohibit their use in products by the same year. These draft targets were comparable to targets set by countries at the forefront of protecting their citizens' health and the environment, including Norway, Sweden, and Switzerland. Sweden, a world leader in reducing environmental impacts on health, has established national objectives and timelines for phasing out mercury, lead, carcinogens, mutagens, and substances that harm reproduction, as well as persistent and bioaccumulative substances.[9] Similarly, the Massachusetts *Toxic Use Reduction Act of 1989* successfully brought a preventive approach to the industrial use of toxic chemicals. Since 1990, releases of chemicals covered by the US Toxics Release Inventory have dropped by 90 percent in Massachusetts, while saving, not costing, industry millions of dollars.[10] The European Union has already prohibited the use of carcinogens, mutagens, and reproductive toxicants in cosmetics and personal care products.[11]

Unfortunately, these ambitious national environmental objectives were never adopted because Martin's government was defeated in 2005. To date, Canada has established a weak and uninspiring mish-mash of environmental objectives. Some of the broad goals are laudable, but many specific targets fail to meet the SMART criteria outlined above. The broad goal for air pollution is to "minimize the threats to air quality so that the air Canadians breathe is clean and supports healthy ecosystems."[12] The specific "target" for outdoor air pollution is to "improve air quality by ensuring compliance with new or amended regulated emission limits by 2020 and thus reducing emissions of air pollutants in support of AQMS [Air Quality Management System] objectives."[13] The problem with this so-called target is that there are no numerical goals identified, making it impossible to measure success or failure. Another weak target, lacking focus and a timeline, is to "reduce levels of human exposure to harmful substances."[14]

Environmental Health Tracking/Surveillance System

As discussed in Chapter 6, environmental health tracking or surveillance refers to the process of systematically collecting, analyzing, and communicating data on environmental hazards, population exposures, and associated health outcomes.[15] Leading experts agree that an environmental health surveillance system is "a fundamental requirement for the practice of public health in Canada ... [and] swift action on the part of government is appropriate."[16] Canada has an opportunity to learn from jurisdictions that are further ahead in developing national or regional environmental health surveillance systems. Canada is at the same point that the United States was at roughly a decade ago, when the Pew Commission on Environmental Health characterized the state of the American public health system's efforts in the field of environmental health as fragmented, neglected, and ineffective.[17]

The federal government, in partnership with the provinces, should establish a national environmental health tracking system.[18] The system would monitor environmental hazards, environmental exposures, and health impacts. Many pieces of this puzzle already exist in Canada, including biomonitoring data from the Canada Health Measures Survey, monitoring of air and water quality, the National Pollutant Release Inventory (NPRI), cancer registries, and waterborne and foodborne disease surveillance. However, this information needs to be systematically integrated in ways that produce and disseminate useful knowledge for health care professionals, policymakers, and researchers. Environmental health tracking systems in the United States, European Union, Japan, and Quebec could serve as models.[19] Quebec has the most advanced environmental health surveillance system in Canada.[20] Adequate funding for collecting, managing, and using environmental health data will require new investments by federal, provincial, and territorial governments.

Elements of the system would include national databases for boil-water advisories, waterborne disease outbreaks, air quality ratings, and poisonings. The federal government has acknowledged that integrating provincial/territorial data on boil-water advisories and violations of drinking water quality standards into a national database is an important step.[21] A report prepared for the Walkerton Inquiry recommended creating an online database of waterborne disease outbreaks.[22] The creation of a national poisoning database was recommended by the North American Commission for Environmental Cooperation and endorsed by the federal government.[23] The United States already maintains a national database of poisonings and produces regular public reports.[24] In contrast, the Canadian Association of

Poison Control Centres lacks adequate funding to function properly, as indicated by the lack of national poisoning data and numerous information gaps on its website.[25] Additional resources would enable data to be collected from provincial poison control centres, hospitals, and emergency medical facilities. All poisonings, including pesticide poisonings, should be designated as reportable events, facilitating proper surveillance and eventually prevention, regulatory, and education programs.[26] In the United States, the National Institute for Occupational Safety and Health recently published a how-to guide for state governments seeking to establish consistent surveillance and monitoring systems for pesticide-related injuries and illnesses. This could serve as a useful model for a Canadian initiative.[27] In 2014, the National Collaborating Centre for Environmental Health (NCCEH) published recommendations for improving food safety systems in Canada.[28]

Canada should develop a robust set of environmental health indicators, building on work that has been done in the United States, Europe, and Australia.[29] Publicizing indicators would contribute to accountability by enabling the public to monitor progress, and would also play a role in public education.

Increased Investments in Environmental Health Research

Several actions need to be initiated immediately to address knowledge gaps. As Dr. Donald Wigle, a leading expert on environmental threats to health, concluded, effective policy and program decisions urgently require "(1) research to better define environmental hazards, susceptible populations, and dose-response relationships and (2) tracking systems to monitor population exposure levels."[30] Canada should conduct a detailed national study to refine the estimates of the environmental burden of disease. This would provide valuable information for use in directing research, informing public education efforts, assisting physicians in providing advice to patients, and guiding health and environmental policymaking. Environmental health specialists across Canada identified this recommendation as a research priority of "high importance" to policymakers.[31]

It is inexcusable that the United States spends over a hundred times as much as Canada on environmental health research, monitoring, and education, given that their population is only nine times larger. Canada must increase funding for research on environmental health issues through the Canadian Institutes of Health Research (CIHR), the National Research Council, Health Canada, the Social Sciences and Humanities Research Council, and the Natural Sciences and Engineering Research Council. The

CIHR should establish an Institute for Environmental Health and make a significant long-term commitment to funding research on the health impacts of ecological change, the relationship between the ecological and social determinants of health, and appropriate strategies for mitigating the health impacts of global ecological change. Research should be focused on informing public policy and assisting medical professionals by identifying pathways from hazards to exposures; understanding the effects of these exposures on health; identifying vulnerable subpopulations; and exploring the health effects of new substances, substances in combination, and gene/environment interactions. Canada should significantly increase support for the NCCEH from its current paltry budget of $1.5 million per year. As pointed out in Chapter 6, its current budget is less than 1 percent of that of a comparable American institution.

Environmental Health Education Initiatives

According to eco-literacy expert Fritjof Capra, "in the coming decades, the survival of humanity will depend on our ecological literacy – our ability to understand the basic principles of ecology and to live accordingly. This means that eco-literacy must become a critical skill for politicians, business leaders, and professionals in all spheres, and should be the most important part of education at all levels – from primary and secondary schools to colleges, universities, and the continuing education and training of professionals."[32] Capra's conclusion has profound implications for both public education and the education and training of workers in the health care system. Norway recognizes the importance of ecological literacy, passing a law in 2006 mandating that sustainable development be taught in day care institutions.[33]

Despite advances in environmental curriculum, Canada's educational system still falls far short of giving people the ecological knowledge needed for society to make a successful transition to a sustainable future. Given the magnitude of the global environmental crisis and Canada's role in exacerbating rather than solving the problems, citizens are needed who can think ecologically, understand the interconnectedness of natural and human systems, and have the will, ability, and courage to act.

A key element of a proactive approach to environmental health is to provide citizens with the knowledge to make better everyday decisions. Disseminating health and environment information should be a priority for the Public Health Agency of Canada, Health Canada, Environment Canada, and their provincial/territorial counterparts. It will be important to find means of conveying the information gathered from the enhanced research, monitoring, and surveillance efforts recommended in this book to health care professionals and the general public. A commendable example of a step in the right direction occurred in November 2013 when Health Canada, in partnership with a number of NGOs, premiered Radon Awareness Month, marking the first substantial effort to educate Canadians about the dangers posed by radon.[34]

Legislative changes discussed in the following section – such as recognition of the right to live in a healthy environment and mandatory labelling of products containing carcinogens, genetically modified organisms, and other potentially hazardous substances – will also give Canadians new tools to protect their health from avoidable environmental threats.

A user-friendly website that provides environmental hazard information by postal code should be developed.[35] The federal government could provide accessible data on air pollution and toxic releases from the National Pollutant Release Inventory. The provincial and territorial governments could provide information on items such as contaminated sites and landfills. Municipalities could contribute reports on drinking water quality, which some provincial laws began to require in the aftermath of the Walkerton disaster. Such a website could develop, over time, into a single integrated window – sharing environmental health information on a geographic basis from all levels of government, businesses, and nongovernmental organizations.

Governments should support public education and outreach programs about environmental health delivered by organizations including the Canadian Cancer Society, Canadian Lung Association, Canadian Institute for Child Health, Learning Disabilities Association of Canada, Canadian Association of Physicians for the Environment, Canadian Partnership for Child Health and the Environment, Pollution Probe, Environmental Defence Canada, David Suzuki Foundation, and similar groups. An excellent example of an online resource is the Canadian Environmental Health Atlas.[36]

Another key educational priority involves strengthening the health care profession's knowledge of environmental health issues. As the Canadian Medical Association pointed out, when it comes to environment/health connections, "public and health care provider information is sorely lacking."[37] The federal and provincial governments should support the development of curricula and teaching capacity in the field of environmental health. They should work with medical associations and academic institutions to integrate environmental health into medical, nursing, and public health education, as well as building graduate programs specializing in environmental health. A recent study showed that attending a single seminar on the health effects of pesticides resulted in Canadian medical students' having increased concerns about the risks associated with pesticide use.[38] In addition to ensuring that all health care professionals have at least a minimum of knowledge in this field, Canada also needs more professionals with specialized training in environmental health. The national environmental health strategy should encourage universities, hospitals, public health departments, and industry to hire appropriately trained environmental health specialists. In recent years, some Canadian universities have developed nodes of expertise in environmental health research and education, including the McMaster Institute of Environment and Health, the Institute of Population Health at the University of Ottawa, the School of Population and Public Health at the University of British Columbia, and the Community Health program at McGill University.

Because of the rapidly evolving landscape of environmental health, ongoing opportunities for professional development are essential. Health Canada should work with medical associations and academic institutions to develop and promote additional opportunities for health professionals to receive training in environmental health, and information about how to integrate knowledge of these issues into day-to-day practice. The NCCEH has a key role to play in these efforts. According to the NCCEH, six universities in Canada offer specialized degrees in environmental health (Simon Fraser University and the Universities of British Columbia, Manitoba, Alberta, Toronto, and Montréal). Five institutions offer degree programs leading to public health inspector certification.[39] The Canadian Medical Association offers online courses on topics such as Air Quality and Health, developed by some of Canada's leading experts in this field.[40]

The Canadian Public Health Association recommends much greater attention to ecological determinants of health, including the following actions:

- Revise core competencies for public health to give greater prominence to the need for public health practitioners to understand the ecological determinants of health.
- Revise the curricula of medical schools, nursing schools, and public health programs to include required courses on the ecological determinants of health.

• Establish a dedicated fund within the Canadian Global Health Research Initiative for research on the health impacts of anticipated global ecological changes.

Stronger Environmental Laws, Regulations, Standards, and Policies

It is obvious from the comparative assessments in Chapters 6, 7, and 8 that Canadian environmental laws and policies need to be substantially strengthened, effectively implemented, and aggressively enforced in order to adequately protect all Canadians – especially the most vulnerable populations – from environmental hazards in air, water, food, and consumer products, as well as threats posed by the built environment, climate change, zoonoses, antibiotic resistance, and biodiversity loss. Increasing access to environmental amenities and benefits also requires stronger laws and policies. To ensure a systemic and effective approach, the enactment, amendment, implementation, and enforcement of environmental laws and policies at all levels of government should be based upon nine guiding principles:

1. Every person has the right to live in a healthy environment.
2. Canadian standards to protect health from environmental hazards must be national in scope, legally enforceable, and as strong as, or stronger than, the highest standards in other OECD countries.
3. The polluter-pays principle must be consistently applied by using environmental taxes to incorporate externalities into prices.
4. The precautionary principle should be applied to prevent potential health and environmental effects in cases where there is scientific uncertainty.
5. Substitution requires the replacement of environmental hazards with safer alternatives.
6. Intergenerational equity should be recognized to protect the rights of future generations.
7. Codifying the public trust doctrine requires governments to manage ecosystems responsibly.
8. The progressivity or nonregression principle must be applied, meaning that today's environmental laws, regulations, and standards represent a baseline that can be strengthened in the future but not weakened.
9. Environmental justice requires the equitable sharing of both environmental burdens and benefits.

Each of these principles is described in greater detail below. Some of these principles are already found in Canadian environmental legislation, leading to the conclusion that principles themselves are not sufficient. This chapter therefore also includes examples of concrete priority actions, guided by these principles, that are necessary to overcome existing weaknesses in Canadian environmental law and policy. The focus is on legislation because, as the Canadian Medical Association recently concluded, "regulatory frameworks should be favoured over voluntary frameworks in order to ensure a level playing field for all manufacturers and to secure rapid and equitable health protection for all Canadians."[41]

1. Every Canadian's Right to Live in a Healthy Environment

The right to live in a healthy environment is a relatively recent addition to the library of fundamental human rights, but has rapidly gained legal recognition over the past four decades, consistent with growing awareness that human activity is causing a global environmental crisis. As discussed in Chapter 6, there are 110 countries where environmental rights enjoy constitutional status, more than 120 countries that have signed legally binding regional human rights agreements including this right, and more than 100 nations whose national environmental laws highlight this right. Canada is not among these countries, yet nine in ten Canadians support constitutional recognition of their right to a healthy environment. A growing body of evidence indicates that constitutional environmental rights and responsibilities lead to improved environmental quality.[42] While constitutional changes are essential and will be discussed in detail in Chapter 11, the right to live in a healthy environment should be recognized in ordinary legislation immediately, as recommended by the Canadian Bar Association in 1990.[43] The National Round Table on the Environment and the Economy noted that the right of all Canadians to breathe clean air should be a basic principle in setting air quality standards.[44] The enactment or strengthening of environmental bills of rights at the federal, provincial, territorial, and municipal levels serves a dual purpose, fleshing out the procedural rights that are essential to fulfilling the substantive right and providing a steppingstone to eventual constitutional recognition. These procedural rights include access to information, the right to participate fully in environmental decision making, and access to justice in situations where a person's right to a healthy environment is threatened or violated.

Legislation recognizing the right to a healthy environment already exists in Quebec, Ontario, the Yukon, the Northwest Territories, and Nunavut, but needs to be strengthened to be effective.[45] Quebec is unique in having added the right to a healthy environment to its *Charter of Human Rights and Freedoms* in 2006. In the remaining provinces, new laws are needed, which could take the form of a stand-alone environmental bill of rights or amendments to existing environmental or human rights laws. A Canadian Environmental Bill of Rights came very close to passing the House of Commons in 2011, was reintroduced in 2014, and enjoys the support of all parties except the Conservatives. Municipal governments can pass by-laws, resolutions, or declarations recognizing the environmental rights of residents, as many cities have done in the United States, from Pittsburgh to Santa Monica. Action at the local level can build pressure for more systemic changes, as demonstrated by the example of laws prohibiting the use of pesticides for cosmetic purposes, which began in one Quebec municipality and now protect the majority of Canadians. In response to a campaign being conducted by the David Suzuki Foundation and Ecojustice, more than fifty Canadian municipalities, including Vancouver, Richmond (BC), and Montreal, have endorsed the right to a healthy environment and pledged actions to protect this right.[46]

Another element of the right to a healthy environment that needs to be enshrined in legislation is the right to know what is in the air we breathe; the water we drink, swim, and fish in; the food we eat; and the consumer products we buy. In the United States, federal and state laws guarantee that every person has the right to know about toxic chemicals that they may be exposed to in the course of ordinary daily activities.[47] Similar laws are in place throughout the European Union.[48] In Canada, regulations passed pursuant to the *Hazardous Products Act* in 1988 created a system called the Workplace Hazardous Materials Information System (WHMIS) to establish standards for hazard classification and communication.[49] The federal WHMIS is complemented by workers' "right-to-know" legislation in every province. Employees are informed about the short- and long-term health impacts of toxic substances they may encounter in the workplace. However, citizens may be using the same or similar products in their homes but do not have access to the same information. The stronger protection provided to employees in the workplace in terms of information about toxic substances should be extended to all citizens.

In 2008, Toronto pioneered the first community right-to-know law in Canada, creating a precedent that other governments should emulate.[50]

Toronto's ChemTRAC program requires local businesses to report releases of specified toxic substances at thresholds far lower than the National Pollutant Release Inventory.[51] ChemTRAC also assists businesses in reducing emissions and preventing pollution.

2. Legally Binding World-Class National Standards

As a general principle, Canadians should enjoy a level of protection from environmental threats that is at least equal to, if not better than, the highest standard enjoyed by the citizens of other wealthy OECD nations. This recommendation echoes the call of the Ontario Task Force on the Primary Prevention of Cancer in 1995, with medical experts urging governments to "adopt the most stringent standards for controlling environmental carcinogens developed by Organisation for Economic Co-operation and Development member countries."[52] The current lack of enforceable national standards for air quality and safe drinking water is unacceptable for one of the world's wealthiest, best-educated, most technologically advanced nations. The United States, Australia, and the European Union all have legally binding standards for air quality. The United States and the European Union have legally binding standards for drinking water quality. There is no valid reason why Canadians should not enjoy the same level of protection. As Justice Dennis O'Connor wrote in his compelling analysis of the Walkerton disaster, matters as important as safe drinking water and public health should be covered by enforceable regulations.[53] The same logic applies to air quality. The National Round Table on the Environment and the Economy recommended that Canada develop enforceable air quality standards because all Canadians have the right to breathe clean air.[54]

Clean Air

The evidence is clear that air pollution is the single largest environmental factor adversely affecting the health of Canadians. Canada would benefit immensely from the implementation of national, legally enforceable air quality standards that are equal to or better than the standards in other wealthy western countries (see Table 10.1). The enforcement of such standards would lead to improvements in air quality that could prevent thousands of premature deaths, prevent millions of unnecessary illnesses, and save billions of dollars in health care costs.

There is no doubt that reducing air pollution saves lives and prevents illnesses. A study of pollution levels and asthma exacerbations in Atlanta before, during, and after the 1996 Summer Olympics showed that reducing

TABLE 10.1
Recommended national standards for air quality

Pollutant	Recommended Canadian standard		Current Canadian guideline
Ozone[1]	50	(WHO)	63
Fine particulate[2]	25	(AUS, WHO)	28
Sulphur dioxide[3]	75	(US)	334
Nitrogen dioxide[4]	21	(EU, WHO)	53
Carbon monoxide[5]	9	(AUS, EU, US)	13
Lead[6]	0.15	(AUS)	–
Arsenic[6]	6	(EU)	–
Benzene[7]	5	(EU)	–
Cadmium[6]	5	(EU)	–
Nickel[6]	20	(EU)	–
Polycyclic aromatic hydrocarbons[6]	1	(EU)[8]	–

Notes: AUS (Australia), EU (European Union), US (United States), and WHO (World Health Organization) refer to the jurisdiction setting the highest air quality standard for the protection of health and the environment for a specific pollutant.
A dash (–) indicates that no standard or guideline has been established.
1   8 hours, parts per billion
2   24 hours, micrograms per cubic metre
3   1 hour, parts per billion
4   Annual, parts per billion
5   8 hours, parts per million
6   Annual average, nanograms per cubic metre
7   Annual average, micrograms per cubic metre
8   European Union, *Directive 2008/50/EC of the European Community and of the Council of 21 May 2008 on Ambient Air Quality and Cleaner Air for Europe.*

vehicle traffic could reduce the number of children going to hospital with breathing difficulties. Temporary measures to reduce traffic and enhance public transportation, such as adding one thousand buses and closing downtown to private vehicles, caused ozone levels to fall by 28 percent and asthma exacerbations fell by 44 percent.[55] An international review of policies and programs implemented to reduce air pollution revealed that reductions in mortality were generally greater than anticipated.[56]

Radon
Radon is the single largest environmental health threat in indoor air in Canada, causing thousands of preventable lung cancer deaths annually. Canada should replace the existing guideline of 200 Bq/m^3 (bequerels per cubic metre) with a recommended intervention level of 100 Bq/m^3 as implemented in Germany and recommended by the World Health Organization. This would reflect the best available scientific knowledge and

provide Canadians with the strongest practical level of protection for their health. Radon testing and remediation should be mandatory for all public buildings (schools, hospitals, long-term care facilities, and other public buildings) as well as private institutional buildings designed for children (e.g., schools, day cares, etc.). Radon concentrations in a home can be measured inexpensively and mitigated effectively at a moderate cost, both in new home construction and in retrofitting of existing buildings.[57] The main methods of reducing radon concentrations in a building are sealing floors and walls; improving ventilation in the house and avoiding the transport of radon from the basement into occupied rooms; increasing ventilation below the building; installing a radon sump system in the basement; and installing a positive pressurization system. High levels of radon in drinking water can be reduced by aeration (either spraying or open air storage).

Health Canada, together with territorial and provincial governments, should also ensure that radon protection measures are incorporated into all building codes in Canada; develop and implement a subsidized radon testing and mitigation program for low-income Canadians; and focus its new public education and outreach campaign in regions known to have high radon concentrations. Based on experiences in British Columbia in renovating a limited number of homes and schools, Health Canada estimates that it will cost roughly $1,000 to renovate the average home to reduce radon risks, and approximately $18,000 per school.[58] Because the number of affected buildings is not currently known, it is difficult to reliably estimate total radon remediation costs for Canada.

Safe Drinking Water

The unenforceable and numerically weak Guidelines for Canadian Drinking Water Quality should be replaced by legally binding national standards for drinking water quality that are equal to or better than the highest standards provided in any other OECD nation. In addition, Canada should develop a set of health-based long-term objectives for drinking water quality. These recommendations will improve the protection of public health, increase the transparency of the process involved in setting the Guidelines for Canadian Drinking Water Quality, and enhance public confidence in tap water, reducing the unnecessary expense and waste associated with bottled water.

Health-Based Long-Term Objectives

New Canadian Drinking Water Objectives should incorporate health-based long-term objectives for drinking water quality similar to the Maximum

Contaminant Level Goals (MCLGs) established by the US Environmental Protection Agency. MCLGs are nonenforceable public health goals that identify the maximum level of a contaminant in drinking water at which no known or anticipated adverse effect on human health would occur, including an adequate margin of safety. These long-term objectives would provide a vision for the future and clarify the distinction between purely health-based objectives and legal standards that represent a compromise between public health, economic costs, and technological constraints.

Legally Binding National Standards
Canada should enact legally binding national standards for maximum acceptable concentrations (MACs) of microbiological, physical, chemical, and radiological contaminants, as well as outcome-based treatment standards. The United States employs legally binding outcome-based treatment standards to address the threat to public health posed by microbiological contaminants, particularly protozoa and viruses. Canadians should enjoy the same level of protection. To ensure that this approach is effective and efficient, a flexibility mechanism should be created, enabling jurisdictions to avoid unnecessary testing and monitoring costs for contaminants that can reasonably be expected to be absent in drinking water. Such an approach would take regional differences into account. This flexibility mechanism would apply to chemical and radiological contaminants, but not microbial contaminants. The US EPA, pursuant to the *Safe Drinking Water Act,* applies this flexible approach in small communities.

In upgrading current MAC guidelines, Canada should adopt the most stringent level established by the United States, the European Union, Australia, or the WHO (see Table 10.2). Federal infrastructure funding for provinces, territories, and municipalities should be made contingent on incorporation of the national standards into law at the appropriate subnational level. A precedent for this kind of arrangement occurred when the federal government required municipalities to have sustainability plans in order to obtain a share of the federal gas tax.[59]

Because guidelines for radiological contaminants use different measurement units, tritium was not included in Table 10.2. However, the current Canadian guideline for tritium of 7,000 Bq/L (becquerels per litre) should be replaced by the EU standard of 100 Bq/L. Canada should also prioritize the development of standards for substances regulated by other countries for which there is currently no Canadian guideline, including di(2-ethylhexyl) phthalate (DEHP), asbestos, beryllium, and thalium.

TABLE 10.2

Recommendations for new Canadian drinking water maximum acceptable concentration standards

Pollutant	Recommended Canadian standard		Current Canadian guideline
2,4-D	0.0001	(EU)	0.1
Antimony	0.003	(AUS)	0.006
Atrazine	0.0001	(EU)	0.005
Azinphos-methyl	0.0001	(EU)	0.02
Barium	0.7	(WHO)	1.0
Benzene	0.001	(EU, AUS)	0.005
Boron	0.5	(WHO)	5.0
Bromoxynil	0.0001	(EU)	0.005
Cadmium	0.002	(AUS)	0.005
Carbaryl	0.0001	(EU)	0.09
Carbofuran	0.0001	(EU)	0.09
Carbon tetrachloride	0.0001	(EU)	0.002
Chlorate	0.0001	(EU)	1.0
Chlorite	0.0001	(EU)	1.0
Chlorpyrifos	0.0001	(EU)	0.09
Cyanide	0.05	(EU)	0.2
Diazinon	0.0001	(EU)	0.02
Dicamba	0.0001	(EU)	0.12
1,2-Dichlorobenzene	0.0001	(EU)	0.2
1,4-Dichlorobenzene	0.0001	(EU)	0.005
1,2-Dichloroethane	0.003	(AUS, EU)	0.005
1,1-Dichloroethylene	0.007	(US)	0.014
Dichloromethane	0.004	(AUS)	0.05
2,4-Dichlorophenol	0.0001	(EU)	0.9
Diclofop-methyl	0.0001	(EU)	0.009
Dimethoate	0.0001	(EU)	0.02
Diquat	0.0001	(EU)	0.07
Diuron	0.0001	(EU)	0.15
Glyphosate	0.0001	(EU)	0.28
Haloacetic acids	0.05	(WHO)	0.06
MCPA	0.0001	(EU)	0.1
Malathion	0.0001	(EU)	0.19
Metolachlor	0.0001	(EU)	0.05
Metribuzin	0.0001	(EU)	0.08
Nitrate	10.0	(US)	45.0
Nitrite	0.5	(EU)	10.0
Nitrilotriacetic acid	0.2	(AUS, WHO)	0.4

Pollutant	Recommended Canadian standard		Current Canadian guideline
Paraquat	0.0001	(EU)	0.01
Parathion	0.0001	(EU)	0.05
Pentachlorophenol	0.0001	(EU)	0.06
Phorate	0.0001	(EU)	0.002
Picloram	0.0001	(EU)	0.19
Simazine	0.0001	(EU)	0.01
Terbufos	0.0001	(EU)	0.001
Tetrachloroethylene	0.005	(US)	0.03
Trifluralin	0.0001	(EU)	0.045
Trihalomethanes	0.08	(US)	0.1
2,4,6-Trichlorophenol	0.0001	(EU)	0.005
2,3,4,6-Tetrachlorophenol	0.0001	(EU)	0.1
Uranium	0.015	(WHO)	0.02
Vinyl chloride	0.0003	(AUS,WHO)	0.002

Notes: AUS (Australia), EU (European Union), US (United States), and WHO (World Health Organization) refer to the jurisdiction setting the highest standard for the protection of health and the environment for a specific pollutant.

All measurements are in milligrams per litre (mg/L).

Federal programs that provide funding for drinking water infrastructure (e.g., treatment and distribution systems) should allow funds to be used for protecting drinking water sources. Experiences in cities from Vancouver to New York to Melbourne indicate that protecting drinking water sources is not only a key element of the multiple-barrier approach but also a good investment. There is a significant backlog of needed improvements to drinking water infrastructure across Canada, particularly with respect to aging distribution systems that both waste valuable water and pose elevated risks of contamination. Federal funding for sustainable infrastructure upgrades should be increased.

Federal funding also should be provided to develop cost-effective, real-time continuous monitoring of water treatment processes to provide early warning of possible treatment failure, as recommended by the Walkerton Inquiry.[60] The US EPA is already investing significant resources in this area, and Canadian research could be designed to be complementary.[61]

3. Implementation of the Polluter-Pays Principle
As detailed in Chapter 8, Canada trails far behind most OECD nations in using taxes to internalize the costs of pollution and environmental damage.

Pollution taxes are widely endorsed by both economists and environment-alists as the most effective, efficient, and equitable way of implementing the polluter-pays principle. While most of the debate in Canada has focused on pricing carbon emissions, there is a far broader suite of toxic substances that should also be the subject of taxes in order to internalize existing external-ities and discourage their production, use, and release. This section recommends the replacement of the current federal fuel excise tax with a new national pollution tax targeting all types of industrial air and water pollution (including carbon emissions). As well, new taxes on pesticides and motor vehicles are proposed. In addition to approving of these kinds of environmental taxes, Canada's Ecofiscal Commission also supports increases in municipal user fees, water prices, and road congestion charges, pointing to the effectiveness of these tools in other countries.[62]

Like France, Canada should establish a National Pollution Tax that applies to industrial releases of specified toxic substances. The tax would be determined by the volume of emissions/releases and their degree of toxicity to humans, wildlife, and ecosystems. Data on pollution gathered by Canada's National Pollutant Release Inventory could serve as the basis for such a new tax, with the initial fees being relatively modest on a per unit basis, but projected to grow over time (as was the case with British Columbia's successful carbon tax). Back in 1998, Parliament's technical committee on business taxation recommended replacing the federal fuel excise tax with broadly based environmental taxes that raise equivalent revenue and are designed to reduce emissions of pollutants and environmentally damaging activities.[63] The Green Budget Coalition, representing many environmental groups from across Canada, has repeatedly recommended establishing a national pollution tax.[64] In 2012, the Drummond report urged the Ontario government to place a greater emphasis on the polluter-pays principle and also to increase the price charged for water and other natural resources by applying the user-pays model and full cost recovery.[65]

A national pollution tax based on the current NPRI would capture only a fraction of total emissions in Canada because the NPRI only covers 371 substances discharged by large polluters and is based on self-reported data. The NPRI should be expanded to cover a broader range of toxic substances, and Environment Canada should be required to conduct audits of the releases reported by industry, to improve the reliability of the information. Provinces and territories should build upon the precedents set by British Columbia and Nova Scotia in establishing charges on industrial emissions and effluent. The fees levied by American states pursuant to federal air and water laws also provide useful precedents for Canada.

Canadian taxpayers are presently on the hook for tens of billions of dollars in liabilities associated with the cleanup and restoration of contaminated sites.[66] The imposition of a very minor environmental income tax, similar to the tax previously collected under the US Superfund legislation, would go a long way towards reallocating the cleanup burden to parties responsible for causing environmental damage. The environmental income tax established in the United States was at a rate of 0.12 percent on taxable income in excess of $2 million (protecting small businesses from an increased tax burden).

Potential revenues from environmental taxes are substantial. British Columbia's carbon tax is already generating over $1 billion in annual revenue, while Quebec's more modest carbon tax generates roughly $200 million per year. Estimates of the annual revenue potential from a federal carbon tax range from $18 billion (National Round Table on the Environment and the Economy) to $46 billion (David Suzuki Foundation and Pembina Institute).[67]

A modest tax on major air pollutants, including sulphur dioxide, nitrogen oxides, fine particulate matter, benzene, and other toxic substances, would also raise billions of dollars in revenue. For example, if Canada applied the tax rates from France's National Pollution Tax to just four categories of air pollution, the annual tax revenue would exceed $725 million (see Table 10.3). While this is a substantial sum of money and would be a good first step, it falls short of fully reflecting the health and environmental damages caused by emissions of these toxic substances. Pollution taxes should be

TABLE 10.3
Estimated Canadian revenues from tax on four classes of air pollutants, using French tax rates

	SOx	NOx	PM	VOCs
Emissions (tonnes per year)[1]	1,130,000	809,000	468,000	693,000
Tax rate (per tonne)[2]	$196.82	$237.57	$376.02	$196.82
Tax generated	$222,406,600	$192,194,130	$175,977,360	$136,396,260

Notes: SOx = sulphur oxides; NOx = nitrogen oxides; PM = particulate matter; VOCs = volatile organic compounds.
1   Canadian emissions data include only industrial sources and electric power generation.
2   French tax rates are current as of 2014. Amounts in euros were converted to Canadian dollars at the exchange rate of December 10, 2014: 1 euro = Cdn$1.42.

Sources: Emissions – Environment Canada, *National Pollutant Release Inventory: 2011 Air Pollutant Emissions for Canada* (Ottawa: Environment Canada, 2013); Tax rates – France (Minister of Economy and Finance), *General Tax on Polluting Activities: 2014 Rates* (2014), http://www.douane.gouv.fr/Portals/0/fichiers/professionnel/fiscalite/tgap-2014.pdf.

adjusted regularly to reflect changes in scientific knowledge, and also indexed to keep pace with inflation. Taxes collected by the federal government could be returned to the provinces for investment in environmental initiatives.

Canada's ineffective Green Levy should be restructured to resemble the motor vehicle purchase taxes found in European countries. A simple first step would be to increase the levy to the level of the US Gas Guzzler Tax. This would lower the threshold for application of the levy from 13 litres per 100 kilometres (L/100 km) to 10.5 L/100 km and increase the maximum levy from $4,000 to $7,700. The tax would then be raised annually and expanded to cover more vehicles, strengthening the incentive to avoid vehicle purchases or buy more fuel-efficient models. Revenues could be used to finance a gas guzzler buy-back program, getting the dirtiest cars off the road.

A modest tax on pesticides in Canada would be an initial move towards internalizing their health and environmental costs. Health Canada's most recent report on pesticide sales indicates that approximately 90 million kilograms of active ingredients were sold in 2011.[68] Canada should eventually implement a sophisticated pesticide tax based on the relative toxicity of active ingredients, as is done in Norway and Denmark. In the interim, Canada should apply Sweden's simple approach ($4.40 per kilogram), plus roughly 2 percent of annual sales revenue to cover administrative costs. This pesticide tax would generate over $400 million annually in revenue. The Scandinavian nations successfully used taxes to achieve major reductions in pesticide use. Sweden reduced pesticide use by over 80 percent since 1980 by charging a special tax on pesticides, offering economic support for organic agriculture, funding research on alternatives to pesticide use, and providing mandatory education programs for pesticide users to assist them in reducing their reliance on these chemicals.[69]

If Canada were to merely raise total environmental taxes (currently 1.2 percent of GDP) to average levels among OECD nations (1.66 percent of GDP), this would represent a total of approximately $8.28 billion in additional tax revenues annually. If Canada raised environmental taxes to a level consistent with European members of the OECD (2.39 percent of GDP), this would double today's environmental tax revenues to approximately $43 billion per year. The International Monetary Fund recently suggested that Canada could generate over $26 billion annually with energy taxes that reflect the damage caused by fossil fuel consumption and traffic congestion.[70] These are substantial sums of money, which would give governments significant fiscal flexibility.

The revenue from new or increased Canadian pollution taxes could be used in five different ways: (1) to reduce other taxes (i.e., revenue recycling), (2) to reduce government debt, (3) to minimize distributional impacts, (4) to avoid or mitigate competitiveness impacts, and (5) to invest in public goods, such as environmental protection efforts or green infrastructure. For example, revenues from taxes on air pollution (including carbon emissions) could be used to reduce emissions, to subsidize renewable energy, to protect low-income Canadians and other households that could suffer disproportionate impacts from rising energy and transportation costs, and to safeguard industries whose international trade profile indicates that such taxes could compromise their competitiveness. Revenues from taxes on water pollution could be targeted towards repairing and upgrading water infrastructure, rehabilitating damaged aquatic ecosystems, or financing improved protection for drinking water sources. Another option would be to finance a just transition strategy for workers who lose jobs due to stronger environmental standards.[71] Many experts recommend offsetting new environmental taxes with cuts to payroll and income taxes. This revenue-neutral approach, employed with British Columbia's carbon tax, is expected to produce both environmental and economic benefits.

In developing new environmental taxes, Canada should adhere to the OECD's key considerations for the design and implementation of environmental taxes:

1. Environmental taxes should target specific pollutants and environmentally damaging behaviours.
2. The tax rate should reflect the extent of health and environmental damage.
3. The tax must be significant and its rate predictable.
4. Distributional impacts should be addressed to avoid creating or exacerbating inequities.
5. Competitiveness concerns need to be carefully assessed.
6. Clear communication is critical to public acceptance.
7. Environmental taxes need to be combined with other policy instruments.[72]

Eliminate Perverse Subsidies

Also consistent with the polluter-pays principle is the elimination of perverse subsidies. Perverse subsidies are government subsidies that provide financial support for activities that cause environmental harm. The most pressing examples are tax breaks benefiting oil, gas, and coal development, which should be terminated. Funds should be redirected to accelerating the development and deployment of zero- or low-emission sources of energy (solar, wind, geothermal, tidal, and micro-hydro). As noted in Chapter 8, Canadian governments provide over $2 billion in annual subsidies for oil, natural gas, and coal despite repeated commitments to end these handouts. Subsidies to other natural resource industries (mining, forestry, fishing, and agriculture) should also be systematically reviewed to eliminate those with adverse environmental effects. Canadian liability limits for environmental damages caused by mining, oil and gas activities, and nuclear energy need to be raised substantially to catch up with other countries and prevent taxpayers from being left on the hook. In the municipal context, subsidies for development that exacerbates urban sprawl should be terminated, resulting in denser communities and healthier people.

4. Precautionary Principle

Canada needs to consistently apply the precautionary principle in decision and policy making involving potential health and environmental threats. The precautionary principle means that "where there are threats of serious or irreversible damage, lack of full scientific certainty should not be used as a reason for postponing measures to prevent environmental degradation."[73] Although commonly found in both federal and provincial environmental legislation and endorsed by the Supreme Court of Canada, implementation has not yet lived up to aspiration.[74] New chemicals and technologies continue to be created and become widely used before their potentially harmful effects on human health and the environment are adequately studied or understood.[75] Hydraulic fracturing, antibiotic resistance, nanotechnology, and replacements for brominated flame retardants offer recent examples where regulation has not kept pace with new developments. Because it is often challenging to reach definitive conclusions about environmental impacts on human health, the application of the precautionary principle is critical in addressing uncertainty. Several concrete recommendations for more rigorous implementation of this principle are provided below.

Food Safety

Pesticides are an excellent example of an environmental health threat where there is extensive evidence regarding adverse chronic health effects but also considerable uncertainty. Although Canada's 2002 *Pest Control Products Act (PCPA)* represented a substantial improvement over the previous pesticide law, the act still has several serious flaws, and its implementation by the

Pest Management Regulatory Agency (PMRA) has been grossly inadequate. The PMRA offers a textbook example of regulatory capture, with the agency favouring the private interests of chemical companies and industrial agriculture over the public interest in health and environmental protection. In 2011, the Federal Court found the PMRA guilty of misinterpreting its own legislation by refusing to conduct special reviews of pesticides registered in Canada but no longer used in other OECD nations.[76] A second lawsuit, filed in 2013, forced the PMRA to initiate special reviews of twenty-three active ingredients whose use is permitted in Canada but not in Europe.[77]

In order to ensure the consistent application of the precautionary principle, the *PCPA* should be amended to immediately suspend the registration of pesticides whose use is no longer permitted in another OECD nation, pending a review by a panel of independent environmental health experts. This would result in the suspension of at least forty-six active ingredients, used in more than a thousand pesticide products in Canada, that have already been banned in other OECD nations for health and environmental reasons (see Table 10.4). Although economic costs would be incurred as a result, there would also be health, environmental, and economic benefits. For example, most nonorganic Canadian apples currently cannot be exported to the European Union because they are sprayed with diphenylamine, which the European Union prohibits on food if residues exceed 0.1 parts per million.[78]

The *PCPA* should also be amended to phase out the registration of cosmetic pesticides used for lawns, gardens, playgrounds, and school fields, as recommended by the Canadian Cancer Society and the Learning Disabilities Association of Canada.[79] The Canadian Medical Association has called on

TABLE 10.4
Pesticide active ingredients whose registration in Canada should
be suspended

Active ingredient	Status
2,4-D*	Pending special review
Acephate*	Pending special review
Aminopyralid*	Pending special review
Amitraz	No review scheduled
Atrazine*	Pending special review
Bifenthrin	No review scheduled
Brodifacoum	No review scheduled

Active ingredient	Status
Bromacil	No review scheduled
Bromethalin	No review scheduled
Bromoxynil*	Pending special review
Carbaryl*	Pending special review
Chlorophacinone	No review scheduled
Chloropicrin*	Pending special review
Chlorthal-dimethyl*	Pending special review
Diazinon*	Pending special review
Dichlobenil*	Pending special review
Dichlorprop	No review scheduled
Dichlorvos*	Pending special review
Difenoconazole*	Pending special review
Difethialone	No review scheduled
Dinocap	No review scheduled
Diphacinone	No review scheduled
Diphenylamine*	Pending special review
Endosulfan	Scheduled to be phased out in Canada by 2016
Ethylene oxide	No review scheduled
Ferbam	No review scheduled
Fluazifop-p-butyl*	Pending special review
Fluazinam*	Pending special review
Hexazinone*	Pending special review
Imazapyr*	Pending special review
Linuron*	Pending special review
Paradichlorobenzene	No review scheduled
Paraquat*	Pending special review
Pentachlorophenol*	Pending special review
Permethrin	No review scheduled
Petroleum oil	No review scheduled
Phorate	No review scheduled
Propoxur	No review scheduled
Quintozene/PCBB*	Pending special review
Simazine*	Pending special review
Sodium chlorate	No review scheduled
Terbacil	No review scheduled
Thiabendazole	No review scheduled
Tributyltin oxide	No review scheduled
Trichlorfon	No review scheduled
Trifluralin*	Pending special review

Note: Following a lawsuit filed by Ecojustice on behalf of Equiterre and the David Suzuki Foundation, the PMRA agreed to initiate special reviews of twenty-three active ingredients, marked with an asterisk, to evaluate whether their registration in Canada should be terminated, as had already been done in the European Union.

the federal government to rescind the registration of combined fertilizer/ pesticide lawn care products.[80] More than 170 Canadian municipalities, as well as Quebec, Ontario, Manitoba, and the four Maritime provinces, have passed laws restricting the cosmetic or nonessential use of pesticides.[81] These laws protect roughly 80 percent of the country's population. Municipal pesticide bylaws have been repeatedly endorsed by the courts, including the Supreme Court of Canada, despite challenges by lawn care and chemical companies.[82] Most importantly, evidence indicates that these laws are working – reducing pesticide use and reducing exposures.[83] For example, the proportion of households in Quebec using chemical pesticides fell from 15 percent to 4 percent after that province's Pesticides Management Code came into effect.[84] Amending the federal pesticide law to prohibit cosmetic pesticide use is necessary to ensure that all Canadians receive the same level of protection, particularly children, who are the most vulnerable to unintentional pesticide poisoning.[85] The American Academy of Pediatrics also recently recommended strengthening of laws and policies to protect children from pesticides.[86]

Canada should review all maximum residue limits (MRLs) for pesticides on food to ensure that Canadian standards are equal to or better than the strongest protection enjoyed by citizens of any other OECD nation. Chapter 7 demonstrated the weakness of Canadian MRLs relative to those established by the European Union, the United States, and Australia. For thirty-nine out of the forty pesticide/food combinations examined, there was a jurisdiction with a more stringent MRL than Canada. Table 10.5 sets out the current Canadian MRL and a recommendation that would align a selected sample of Canadian MRLs with the strongest standards available in other industrialized nations.

The federal government should also require that all pesticide products sold or imported into Canada or exported from Canada be sold in childproof containers with labels that provide information on safe storage and specific risks to children, to minimize the risk of accidental exposures (as is done with pharmaceutical products).[87]

Improve Government's Recall Powers

Under current legislation, the federal government lacks the authority to order the mandatory recall of a consumer product, even if there is strong evidence of potential harm to health. Canada has been slow to respond to products that pose health threats, including lead in a wide variety of products, polybrominated diphenyl ethers (PBDEs) in electronics and home

TABLE 10.5

Proposed maximum residue limits (MRLs) for pesticides on Canadian food products

Pesticide	Food	Current MRL	Recommended MRL	
Aldicarb	Potatoes	0.5	0.02	(EU)
Atrazine	Corn	0.2	0.1	(EU, AUS)
Azinphos-methyl	Grapes	5.0	0.05	(EU)
Bromoxynil	Eggs	0.1	0.02	(AUS)
	Milk	0.1	0.01	(EU)
	Meat	0.1	0.02	(AUS)
Captan	Cranberries	5.0	0.2	(EU)
Carbaryl	Citrus fruit	10.0	0.1	(EU)
Carbofuran	Strawberries	0.4	0.01	(EU)
Chlorothalonil	Celery	15.0	10.0	(AUS)
Chlorpyrifos	Lemons	1.0	0.2	(EU)
Diazinon	Apples	0.75	0.01	(EU)
	Strawberries	0.75	0.01	(EU)
Dichlorvos	Tomatoes	0.25	0.01	(EU)
Dicofol	Cucumber	3.0	0.02	(EU)
	Strawberries	3.0	0.02	(EU)
Diquat	Lentils, dry	0.2	0.05	(US)
Diuron	Asparagus	7.0	2.0	(EU, AUS)
Endosulfan	Pears	2.0	0.05	(EU)
Ferbam	Peaches	7.0	4.0	(US)
Glyphosate	Soybeans	20.0	10.0	(AUS)
Heptachlor	Dairy products	0.1	0.004	(EU)
Imidacloprid	Cherries	3.0	0.5	(EU, AUS)
Iprodione	Lettuce	25.0	5.0	(AUS)
Malathion	Blueberries	8.0	0.02	(EU)
Methamidophos	Broccoli	1.0	0.01	(EU)
Metribuzin	Potatoes	0.5	0.1	(EU)
Nicosulfuran	Corn	0.1	0.05	(AUS)
Paraquat	Onions	0.1	0.02	(EU)
Permethrin	Leaf lettuce, spinach	20.0	0.05	(EU)
Phosmet	Grapes	10.0	0.05	(EU)
Propiconazole	Plums	1.0	0.05	(EU)
Quinclorac	Barley	2.0	0.01	(EU)
Spinosad	Kale	7.0	2.0	(EU)
Thiabendazole	Apples, pears	10.0	5.0	(US, EU)
Thiram	Tomatoes	7.0	0.1	(EU)
Vinclozolin	Apricots	5.0	0.05	(EU)
Ziram	Fruit and vegetables	7.0	0.1	(EU)

Notes: All MRLs are measured in parts per million (ppm). EU (European Union), AUS (Australia), and US (United States) refer to the jurisdictions with the strongest standards in terms of MRLs.

furnishings, and perfluorochemicals (PFCs) in nonstick cookware. The Auditor General of Canada recently criticized this country's voluntary system for recalling food products in major cases involving foodborne illnesses.[88] The *Food and Drugs Act, Canada Consumer Product Safety Act,* and *Hazardous Products Act* should be amended to ensure mandatory recall of products when Health Canada determines that they pose a threat to human health.

New Substances

Another priority area for improved environmental regulation relates to new products and substances, such as those produced through the relatively new field of nanotechnology. A recent audit by KPMG found that the Canadian government was falling behind in "the development and implementation of regulations to address environmental risks of new substances in pharmaceutical and personal care products."[89]

5. Substitution

All environmental laws governing chemicals and pollution should explicitly incorporate the substitution principle, requiring toxic products, processes, inputs, and types of energy to be replaced with safer alternatives. The substitution principle originated in Swedish chemicals legislation, which is regarded as the most stringent in the world, and is now entrenched in EU legislation.[90] For almost every application or use of toxic substances in today's society, there are less hazardous and yet economically viable alternatives, particularly when hidden health and environmental costs are considered. For example, researchers have identified viable alternatives to the world's most widely used brominated flame retardant (decaBDE).[91] A study commissioned by the state of Massachusetts found that there are economically feasible substitutes for five commonly used but hazardous materials (lead, formaldehyde, perchloroethylene, DEHP, and hexavalent chromium).[92]

Canada should use the *Canadian Environmental Protection Act, 1999* to phase out the production, use, sale, import, or release of substances when it is known or probable that these substances cause cancer; birth defects; abnormal development; damage to the brain, nervous system, reproductive system, or immune system; or interference with the endocrine system. In 1995, the Ontario Task Force on the Primary Prevention of Cancer, composed of more than twenty medical experts, called on government to set timetables for the elimination of carcinogens, chlorine, and persistent, bioaccumulative, toxic substances. As the task force concluded, "the only prudent approach to safeguarding the health of the public from known and suspected environmental carcinogens is to be precautionary while the necessary research efforts are being made to resolve the uncertainty."[93] Citizens should be able to trigger the substitution process by submitting evidence that safer alternatives exist or that another OECD nation has prohibited a substance or product that continues to be permitted in Canada.

Substances that have not been adequately tested for health impacts should be removed from the Canadian market by 2020, effectively reversing the current burden of proof, which considers chemicals innocent until proven guilty of harming human health. All chemicals should be tested to assess whether they are carcinogenic, mutagenic, endocrine disrupting, or neurotoxic, or have developmental effects. Sweden has already adopted this policy.[94]

Eliminate Exposure to Carcinogens

Given that environmental hazards cause thousands of premature deaths from cancer every year in Canada, it seems obvious that laws and policies should seek to reduce and eventually eliminate involuntary exposures to carcinogens. Priorities should include all substances designated as human carcinogens by the world's leading authority, the International Agency for Research on Cancer (IARC). Examples of known carcinogens where Canadian laws and policies are weaker than other countries include air pollution, asbestos, formaldehyde, benzene, and diesel fuel.

Prohibit all uses of all types of asbestos

All types of asbestos fibres are carcinogenic. As more than fifty countries have banned all uses of asbestos, there are obviously effective and affordable substitutes available. All remaining lawful uses in Canada should therefore be eliminated.

Discourage the use of diesel fuel

Canada currently subsidizes the use of diesel fuel by charging a lower excise tax compared with regular gasoline. This perverse subsidy should be rectified immediately, as recommended by the OECD. In addition, diesel-burning vehicles should be subject to a special surcharge to reflect the additional health costs caused by exposure to diesel exhaust.

Eliminate Exposure to Developmental Neurotoxins

It is well established that some industrial chemicals – including lead, mercury, manganese, arsenic, PCBs, and toluene – cause neurological disorders and brain dysfunction in babies and young children.[95] Hundreds of other industrial chemicals – including pesticides, solvents, and heavy metals – are suspected of being developmental neurotoxins but the evidence is not yet conclusive. The adverse effects caused by developmental neurotoxins include ADHD, cerebral palsy, autism spectrum disorders, and decreased cognition, memory, and intelligence. Because neurodevelopmental damage is often permanent, preventing exposure is essential. Canada needs to eliminate all exposures to lead, mercury, arsenic, toluene, and other developmental neurotoxins. Canada could be a global leader by pushing for an international agreement that protects the developing brains of the world's children.

Eliminate Exposure to Endocrine-Disrupting Chemicals
In recent years, scientists have identified a growing number of manmade chemicals that interfere with the endocrine systems of humans and wildlife, leading to disease or interfering with normal development.[96] Endocrine-disrupting chemicals have been shown to interfere with reproductive systems, increase fat development and weight gain, raise the risk of cancer, and harm both immune and cardiovascular systems. Some endocrine disruptors operate at very low doses and can have multigenerational or transgenerational effects, underscoring the importance of preventing exposures and taking a precautionary approach.[97] Among the known or suspected endocrine disruptors are phthalates, triclosan, pesticides, flame retardants, and eight hundred other industrial chemicals.[98] The European Union's progress in banning or restricting the use of endocrine disruptors should be emulated.[99]

Prohibit the Manufacturing, Import, Sale, and Use of All PBDEs in Canada
All PBDEs should be designated for virtual elimination under the *Canadian Environmental Protection Act, 1999* in order to protect human health and the environment. Regulations already prohibit the manufacture, import, sale, and use of two commercial mixtures of PBDEs (pentaBDE and octaBDE). However, Canada has dragged its feet in regulating decaBDE – the predominant PBDE on the market and a substance that degrades into the very substances that the federal government has already regulated. Canada should support the listing of decaBDE pursuant to the Stockholm Convention on Persistent Organic Pollutants, which would result in a global ban on this entire family of toxic substances. Unless a worldwide effort

is made to eliminate PBDEs from the environment, global systems (atmospheric transport, food webs) will continue to bring these harmful chemicals into Canadian ecosystems (particularly the Arctic) and into food consumed by Canadians.

Prohibit the Manufacturing, Import, Sale, and Use of All PFCs in Canada

Canada should replace the current piecemeal approach to PFCs with a regulation that prohibits the manufacturing, import, sale, and use of all PFCs, including perfluorooctanoic acid (PFOA), perfluorooctane sulphonate (PFOS), and their precursors. There are safer alternatives for all of these hazardous chemicals.

Eliminate the Use of Hazardous Phthalates

Canada should emulate the European Union and phase out all uses of butylbenzyl phthalate (BBP), dibutyl phthalate (DBP), diisodecyl phthalate (DIDP), and DEHP. While the use of DEHP in children's products was banned by Canada in 2010, its continued use in a wide range of applications, from food packaging to medical devices, can no longer be justified.

Require Mandatory Labelling of All Products Containing Toxic Substances

As an immediate interim step, pending the actions outlined above, Canada should require mandatory hazard labelling of all consumer products (including food) containing substances known to cause or suspected of causing adverse health effects. Similar labelling requirements already exist in Europe and California. The Canadian Strategy for Cancer Control recommended legislation requiring full disclosure of all known and probable carcinogens in consumer products.[100] Mandatory labelling could be included in the right-to-know legislation described earlier in this chapter.

6. Intergenerational Equity

The principle of intergenerational equity states that "each generation has an obligation to future generations to pass on the natural and cultural resources of the planet in no worse condition than received and to provide reasonable access to the legacy for the present generation."[101] An example of environmental legislation that incorporates this principle is the *Canada National Parks Act*, which requires that national parks "shall be maintained and made

use of so as to leave them unimpaired for the enjoyment of future generations."[102] Among the various environmental threats to public health, climate
change probably has the greatest long-term consequences. The most devastating impacts of climate change are not projected to occur for decades and
possibly centuries due to lags between rising concentrations of atmospheric
greenhouse gases, rising global temperatures, rising sea levels, and ocean
acidification.

Effective Climate Policy

In order to minimize adverse health effects imposed on future generations,
Canada urgently needs to implement effective laws and policies to accelerate the transition to an energy-efficient, low-carbon economy. Canada is
a very fortunate country in that renewable energy supplies – solar, wind,
biomass, geothermal, and hydroelectric – are far larger than current or
anticipated energy needs.[103] Mitigation (reducing greenhouse gas emissions and preventing deforestation) and adaptation (preparing for the
impacts of climate change) are both necessary. As described in Chapter 7,
Canada has a twenty-five-year track record of broken promises on climate
change, with a high likelihood that we will fail to meet our current target of
reducing emissions 17 percent below 2005 levels by 2020.[104] The approach
of relying primarily upon information programs, voluntary initiatives, and
consumer subsidies was ineffective.[105] Comprehensive recommendations
for effective climate policy in Canada have been published by the Pembina
Institute, the David Suzuki Foundation, the International Institute for Sustainable Development, and the National Round Table on the Environment
and the Economy.[106] The Intergovernmental Panel on Climate Change identified three actions that would reduce GHG emissions and provide major
health benefits: (1) reducing air pollution by shifting to cleaner sources of
energy and increasing efficiency; (2) shifting to healthier diets by reducing
meat consumption; and (3) designing transport systems that reduce motor
vehicle use and favour active transport (walking, cycling, etc.).[107]

Canada should immediately develop and implement an ambitious climate
change strategy with scientifically robust emission reduction goals, rigorous
regulations, strong economic instruments that put a price on all carbon
emissions, and carefully targeted subsidies to encourage the development
and diffusion of low- or zero-carbon alternatives. Large industry should be
subject to emission caps that decline over time and contribute an appropriate share of emission reductions (roughly half of Canada's emissions).

However, regulations and carbon pricing need to apply to all sources in order to achieve deep emission reductions. As discussed earlier in this chapter, carbon emissions should be taxed, with a rebate mechanism to protect low-income Canadians, and possibly concessions for industrial sectors whose competitiveness would otherwise be compromised. Subsidies currently enjoyed by the fossil fuel industry should be redirected in their entirety to promotion of renewable energy sources as well as energy efficiency initiatives. Major challenges will be tackling the rapid growth of Alberta's oil sands and fracking for natural gas. International analysis suggests that these unconventional fossil fuel resources must be left undeveloped if the world is to avoid dangerous levels of climate disruption.[108] Transportation emissions need to be addressed with a variety of policies to support denser urban communities, walking and cycling, improved public transit, car-sharing programs, electric vehicles, and rapid gains in vehicle fuel efficiency. Building codes need to be revamped so that Canada can keep up with world leaders. In California and Europe, laws require all new construction beginning in 2020 to meet near-zero standards for energy use.[109]

Federal, Provincial, and Territorial Futures Funds

Another key element of intergenerational equity is to ensure that future generations benefit from today's use of nonrenewable resources, particularly in countries that rely heavily on oil, gas, coal, and mining. Forward-thinking countries have allocated a portion of revenues from these industries to government-owned investment funds (often called "sovereign wealth funds"). These funds are intended to address the high volatility of commodity prices, the unpredictability of rates of extraction, and the finite nature of nonrenewable resources.[110] Establishing a futures fund preserves assets for future generations, stabilizes government revenues, and reduces the potential impacts that commodity price fluctuations can have on a country's currency and rate of inflation.[111]

Norway established a sovereign wealth fund in 1990 that includes all government revenues from the petroleum sector (taxes, royalties, licence fees, and dividends from the government-owned Statoil corporation). The special corporate income tax rate for the oil and gas industry is 78 percent in Norway. The Norwegian fund is now worth over $1 trillion.[112] Inspired by Norway's tremendous success, more and more nations are creating similar funds. There are more than sixty resource-backed sovereign wealth funds in the world, with more being created.[113] Saudi Arabia, Kuwait, and the United

Arab Emirates also have enormous sovereign wealth funds (measured in the hundreds of billions of dollars), generated through income from oil and gas activities.

Ironically, Norway took its initial inspiration from Alberta's Heritage Fund, created by Premier Peter Lougheed in the 1970s. The Heritage Fund received 30 percent of nonrenewable resource royalties, but Lougheed's successors began dipping into the fund for infrastructure projects. Contributions were reduced to 15 percent, and in 1987 the government stopped adding resource royalties to the fund. In the 1990s, governments began removing the annual income from the fund and adding it to general revenues. The Heritage Fund currently sits at roughly $16 billion. Quebec began a similar fund in 2006, using revenue from hydroelectricity and mining royalties. As of 2014, the Generations Fund was worth $5.7 billion, with projections that it would reach $14 billion by 2018 as a result of additional revenue streams (100 percent of mining royalties beginning in 2015, savings from the planned closure of the Gentilly-2 nuclear power plant, and an increased tax on alcoholic beverages).[114]

It is mind-boggling to consider that Canada, despite decades of exploiting its extraordinary natural wealth, has a combined federal/provincial debt exceeding $1 trillion, while Norway has no debt and a future fund worth in excess of $1 trillion. The International Monetary Fund, in a recent review of Canada's economic performance, urged the creation of a sovereign wealth fund. In 2012, however, Natural Resources Minister Joe Oliver rejected the idea, arguing that the government needs to spend the money now for social programs such as health care and education.[115] In the meantime, foreign sovereign wealth funds, from Norway to China, are investing in Canadian resources and generating revenue for citizens and future generations in other countries.

The federal government, as well as provincial and territorial governments other than Alberta and Quebec, should take immediate steps to allocate specified revenues to future funds.[116] Saskatchewan appears poised to move in this direction. A recent report prepared for the Saskatchewan government recommended the creation of "a permanent fund for saving a portion of the revenues from non-renewable resources to be invested for the benefit of future as well as present residents of our province for generations to come, hopefully forever."[117] The report warned that the fund should not be plundered opportunistically by governments seeking to maintain unsustainable levels of spending.

7. Codifying the Public Trust

The roots of the public trust doctrine, which has played a central role in environmental management in the United States but not in Canada, go back many centuries.[118] The essence of the concept is that the elements of a healthy environment – fresh water, oceans, the atmosphere, and fertile soil – are vital to human well-being, health, and even survival. Therefore, governments have a fiduciary duty to manage these public resources in a manner that ensures their availability for the use and enjoyment of both present and future generations.[119] Management decisions must prioritize the public good rather than private interests, providing protection against the potential domination of property rights. According to environmental lawyers Oliver Brandes and Randy Christensen, recognition and implementation of the public trust doctrine would be "of invaluable assistance in protecting ecological values, ensuring water for future needs, engaging the public and protecting public interests."[120]

While not yet widely recognized in Canadian law, the public trust doctrine is incorporated in the Yukon's *Environment Act* and the *Environmental Rights Acts* of the Northwest Territories and Nunavut. The Supreme Court of Canada commented favourably on the public trust in a case involving damages to publicly owned resources.[121] The public trust is also consistent with Indigenous law regarding the stewardship obligations of present generations towards the natural world.[122]

Given its potential utility, the public trust concept should be explicitly incorporated into all Canadian legislation governing land, water, wildlife, and natural resources, making it clear that present and future generations are the beneficiaries of a public trust comprising air, water, soil, and biodiversity, with governments required to act as trustees. For example, incorporating the public trust into provincial and territorial water laws would ensure that essential public uses of water, such as drinking water, take priority over private uses.[123] As well, the public trust doctrine would help ensure that the long-term water needs of ecosystems (e.g., minimum flows for rivers) are respected and protected.[124]

8. Progressivity/Nonregression

A growing number of nations recognize that in light of today's severe ecological problems, existing environmental laws and policies must be viewed as a baseline that can be strengthened in the future but never weakened. In France, this concept is described as the principle of nonregression.[125] This principle is known in Mexico as progressivity and was added to the Mexican Constitution in 2011. In other European and Latin American nations, courts have ruled that nonregression is an implicit consequence of constitutional recognition of the right to a healthy environment and government's corresponding obligation to respect this right.[126]

Incorporating the principle of nonregression in Canadian environmental law and policy could have a powerful positive effect. Attempts to weaken environmental laws, regulations, or standards should be prohibited. For example, the two omnibus budget implementation bills enacted in 2012 (Bills C-38 and C-45) substantially weakened the *Canadian Environmental Assessment Act, Fisheries Act, Navigable Waters Protection Act, Species at Risk Act,* and other environmental laws. Amendments to the *National Energy Board Act* reduced public participation in decision making and fast-tracked oil and gas projects. Given the immense health and environmental problems facing Canada, such legal changes should have been stopped in their tracks. At the provincial level, examples of damaging environmental law rollbacks occurred in British Columbia under Premier Gordon Campbell (e.g., weaker logging practices, loosening of air quality regulations), in Ontario under Premier Mike Harris (e.g., cuts to drinking water protection), in Alberta under Premier Ralph Klein, and in Nova Scotia under Premier Darrell Dexter (delaying regulations reducing mercury emissions from power plants). Prohibiting changes that weaken environmental laws and regulations in Canada probably requires a constitutional amendment (discussed in Chapter 11), but would prevent governments from putting private interests ahead of public rights.

9. Environmental Justice

Unfortunately, as documented in Chapter 4, socially and economically marginalized communities in Canada bear a disproportionate burden of environmental harm and lack access to environmental goods and services such as public green spaces and safe drinking water.[127] While not yet enshrined in any Canadian laws or regulations, the principle of environmental justice was defined in the proposed Canadian Environmental Bill of Rights as "the principle that there should be a just and consistent distribution of environmental benefits and burdens among Canadians, without discrimination on the basis of any ground prohibited by the *Canadian Charter of Rights and Freedoms.*"[128] The World Health Organization recommends completing a national environmental health inequality assessment to comprehensively identify problem areas, followed by laws and policies that improve environmental quality for everyone but provide additional assistance to the most exposed and vulnerable populations.[129]

All Canadian health, safety, and environmental legislation should be amended to explicitly require that steps be taken to protect children, pregnant women, people with compromised immune systems, and other disadvantaged or vulnerable populations when establishing priorities, setting standards, and assessing health and environmental impacts. Key examples include the *Canadian Environmental Protection Act, 1999*, the *Food and Drugs Act*, and the *Canada Consumer Product Safety Act*. The *Canadian Environmental Assessment Act, 2012* and all provincial environmental assessment laws should be amended to require the evaluation of potential equity concerns associated with environmental impacts on disadvantaged and vulnerable populations.[130] These assessments must not myopically focus on single projects or activities but take cumulative health and environmental effects into consideration.

Although changes to federal, provincial, and territorial laws are needed to provide equal protection for all Canadians, much can be done at the local level as well.[131] In communities already facing above-average levels of pollution, no additional pollution should be authorized by governments until air and water quality have been improved to levels as good as or better than the Canadian average. The Canadian Institute for Health Information published a framework that offers useful guidance for addressing health inequities in the context of urban environments.[132]

At the municipal level, land-use and zoning bylaws need to be revised to promote environmental justice and to reflect advances in our knowledge and understanding of environmental impacts on health. A leading example is the fact that exposure to air pollutants caused by traffic on busy roads is now known to cause premature births and asthma as well as other adverse impacts on respiratory health. New schools, day-care facilities, hospitals, and seniors' housing should not be permitted within a certain distance of busy roads. If possible, traffic should be re-routed away from these facilities. All local zoning, land-use, and transportation bylaws and decisions should take air pollution into consideration. Similarly, municipalities should conduct map-based inventories of green spaces, urban forest cover, and healthy food assets (e.g., farmers' markets and community gardens) and take action to ensure that socially and economically disadvantaged populations gain access to these vital environmental amenities. The US Environmental Protection Agency published a set of recommendations for achieving environmental justice in urban settings, including ensuring meaningful community involvement in planning and land-use decisions, focusing on zoning that reduces exposures, priority restoration of contaminated sites, improving infrastructure, reusing vacant properties, reducing barriers to healthy food, and offering safe active transportation options.[133]

The United States has spent millions on lead abatement programs focused on lead paint hazards in low-income housing. A recent American study concluded: "If we continue to permit children and, by extension, pregnant women to maintain up to 10 μg/dL blood lead level without aggressive intervention to lower exposure, we are still allowing most of the preventable sub-clinical damage to occur."[134] Canada has never made a similar investment in lead abatement, despite the fact that the government estimates that as many as one in four children may be at risk from this environmental hazard. The remediation of lead hazard hotspots where children suffer from elevated blood lead levels (e.g., Trail, BC, and Belledune, New Brunswick) should be a priority.[135] Regulations under the *Food and Drugs Act* allowing lead concentrations in apple juice at levels twenty times higher than permissible in drinking water should be amended immediately. The American experience and Health Canada research indicate that the health, environmental, and economic benefits of reducing blood lead levels are likely to be measured in billions of dollars.

Another environmental justice priority is to improve drinking water quality on Aboriginal reserves. Although some progress has been made, both in terms of law (the 2013 *Safe Drinking Water for First Nations Act*) and on the ground, Canada needs to accelerate efforts to ensure the provision of adequate drinking water in these communities. Further investments in infrastructure, training, distribution systems, testing, and monitoring are urgently required.

Effective Enforcement of Environmental Laws

Even the strongest environmental laws in the world would be meaningless if they were not enforced. Canada has a long-standing record of failing to enforce environmental laws, as detailed in Chapter 8. When polluters are out of compliance with their permits, the general practice is not to prosecute them but to amend the permit to authorize higher volumes of pollution. In the rare cases where regulators have taken enforcement action, courts have often failed to respond effectively, permitting a panoply of defences and levying fines that are little more than slaps on the wrist.

To address these problems, two major innovations are recommended, including the creation of independent environmental enforcement agencies and a system of green courts. An independent enforcement agency would eliminate the problem of governments being soft on crime, and ensure that when environmental laws are broken, lawbreakers will face consequences. An intriguing model is Brazil's Ministério Público, or Public Ministry, which has been compared to a fourth branch of government and is responsible for protecting human rights, such as the right to a healthy environment. It receives public complaints, conducts investigations, and prosecutes cases. The constitutional changes in 1988 that empowered the Ministério Público to defend environmental rights have resulted in a dramatic increase in enforcement of environmental laws.[136] A Brazilian judge wrote that "hundreds of pages would be needed to mention all the precedents" set by Brazilian courts in recent years dealing with constitutional protection for the environment.[137] In the state of São Paulo alone, between 1984 and 2004, the Ministério Público filed over four thousand public civil actions in environmental cases addressing issues ranging from deforestation to air pollution.[138] Brazil's public ministry has been emulated by Portugal, Colombia, and many Latin American nations in recent years.

Effectively enforcing environmental laws also depends on the existence of impartial adjudicative bodies, which can be either courts or administrative tribunals with quasi-judicial powers. Courts have a long history of impartially resolving disputes between parties, but judicial proceedings are expensive and time-consuming. Many judges have limited expertise in environmental matters. Administrative tribunals offer the potential for more informal, accessible, timely, and inexpensive resolution of environmental disputes.[139] Appointees to an environmental tribunal should possess either environmental or legal expertise, and ideally both. Tribunals "can provide an important check on bureaucratic decisions, and the mere availability of appeals can improve the integrity of decision-making in the knowledge that some independent oversight and scrutiny might be applied in the future."[140]

There are no environmental courts in Canada, although several Canadian jurisdictions employ administrative tribunals that specialize in subjects related to environmental protection. For example, Ontario has five tribunals that make up the Environment and Land Tribunals system, including the Environmental Review Tribunal, the Assessment Review Board, Board of Negotiation, Conservation Review Board, and Ontario Municipal Board. British Columbia has ten administrative tribunals with mandates that relate, to varying degrees, to environmental protection.

There is an increasing trend in other nations to establish specialized environmental courts or tribunals.[141] Over 360 specialized environmental courts and tribunals have been established in forty-one countries, in every major type of legal system, and in developed as well as developing nations.[142] Sweden, New Zealand, and three Australian states (New South Wales, Queensland, and South Australia) have established specialized environmental courts.[143] The Netherlands, Finland, Thailand, Kenya, and Bangladesh have judges within the regular court system who specialize in adjudicating environmental cases.[144]

The reasons for establishing specialized environmental courts and tribunals include:

Efficiency – Reduce time required for decision making.

Economy – Reduce costs through more efficient handling of cases, aggressive case management, more efficient use of experts, and use of alternative dispute resolution (ADR).

Expertise – Increase decision quality with judges who have specialized expertise.

Uniformity – Increase consistency in the interpretation and application of environmental law, and discourage forum shopping.

Access to justice – Improve access to justice for citizens, NGOs, and businesses.

Commitment – Demonstrate government's commitment to protecting the environment.

Problem-solving approach – Open up more flexible ways of resolving environmental disputes than the traditional adversarial process (ADR, collaborative planning and decision making, hybrid civil/criminal prosecution, creative sentencing and enforcement options, court-appointed special commissions, and facilitated settlement agreements).

Public participation – Encourage greater public participation and support for the decision-making process through broad standing, use of community expert committees, limited cost awards, and so on.

Public confidence – Increase public confidence in the government's environmental efforts by having a transparent, effective, expert decision-making body.

A comprehensive global study of environmental courts and tribunals concluded that an integrated environmental and land-use planning court, with civil, administrative, and criminal jurisdiction and enforcement powers adequate to the task, is best equipped to provide comprehensive access to environmental justice.[145]

Specialized rules may be required for courts to handle environmental cases effectively and efficiently. For example, the Philippines established special procedures for environmental litigation, with four objectives: (1) protecting and advancing the constitutional right to a healthy environment; (2) providing a simplified, speedy, and inexpensive procedure for enforcing environmental rights; (3) adopting innovations and best practices for enforcing environmental laws; and (4) enabling courts to monitor and ensure compliance with orders in environmental cases.[146] Among the innovative rules is a requirement that all civil cases be referred to mediation for a period of thirty days.[147]

International Leadership: Prioritize Environmental Health in Canadian Foreign Policy

Another key environmental law principle is common but differentiated responsibility, which means that all nations share a duty to protect the environment but wealthier countries need to shoulder a heavier share of the burden. As Norway has acknowledged: "The rich countries are largely responsible for generating these problems and have the most extensive economic resources."[148] Reducing environmental impacts on health in developing countries should be a priority of Canada's development assistance programs – focusing on air quality, clean water, adequate sanitation, and developmental neurotoxins. Canada should establish a strategy, including a legislated timeline, for meeting the internationally accepted target for development assistance of 0.7 percent of GDP; conduct an environmental audit of our international trade profile to ensure that we are not shifting polluting industries or exporting harmful substances to developing nations, where health and environmental policies are weaker or rarely enforced; and continue to forgive the debt of developing nations that meet human rights and corruption criteria.

Canada must also re-evaluate its positions in international negotiations where we are interfering with global efforts to reduce environmental impacts on health. Embarrassing examples include Canada's opposition to recognition of the right to a healthy environment and its obstructive role in climate change and biodiversity negotiations. Following our leadership in developing the "responsibility to protect" doctrine requiring nations to take positive actions to protect their citizens from genocide, war crimes, crimes against humanity, and ethnic cleansing, Canada should be a global leader in advocating a new international agreement to phase out the production, use, and release of developmental neurotoxins such as lead, mercury, arsenic, PCBs, and toluene.[149] The new agreement could be similar to the successful and widely supported Stockholm Convention on Persistent Organic Pollutants. Finally, Canada should reverse its position of opposing the listing of chrysotile asbestos under the Rotterdam Convention. A promising sign that more ethical foreign policy positions are possible was Canada's recent reversal on the right to water, which it previously opposed but now supports.

Canada should also revise its position on free trade by supporting the ability of countries to enact stronger environmental laws and policies to protect the health and well-being of citizens without having to pay compensation to corporations whose profits may be adversely affected by such laws. This would require Canada to reject investor-state dispute settlement provisions that allow foreign corporations to bypass domestic legal systems and pursue huge damages awards through international arbitration mechanisms. In recent years, there has been an explosion of these cases, mainly related to mining, oil, and gas projects.[150] A growing number of cases are being filed against Canada.[151] For example, Lone Pine Resources sued Canada in 2013 because of Quebec's moratorium on hydraulic fracturing (fracking).[152] Canadian resource companies have filed many investor-state lawsuits against governments in developing countries (particularly in Latin America) for blocking projects because of health and environmental concerns.[153] For example, a Canadian mining company is seeking approximately $1 billion in damages from Costa Rica for that nation's refusal to license an open-pit gold mine.[154]

Foreign corporations have forced Canada to pay hundreds of millions of dollars in compensation and repeal environmental laws pursuant to provisions in the North American Free Trade Agreement.[155] NAFTA should be renegotiated to limit these lawsuits to cases of intentional discrimination or unwarranted expropriation without compensation, and Canada should avoid these types of provisions in negotiating future trade agreements. Australia set a useful precedent by rejecting the inclusion of investor-state dispute settlement provisions in free trade agreements based on the arbitrary nature of decisions rendered by three-person international arbitration panels, who need not consider a nation's constitutional law or precedents from domestic courts.[156] Other countries, from Latin America to the European Union, are also refusing to sign trade agreements that include investor-state dispute resolution provisions.[157]

Conclusion

The information generated by the environmental health research and surveillance initiatives outlined in this chapter will strengthen the scientific basis for health and environmental policymaking for generations to come. Canada needs to integrate and disseminate data on environmental hazards and amenities, exposures, disease outcomes, and the effectiveness of environmental health policies. Enhanced understanding of this information will facilitate improvements to risk assessment, health and environmental laws, policies, and programs, and the establishment of regulatory standards. However, there is no question that much can be done in Canada right now to protect people's health from environmental harms on the basis of existing knowledge and lessons learned from the experiences of other nations.

The stronger laws, regulations, policies, and programs identified in this chapter will decrease exposure to environmental hazards, increase access to environmental amenities, alleviate environmental injustices, and ensure systematic implementation of the polluter-pays and precautionary principles. The net result will be unprecedented protection of Canadians' right to a healthy environment. Thousands of premature deaths can be prevented. Billions of dollars in health care costs can be avoided. The potential improvements in Canadians' quality of life are worth many more billions of dollars, according to the calculations of economists, or can be considered invaluable, according to the understanding of many ordinary people.

11

Systemic Changes in Pursuit of Sustainability

Sustainability in Canada, as elsewhere, will likely only arise if people are prepared to choose fundamentally different goals for their society, including a fundamentally different economic model in which maintaining ecological integrity is a precondition to all development.

– PROFESSORS STEPAN WOOD, GEORGIA TANNER, AND BEN RICHARDSON (2010)

Chapter 10 identified short-term law and policy changes that would improve Canada's environmental record and decrease the burden of illnesses, premature deaths, and socio-economic costs caused by environmental degradation. Although implementing these actions would produce much-needed improvements, it is unlikely that – even collectively – they would solve the underlying problems. Long-term solutions will require a suite of systemic economic, legal, political, and social changes, which are introduced in this chapter:

- focusing on Canadian well-being instead of myopically pursuing GDP growth
- shifting to a circular, steady-state economy

- reforming corporate law and governance to benefit society and the environment
- accelerating the transition to renewable energy
- enshrining environmental rights and responsibilities in the Constitution
- resuscitating Canadian democracy from its current malaise
- reducing inequality, both within Canada and internationally
- promoting peace and investing the savings in societal projects.

None of these systemic changes will come easily, yet they lie within reach if Canadians act upon their concerns about the environment, their health, and their children's futures. Ultimately, Canada's challenge is to transform the relationship between people and the natural environment from the current approach of minimizing harm to a future based on maximizing harmony. Instead of attempting to merely limit the ecological damage caused by contemporary industrial society, Canada should challenge the pervasive belief that human activities must inevitably damage the natural world, and strive to do things in ways that avoid creating environmental problems in the first place. In the words of William McDonough and Michael Braungart, "to be less bad is to accept things as they are, to believe that poorly designed, dishonorable, destructive systems are the best humans can do. This is the ultimate failure of the 'be less bad' approach: a failure of the imagination."[1] The policies outlined in this chapter are intended to facilitate processes, products, and patterns of behaviour that are good for society and the planet.

Focus on Quality of Life, not Economic Growth

> GDP sheds no light on the health of our population, on the vibrancy of our democracy and our communities, on the growing inequality within our country, on the sustainability of our environment, or on other aspects of the quality of life of Canadians.
>
> – CANADIAN INDEX OF WELLBEING (2012)

As noted in Chapter 9, endless economic growth on a finite planet is impossible. Climate change, biodiversity loss, and ecological footprint analysis prove beyond a reasonable doubt that further economic growth for wealthy countries is unsustainable.[2] In the words of Stanford University ecologist

Gretchen Daily, "the physical pressure that human activities put on the environment can't possibly be sustained."[3] And yet in most government, business, and economic circles, growth continues to be viewed as imperative, a prerequisite for addressing every problem faced by society, from unemployment and poverty to improved health and environmental restoration. Lawrence Summers, economist, former head of the World Bank, and adviser to President Barack Obama, said: "The idea that we should put limits on growth because of some natural limit is a profound error, and one that, were it ever to prove influential, would have staggering social costs."[4] Political leaders in Canada and the United States continue to stress the paramount importance of continuing and even accelerating economic growth.

Outside North America, calling for an end to economic growth is no longer a radical idea. Nobel Prize–winning economists Joseph Stiglitz and Amartya Sen led France's Commission on the Measurement of Economic Performance and Social Progress, which criticized GDP as inadequate because of its exclusion of social and environmental factors and described society's emphasis on this single indicator as "fetishism."[5] Economist Tim Jackson, who led the British government's Sustainable Development Commission, argued that the "narrow pursuit of growth represents a horrible distortion of the common good and our underlying human values."[6] Governments in Bhutan, the United Kingdom, France, Brazil, Germany, Ecuador, Bolivia, and Italy have recognized that increases in GDP were never intended to serve as a proxy for human progress. These countries are supplementing or replacing GDP and the focus on economic growth with a more holistic approach intended to respect environmental limits and improve quality of life for both present and future generations.[7] Although the Organisation for Economic Co-operation and Development continues to promote growth, it created a Better Life Initiative that may prompt a re-examination of conventional wisdom about progress.[8] Even China recognizes that blind pursuit of economic growth is self-defeating.[9]

The end of material growth must not be confused with the end of human development. Indeed, the opposite outcome can and should be envisioned: by refocusing society's remarkable ingenuity on the pursuit of justice, sustainable prosperity, and genuine wealth, we should achieve higher levels of fulfillment and happiness. Many studies have shown that there is a point where higher incomes and consumption do not increase happiness, and average per capita income in Canada is well past that point.[10]

There are many comprehensive indices already available to supplement or supersede GDP, including the Canadian Index of Wellbeing (CIW), the

Genuine Progress Indicator, the concept of genuine wealth, the Happy Planet Index, and the Index of Sustainable Economic Welfare.[11] These holistic measures often tell a different, more nuanced story than the triumphalist version of eternal economic growth. For example, the CIW tracks sixty-four indicators in eight areas of life in Canada: living standards, health, community vitality, education, time use, democratic engagement, leisure and culture, and the environment.[12] These domains were chosen based on in-depth public consultations with Canadians about the things they value. While Canada experienced relatively robust economic growth of 28.9 percent between 1994 and 2010, the CIW rose only 5.7 percent, with declines in the environmental, leisure, and culture indicators.[13]

The false dilemma of growth is that we appear to be caught between the desire for economic stability and the need to remain within ecological limits. Professor Peter Victor of York University wrote a book called *Managing without Growth*, about the consequences if Canada were to end its fixation on GDP. Victor's extensive economic modelling demonstrated that ending growth abruptly would be very painful. However, he reached a remarkable conclusion: "Slower growth, leading to stability around 2030, can also be consistent with attractive economic, social, and environmental outcomes: full employment, virtual elimination of poverty, more leisure, considerable reduction in GHG emissions and fiscal balance."[14] Victor identified an array of policies that would be required to effectively manage the transition, first to slower growth and eventually to no growth, including quantitative limits on resource inputs and waste outputs, reduced work hours, and a stable population (where immigration would offset Canada's low birth rate). Increasing efficiency is a popular but insufficient solution because gains cannot keep pace with expansions in overall scale. For example, oil sands companies may use less energy and water per barrel of oil, but expansion in the rate of extraction means that their overall use of water and energy continues to grow.

Like Victor, Tim Jackson recommended a suite of changes to replace economic growth with the pursuit of sustainable well-being, including a shorter working week, shorter working hours, increased leisure time, taxes on resource use and pollution, accounting for the value of natural capital and ecosystem services, investing in green skills and jobs, creating a tax on international currency transfers to reduce excessive mobility of capital and fund sustainable development initiatives, dismantling the culture of consumerism (e.g., by restricting advertising directed at children), requiring durability and repair instead of planned obsolescence, prioritizing local production

and consumption, focusing on services, not goods, and investing in ecological assets.[15] These changes would reshape economic activity to promote
human development and provide decent livelihoods, but with much lower
resource and energy throughput. Making these changes also would have a
profound impact on investment decisions. Many investments avoided today
because of low rates of financial return would be viewed through a different
lens. When externalities are internalized, investments in renewable energy,
building retrofits, electricity grid upgrades, public transit, public spaces,
and ecosystem restoration become more attractive. Both Victor and Jackson
emphasize that a strategy of contraction and convergence is needed, meaning that resource use needs to decline in wealthy nations while rising in
developing nations to narrow the enormous wealth gap.

Creating a Circular, Steady-State Economy

> The richest nations are putting so much pressure on the
> environment and natural resources that other nations cannot
> improve their welfare without exceeding environmental
> tolerance limits.
>
> – GOVERNMENT OF NORWAY, STRATEGY FOR
> SUSTAINABLE DEVELOPMENT

Canada needs to move away from today's linear economy, treating the natural world as nothing more than an endless inventory of resources for our
use and a garbage can for our wastes. Ecological footprint analysis demonstrates that Canada is currently consuming resources several times faster
than the sustainable rate. The quantity and qualities of humanity's waste and
pollution are no longer within nature's assimilative capacity, as climate
change, ozone depletion, and the accumulation of persistent organic pollutants in the Arctic demonstrate. In contrast, in natural systems the quantity and quality of "wastes" are such that they can all be recycled into useful
resources, resulting in a circular and inherently sustainable process powered by solar energy. By intelligently redesigning systems of production and
consumption, using natural cycles as models, humans can ensure that our
"wastes" are also of a quality and quantity capable of being recycled as useful inputs. McDonough and Braungart describe two "waste" streams: industrial and biological.[16] The industrial stream consists of products that
can be repeatedly recycled, such as metals. The biological stream consists of

biodegradable materials that can be safely composted and added to soil to grow food, trees, or other useful products.

A circular, one-planet, or biosphere economy would recognize that the Earth is finite – that there are physical limits to nonrenewable substances like fossil fuels and minerals, and limits to the productive capacity of eco-systems. As well, there are the limits to Earth's assimilative capacity, which humans exceed at our collective peril. Explicitly recognizing biophysical limits would require reversing current trends of growing resource con-sumption and population.[17] Scandinavian nations are ahead of Canada in this regard. Norway recognizes that "if environmental limits are exceeded, the consequences may be irreversible ... Norway's sustainable development policy, including its environmental protection policy, are therefore based on environmental targets that take account of the tolerance limits of the environment."[18] Similarly, Sweden admits that "it is becoming ever more apparent that, when the consumption patterns of the industrialised world are adopted by the developing countries, the aggregate extraction of re-sources worldwide will exceed planetary limits."[19]

It is difficult to determine the planet's productive and assimilative limits, as illustrated by ongoing debates about "peak oil" and the pace of global climate change.[20] A more productive approach is to identify the basic con-ditions necessary for attaining sustainability. There has been a tremendous outpouring of scholarship about the meanings of sustainable development and sustainability since the words came into prominence with the publica-tion of the Brundtland Commission's report *Our Common Future* in 1987. The original definition – "development that meets the needs of the present without compromising the ability of future generations to meet their own needs" – is insufficiently detailed to provide concrete guidance.[21] A group of Swedish scientists identified four system conditions that establish the basis for sustainability:

System Conditions

In the sustainable society, nature is not subject to systematically increasing ...

1. concentrations of substances extracted from the Earth's crust
2. concentrations of substances produced by society
3. degradation by physical means

and, people are not subject to conditions that systematically

4. undermine their capacity to meet their needs.[22]

If the system conditions are being violated, then the society is not sustainable. Period.

It follows from the system conditions that the environmental imperative in industrialized nations like Canada is to reduce our consumption of resources (dematerialization) and substitute safe, renewable substances for substances that are known or suspected to be toxic, persistent, or bioaccumulative. In order to achieve dematerialization and substitution, two things need to happen: (1) the modification of individual, business, and government behaviour; and (2) the invention and diffusion of new technologies. Stronger environmental laws and policies can stimulate both kinds of action. The European Union and Japan are world leaders in developing policies and plans for the transition to a circular economy, while China is also keenly interested in this approach.[23]

The Renewable Energy Revolution

> I'd put my money on the sun and solar energy.
> – THOMAS EDISON

A shift towards renewable energy is inevitable because fossil fuels, by their very nature, are finite. There is a lively debate about "peak oil" but the controversy focuses on when petroleum will begin running out, not whether this will happen. Since the lion's share of adverse health effects from environmental hazards in Canada are caused by burning fossil fuels, shifting to renewables will substantially reduce health costs. Phasing out fossil fuels will dramatically reduce negative externalities, including air pollution, water pollution, and climate change. It is important to emphasize that adding renewable energy capacity should always be complemented by reductions in overall energy use through behavioural change and greater efficiency (e.g., buildings, vehicles, and consumer products).

Professors Mark Jacobson and Mark Delucchi have demonstrated that the entire world could shift to 100 percent renewable energy for all needs – residential, commercial, industrial, and transportation – by 2050.[24] Jacobson has published plausible plans for the United States and each of the fifty states to accomplish this ambitious goal. His conclusions have been confirmed by US government agencies and other research institutes. For example, the US National Oceanic and Atmospheric Administration indicated that 80 percent of American electricity needs could be generated by renewables by 2030 (with the remainder from fossil fuels and nuclear power). A collaboration by 110 researchers from thirty-five institutions published by the highly respected US National Renewable Energy Laboratory (NREL) concluded that existing renewable energy technologies could easily meet 80 percent of American electricity needs by 2050.[25] The resulting system would produce 90 percent less greenhouse gas emissions and reduce water use by 50 percent. Wind and solar dominate, with smaller contributions from geothermal, hydropower, and biomass. The study did not include emerging technologies such as enhanced geothermal systems, wave and tidal power, offshore wind turbines, and solar nanotechnology. American renewable energy potential is estimated to be roughly 128 times the generating capacity of the current US electrical system. The shift to renewables is underway, as wind power tripled between 2007 and 2012, while solar power quadrupled.[26]

In Australia, a federal government study published in 2013 indicated that the transition to 100 percent renewable electricity by 2030 would be on par economically with the investments needed to maintain today's system based predominantly on fossil fuels.[27] Other studies show that solar and wind power are now cheaper than coal and gas in Australia, even before health and environmental externalities are factored into the comparison. Even without a carbon tax, wind energy was 14 percent cheaper than new coal and 18 percent cheaper than new natural gas.[28] "The perception that fossil fuels are cheap and renewables are expensive is now out of date," said Michael Liebreich, chief executive of Bloomberg New Energy Finance.[29] Liebreich added: "The fact that wind power is now cheaper than coal and gas in a country with some of the world's best fossil fuel resources shows that clean energy is a game changer which promises to turn the economics of power systems on its head."[30]

Germany has a binding target to produce at least 35 percent of its electricity from renewable sources by 2020 – with the target rising to 50 percent by 2030, and 80 percent by 2050.[31] Since 2000, Germany has quadrupled the portion of electricity generated by renewable sources, going from 6 percent to over 25 percent.[32] On one day in May 2014, wind and solar reached a record 75 percent of total electricity supply in Germany.[33] This progress was propelled primarily by government policies, including a feed-in tariff mandating substantial subsidies for wind and solar. Although Germany's experience has generated controversy, the OECD calculates that there has been a tiny negative impact on Germany's GDP (approximately 0.2 percent).[34] Jobs in Germany's renewable energy industry have more than tripled over the past decade, to 367,400 in 2010, and are projected to grow to 500,000 by 2020.[35]

Other countries are also making tremendous progress. Fifteen countries – from Albania to Zambia – generate over 90 percent of their electricity from renewables. Costa Rica set a target of generating all electricity from renewable sources by 2020 and is already at 99 percent. Iceland and Paraguay already generate 100 percent of their electricity from renewable sources, while Norway is at 97 percent.[36] Denmark is aiming to produce 50 percent of its electricity from wind by 2025 – and 100 percent of its electricity from renewable energy by 2050. Wind power is now the leading producer of electricity in Spain.[37] In the aftermath of the Fukushima nuclear disaster, the Japanese government moved quickly to expand its feed-in tariff program for renewables. Over 4 gigawatts of new solar electricity generating capacity were added in the first year, the equivalent of four large nuclear reactors. Another 25 gigawatts of clean energy projects (mostly wind and solar) have been approved.[38]

These are extraordinary findings. Today's renewable energy technologies, which are certain to improve and fall further in cost due to improving technology and economies of scale, are already capable of providing 100 percent of the world's electricity needs within the relatively short span of a few decades. Solar power rose by a factor of five globally between 2009 and 2012.[39] When the health and environmental externalities of burning fossil fuels are taken into consideration, the economic rationale for switching to renewable energy is even more compelling.[40] The International Energy Agency estimated that it would cost $44 trillion to switch the global energy systems to renewables by 2050, but would save $115 trillion in fuel costs, for net savings of $71 trillion.[41] Challenges related to grid access, intermittency, and storage are being addressed. For example, although the wind blows intermittently, it dovetails with hydroelectric power, as reservoirs can serve as de facto batteries. The world's first solar power plant that produces electricity around the clock came online in 2011 in Spain, and is being emulated in the United States and elsewhere.

Fortunately, Canada is well positioned for the transition to using renewable energy for 100 percent of its energy needs, with tremendous wind, solar, geothermal, biomass, wave, and tidal energy resources. These resources "are many times larger than current or projected levels of total fuel and electricity consumption."[42] As of 2014, almost two-thirds of Canadian electricity consumption was generated from renewable sources. Sixty percent of Canada's electricity was produced by hydroelectricity, with wind, biomass, and solar photovoltaic far behind at 1.6 percent, 1.4 percent, and 0.5 percent, respectively. Burning fossil fuels generates roughly one-quarter of Canadian electricity and nuclear provides the remaining 15 percent.[43] Transportation is almost entirely fossil-fuel based, although sales of electric vehicles are growing rapidly. A UN-sponsored study identified several plausible pathways for Canada to reduce GHGs 90 percent by 2050, by completely shifting to renewable electricity and biofuels.[44]

Wind and solar power have experienced rapid growth in Canada in recent years, while wave and tidal power are just beginning to be deployed. In 1997, Canada had 23 megawatts of installed wind capacity. By the end of 2014, that number had grown to 9,694 megawatts, placing Canada seventh in the world. For the year 2014, Canada ranked sixth in the world in adding new wind capacity, behind China, Germany, the United States, Brazil, and India.[45] In 2003, Canada had 12 megawatts of installed solar photovoltaic capacity. By 2013, that number had leapt to 1,200 megawatts, a hundred times higher. Ninety percent of that leap was made in the most recent five-year period. Wave and tidal current technology demonstration projects are under way in British Columbia and Nova Scotia. In BC, there is a wave energy device with a capacity of 100 kilowatts. In Nova Scotia, there is a tidal power plant with a generating capacity of 20 megawatts. The elimination of coal-fired electricity generation in Ontario was a major step forward, and should be emulated by other Canadian provinces. Accelerating Canada's transition to renewable energy in order to meet established government GHG reduction targets would create 620,000 person-years of construction jobs and 34,000 permanent jobs by 2022.[46]

Policies that have proven successful in accelerating the adoption of renewable energy are renewable energy targets, coal power phaseouts, feed-in tariffs, and guaranteed grid access. First enacted in 1991 and adjusted several times since, Germany's feed-in tariff gives renewable energy projects priority access to the power grid, and provides a guaranteed price for the power for up to twenty years. Ontario's *Green Energy Act,* modelled after German and Japanese legislation, provides a leading Canadian example.[47] Providing support and minimizing barriers to the adoption of municipal- and community-scale renewable energy products should also be prioritized.

Moving towards a transportation system that is entirely based on renewable energy represents a stiffer challenge. Electric vehicles are coming on stream in record numbers but still represent a small proportion of new vehicles, with the exception of Norway, where the Tesla sedan and the Nissan Leaf are the top-selling cars.[48] Electric vehicle technology will ultimately also provide part of the solution to energy storage, as millions of these cars can be used to store electricity and then return it to the grid at different times based on supply and demand in the system as a whole.

It should be noted that some high-profile environmentalists – such as James Lovelock – support nuclear energy. However, nuclear energy faces daunting obstacles, including the risk of catastrophic accidents, the risk of terrorist attacks, the unsolved dilemma of storing nuclear waste, and the astronomical costs.[49]

The Canadian Charter of Environmental Rights and Responsibilities

The overhaul of Canada's environmental laws and policies outlined in Chapter 10 needs to start at the very top, with the incorporation of environmental rights and responsibilities into the Constitution.[50] As the supreme law of Canada, the Constitution establishes the rules that guide and constrain government powers and it protects individual rights. A constitution also reflects and reinforces a society's deepest and most cherished values, acting as a mirror of a country's soul.[51] The logical argument for according constitutional status to the right to a healthy environment is straightforward.[52] Fundamental human rights should enjoy the strongest legal status available in today's society – constitutional protection – to ensure that they are respected and fulfilled. The right to live in a healthy environment meets the three criteria for recognition as a fundamental human right (moral importance, universality, practicability). Therefore, it should be protected by Canada's Constitution. As well, empirical evidence based on the experiences of more than a hundred nations indicates that constitutional entrenchment of environmental rights and responsibilities contributes to stronger laws, increased enforcement, an enhanced role for citizens, and improved environmental performance.

Environmental rights and responsibilities could be incorporated into the *Canadian Charter of Rights and Freedoms* by adding the following provision to section 7:

7.1 Everyone has the right to live in a healthy and ecologically balanced environment, including clean air, safe water, fertile soil, nutritious food, a stable climate, and flourishing biodiversity.

This approach offers the advantage of consistency with the current style of the *Charter*, which is concise and focused on individual rights. Government's duty to protect the environment is implicit, and it is left to legislatures, courts, and citizens to fill in the details. A second option would be to take a more comprehensive approach, comparable to the extensive provisions of the *Charter* dealing with official languages.[53] An example of a more detailed set of provisions is provided below:

The Canadian Charter of Environmental Rights and Responsibilities

The people of Canada understand that:

The beauty, vastness, and diversity of Nature are at the heart of the Canadian identity;

We are stewards of a sacred trust, safeguarding Canada's unique and magnificent natural heritage on behalf of the world;

The air we breathe, the water we drink, and the food we eat make us part of, and dependent upon, the environment;

The choices we make to meet our needs must not compromise the capacity of future generations and other peoples to satisfy their needs;

Our future health, well-being, and prosperity depend on reducing our pressure on the Earth's ecosystems and living graciously within Nature's limits;

Therefore we proclaim:

1 Everyone has the right to live in a healthy and ecologically balanced environment, including clean air, safe water, fertile soil, nutritious food, a stable climate, and flourishing biodiversity.

2 Everyone has a responsibility to protect and, where possible, restore the environment.

3 Everyone has the following rights: to information about the state of the environment; to participate in public decision making that affects the environment; and access to justice in response to violations or anticipated violations of their right to live in a healthy environment.

4 Governments at all levels, according to their jurisdiction under the *Constitution Act, 1867*, are trustees who share the responsibility for protecting and restoring the environment, for the benefit of present and future generations.

5 Government laws, regulations, policies, and decisions shall apply the polluter-pays principle, so that any individual, private enterprise, or public entity that damages human health or the environment is responsible

for paying for the full costs of restoring, rehabilitating, or paying compensation for damages inflicted.

6 Government laws, regulations, policies, and decisions shall follow the precautionary principle, so that where there is evidence of potentially significant environmental harm, a lack of scientific certainty shall not be used to avoid or delay the implementation of effective and efficient measures to prevent or mitigate the harm.

7 Governments shall ensure that the costs of pollution and environmental damage are fairly distributed, that existing environmental injustices are alleviated, and that the benefits of environmental goods and services are enjoyed equitably.

8 Educational programs at all levels, from preschool to university, must contribute to the implementation of the rights and responsibilities defined by this *Charter.*

9 The rights of future generations and Nature shall be respected by governments when enacting laws or regulations, making decisions, developing policies, and implementing programs or budgets.

10 Canada shall comply with the principles articulated in this *Charter* when engaged in negotiations or actions at the international level.

This draft charter resembles France's Charter for the Environment, which has already had a substantial positive impact since its enactment in 2005.[54] Both documents set forth the rationale for constitutional change as a response to pressing national and global ecological challenges. Both articulate substantive and procedural environmental rights and responsibilities. The draft Canadian Charter of Environmental Rights and Responsibilities addresses the complex question of constitutional jurisdiction by clarifying that governments at all levels are trustees for environmental protection within their fields of responsibility. It also identifies a number of established legal principles – polluter-pays, the precautionary principle, environmental justice, and intergenerational equity – and elevates them to constitutional status to ensure that they consistently guide government decision making. Inspired by Indigenous law as well as recent legal developments in Bolivia, Ecuador, and New Zealand, it also recognizes the rights of Nature (discussed in detail below). Like the French charter, it emphasizes the critical role of education. Finally, Canada would be constitutionally bound to act in an environmentally responsible manner on the international stage, reversing a recent pattern of violating commitments, withdrawing from treaties, and obstructing negotiations.

Achieving constitutional change is challenging in Canada because the amending formula requires the support of Parliament and the legislatures of at least two-thirds of the provinces (with at least 50 percent of the population), which must be achieved within a three-year period. As of 2014, no province has a veto under the amending formula (i.e., no province has 50 percent of Canada's population). Given the problems plaguing the Senate, it is worth noting that the requirement of Senate approval can be overridden. If 180 days pass after the House of Commons adopts its authorizing resolution and the Senate has not concurred, the House may adopt a second resolution, eliminating the need for Senate approval.

The Supreme Court of Canada has repeatedly endorsed recognition of the right to live in a healthy environment.[55] In 1990, the Canadian Bar Association made the following recommendation:

> The Government of Canada should adopt a long-term strategy to entrench the right to a healthy environment in the Canadian Constitution. In the interim it should enact a statute enunciating the right of every Canadian to a healthy environment. No statute should be enacted that is inconsistent with that right.[56]

A coalition of environmental organizations led by the David Suzuki Foundation and Ecojustice has commenced a national campaign to secure constitutional recognition of the right to a healthy environment. A public opinion poll indicates that nine in ten Canadians support this objective.[57] Momentum could be built by securing recognition of the right to a healthy environment at the local and provincial/territorial level, as suggested in Chapter 10.

Rights of Nature
Something is clearly amiss in humanity's relationship with the rest of the natural world. We treat Nature as separate from humans when we are but one species among millions, all biologically dependent on ecosystems that produce water, air, food, and a stable climate. One option for repairing our relationship with Nature and living in harmony with other species is to recognize that Nature has rights that give rise to human responsibilities. Acknowledging Nature's rights has deep roots in cultures around the world, including Canada. Over a thousand years ago, a scholar wrote a book in Arabic in which the animal kingdom sued humankind for violating its rights.[58]

According to Professor John Borrows, author of *Canada's Indigenous Constitution*, a key element of many Aboriginal legal systems is a set of reciprocal rights and responsibilities between humans and other species, as well as nonliving elements of the environment: "The land's sentience is a fundamental principle of Anishinabek law," and it contributes to "a multiplicity of citizenship rights and responsibilities for Anishinabek people and the Earth."[59] Similarly, Mi'kmaq law is rooted in ecological relationships, extending legal personality to animals, plants, insects, and rocks, and imposing legal obligations on Mi'kmaq persons.[60]

The first modern suggestion that the rights of Nature be recognized came from American law professor Christopher Stone in 1972, and was echoed by US Supreme Court justice William Douglas.[61] Stone argued that there was no legal barrier to granting rights to Nature, given that other nonhuman entities such as corporations and ships had legal rights conferred upon them.[62] More recently, constitutional reforms in Bolivia and Ecuador explicitly recognized the rights of nonhuman species. Ecuador's constitution provides a detailed articulation of the "Rights of Nature" (Pachamama):

Chapter Seven: Rights of Nature

Article 71. Nature or Pachamama, where life plays and performs, is entitled to full respect, existence, and the maintenance and regeneration of its vital cycles, structure, functions, and evolutionary processes. Any person, community, or nation may require the public authority to comply with the rights of nature. The principles enshrined in the Constitution will be used to apply and interpret these rights, as appropriate. The State will encourage individuals, legal persons, and collective entities to protect nature and promote respect for all the elements that form an ecosystem.[63]

Several court decisions have enforced this right, although there are concerns regarding its inconsistent implementation.[64] Bolivia enacted a *Law on the Rights of Mother Earth* in 2010 that enumerated seven specific rights to which Mother Earth and her constituent life systems (including human communities) are entitled, including life, diversity, clean water, clean air, equilibrium, restoration, and freedom from contamination.[65] In New Zealand, an agreement between the government and the Maori recognized the legal rights of the Whanganui River, and established a trustee to ensure that the river's rights are respected. In 2014, New Zealand enacted a law recognizing that Te Urewera, formerly a national park, is a legal entity with "all the rights, powers, duties, and liabilities of a legal person."[66] Building on these precedents, advocates in Australia are seeking recognition of the rights of the Great Barrier Reef.[67] In the United States, more than three dozen local governments – from Pittsburgh to Santa Monica – have passed ordinances that explicitly recognize the rights of Nature.[68] For example, an ordinance passed by a town in New Hampshire states:

> Natural communities and ecosystems possess inalienable and fundamental rights to exist and flourish within the Town of Barnstead. Ecosystems shall include, but not be limited to, wetlands, streams, rivers, aquifers, and other water systems.

While many questions remain regarding the legal implications of recognizing Nature's rights, these developments have been complemented by calls for a UN Declaration of the Rights of Mother Earth, which is the subject of ongoing discussions.

Resuscitating Canadian Democracy

> The current electoral system no longer responds to 21st century Canadian values.
>
> – LAW REFORM COMMISSION OF CANADA (2004)

With a mandate from less than one-quarter of eligible Canadian voters and less than 40 percent of those who voted, Prime Minister Stephen Harper's Conservative government weakened many of Canada's most important environmental laws (e.g., the *Fisheries Act* and the *Canadian Environmental Assessment Act*), withdrew Canada from international treaties on climate change and desertification, made false statements about carbon taxes, and placed oil and gas development ahead of renewable energy. The propensity of the first-past-the-post electoral system to generate powerful false majorities (described in Chapter 9) should not be tolerated in a genuinely democratic nation, where each citizen's vote should be respected.

A panel composed of citizens and experts should be established with a mandate to prepare several clear options for a national referendum on electoral reform. Proportional representation systems maximize the extent to which every person's vote is reflected in election outcomes and offer several other advantages:

- Voters choose their preferred candidate instead of engaging in strategic voting.
- Parliament reflects the popular vote and fairly represents the will of the people.
- Parliament comes closer to embodying diverse populations (women, minorities, young and old).
- There is a higher likelihood that all regions are represented in government.
- Voter turnout is higher.
- Majority governments represent a genuine majority of the public.
- Government decisions are reached through cooperation, negotiation, and compromise.

More than eighty countries use proportional representation systems when electing their national assembly, including most long-term democracies, most European countries, and most of the major nations of the Americas. Most of these have used it for decades. Newly democratic countries almost never opt for a system like Canada's when setting up their electoral system.

New Zealand provides a promising example of a country that switched from first-past-the-post to a mixed-member proportional representation system (MMP). In a 1992 referendum, over 80 percent voted to change the electoral system, with over 70 percent selecting MMP.[69] In a 2011 referendum, a majority confirmed their preference for the MMP system. Citizens vote for both an individual representative and a party. In 2011, 97 percent of New Zealand voters cast a vote that elected someone to represent them.

Criticisms of proportional representation are often misguided or ill-informed. For example, concerns are expressed about unstable minority governments, yet nations relying on proportional representation are just as stable as nations using the first-past-the-post system. Italy, often held out as an exemplar of instability, has had fewer national elections than Canada in the past forty years. Similarly, studies demonstrate that the type of electoral system does not affect economic performance.[70]

Other problems undermining Canadian democracy include the influence of private money in politics, the excessive power wielded by the Prime Minister's Office, the use of omnibus bills to suppress public debate, and the Senate's lack of effectiveness and accountability. To make matters worse, the *Fair Elections Act*, enacted in 2014, removed investigative powers from Elections Canada, tilted the playing field in favour of the Conservatives, and may disenfranchise thousands of voters.[71] Canada moved towards public funding of election campaigns under Prime Minister Jean Chrétien but this progress was reversed by the Harper government in 2012. In many European countries, election campaigns are publicly funded, political advertising is prohibited, media must provide equal access for candidates, and private donations are not allowed.[72] Adopting these policies would help revitalize Canadian democracy.

Steps also need to be taken to rein in the growing powers of the Prime Minister's Office. Under Prime Minister Harper, the PMO has reached unprecedented size and asserted unparalleled control over the federal government's operations and communications. Because of quirks in Canada's political system, a prime minister with a majority government controls all three branches of government, through the power to appoint judges, choose cabinet ministers, and appoint deputy ministers. In 2013, Conservative backbencher Michael Chong introduced a private member's bill containing three laudable reforms that would restore local control over party nominations, strengthen party caucuses as decision-making bodies, and reinforce the accountability of party leaders.[73] While these changes would restore some degree of accountability, they are only a first step towards reining in the prime minister's power.

Omnibus bills that wrap sweeping changes to dozens of disparate laws in a single piece of legislation are fundamentally undemocratic because they preclude fulsome analysis and public debate. In general, there is no justification for bundling a broad array of unrelated legislative changes into a single bill. This is particularly true for budget implementation legislation, which entails a confidence vote and thus prevents opposition parties from voting against a bill (in a minority government situation) unless they are willing to trigger a federal election. Omnibus bills should be prohibited unless there are exceptional circumstances that warrant bypassing normal parliamentary scrutiny.

The fate of Canada's unelected and unaccountable Senate is also a major democratic issue.[74] The Senate has lost its credibility because of repeated scandals, making it hard to see how the institution adds value. It should be either abolished altogether or replaced by a body of representatives elected through a process in which party affiliations and advertising are prohibited. According to the Supreme Court, these changes will require constitutional reform.[75]

Reform of Corporate Law and Governance
Business is a powerful force in today's world but the corporate model too often benefits shareholders at the expense of the public, human rights, and

the environment. The law of corporations requires, or is perceived to require, the maximization of value for shareholders, which results in other stakeholders and interests, from employees to the environment, being sacrificed, disregarded, or given insufficient priority. As the Supreme Court of Canada stated: "Often the interests of shareholders and stakeholders are co-extensive with the interests of the corporation. But if they conflict, the directors' duty is clear – it is to the corporation."[76] Putting profits on a pedestal above other societal goals has proven increasingly counterproductive, and is unnecessary for the basic corporate purpose of organizing people into groups to achieve common goals. Current corporate structures undermine democracy through excessive political influence, damage human and ecosystem health by externalizing costs, and exacerbate inequality through the concentration of wealth. A variety of changes to legislation governing corporations and their behaviour are needed, including:

- authorizing fair returns for shareholders, not maximum returns
- the obligation to recognize public interests, including healthy environments, human rights, the best interests of children, gender equity, and fair wages
- withdrawal of personhood and constitutional rights (e.g., freedom of expression) from corporations
- prohibition of corporate involvement in lobbying, political finances, and election campaigns
- capping the maximum salary ratio between executives and employees.

One potential solution is a reformed corporate model called a benefit corporation. Benefit corporations are for-profit enterprises that undergo legal changes clarifying their ability to take societal and environmental interests into account and requiring them to make "a material positive impact on society."[77] These enterprises agree to meet higher standards of transparency, accountability, and performance. Benefit corporations must (1) have a corporate purpose to create a material positive impact on society and the environment; (2) expand the duties of directors to require consideration of nonfinancial stakeholders as well as the financial interests of shareholders; and (3) report on their social and environmental performance using a credible, independent, and transparent third-party standard.[78] As of 2014, thirty-one US states had passed benefit corporation legislation and twelve were in the process of doing so.[79] "B Corps" is not an abbreviation but refers to benefit corporations that have been certified by an independent organization (B Lab). There are now more than a thousand B Corps in thirty-two countries, including Seventh Generation, Patagonia, and Canada's Bullfrog Power.[80] British Columbia amended its *Business Corporations Act* to enable the creation of "community contribution companies," whose characteristics resemble benefit corporations.[81] In the United Kingdom, community interest companies enjoy the benefits of the corporate model but are required to pursue public interests.[82]

Another promising model is the cooperative, where members are democratically involved in the oversight of the business. Cooperatives are intended to meet the common needs of their members and operate on a one-member, one-vote basis rather than a one-share, one-vote basis. Profits are distributed on the basis of usage of the co-op's services rather than the number of shares owned. There are roughly nine thousand cooperatives in Canada with 18 million members.[83] Prominent Canadian cooperatives include Mountain Equipment Coop, VanCity Credit Union (Canada's largest credit union), Federated Cooperatives Limited, and Desjardins (Canada's sixth-largest financial institution).

Reducing Inequality
Research on the benefits of equality in OECD nations has produced startling results: life expectancy, literacy, child well-being, trust, and social mobility are all better in more equal societies.[84] Rates of obesity, infant mortality, teen pregnancy, homicide, and mental illness are all worse in less equal societies. There is also evidence that the collapse of societies is more likely where there is a combination of environmental degradation and a growing gap between a small elite and the majority of the population.[85] These research findings highlight the fact that stronger government policies to reduce inequality in Canadian society would produce health and environmental benefits.

The Conference Board of Canada ranks Canada twelfth out of seventeen countries in income inequality, describing our record as mediocre and noting that Canada is alone among wealthy industrialized nations in that the situation has worsened since the mid-1990s.[86] The Conference Board also concludes that Canada's "D" grade on working-age poverty and "C" grades on child poverty and income inequality are troubling for a wealthy country."[87] In 2014, data released by Statistics Canada revealed that the eighty-six richest Canadians collectively possessed greater wealth than the poorest 11 million Canadians.[88] Canada's tax system is failing to adequately redistribute income, because of a dramatic decline in corporate taxation, extensive tax loopholes that benefit the rich, the fact that Canada is one of the few countries without an inheritance tax, the fact that rules regarding offshore tax havens are frequently not enforced, and the fact that capital gains are currently taxed at half the rate of employment income. The top marginal tax rate on capital gains in Canada is almost half the rate in Denmark and France, and lower than the top marginal rates in the United States, United Kingdom, Germany, Ireland, Finland, Sweden, Norway, Spain, Austria, Israel, and the Slovak Republic.[89]

The policy changes required to address Canada's inequality gap are well known, with a history of achieving the desired results both in Canada and in other nations. These policies include establishing more progressive income tax rates, closing the tax loopholes that disproportionately benefit the wealthy, raising the capital gains tax, raising labour and employment standards (including the minimum wage), re-establishing an inheritance tax on large estates, creating a modest financial transaction tax, restricting the use of foreign temporary workers and ensuring that such workers enjoy full and equal rights, subsidizing affordable housing for low-income Canadians, increasing investment in training and higher education (making tuition affordable), subsidizing universal child care, and creating a basic income program (e.g., guaranteed annual income) to replace today's broad array of ineffective and inefficient welfare programs.[90] To promote equality, the OECD recommends affordable access to early childhood education and postsecondary education; investments in child care, parental support, and flexible employment; and policies that diminish the unequal treatment of employment and investment income.[91] These equality-promoting policies are being successfully implemented in Scandinavian nations. Nine in ten Canadians support government action to reduce poverty and inequality.[92]

Promote Peace

The Cold War is over and armed conflicts (both international wars and civil wars) are in decline, with fewer war-related deaths between 2000 and 2014 than in any decade of the twentieth century.[93] However, the Department of National Defence still has the largest budget of any Canadian government department. In 2008, the Conservative government unveiled its Canada First Defence Strategy, with a plan to expand the armed forces and spend $490 billion over a twenty-year period.[94] Included in this budget are over $100 billion for new warships and over $30 billion for new fighter planes.[95]

Defence budgets could be reallocated in ways that increase the well-being of Canadians and the sustainability of Canadian society. Costa Rica offers a fascinating precedent. In 1948, this Latin American nation decided to eliminate its armed forces. In hindsight, it was a courageous and brilliant decision.[96] Costa Rica has not been invaded nor (unlike many of its neighbours) has the government been overthrown by a military coup. Instead, Costa Rica has enjoyed a period of unprecedented democracy and stability. Other Latin American nations have spent billions on war over the past seven decades, while Costa Rica has invested in health, education, and environmental protection. The results are inspiring – levels of life expectancy and literacy that rival Canada and the United States despite far lower income and wealth levels.[97] Another indicator of the success of Costa Rica's approach is that the country ranks number one on the global Happy Planet Index, which incorporates data on life expectancy, ecological footprints, and happiness.[98]

The peace dividend derived from dramatically reducing Canadian military spending could be invested in retraining members of the armed forces for civilian jobs, or directed towards various national priorities such as strengthening the health care system, rebuilding municipal infrastructure, improving the energy efficiency of existing buildings, harnessing renewable sources of energy, tackling inequality, addressing child poverty, or reducing the national debt.

Conclusion

There is a dynamic tension between the structural economic, political, and legal changes identified in this chapter and the incremental improvements to Canadian environmental law and policy detailed in Chapter 10. Some will view the former as radical, while others will see the latter as inadequate. There is a danger that focusing on short-term solutions at the expense of systemic changes will result in limited incremental progress. Conversely, working solely on long-term changes could mean failing to enact and implement laws and policies that offer immediate benefits for Canadians' health and the environment. What both sets of recommendations have in common is that they are being employed successfully in other countries. Coordinated market economies (such as those found in Scandinavia and Germany) produce a wide range of more attractive outcomes than liberalized market economies (Canada and the United States), although both are subspecies of capitalism.[99] Coordinated market economies have less debt (both public and private), lower rates of unemployment, lower per capita carbon dioxide emissions, lower infant mortality, lower rates of teenage pregnancy, and a lower percentage of people who report feeling like an outsider.

In conclusion, Canadians should not be swayed by arguments that they must choose between the immediate steps that can and should be taken to reduce the environmental burden of disease and beginning efforts intended to achieve the structural changes outlined in this chapter. If other countries can successfully move forward on both aspects of a comprehensive environmental health agenda, then Canada also has this ability.

12

The Time for Action Is Now

Once people recognize how much is at stake with their health
and lives, and with the health and lives of their children, they will
do everything in their power to protect the global environment.

– ERIC CHIVIAN, MD, AND AARON BERNSTEIN, MD,
EDITORS OF *SUSTAINING LIFE: HOW HUMAN HEALTH
DEPENDS ON BIODIVERSITY*

In 2005, Canadian governments pledged to achieve the following health
goal: "The air we breathe, the water we drink, the food we eat, and the places
we live, work and play are safe and healthy – now and for generations to
come." Safe and healthy air must mean that no Canadians face increased
risks of cancer, cardiovascular disease, or respiratory illness simply from
breathing, whether indoors or outside. Safe and healthy food and water would
enable all Canadians to drink tap water and eat meals with complete confidence, knowing there was no short-term risk of gastrointestinal illness or
long-term risk of cancer. Ensuring that homes, schools, workplaces, and
recreational facilities are safe and healthy would mean that toxic substances
in all consumer products and construction materials had been eliminated.
Healthy environments require more than the mere absence of pollution and
toxic substances. Canadians need to be able to smell flowers, hear birdsong,
watch trees grow in height, girth, and majesty, marvel at stars in the night

sky, feel the subtle signs of changing seasons, revel in the laughter of children playing outdoors, and witness the myriad wonders of Nature in our daily lives. The overwhelming majority of Canadians support these health objectives, believing that a healthy environment is not just a policy goal but also a fundamental human right that deserves constitutional protection.

Despite being one of the wealthiest, best educated, and most technologically advanced nations in the history of humankind, Canada trails other industrialized nations in protecting human health from environmental hazards. The environmental rights of Canadians are neither recognized nor respected. Environmental hazards are ubiquitous, pervasive, and largely invisible, odourless, and tasteless, making it difficult for individuals to protect themselves and their families. Governments therefore have a duty to ensure that Canadians are not involuntarily subjected to environmental risks. Governments also have a duty to ensure that all Canadians enjoy equitable access to environmental amenities, including safe drinking water, clean air, green spaces, and the inspiring wonders of the natural world. These duties are especially vital in safeguarding and enriching the lives of infants and children, who are the most vulnerable to environmental hazards, the least able to protect themselves, and the most likely to benefit from healthy environments.

Examination

The magnitude of the adverse health impacts caused by air pollution and other environmental hazards in Canada is breathtaking. These impacts include thousands of premature deaths and millions of preventable illnesses annually. The environmental burden of disease includes cancer, cardiovascular disease, respiratory illness, birth defects, neuropsychiatric conditions, and gastrointestinal illness. The direct health care expenses related to visiting doctors, emergency rooms, and hospitals for a subset of these diseases range from $2.6 billion to $6.9 billion. The indirect costs, such as productivity losses, school absences, and decreased intelligence range from $3.3 billion to $8.5 billion. When the direct, indirect, and intangible costs (estimating the value of lives lost) are added together, the total damage ranges from $70.9 billion to $175.3 billion each year, with a mean estimate of $123 billion, or 6 percent of Canada's GDP ($1.9 trillion in 2013). These costs, calculated using methods regularly employed by governments to conduct cost-benefit analyses, are staggering. Also disturbing is the profoundly inequitable distribution of these costs. Poor Canadians, recent immigrants, and Aboriginal communities suffer a disproportionate burden of pollution while also being deprived of a fair share of the health benefits provided by ecosystems.

Diagnosis

Canada's environmental laws and policies are strikingly substandard compared with laws found in other wealthy industrialized countries. On almost every health-related environmental law, regulation, standard, tax, and policy, Canada has fallen behind. Canada is not among the hundred-plus countries where the right to live in a healthy environment enjoys constitutional protection. Unlike the United States, the European Union, and Australia, Canada lacks a comprehensive national health and environment strategy. In contrast to the United States, European Union, and Japan, Canada has no national environmental health surveillance system to monitor hazards, exposures, and outcomes. Some of the pieces are in place but they have not been integrated. There is not a single law, regulation, or policy in Canada that directly aims to ameliorate or prevent environmental injustices. Canada has refused to make adequate investments in environmental health research, monitoring, and education. At the international level, Canada has been miserly in providing foreign aid, obstructed vital environmental negotiations, and implemented policies that have contributed to deaths and illnesses in developing countries.

Comparative analysis reveals that Canada lags far behind the United States, the European Union, and Australia in enacting, implementing, and enforcing key laws and policies to prevent environmental impacts on health. Laws and regulations governing air quality, drinking water safety, pesticides, toxic substances, climate change, and biodiversity are weaker than in comparable wealthy nations. Unlike the United States, European Union, and Australia, Canada has no legally binding national standards for air quality or drinking water safety. Instead, Canada has voluntary guidelines. This is akin to wearing a ninety-nine-cent dust mask from your local hardware store instead of a firefighter's high-tech respiratory equipment. Both are intended to protect an individual's ability to breathe but one is obviously far more effective. Some might argue that the high-tech mask is more expensive, but a closer look at the overall costs and benefits reveals the fallacy of that argument. Despite their voluntary status, Canada's air quality guidelines set weaker targets than the legally binding American, European, and Australian standards for five out of six air pollutants (ozone, particulate matter, sulphur oxides, nitrogen oxides, lead, and carbon monoxide). Canada lacks even voluntary guidelines for additional air toxics regulated by the

European Union, including benzene and polycyclic aromatic hydrocarbons (PAHs). National guidelines for Canadian drinking water are not only voluntary but also numerically weaker and less comprehensive than the legally binding standards in other jurisdictions. There are more than fifty contaminants for which Canada has weaker drinking water guidelines than at least one other jurisdiction. These contaminants include bacteria, pesticides, carcinogenic industrial chemicals, and a radioactive substance released by nuclear reactors. Canadian drinking water guidelines are up to one thousand times weaker than European standards.

Canada still permits the use of at least forty-six active ingredients in pesticides that other nations have banned, including 2,4-D, atrazine, carbaryl, dichlorvos, permethrin, and propoxur. These active ingredients are used in more than a thousand commercial pesticide products sold in Canada. Canadian maximum residue limits for pesticides on food are significantly weaker than residue limits in other nations. In some cases, Canada allows up to a thousand times the European limit. Canadian regulations and policies are also weaker for many other hazardous substances, including asbestos, lead, formaldehyde, polybrominated diphenyl ethers (PBDEs), phthalates, radon, and PAHs.

Canada endorses the polluter-pays principle in theory but refuses to implement it in practice by putting an appropriate price on environmentally damaging activities or rigorously enforcing environmental laws. Leading OECD nations garner over 10 percent of total tax revenues through environmental taxes, while Canada collects less than 4 percent (and that figure is declining). Taxes on fuel, new vehicles, carbon dioxide emissions, pesticides, air emissions, and discharges into water are either absent in Canada or substantially lower than in other countries. Fuel taxes in Canada are two to twelve times lower than in thirty-two of thirty-four OECD nations. Instead of taxing pesticides, Canada exempts them from the GST. Only two provinces charge a tax on nitrogen oxide emissions, and that tax is at least twenty times smaller than the French tax and five hundred times smaller than the Swedish tax. Canada also has a track record of lax enforcement of environmental laws.

The results of these comparisons put to rest, conclusively, any remaining notion that Canada is an environmental leader. Canada's systemic failure to protect people's health and well-being from environmental hazards can be explained by deep-seated economic, political, legal, and social problems. Powerful vested interests have dominated the enactment, implementation, and enforcement of environmental law and policy in Canada to a greater extent than in many other nations. In recent years, Canada's renewed dependence on natural resource industries, particularly for exports, motivated the weakening of key environmental laws. The Constitution's silence on environmental matters has enabled both federal and provincial governments to pass the buck, while empowering corporations to mount legal challenges against new environmental laws. Canada's parliamentary system, with a powerful prime minister, an unelected Senate, and a lack of separation of powers results in the absence of effective checks and balances. The first-past-the-post electoral system exacerbates these political problems by facilitating false majorities and disenfranchising Canadian voters. Another problem is the cultural myth that Canada is a vast and unpolluted land, a misperception that reflects widespread ecological illiteracy.

Prescription

Fortunately, the overwhelming majority of adverse health effects caused by environmental hazards could be prevented through stronger environmental laws and policies, rigorously implemented and enforced. Canada can draw on its own history of environmental health success stories as well as the positive experiences of other nations, which offer a wealth of insights into the kinds of environmental rules and approaches that can achieve effective, efficient, and equitable results. If other nations can reduce the environmental burden of disease, then surely Canada also has this ability.

The blueprint for a future where environmental health problems recede into history is surprisingly simple. First, Canada needs a comprehensive national environmental health action plan that includes ambitious targets and timelines, measurable indicators, and an environmental health surveillance system. Funding must be provided to bolster research into both the causes of, and effective responses to, environmentally related illnesses. The Canadian Institutes for Health Research should establish an Institute for Environmental Health. The National Collaborating Centre for Environmental Health should receive a major increase in funding, enabling it to lead a national education initiative to bolster the ecological literacy of all Canadians, with an initial emphasis on health care professionals and policymakers.

Instead of burdening society and future Canadians with health and environmental costs – which is the business-as-usual approach – environmental laws must be amended to put prevention first and to ensure that those responsible for environmental degradation bear the full costs. Years of lip service to environmental protection need to be supplanted by vigorous application of the key principles identified in Chapter 10, including the right to live in a healthy environment; national, legally enforceable environmental health standards that are as strong as or stronger than the highest standards in other OECD countries; the polluter-pays principle; the precautionary principle; substituting safe alternatives for environmental hazards; intergenerational equity; the public trust doctrine; nonregression; and environmental justice. These principles must be applied through a series of concrete actions, including legally binding national standards for air quality and safe drinking water; a national pollution tax on releases of toxic substances, pesticides, and the sale of vehicles; banning the use of pesticides that are no longer permitted in the European Union; eliminating the overuse of antibiotics in agriculture; and phasing out the manufacture, use, sale, import, or release of all toxic substances that are known or probable causes of cancer, birth defects, respiratory illnesses, cardiovascular disease, impacts on development, neuropsychiatric conditions, or harm to the reproductive, immune, or endocrine systems. For most of the toxic chemicals, processes, and products in use today, affordable substitutes are available that will save lives, prevent illnesses, and, by any comprehensive measure, benefit our economy. For the remainder, we can be confident that human ingenuity will identify a safer solution. Intergenerational equity demands aggressive climate change policies and futures funds financed by revenue from nonrenewable resources. Environmental laws and policies must not only be strong on paper but also conscientiously implemented and rigorously enforced. To ensure that these principles are put into practice will require the creation of independent environmental enforcement agencies and a system of green courts or tribunals.

Two other conclusions can be drawn regarding future policy priorities. First, it is clear that air pollution inflicts the highest economic cost of any current environmental problem afflicting human health in Canada. Reducing air pollution from industry and vehicles will require efforts from every level of government and changes in public behaviour. Second, the neurodevelopmental impacts of exposure to toxic substances such as lead, mercury, and toluene not only afflict a vulnerable population (infants and children) but also have lifelong and extensive economic costs.[1] Canada could play an inspiring role globally by taking swift steps to reduce children's exposure to these toxic substances, advocating for international agreements to eliminate their use, and assisting poorer countries in phasing them out.

The implementation of the foregoing recommendations has the potential to prevent thousands of premature deaths, millions of episodes of ill health, and the wasteful spending of billions of dollars on health care every year. This low-hanging fruit should be harvested immediately. However, the full benefits of these reforms will not be realized unless the systemic problems identified in Chapter 9 are also addressed. Chapter 11 therefore offered recommendations that include specific actions to focus on Canadian well-being instead of GDP growth; create a circular, steady-state economy; accelerate the shift towards renewable energy; recognize constitutional environmental rights and responsibilities as well as the rights of Nature; secure the peace dividend through demilitarization; reform corporations to ensure greater social responsibility; resuscitate Canadian democracy; and reduce inequality. Some of the more challenging systemic changes may take years or even decades, but the foundations can be laid today.

The overarching goal of the recommendations in this book is to ensure that Canadians receive a level of protection for their health that is consistent with the highest standards found in other nations in the Organisation for Economic Co-operation and Development. This is not asking for the moon. It is not asking Canada to go beyond the standards established by other wealthy nations. Canadians simply should not be governed by laws and policies that are substantially inferior to those implemented by other nations. Canadians should not be second-class citizens when it comes to their health or the health of the environment.

Inspiration from Other Nations

Canada ranks tenth out of seventeen wealthy industrialized countries in health performance, trailing countries that are both health and environmental leaders, such as Sweden, Finland, and France.[2] Each of these countries spends less money on health care, per capita, than Canada.[3] According to the Conference Board of Canada, "most top-performing countries have achieved better health outcomes through actions on the broader determinants of health such as environmental stewardship and health-promotion programs."[4] The Nordic nations offer inspiring examples for Canada. Norway, Sweden, Finland, and Denmark employ strong environmental laws and policies, provide citizens with remarkably generous social programs, and are world leaders in development assistance to poor countries. Norway and Sweden explicitly acknowledge that there are ecological limits to economic growth. Both countries elect governments with proportional representation voting systems. Norway and Sweden have strong constitutional provisions establishing environmental rights and responsibilities, and actively account for future generations in policymaking. Both countries have imposed carbon taxes for more than two decades, as well as a plethora of other carefully crafted and effective environmental taxes. Sweden aims to be fossil fuel–free by 2050, while Norway has pledged to become carbon-neutral by that date (offsetting any remaining carbon emissions through reforestation). Sweden finetuned its ambitious plan to achieve a sustainable future within a generation by pledging not to export its environmental problems to other countries. Denmark dramatically reduced the use of antibiotics in the livestock industry while increasing production.[5] Canada should emulate Norway by taking a larger share of the revenue from the exploitation of publicly owned nonrenewable resources. Investing this revenue in federal and provincial futures funds would provide a vital cushion for the transition from today's ecologically and socially unsustainable economy predicated on endless growth to tomorrow's steady-state economy. While Canada is distinct from Scandinavia in many ways, there are compelling reasons for adopting or adapting the kinds of environmental laws and policies that have been so successful in that region.

Strong regulatory action can produce swift results. In Sweden, when scientists observed that concentrations of PBDEs in women's breast milk were doubling every five years, the government moved to ban the use of PBDEs.[6] Sweden inspired Germany, Denmark, Norway, and the Netherlands to also take early preventive action to limit the use of PBDEs, leading to an EU ban. The result: a rapid decline in the concentration of PBDEs in the breast milk of Swedish women, and no noticeable negative economic impacts.[7] Another promising example: Swedish cancer experts believe that early regulatory action on pesticides and other toxic substances by the government of Sweden may have contributed to declining rates of some cancers, particularly non-Hodgkin's lymphoma.[8]

Costa Rica is another country widely recognized as an environmental leader, as a result of two decades of determined effort, including providing constitutional recognition of the right to a healthy environment, enacting and implementing strong laws (such as prohibitions on open-pit mining and offshore oil and gas activity), placing over one-quarter of its land in parks and protected areas, reversing the trend of deforestation, and producing 99 percent of its electricity from renewable energy. Costa Rica's most valuable export is computer chips, as high-tech giants have located manufacturing facilities to take advantage of the country's clean air and water.[9] Costa Rica is the top-ranked country in the world on the Happy Planet Index, which integrates measures of life expectancy, self-rated happiness, and per capita ecological footprints.[10] While Costa Rica is not an ecological utopia, its successful pursuit of human well-being does offer some inspiring lessons for Canada.

Other nations have also shown leadership, though less consistently. Empowered by its constitutional Charter for the Environment, France became the first country in the world to pass a law banning fracking, passed a national law prohibiting the sale of cosmetic pesticides, and has climbed into the top three in the Conference Board of Canada's environmental rankings. Ecuador, Bolivia, and New Zealand are leading the way in recognizing the rights of Nature. Australia set a key precedent by refusing to include investor-state dispute resolution mechanisms in free trade agreements.

The best news provided by this book is that the solutions necessary to prevent adverse environmental effects on our health are known, affordable, and effective. By embracing the recommendations for reducing air pollution, protecting water quality, improving food safety, addressing threats posed by consumer products, and eliminating releases of the most hazardous substances into our environment, Canada could join other world leaders in protecting public health.

Moving Forward

Canadians need to recognize, understand, and respect the intimate connections between our health and the ecosystems that we inhabit. The air we breathe, the water we drink, and the food we eat all depend on natural ecological functions, from pollination and genetic diversity in food crops to the water and carbon cycles that are integral to all life on Earth. Our mental health and our happiness are dependent on access to green spaces. Our ability to recover from illnesses often depends on medicines or treatments derived from or inspired by the natural world. To the extent we harm natural ecosystems, eliminate species, or disrupt ecological processes, we indirectly harm our health as well. When we release toxic substances into the environment, there is a boomerang effect. Every person in Canada has traces of pesticides, phthalates, flame retardants, and byproducts from burning fossil fuels in their body. While ignorance of the adverse environmental and health consequences of our actions may once have been a plausible excuse, our level of knowledge today surely demands that we do better.

Preventing adverse environmental health consequences is technologically possible, economically feasible, and socially imperative. Despite the daunting evidence about the scale and scope of environmental impacts on health in Canada, there are grounds for cautious optimism. Canadians have demonstrated an ability to solve environmental problems and reduce threats to human health. Improvements in drinking water treatment and sanitation have dramatically reduced waterborne illnesses. Concentrations of some air pollutants in Canadian cities – sulphur dioxide, nitrogen oxides, and carbon monoxide – have decreased by over 50 percent since the 1970s.[11] Banning the use of lead as a gasoline additive caused precipitous declines in children's blood lead levels. Production and use of ozone-depleting chemicals is down 99 percent in Canada since the Montreal Protocol was negotiated in 1987, leading to positive forecasts for the recovery of Earth's ozone layer. Dioxins and furans in effluent from pulp and paper mills are down 99 percent since the 1980s. Canada was the first country to ban the use of bisphenol A (BPA) in baby bottles, and was one of the pioneers in regulating perfluorochemicals (PFCs).

In each of these success stories, opponents of regulatory action launched vitriolic attacks arguing that the environmental problems and associated health consequences were being exaggerated.[12] When the scientific evidence accumulated to the point where it could no longer be dismissed, industries and their apologists claimed that the technology required to solve the problem had yet to be developed, that there was no alternative to business as usual. For example, the automobile industry took years to acknowledge that cars caused air pollution, and then argued that no clean technology was available.[13] When technological denial was no longer tenable, industry's last stand was to argue that change was unaffordable, or that the costs exceeded the benefits. A classic example, absurd in retrospect, was the Fraser Institute's assertion that banning chlorofluorocarbons (CFCs) to protect the ozone layer would backfire by causing deaths due to a lack of refrigeration for foods and medicines.[14] In fact, protecting the Earth's ozone layer has provided net benefits totalling trillions of dollars.[15]

Understanding this historical pattern is essential for solving today's environmental health problems in a timely and effective manner. Politicians and policymakers need to treat industry's claims – on science, technology, and economics – with a healthy dose of skepticism. For too long, private economic interests have trumped public health and environmental interests in Canada. Governments must prioritize the health and well-being of real people, not the financial health of corporate persons. We must learn from the mistakes of the past – our failure to regulate lead, asbestos, benzene, air pollution, CFCs, mercury, PCBs, and other substances until terrible damages were incurred – and adopt a preventive, precautionary approach to our future. Vigilance is required to address emerging environmental threats ranging from antibiotic resistance and nanotechnology to zoonoses. Every year that Canada drags its feet and refuses to join leading countries in protecting health from environmental pollution and degradation sentences thousands of Canadians to unnecessary premature deaths and millions to avoidable illnesses.

Time for Change

This book reveals a shocking abdication of responsibility by Canadian governments. There is no possible justification for permitting today's unconscionable state of affairs – treating Canadians like second-class citizens – to continue. This is not the Canada that a vast majority of Canadians want. Three-quarters of Canadians want stronger environmental laws and nine in ten support recognition of their right to live in a healthy environment. Yet successive Conservative governments have gutted scientific capacity, eviscerated environmental protection budgets, and repealed or weakened key federal environmental laws. Their Liberal predecessors avoided such direct attacks but were also guilty of failing to take adequate actions to protect Canadians' health from environmental hazards. The NDP has failed to consistently articulate and support more effective approaches to protecting environmental health, illustrated by their opposition to carbon taxes. As is the case in the United States, "environmental health objectives are ill served by our dysfunctional and increasingly partisan national politics."[16] All political parties should support improved environmental health policies. The chasm between what the majority of Canadians want – environmental health leadership – and what Canadian governments deliver reinforces the conclusion that Canada has a serious democratic deficit.

Implementing the recommendations in this book will cost hundreds of millions of dollars over the course of the next decade. This represents a significant outlay of taxpayers' money. With annual health care spending spiralling above $200 billion, there is plenty of incentive to take a more preventive approach. Investments in a healthy environment are neither risky nor speculative. The proposed environmental health laws, policies, and programs are guaranteed to provide a return measured in thousands of lives saved, millions of illnesses prevented, and improved quality of life for all Canadians, particularly the most vulnerable in our society. The value of these benefits will be viewed by many Canadians as infinite – incapable of being calculated in dollars and cents. In the course of making the case for revamping Canada's approach to environmental law and policy, this book has presented a prodigious volume of information, including extensive use of statistics and abstract economic valuations. But behind every number are individual flesh and blood Canadians, with hopes and dreams, families and friends. Neither statisticians nor economists can capture adequately the pain and suffering inflicted when a child suffers from asthma, when a relative is diagnosed with cancer, or when a friend dies prematurely because of heart or lung disease. Everyone in Canada knows someone affected by these afflictions.

Yet even reduced to cold monetary terms, using conservative valuation techniques, the economic benefits of improved environmental laws and policies will dwarf the costs. Numerous studies confirm that stronger environmental protection offers one of the most cost-effective approaches to reducing health care expenditures.[17] These studies point to a compelling conclusion – it will cost less to prevent environmental impacts on our health than to pay for the enormous costs of illness, disability, and death caused by exposure to environmental hazards. If the recommendations in this book reduce Canadian health care costs by even 1 percent, that would represent savings of over $2 billion annually.

Leaders of large corporations, industry associations, right-wing think tanks, and some elected representatives may oppose stronger environmental laws and policies despite demonstrable net benefits to Canada and Canadians. Their opposition is rooted in defending the private gains being reaped under today's unsustainable system. Overcoming their political power will require a concerted effort over the course of the next generation by Canadians of all stripes, particularly doctors, nurses, researchers, and others in the health care community. Research shows that focusing on the health benefits of environmental laws will further strengthen public support for these changes.[18] Responsible business leaders need to break ranks with their colleagues and acknowledge that the societal dividends justify environmental taxes and stronger environmental rules. Contrary to conventional wisdom in Canada, many businesses will benefit and even flourish as rigorous environmental laws and policies inspire innovation, produce productivity gains, and enhance competitiveness.[19] Indirect benefits will include making Canada an even more attractive destination for talented immigrants and principled investors.

Many of the prescriptions found in this book are not new. Medical experts, scientists, environmental groups, the Canadian Lung Association, the Canadian Cancer Society, the Canadian Institute for Child Health, the Asthma Society of Canada, the Commission on the Future of Health Care in Canada, the Canadian Public Health Association, the Canadian Partnership for Child Health and the Environment, the Canadian Association of Physicians for the Environment, and concerned citizens have been urging governments to take action on environmental health for years. Too often, these pleas fell on deaf ears.

In the absence of a sustained effort, our children and grandchildren will inherit a nation, and indeed a world, where environmental impacts on health are even worse than they are today. We can and must do better. By recognizing that Canadians have a fundamental human right to live in a healthy environment, taking a comprehensive, preventive, and proactive approach, investing in urgently needed research and surveillance, strengthening environmental laws and regulations, shifting from a linear to a circular economy powered by renewable energy, and abandoning the myopic focus on economic growth, Canada could not only reduce but virtually eliminate the majority of environmental threats to human health. The results of taking these preventive and precautionary actions would include better health, a more resilient economy, a cleaner environment, and, perhaps most important, improved quality of life for ourselves, our children, and our grandchildren. Canada still has the potential and the opportunity to change course, evolve from environmental laggard to leader, and once again become a country that instills pride in its citizens and enjoys the respect of the global community. There is still time, but the hour is late.

Notes

Chapter 1: A Neglected but Vital Issue

1 See the Canadian Environmental Health Atlas, http://www.ehatlas.ca.

2 S. Janssen, G. Solomon, and T. Schettler, "CHE Toxicant and Disease Database" (Collaborative on Health and the Environment, 2013), http://www.healthand environment.org/tddb/.

3 Conference Board of Canada, *How Canada Performs: A Report Card on Canada* (Ottawa: Conference Board, 2008).

4 D.R. Boyd, *The Air We Breathe: An International Comparison of Air Quality Standards and Guidelines* (Vancouver: David Suzuki Foundation, 2006); Canadian Medical Association, *No Breathing Room: National Illness Costs of Air Pollution* (Toronto: CMA, 2008).

5 Health Canada, *Respiratory Disease in Canada* (Ottawa: Health Canada, 2001).

6 C.G. Schuster, A.G. Ellis, W.J. Robertson, et al., "Infectious Disease Outbreaks Related to Drinking Water in Canada 1974–2001," *Canadian Journal of Public Health* 96, 4 (2005): 254–58.

7 Environment Canada, "The National Pollutant Release Inventory" (2014), http://www.ec.gc.ca.

8 Canadian Institute for Health Information, *Urban Physical Environments and Health Inequality* (Ottawa: CIHI, 2011).

9 Environmental Defence Canada, *Toxic Nation: A Report on Pollution in Canadians* (Toronto: EDC, 2005); Environmental Defence Canada, *Polluted Children, Toxic Nation: A Report on Pollution in Canadian Families* (Toronto: EDC, 2006). Both documents available at http://environmentaldefence.ca/.

10 US Centers for Disease Control and Prevention, Department of Health and Human Services, "Third National Report on Human Exposure to Environmental Chemicals" (2009), http://www.cdc.gov/exposurereport/.

11 Environmental Defence Canada, *Pre-Polluted: A Report on Toxic Substances in the Umbilical Cord Blood of Canadian Newborns* (Toronto: EDC, 2013); Environmental Working Group, *Body Burden 2: The Pollution in Newborns* (Washington, DC: EWG, 2005), http://www.ewg.org.

12 K. Cook, "Testimony" (Subcommittee on Superfund, Toxics, and Environmental Health, Senate Environment and Public Works Committee, February 4, 2010), 3.

13 For an excellent sample of new studies, see the peer-reviewed scientific journal *Environmental Health Perspectives*, available at http://ehp.niehs.nih.gov/.

14 A.G. Fitzmaurice, S.L. Rhoes, M. Cockburn, et al., "Aldehyde Dehydrogenase Variation Enhances Effects of Pesticides Associated with Parkinson disease," *Neurology* 82, 5 (2014): 419–26.

15 C.T. Wong, E. Ahmad, H. Li, D.A. Crawford, "Prostaglandin E2 Alters Wnt-Dependent Migration and Proliferation in Neuroectodermal Stem Cells: Implications for Autism Spectrum Disorders," *Cell Communication and Signaling* 12, 1 (2014): 19. doi:10.1186/1478-811X-12-19.

16 C. Schiffer, A. Müller, D.L. Egeberg, et al., "Direct Action of Endocrine Disrupting Chemicals on Human Sperm," *EMBO Reports* (2014), doi:10.15252/embr.201438869.

17 P.J. Landrigan and R.A Etzel, eds., *The Textbook of Children's Environmental Health* (Oxford: Oxford University Press, 2014), 560.

18 US President's Cancer Panel, *Reducing Environmental Cancer Risk: What We Can Do Now. 2008–2009 Annual Report* (Washington, DC: Department of Health and Human Services, 2010).

19 T.J. Murray, M.V. Maffini, A.A. Ucci, et al., "Induction of Mammary Gland Ductal Hyperplasias and Carcinoma in Situ Following Fetal Bisphenol A Exposure," *Reproductive Toxicology* 23, 3 (2007): 383–90.

20 M.D. Anway and M.K. Skinner, "Epigenetic Transgenerational Actions of Endocrine Disruptors," *Endocrinology* 147, 6 (2006): s43–s49; M.D. Anway, M.A. Memon, M. Uzumcu, and M.K. Skinner, "Transgenerational Effect of the Endocrine Disruptor Vinclozolin on Male Spermatogenesis," *Journal of Andrology* 27, 6 (2006): 868–79.

21 T. Bach, "Protecting Human Health and Stewarding the Environment: An Essay Exploring Values in US Environmental Protection Law," *Michigan Journal of Environmental and Administrative Law* 3, 2 (2014): 19–30.

22 T. Gunton and K.S. Calbrick, *The Maple Leaf in the OECD: Canada's Environmental Performance* (Vancouver: David Suzuki Foundation, 2010).

23 Organisation for Economic Co-operation and Development, *Environmental Performance Review: Canada* (Paris: OECD, 2004).

24 J. Burck, F. Marten, and C. Balss, *The Climate Change Performance Index: Results 2014* (Bonn: Germanwatch and Climate Action Network Europe, 2013), 6.

25 Center for Global Development, "Commitment to Development Index" (2013), http://www.cgdev.org/publication/commitment-development-index-2013.

26 Conference Board of Canada, "How Canada Performs" (2013), http://www.conferenceboard.ca/hcp/default.aspx.

27 I. Weibust, *Green Leviathan: The Case for a Federal Role in Environmental Policy* (Burlington, VT: Ashgate, 2009), 119.

28 A. McAllister, *Global Thought Leader Survey* (survey commissioned by the Pembina Institute) (Vancouver: McAllister Opinion Research, 2010).

29 OECD, *Environmental Data Compendium* (Paris: OECD, 2007).

30 Environment Canada, *The 2012 Progress Report of the Federal Sustainable Development Strategy* (Ottawa: Environment Canada, 2013); Environment Canada, "Air Quality Indicators" (2010), https://www.ec.gc.ca/indicateurs-indicators/default.asp?lang=en&n=7DCC2250-1.

31 I.J. Simpson, J.E. Marrero, S. Batterman, et al., "Air Quality in the Industrial Heartland of Alberta, Canada and Potential Impacts on Human Health," *Atmospheric Environment* 81 (2013): 702–9.

32 Canadian Environmental Law Association and Environmental Defence, *Partners in Pollution 2: An Update on the Continuing Canadian and United States Contributions to Great Lakes–St. Lawrence River Ecosystem Pollution* (Toronto: CELA and ED, 2010).

33 D.R. Boyd, "No Taps, No Toilets: First Nations and the Constitutional Right to Water in Canada," *McGill Law Journal* 57, 1 (2011): 81–134.

34 World Wildlife Fund, Zoological Society of London, and Global Footprint Network, *Living Planet Report 2010* (London: World Wildlife Fund, 2010).

35 L. McDonald, "Crimes against Ecology: Is the Harper Government Guilty?" *Alternatives* 39.6 (2013), http://www.alternativesjournal.ca/policy-and-politics/crimes-against-ecology.

36 S. Wood, G. Tanner, and B.J. Richardson, "What Ever Happened to Canadian Environmental Law?" *Ecology Law Quarterly* 37 (2010): 981–1040.

37 D.R. Boyd, A. Attaran, and M. Stanbrook, "Asbestos Mortality: A Canadian Export," *Canadian Medical Association Journal* 179, 9 (2008): 871–72.

38 Canadian Press, "Harper Defends Climate-Change Efforts amid Criticism Canada Is Lagging," September 23, 2009; A. Gurzu, "Climate Change Criticism Reaches New Level: Leaders' Comments Show International Frustration over Canada's Position, Experts Say," *Hill Times Online*, May 19, 2010, http://www.hilltimes.com/news/2010/05/19/climate-change-criticism-reaches-new-level/23870.

39 Public Health Agency of Canada, "Canada Signs UN Declaration on Preventing and Controlling Chronic Diseases" (2011), http://www.phac-aspc.gc.ca/media/nr-rp/2011/2011_0919-eng.php; Public Health Agency of Canada, "Reports on Plans and Priorities" (2007), http://www.tbs-sct.gc.ca/rpp/0607/phac-aspc/phac-aspc01_e.asp#s1.

40 D. Dodge and R. Dion, *Chronic Healthcare Spending Disease: A Macro Diagnosis and Prognosis* (Toronto: C.D. Howe Institute, 2011).

41 M. Jerrett, J. Eyles, C. Dufournaud, and S. Birch, "Environmental Influences on Healthcare Expenditures: An Exploratory Analysis from Ontario, Canada," *Journal of Epidemiology and Community Health* 57, 5 (2003): 334–38.

42 European Environment Agency and European Commission, *Environment and Human Health* (Copenhagen: European Environment Agency, 2013), 11.

43 J. Hume, "Health Care Top Priority at Polls: Survey," *Toronto Sun*, January 24, 2014, http://www.torontosun.com/2014/01/24/health-care-top-priority-at-the-polls-survey.

44 "Health Care in Canada Survey" (2007), http://www.hcic-sssc.ca/english/Content.aspx?l0=1&l1=14&tid=14&l=1.

45 A. McAllister, *A Backyard Field Guide to Canadians* (Vancouver: McAllister Opinion Research, 2010); Health Canada, "Health and the Environment: Critical Pathways," *Health Policy Research Bulletin* 4 (2002): 1–2.
46 "Health Care in Canada Survey" (2007), http://www.hcic-sssc.ca/english/Content. aspx?l0=1&l1=14&tid=14&l=1.
47 D. Krewski, L. Lemyre, M.C. Turner, et al., "Public Perception of Population Health Risks in Canada: Health Hazards and Information," *Human and Ecological Risk Assessment* 12, 4 (2006): 626–44.
48 Ipsos Reid, *7th Annual National Report Card on Health Care* (prepared for the Canadian Medical Association) (Toronto: Ipsos Reid, 2007).
49 McAllister Opinion Research, "Increasing Majority Call Canada's Pollution Laws Inadequate" (media release for *Environmental Monitor*, Globescan Incorporated) (2007).
50 I. Buka, W.T. Rogers, A.R. Osornio-Vargas, et al., "An Urban Survey of Paediatric Environmental Health Concerns: Perceptions of Parents/Guardians and Health Care Professionals," *Paediatrics and Child Health* 11, 4 (2006): 235–38.
51 Public Health Agency of Canada, "Departmental Performance Report 2006–2007" (2007), http://www.tbs-sct.gc.ca/dpr-rmr/2006-2007/inst/ahs/ahs01-eng.asp#_Toc 177793130; Canadian Public Health Association, "Policy Resolutions: Motion No. 1, Children's Environmental Health" (1999), http://www.cpha.ca/english/policy/ resolu/1990s/1999page6.htm; Commissioner of the Environment and Sustainable Development, "Chapters 3 and 4: Managing Toxic Substances," in *Report to the House of Commons* (Ottawa: Office of the Auditor General of Canada, 1999); International Joint Commission, *Ninth Biennial Report on Great Lakes Water Quality* (Ottawa: International Joint Commission, 1998); National Round Table on the Environment and the Economy, *Managing Potentially Toxic Substances in Canada* (Ottawa: NRTEE, 2001); Royal Society of Canada, *Implications of Global Change for Human Health: Final Report of the Health Issues Panel of the Canadian Global Change Program*, Incidental Report Series IR95-2 (Ottawa: Royal Society of Canada, 1995).
52 K.K. Leitch, *Reaching for the Top: A Report by the Advisor on Children and Youth* (report prepared for the Minister of Health) (Ottawa: Health Canada, 2008), 89.
53 Canadian Cancer Society, Canadian Lung Association, and Heart and Stroke Foundation of Canada, "The Big Three Fuel the Air Pollution and Health Debate: Major Canadian Health Groups Launch New Campaign on Environmental Health" (press release, March 6, 2008); Canadian Public Health Association, "Brief to the Senate Standing Committee on Energy, the Environment, and Natural Resources on Recommended Changes to the Canadian Environmental Protection Act 1999" (November 7, 2006).
54 J. Wood, *Canadian Environmental Indicators: Air Quality* (Vancouver: Fraser Institute, 2012); J. Schwarcz, *An Apple a Day: The Truths, Misconceptions, and Outright Exaggerations about Diet, Nutrition, and the Foods We Eat* (Toronto: HarperCollins Canada, 2007); American Council on Science and Health, http://acsh.org/.
55 M. Lalonde, *A New Perspective on the Health of Canadians* (Ottawa: Minister of National Health and Welfare, 1974).

56 C. Bennett, *Strengthening the Pan-Canadian Health System: Discussion Paper* (Ottawa: Minister of State for Public Health, 2004).

57 J. Simpson, *Chronic Condition: Why Canada's Health-Care System Needs to be Dragged into the 21st Century* (Toronto: Penguin, 2013).

58 Canadian Institute of Health Information, *Health Care Cost Drivers: The Facts* (Ottawa: CIHI, 2013).

59 J.M. Last, *A Dictionary of Epidemiology* (Oxford: Oxford University Press, 2001).

60 This assertion is frequently found on the Internet. For example, see http://www.allergykids.com/blog/90-of-all-cancers-are-caused-by-environmental-factors/.

61 M. Lippman, B. Cohen, and R.B. Schlesinger, *Environmental Health Science: Recognition, Evaluation, and Control of Chemical and Physical Health Hazards* (Oxford: Oxford University Press, 2003), 164–65.

62 A. Prüss-Üstün and C. Corvalan, *Preventing Disease through Healthy Environments: Towards an Estimate of the Environmental Burden of Disease* (Geneva: World Health Organization, 2006).

63 D. Haines, "Environmental Health Surveillance, Biomonitoring and Indicators: National Policy Consultation on Children's Health and the Environment" (Edmonton, April 18–19, 2007), https://www.yumpu.com/en/document/view/34134557/doug-haines-pollution-probe.

64 World Health Organization, *A Global Strategy: Health, Environment, and Development* (Geneva: WHO, 1993).

65 N.A. Ross, S. Tremblay, S. Khan, et al., "Body Mass Index in Urban Canada: Neighborhood and Metropolitan Area Effects," *American Journal of Public Health* 97, 3 (2007): 500–8.

66 D. Quammen, *Spillover: Animal Infections and the Next Human Pandemic* (New York: W.W. Norton, 2012).

67 H. Frumkin, "Beyond Toxicity: Human Health and the Natural Environment," *American Journal of Preventive Medicine* 20 (2001): 234–40; T. Takano, K. Nakamura, and M. Watanabe, "Urban Residential Improvements and Senior Citizens' Longevity in Megacity Areas: The Importance of Walkable Green Spaces," *Journal of Epidemiology and Community Health* 56 (2002): 913–18.

68 E.K.L. Nisbet and J.M. Zelenski, "Nature Relatedness and Subjective Well-Being: Are Nature Lovers Happier People?" (paper presented at the annual meeting of the Canadian Psychological Association, St. John's, 2004).

69 Federal, Provincial and Territorial Ministers of Health, *Health Goals for Canada* (Ottawa: Public Health Agency of Canada, October 2005), http://www.phac-aspc.gc.ca/publicat/sds-sdd/sds-sdd2-app-ann2-3-4-eng.php.

Chapter 2: Environmental Influences on Human Health

1 C. Soskolne and R. Bertollini, *Global Ecological Integrity and Sustainable Development: Cornerstones of Public Health* (Rome: World Health Organization and European Centre for Environment and Health, 1999).

2 O.E. Sala, L.A. Meyerson, and C. Parmesan, "Changes in Biodiversity and Their Consequences for Human Health," in *Biodiversity Change and Human Health: From Ecosystem Services to Spread of Disease,* ed. O.E. Sala, L.A. Meyerson, and C. Parmesan (Washington: Island Press, 2009), 2.

3 M.B. Dunbar, P. Panagos, and L. Montanarella, "European Perspectives of Ecosystem Services and Related Policies," *Integrated Environmental Assessment and Management* 9, 2 (2013): 231–36.

4 Millennium Ecosystem Assessment, *Ecosystems and Human Well-Being: Synthesis* (Washington, DC: Island Press, 2005).

5 E. Chivian and A. Bernstein, eds., *Sustaining Life: How Human Health Depends on Biodiversity* (Oxford: Oxford University Press, 2008).

6 Ibid.

7 K. Levy, G. Daily, and S.S. Myers, "Human Health as an Ecosystem Service: A Conceptual Framework," in *Integrating Ecology and Poverty Reduction: Ecological Dimensions,* ed. J.C. Ingram, F. DeClerck, and C. Rumbaitis del Rio (New York: Springer, 2012), 231–51.

8 Ibid.

9 Ibid., 241.

10 Chivian and Bernstein, *Sustaining Life* (see n. 5 above).

11 E.J. Brunner, P.J. Jones, S. Friel, and M. Bartley, "Fish, Human Health and Marine Ecosystem Health: Policies in Collision," *International Journal of Epidemiology* 38, 1 (2009): 93–100.

12 G. Tan, C. Gyllenhaal, and D.D. Soejarto, "Biodiversity as a Source of Anticancer Drugs," *Current Drug Targets* 7, 3 (2006): 265–77.

13 Chivian and Bernstein, *Sustaining Life* (see n. 5 above); R. Montaser and H. Luesch, "Marine Natural Products: A New Wave of Drugs?" *Future Medicinal Chemistry* 3, 12 (2011): 1475–89.

14 R. Alves and I. Rosa, "Biodiversity, Traditional Medicine and Public Health: Where Do They Meet?" *Journal of Ethnobiology and Ethnomedicine* 3, 14 (2007), http://www.ethnobiomed.com/content/3/1/14.

15 Chivian and Bernstein, *Sustaining Life* (see n. 5 above).

16 A.S. Bernstein and D.S. Ludwig, "The Importance of Biodiversity to Medicine," *Journal of the American Medical Association* 300, 19 (2008): 2297–99.

17 Chivian and Bernstein, *Sustaining Life* (see n. 5 above).

18 Ibid.

19 Ibid.

20 D. Jain and S. Kumar, "Snake Venom: A Potent Anticancer Agent," *Asian Pacific Journal of Cancer Research* 13, 10 (2010): 4855–60.

21 Chivian and Bernstein, *Sustaining Life* (see n. 5 above).

22 Ibid.

23 Ibid.

24 Ibid.

25 Ibid.

26 Bernstein and Ludwig, "The Importance of Biodiversity to Medicine," 2297–99 (see n. 16 above).

27 Chivian and Bernstein, *Sustaining Life* (see n. 5 above).

28 Ibid.

29 Bernstein and Ludwig, "The Importance of Biodiversity to Medicine," 2297 (see n. 16 above).

30 G.M. Cragg and D.J. Newman, "Biodiversity: A Continuing Source of Novel Drug Leads," *Pure and Applied Chemistry* 77, 1 (2005): 7–24.

31 Chivian and Bernstein, *Sustaining Life* (see n. 5 above).

32 V.O. Ezenwa, M.S. Godsey, R.J. King, and S.C. Guptill, "Avian Diversity and West Nile Virus: Testing Associations between Biodiversity and Infectious Disease Risk," *Proceedings of the Royal Society B – Biological Sciences* 273 (2006): 109–17.

33 R.S. Ostfeld and F. Keesing, "Biodiversity and Disease Risk: The Case of Lyme Disease," *Conservation Biology* 14, 3 (2000): 722–28.

34 C. Maller, M. Townsend, A. Pryor, et al. "Healthy Nature Healthy People: 'Contact with Nature' as an Upstream Health Promotion Intervention for Populations," *Health Promotion International* 21, 1 (2006): 45–54.

35 World Health Organization, *Depression*, Fact Sheet No. 369 (Geneva: WHO, 2012), http://www.who.int/mediacentre/factsheets/fs369/en/index.html.

36 R. Mitchell, "Is Physical Activity in Natural Environments Better for Mental Health than Physical Activity in Other Environments?" *Social Science and Medicine* 91 (2012): 30–34.

37 P. O'Campo, C. Salmon, and J. Burke, "Neighbourhoods and Mental Well-Being: What Are the Pathways?" *Health and Place* 14, 1 (2009): 56–68.

38 L.E. Keniger, K.J. Gaston, K.N. Irvine, and R.A. Fuller, "What Are the Benefits of Interacting with Nature?" *International Journal of Environmental Research and Public Health* 10, 3 (2013): 913–35.

39 Ibid.

40 G.N. Bratman, J.P. Hamilton, and G.C. Daily, "The Impacts of Nature Experiences on Human Cognitive Function and Mental Health," *Annals of the New York Academy of Sciences* 1249, 1 (2012): 118–36; E. Karjalainen, T. Sarjala, and H. Raitio, "Promoting Human Health through Forests: Overview and Major Challenges," *Environmental Health and Preventive Medicine* 15, 1 (2010): 1–8.

41 Keniger et al., "What Are the Benefits of Interacting with Nature?" 913–35 (see n. 38 above).

42 Ibid.

43 Ibid.

44 V.I. Lohr, "Benefits of Nature: What We Are Learning about Why People Respond to Nature," *Journal of Physiological Anthropology* 26, 2 (2007): 83–85.

45 C.W. Thompson, J. Roe, P. Aspinall, et al., "More Green Space Is Linked to Less Stress in Deprived Communities: Evidence from Salivary Cortisol Patterns," *Landscape and Urban Planning* 105, 3 (2012): 221–29; F.E. Kuo, *Parks and Other Green Environments: Essential Components of a Healthy Human Habitat* (Ashburn, VA: National Recreation and Parks Association, 2010).

46 Thompson et al., ibid., 221–29.

47 Kuo, *Parks and Other Green Environments* (see n. 45 above).

48 Ibid.

49 Karjalainen, Sarjala, and Raitio, "Promoting Human Health through Forests" (see n. 40 above).

50 Bratman, Hamilton, and Daily, "The Impacts of Nature Experiences" (see n. 40 above).

51 J. Barton and J. Pretty, "What Is the Best Dose of Nature and Green Exercise for Improving Mental Health? A Multi-Study Analysis," *Environmental Science and Technology* 44, 10 (2010): 3947–55.

52 D.E. Bowler, L.M. Buyung-Ali, T.M. Knight, and A.S. Pullin, "A Systematic Review of Evidence for the Added Benefits to Health of Exposure to Natural Environments," *BMC Public Health* 10 (2010): 456–66.

53 R. Louv, *Last Child in the Woods* (Chapel Hill, NC: Algonquin Books, 2008); H Frumkin, "Healthy Places: Exploring the Evidence," *American Journal of Public Health* 93, 9 (2003): 1451–56.

54 L.E. McCurdy, K.E. Winterbottom, S.S. Mehta, and J.R. Roberts, "Using Nature and Outdoor Activity to Improve Children's Health," *Current Problems in Pediatric and Adolescent Health Care* 40, 5 (2010): 102–17.

55 N.M. Wells and G.W. Evans, "Nearby Nature: A Buffer of Life Stress among Rural Children," *Environment and Behavior* 35, 3 (2003): 311–30.

56 Kuo, *Parks and Other Green Environments* (see n. 45 above).

57 Keniger et al., "What Are the Benefits of Interacting with Nature?," 913–35 (see n. 38 above); A.F. Taylor and F.E. Kuo, "Could Exposure to Everyday Green Spaces Help Treat ADHD? Evidence from Children's Play Settings," *Applied Psychology: Health and Well-Being* 3, 3 (2011): 281–303; Kuo, *Parks and Other Green Environments* (see n. 45 above).

58 A.F. Taylor and F. Kuo, quoted in Louv, *Last Child in the Woods,* 110 (see n. 53 above).

59 J. Nurse, D. Basher, A. Bone, and W. Bird, "An Ecological Approach to Promoting Population Mental Health and Well-Being – A Response to the Challenge of Climate Change," *Perspectives in Public Health* 130, 1 (2010): 27–33.

60 J. Dean, K. van Dooren, and P. Weinstein, "Does Biodiversity Improve Mental Health in Urban Settings?" *Medical Hypotheses* 76, 6 (2011): 877–80.

61 Nurse et al., "An Ecological Approach," 27–33 (see n. 59 above).

62 Ibid.

63 K.J. Doyle and L. Van Susteren, *The Psychological Effects of Global Warming in the United States: And Why the US Mental Health Care System Is Not Adequately Prepared* (Washington, DC: National Wildlife Federation, 2012).

64 E.G. Knox, "Childhood Cancers and Atmospheric Carcinogens," *Journal of Epidemiology and Community Health* 59, 2 (2005): 101–5; E.G. Knox, "Roads, Railways, and Childhood Cancers," *Journal of Epidemiology and Community Health* 60, 2 (2006): 136–41; E.G. Knox, "Oil Combustion and Childhood Cancers," *Journal of Epidemiology and Community Health* 59, 9 (2005): 755–60.

65 Environment Canada, "The National Pollutant Release Inventory" (2014), http://www.ec.gc.ca.

66 H. Koren and M. Bisisi, *Handbook of Environmental Health: Biological, Chemical, and Physical Agents of Environmentally Related Disease,* 4th ed. (Boca Raton, FL: National Environmental Health Association and Lewis Publishers, 2002).

67 Government of Canada, *Children's Health and the Environment in North America: A First Report on Available Indicators and Measures. Country Report: Canada* (Gatineau, QC: Environment Canada, 2005).

68 P.E. Rasmussen, K.S. Subramanian, and B.J. Jessiman, "A Multi-Level Profile of Housedust in Relation to Exterior Dust and Soils in the City of Ottawa, Canada," *Science of the Total Environment* 267 (2001): 125–40.

69 K. Fulcher and H. Gibb, "Setting the Research Agenda on the Health Effects of Chemicals," *International Journal of Environmental Research and Public Health* 11, 1 (2014): 1049–57.

70 P. Grandjean, *Only One Chance: How Environmental Pollution Impairs Brain Development* (Oxford: Oxford University Press, 2013).

71 B. Lanphear, R. Hornung, J. Koury, et al., "Low-Level Environmental Lead Exposure and Children's Intellectual Function: An International Pooled Analysis," *Environmental Health Perspectives* 113, 7 (2005): 894–99; US Environmental Protection Agency, *America's Children and the Environment: Measures of Contaminants, Body Burdens, and Illnesses* (Washington, DC: US EPA, 2003).

72 R.L. Canfield, C.R. Henderson, D.A. Cory-Slechta, et al., "Intellectual Impairment in Children with Blood Lead Concentrations below 10 ug per Deciliter," *New England Journal of Medicine* 348 (2003): 1517–26; B.P. Lanphear, K. Dietrich, P. Auinger, and C. Cox, "Cognitive Deficits Associated with Blood Lead Concentrations <10 microg/ dL in US Children and Adolescents," *Public Health Reports* 115, 6 (2000): 521–29; S.J. Rothenberg and J.C. Rothenberg, "Testing the Dose-Response Specification in Epidemiology: Public Health and Policy Consequences for Lead," *Environmental Health Perspectives* 113 (2005): 1190–95.

73 A. Spivey, "The Weight of Lead: Effects Add Up in Adults," *Environmental Health Perspectives* 115, 1 (2007): A30-A36; A. Picard, "Decades Later, Lead Is Stalking Our Kids," *Globe and Mail*, April 14, 2005, A17.

74 Rothenberg and Rothenberg, "Testing the Dose-Response Specification in Epidemiology," 1190–95 (see n. 72 above).

75 Labour Environmental Alliance Society, *The CancerSmart Consumer Guide* (Vancouver: LEAS, 2005).

76 X. Tian, L. Neng, and A.E. Nel, "Potential Health Impacts of Nanoparticles," *Annual Review of Public Health* 30 (2009): 137–50.

77 C. Watson, J. Ge, J. Cohen, et al. 2014. "High-Throughput Screening Platform for Engineered Nanoparticle-Mediated Genotoxicity Using CometChip Technology," *ACS Nano* 8, 3 (2009): 2118–33; H. Wang, F. Wu, W. Meng, et al., "Engineered Nanoparticles May Induce Genotoxicity," *Environmental Science and Technology* 47, 23 (2013): 13212–14.

78 S.M. Choi, S.D. Yoo, and B.M. Lee, "Toxicological Characteristics of Endocrine-Disrupting Chemicals: Developmental Toxicity, Carcinogenicity, and Mutagenicity," *Journal of Toxicology and Environmental Health, Part B* 7, 1 (2004): 1–32.

79 World Health Organization and UN Environment Programme, *State of the Science on Endocrine Disrupting Chemicals – 2012* (Geneva: WHO/UNEP, 2013).

80 J.W. Thornton, M. McCally, and J. Houlihan, "Biomonitoring of Industrial Pollutants: Health and Policy Implications of the Chemical Body Burden," *Public Health Reports* 117 (2002): 315–23.

81 World Health Organization and UN Environment Programme, *State of the Science* (see n. 79 above).

82 M. Sun, C.X. Song, H. Huang, et al., "HMGA2/TET1/HOXA9 Signaling Pathway Regulates Breast Cancer Growth and Metastasis," *Proceedings of the National Academy of Sciences* 110, 24 (2013): 9920–25.

83 F. Perera, W. Yang, J. Herbstman, et al., "Relation of DNA Methylation of 5'-CpG Island of *ACSL3* to Transplacental Exposure to Airborne Polycyclic Aromatic Hydrocarbons and Childhood Asthma," *PLOS One* (August 18, 2009), doi:10.1371/annotation/6a678269-9623-4a13-8b19-4e9431ff3cb6.

84 Sun et al., "HMGA2/TET1/HOXA9 Signaling Pathway," 9920–25 (see n. 82 above).

85 L. Curtis, W. Rea, P. Smith-Willis, et al., "Adverse Health Effects of Outdoor Air Pollutants," *Environment International* 32, 6 (2006): 815–30; D. Krewski, R. Burnett, M. Jerrett, et al., "Mortality and Long-Term Exposure to Ambient Air Pollution: Ongoing Analyses Based on the American Cancer Society Cohort," *Journal of Toxicology and Environmental Health, Part A* 68 (2005): 1093–1109.

86 S. Koranteng, A.R. Osornio Vargas, and I. Buka, "Ambient Air Pollution and Children's Health: A Systematic Review of Canadian Epidemiological Studies," *Paediatric Child Health* 12, 3 (2007): 225–33.

87 H. Chen, M.S. Goldberg, and P.J. Villeneuve. 2008. "A Systematic Review of the Relation between Long-Term Exposure to Ambient Air Pollution and Chronic Diseases," *Review of Environmental Health* 23, 4 (2007): 243–97.

88 Ibid.

89 D. Stieb, L. Chen, M. Eshoul, and S. Judek. 2012. "Ambient Air Pollution, Birth Weight and Preterm Birth: A Systematic Review and Meta-Analysis," *Environmental Research* 117 (2007): 100–11; M. Brauer, C. Lencar, L. Tamburic, et al., "A Cohort Study of Traffic-Related Air Pollution Impacts on Birth Outcomes," *Environmental Health Perspectives* 116, 5 (2008): 680–86; S. Liu, D. Krewski, Y. Shi, Y. Chen, and R.T. Burnett, "Association between Gaseous Ambient Air Pollutants and Adverse Pregnancy Outcomes in Vancouver, Canada," *Environmental Health Perspectives* 111 (2003): 1773–78.

90 A.M. Gowers, P. Cullinan, J.G. Ayres, et al., "Does Outdoor Air Pollution Induce New Cases of Asthma? Biological Plausibility and Evidence; a Review," *Respirology* 17 (2012): 887–98.

91 M. Jerrett, K. Shankardass, K. Berhane, et al., "Traffic-Related Air Pollution and Asthma Onset in Children: A Prospective Cohort Study with Individual Exposure Measurement," *Environmental Health Perspectives* 116, 10 (2009): 1433–38; N. Kunzli, P.-O. Bridevaux, L.-J.S. Liu, et al., "Traffic-Related Air Pollution Correlates with Adult Onset Asthma in Never-Smokers," *Thorax* 64 (2009): 664–70.

92 M. Masoli, D. Fabian, S. Holt, and R. Beasley, "The Global Burden of Asthma," *Allergy* 59 (2004): 469–78.

93 K. Weir, "Smog in Our Brains," *Monitor on Psychology* 43, 7 (2012): 32.

94 Heart and Stroke Foundation of Canada, *The Changing Face of Heart Disease and Stroke in Canada 2000* (Ottawa: Heart and Stroke Foundation of Canada, 2000).

95 H. Mustafic, P. Jabre, C. Caussin, et al., "Main Air Pollutants and Myocardial Infarction: A Systematic Review and Meta-Analysis," *JAMA* 307, 7 (2012): 713–21; C.A. Pope III, R.T. Burnett, G.D. Thurston, et al., "Cardiovascular Mortality and Long-Term Exposure to Particulate Air Pollution: Epidemiological Evidence of

General Pathophysiological Pathways of Disease," *Circulation* 109 (2004): 71–77; R.D. Brook, B. Franklin, W. Cascio, et al., "Air Pollution and Cardiovascular Disease: A Statement for Healthcare Professionals from the Expert Panel on Population and Prevention Science of the American Heart Association," *Circulation* 109 (2004): 2655–71.

96 A.J. Cohen, H. Ross Anderson, B. Ostro, et al., "The Global Burden of Disease Due to Outdoor Air Pollution," *Journal of Toxicology and Environmental Health* 68, 13–14 (2005): 1301–7.

97 Pope et al., "Cardiovascular Mortality and Long-Term Exposure to Particulate Air Pollution," 71–77 (see n. 95 above).

98 D. Jaffe, T. Anderson, D. Covert, et al., "Transport of Asian Air Pollution to North America," *Geophysical Research Letters* 26, 6 (1999): 711-14.

99 C.A. Pope III, R.T. Burnett, M.J. Thun, et al., "Lung Cancer, Cardiopulmonary Mortality, and Long-Term Exposure to Fine Particulate Air Pollution," *JAMA* 287, 9 (2002): 1132–41; M. Brauer, C. Avila-Casado, T.I. Fortoul, et al., "Air Pollution and Retained Particles in the Lung," *Environmental Health Perspectives* 109 (2001): 1039–43; A. Churg, M. Brauer, M. del Carmen Avila-Casado, et al., "Chronic Exposure to High Levels of Particulate Air Pollution and Small Airway Remodeling," *Environmental Health Perspectives* 111 (2003): 714–18.

100 Ibid.

101 Pope et al., "Lung Cancer, Cardiopulmonary Mortality," 1132–41 (see n. 99 above).

102 Ibid.

103 Ibid.

104 M.L. Bell, F. Dominici, and J.M. Samet, "A Meta-Analysis of Time-Series Studies of Ozone and Mortality with Comparison to the National Morbidity, Mortality, and Air Pollution Study," *Epidemiology* 16 (2005): 436–45; K. Ito, S.F. De Leon, and M. Lippmann, "Associations between Ozone and Daily Mortality: Analysis and Meta-Analysis," *Epidemiology* 16 (2005): 446–57; J.I. Levy, S.M. Chemerynski, and J.A. Sarnat, "Ozone Exposure and Mortality: An Empirical Bayes Meta-Regression Analysis," *Epidemiology* 16 (2005): 458–68.

105 L. Curtis, W. Rea, P. Smith-Willis, et al., "Adverse Health Effects of Outdoor Air Pollutants," *Environment International* 32, 6 (2006): 815–30.

106 Environment Canada, National Air Pollution Surveillance Network, http://www.ec.gc.ca/rnspa-naps/.

107 R. Ambrose, "A Breath of Fresh Air" (speech given at GLOBE 2006, Vancouver, BC, March 31, 2006).

108 US Environmental Protection Agency, "National-Scale Air Toxics Assessment" (2005), http://epa.gov/ttn/atw/nata2005/05pdf/sum_results.pdf.

109 J.I. Levy, K. Lee, Y. Yanagisawa, et al., "Determinants of Nitrogen Dioxide Concentrations in Indoor Ice Skating Rinks," *American Journal of Public Health* 88, 12 (1998): 1781–86; K.W. Rundell, "High Levels of Airborne Ultrafine and Fine Particulate Matter in Indoor Ice Arenas," *Inhalation Toxicology* 15 (2003): 237–50.

110 W.J. Fisk, Q. Lei-Gomez, and M.J. Mendell, "Meta-Analyses of the Associations of Respiratory Health Effects with Dampness and Mold in Homes," *Indoor Air* 17, 4 (2007): 284–96.

111 J. La Dou, ed., *Current Occupational and Environmental Medicine* (New York: McGraw-Hill, 2004).

112 S.J. Genuis, "Clinical Medicine and the Budding Science of Indoor Mold Exposure," *European Journal of Internal Medicine* 18 (2007): 516–23.

113 Health Canada, *Canadian Tobacco Use Monitoring Survey: CTUMS 2012 Results* (Ottawa: Health Canada, 2014).

114 D. Krewski, J.H. Lubin, J.M. Zielinski, et al., "Residential Radon and Risk of Lung Cancer: A Combined Analysis of 7 North American Case-Control Studies," *Epidemiology* 16, 2 (2005): 137–45; S.C. Darby, D. Hill, A. Auvinen, et al., "Radon in Houses and Risk of Lung Cancer: Collaborative Analysis of Data from 13 European Case-Control Studies," *British Medical Journal* 330 (2005): 223–26.

115 Krewski et al., ibid., 137–45.

116 International Agency for Research on Cancer, *Radon-222 and Its Decay Products*, IARC Monographs, vol. 78 (2001), http://www.iarc.fr.

117 World Health Organization, *Air Quality Guidelines for Europe*, 2nd ed. (Copenhagen: WHO Regional Office for Europe, 2000), 215; National Research Council, Board of Biological Effects of Ionizing Radiation of the National Academy of Sciences, *BEIR VII Report: The Health Effects of Exposure to Indoor Radon* (Washington, DC: National Academies Press, 2005).

118 BC Lung Association, *Prince George: Community-Wide Radon Testing Results* (Vancouver: BC Lung Association, 2014); BC Lung Association, *Castlegar: Community-Wide Radon Testing Results*, (Vancouver: BC Lung Association, 2014).

119 J.M. Samet, J. Spengler, and C. Mitchell, "Indoor Air Pollution," in *Environmental and Occupational Medicine*, ed. William N. Rom (Philadelphia: Lippincott-Raven Publishers, 1998).

120 World Health Organization, *Air Quality Guidelines for Europe* (see n. 117 above).

121 Pollution Probe, *Volatile Organic Compounds: A Primer* (Toronto: Pollution Probe, 2005), http://www.pollutionprobe.org; US Environmental Protection Agency, "An Introduction to Indoor Air Quality," http://www.epa.gov/iaq/voc.html.

122 SE. Hrudey and E.J. Hrudey, *Safe Drinking Water: Lessons from Recent Outbreaks in Affluent Nations* (London: IWA Publishing, 2004), 4.

123 Ibid.

124 Commissioner of the Environment and Sustainable Development, "Drinking Water in First Nations Communities," in *Report to the House of Commons* (Ottawa: CESD, 2005); D.R. Boyd, *Unnatural Law: Rethinking Canadian Environmental Law and Policy* (Vancouver: UBC Press, 2003), ch. 2.1, "Drinking Water."

125 R. Christensen, *Waterproof 3: Canada's Drinking Water Report Card* (Vancouver: Ecojustice, 2011). An updated map is available at http://www.watertoday.ca/map-graphic.asp.

126 Commissioner of the Environment and Sustainable Development, "Drinking Water in First Nations Communities" (see n. 124 above).

127 Commission for Environmental Cooperation, *Children's Health and the Environment in North America: A First Report on Available Indicators and Measures* (Montreal: CEC, 2006), http://www.cec.org.

128 Hrudey and Hrudey, *Safe Drinking Water* (see n. 122 above); D. Krewski, J. Balbus, D. Butler-Jones, et al., "Managing Health Risks from Drinking Water: A Report to

the Walkerton Inquiry," *Journal of Toxicology and Environmental Health Part A* 65 (2002): 1635–1823.

129 Krewski et al., ibid., 1635–1823.

130 World Health Organization, *Emerging Issues in Water and Infectious Disease* (Geneva: WHO, 2003).

131 P.E. Rasmussen and H.D. Gardner, "International Year of Planet Earth 2. Earth and Health: Building a Safer Canadian Environment," *Geoscience Canada* 35, 2 (2008): 61–72.

132 G.A. Wasserman, X. Liu, N.J. LoIacono, et al., "A Cross-Sectional Study of Well Water and Child IQ in Maine Schoolchildren," *Environmental Health* 13 (2014): 23, doi:10.1186/1476-069X-13-23; International Agency for Research on Cancer, "Arsenic in Drinking-Water," *IARC Monographs on the Evaluation of Carcinogenic Risks to Humans* 84 (2004): 39–267.

133 A. Aschengrau, C. Rogers, and D. Ozonoff, "Perchloroethylene-Contaminated Drinking Water and the Risk of Breast Cancer: Additional Results from Cape Cod Massachusetts," *Environmental Health Perspectives* 111 (2003): 167–73; K. Costas, R.S. Knorr, and S.K. Condon, "A Case Control Study of Childhood Leukemia in Woburn, Massachusetts: The Relationship between Leukemia Incidence and Exposure to Public Drinking Water," *Science of the Total Environment* 300 (2002): 23–25.

134 K.P. Cantor, C.F. Lynch, M.E. Hildesheim, et al., "Drinking Water Source and Chlorination Byproducts. I. Risk of Bladder Cancer," *Epidemiology* 9 (1998): 21–28.

135 World Health Organization, *Guidelines for Drinking-Water Quality*, 3rd ed. (Geneva: WHO, 2004), http://www.who.int/water_sanitation_health/dwq/gdwq3rev/en/.

136 Environment Canada, *Shellfish Water Quality Protection Program* (Ottawa: Environment Canada, 1999).

137 J. Muzzin, "Public Health Concern Behind the Exposure to Persistent Organic Pollutants and the Risk of Metabolic Diseases," *BMC Public Health* 12 (2012): 298.

138 A. Lukacsovics, M. Hatcher, and A. Papadopolous, *Risk Factors and Surveillance Systems for Foodborne Illness Outbreaks in Canada* (Vancouver: National Collaborating Centre for Environmental Health, 2014).

139 P.S. Mead, L. Slutsker, V. Dietz, et al., "Food-Related Illness and Death in the United States," *Emerging Infectious Diseases Journal* 5, 5 (1999): 1–19.

140 Lukacsovics, Hatcher, and Papadopolous, *Risk Factors and Surveillance Systems* (see n. 138 above).

141 Foodnet Canada, *2012 Short Report* (Ottawa: Public Health Agency of Canada, 2014).

142 Ibid.

143 K.S. Schafer and S.E. Kegley, "Persistent Toxic Chemicals in the US Food Supply," *Journal of Epidemiology and Community Health* 56, 11 (2002): 813–17.

144 World Health Organization, *Dioxins and Their Effects on Human Health*, Fact Sheet No. 225 (Geneva: WHO, 2010).

145 R. Copes, "Health and Environment: What Are the Links?" *BC Medical Journal* 48, 2 (2006): 82.

146 L.L. Aylward, and S.M. Hays, "Temporal Trends in Human TCDD Body Burden: Decreases over Three Decades and Implications for Exposure Levels," *Journal of Exposure Analysis and Environmental Epidemiology* 12, 5 (2002): 319–28.

147 Environmental Defence Canada, *Polluted Children, Toxic Nation: A Report on Pollution in Canadian Families* (Toronto: EDC, 2006), http://environmentaldefence.ca/; Environmental Defence Canada, *Toxic Nation: A Report on Pollution in Canadians* (Toronto: EDC, 2005), http://environmentaldefence.ca/.

148 Environmental Defence Canada, *Pre-Polluted: A Report on the Toxic Substances in the Umbilical Cord Blood of Canadian Newborns* (Toronto: EDC, 2013); Environmental Working Group, *Body Burden 2: The Pollution in Newborns* (Washington, DC: EWG, 2005).

149 M.O. Enrique, V. Morales, E. Ngoumgna, et al., "Prevalence of Fetal Exposure to Environmental Toxic Substances as Determined by Meconium Analysis," *Neurotoxicology* 23, 3 (2002): 329–39.

150 R. Reigart and J. Roberts, eds., *Recognition and Management of Pesticide Poisoning*, 5th ed. (Washington, DC: US EPA, 1999).

151 Ibid.

152 J.D. Buckley, A.T. Meadows, M.E. Kadin, et al., "Pesticide Exposures in Children with Non-Hodgkin Lymphoma," *Cancer* 89, 11 (2000): 2315–21; X. Ma, P. Buffler, R. Gunier, et al., "Critical Windows of Exposure to Household Pesticides and Risk of Childhood Leukemia," *Environmental Health Perspectives* 110, 9 (2002): 955–60; M. Sears, C.R. Walker, R. van der Jagt, and P. Claman, "Pesticide Assessment: Protecting Public Health on the Home Turf," *Paediatrics and Child Health* 11, 4 (2006): 229–35; M. Sanborn, D. Cole, K. Kerr, et al., *Ontario College of Family Physicians: Pesticides Literature Review* (Toronto: Ontario College of Family Physicians, 2004); C. Infante-Rivard, D. Labuda, M. Krajinovic, et al., "Risk of Childhood Leukemia Associated with Exposure to Pesticides and Gene Polymorphisms," *Epidemiology* 10 (1999): 481–87.

153 M. van der Mark, M. Brouwer, H. Kromhout, et al., "Is Pesticide Use Related to Parkinson's Disease: Some Clues to Heterogeneity in Study Results," *Environmental Health Perspectives* 120, 3 (2012): 340–47.

154 L. Fritschi, G. Benke, A.M. Hughes, et al., "Occupational Exposure to Pesticides and Risk of Non-Hodgkin's Lymphoma," *American Journal of Epidemiology* 162, 9 (2005): 849–57.

155 Sears et al., "Pesticide Assessment," 229–35 (see n. 152 above).

156 R.P. Bull, B. Ritz, and G.M. Shaw, "Neural Tube Defects and Maternal Residential Proximity to Agricultural Pesticide Applications," *American Journal of Epidemiology* 163, 8 (2006): 743–53; E.M. Bell, I. Hertz-Picciotto, and J.J. Beaumont, "A Case-Control Study of Pesticides and Fetal Death Due to Congenital Anomalies," *Epidemiology* 12, 2 (2001): 148–56.

157 National Research Council, *Pesticides in the Diets of Infants and Children* (Washington, DC: National Academies Press, 1993); C. Lu, K. Toepel, R. Irish, et al., "Organic Diets Significantly Lower Children's Dietary Exposure to Organophosphorous Pesticides," *Environmental Health Perspectives* 114, 2 (2006): 260–63.

158 B.P. Jackson, V.F. Taylor, M.R. Karagas, T. Punshon, and K.L. Cottingham, "Arsenic, Organic Foods, and Brown Rice Syrup," *Environmental Health Perspectives* 120, 5 (2012): 623–26.

159 P. Grandjean and P.J. Landrigan, "Neurobehavioral Effects of Developmental Toxicity," *Lancet Neurology* 13, 3 (2013): 330–38.

160 Environment Canada, *The Status of Mercury in Canada: Report No. 2* (Ottawa: Environment Canada, 2000).

161 Ontario Ministry of Environment, *Guide to Eating Ontario Sport Fish, 2013–2014* (Toronto: Queen's Printer, 2013).

162 B. Lourie, *Mercury in the Environment: A Primer* (Toronto: Pollution Probe, 2003).

163 M. Munro, "As Canada Dawdles, Denmark Shows the World How to Stop Mass Medicating Animals," *Saskatoon Star Phoenix*, April 18, 2014.

164 World Health Organization, *Antimicrobial Resistance: Global Report on Surveillance* (Geneva: WHO, 2014).

165 J.L. Domingo, "Human Health Effects of Genetically Modified (GM) Plants: Risk and Perception," *Human and Ecological Risk Assessment: An International Journal* 17, 3 (2011): 535–37; M. Kramkowska, T. Grzelak, and K. Czyzewska, "Benefits and Risks Associated with Genetically Modified Food Products," *Annals of Agricultural and Environmental Medicine* 20, 3 (2013): 413–19.

166 A. Dona and I.S. Arvanitoyannis, "Health Risks of Genetically Modified Foods," *Critical Reviews in Food Science and Nutrition* 49, 2 (2009): 164–75.

167 A. Nicolia, A. Manzo, F. Veronisi, and D. Rosellini, "An Overview of the Last 10 Years of Genetically Engineered Crop Safety Research," *Critical Reviews in Biotechnology* 34, 1 (2014): 84.

168 European Commission, "A Decade of EU-Funded GMO Research" (2010), http://ec.europa.eu/research/biosociety/pdf/a_decade_of_eu-funded_gmo_research.pdf.

169 Frank R. de Gruijl and Jan C. van der Leun, "Environment and Health: Ozone Depletion and Ultraviolet Radiation," *Canadian Medical Association Journal* 163, 7 (2000): 851–55.

170 T.L. Diepgen and V. Mahler, "The Epidemiology of Skin Cancer," *British Journal of Dermatology* 146, s61 (2002): 1–6.

171 H. Slaper, G. Velders, J. Daniel, et al., "Estimates of Ozone Depletion and Skin Cancer Incidence to Examine the Vienna Convention Achievements," *Nature* 384 (1996): 256–58.

172 UN Environment Programme and World Meteorological Organization, "Ozone Layer on Track to Recovery: Success Story Should Encourage Action on Climate" (joint press release, September 10, 2014).

173 For example, the most recent article in the *Canadian Medical Association Journal* dealing with noise in an environmental context is from 1991: J. Rosenberg, "Jets over Labrador and Quebec: Noise Effects on Human Health," *Canadian Medical Association Journal* 144, 7 (1991): 869–75.

174 H. Ising and B. Kruppa, "Health Effects and Noise: Evidence in the Literature from the Past 25 Years," *Noise and Health* 6, 22 (2004): 5–13; S.A. Stansfeld and M.P. Matheson, "Noise Pollution: Non-Auditory Effects on Health," *British Medical Bulletin* 68 (2003): 243–57.

175 *Montréal (City) v. 2952-1366 Québec Inc.* [2005], 3 S.C.R. 141.

176 Cancer Care Ontario, *Insight on Cancer: Environmental Exposures and Cancer* (Toronto: Canadian Cancer Society, Ontario Division, 2005).

177 L. Hardell, M. Carlberg, and K.H. Mild, "Pooled Analysis of Two Case-Control Studies on Use of Cellular and Cordless Telephones and the Risk for Malignant Brain

Tumours Diagnosed in 1997–2003," *International Archives of Occupational and Environmental Health* 79, 8 (2006): 630–39.

178 J. Schuz, R. Jacobsen, J.H. Olsen, et al., "Cellular Telephone Use and Cancer Risk: An Update of a Nationwide Danish Cohort," *Journal of the National Cancer Institute* 98 (2006): 1707–13; C. Wild, *IARC Report to the International Union for Cancer Control (IUCC) on the Interphone Study* (Lyon, FR: International Agency for Research on Cancer, 2011).

179 M.A. Papas, A.J. Alberg, R. Ewing, et al., "The Built Environment and Obesity," *Epidemiologic Reviews* 29, 1 (2007): 129–43.

180 P.G. Sainsbury, "Ethical Considerations Involved in Constructing the Built Environment to Promote Health," *Bioethical Inquiry* 10, 1 (2013); 39–48; J. Kent and S. Thompson, "Health and the Built Environment: Exploring Foundations for a New Interdisciplinary Profession," *Journal of Environmental and Public Health,* Article ID 958175 (2012), doi:10.1155/2012/958175.

181 Papas et al., "The Built Environment and Obesity," 130 (see n. 179 above).

182 A.E. van den Berg, J. Maas, R.A. Verheij, and P.P. Groenewegen, "Green Space as a Buffer between Stressful Life Events and Health," *Social Science and Medicine* 70, 8 (2010): 1203–10; J. Maas, R.A. Verheij, S. de Vries, et al., "Morbidity Is Related to a Green Living Environment," *Journal of Epidemiology and Community Health* 63, 12 (2009): 967–73; R. Mitchell and F. Popham, "Effect of Exposure to Natural Environment on Health Inequalities: An Observational Population Study," *Lancet* 372, 9650 (2008): 1655–60.

183 Sainsbury, "Ethical Considerations," 39–48 (see n. 180 above).

184 J. Kent, S.M. Thompson, and B. Jalaludin, *Healthy Built Environments: A Review of the Literature* (Sydney: Healthy Built Environments Program, City Futures Research Centre, University of New South Wales, 2011).

185 Papas et al., "The Built Environment and Obesity," 129–43 (see n. 179 above); J.F. Sallis, B.E. Saelens, L.D. Frank, et al., "Neighbourhood Built Environment and Income: Examining Multiple Health Outcomes," *Social Science and Medicine* 68, 7 (2009): 1285–93.

186 D. Farr, *Sustainable Urbanism: Urban Design with Nature* (Hoboken, NJ: John Wiley and Sons, 2008).

187 M. Roseland, *Toward Sustainable Communities: Resources for Citizens and Their Governments,* rev. ed. (Gabriola Island, BC: New Society Publishers, 2005).

188 A. Berland, "Foundations for a Healthier Built Environment: Summary Paper" (prepared for BC Provincial Health Services Authority, 2009).

189 M. Simmons, K. Baughman, and J. Hight, "Healthy Neighbourhoods," in *Sustainable Urbanism: Urban Design with Nature,* ed. D. Farr (Hoboken, NJ: John Wiley and Sons, 2008), 148.

190 Sainsbury, "Ethical Considerations," 39–48 (see n. 180 above).

191 Papas et al., "The Built Environment and Obesity," 129–43 (see n. 179 above).

192 A. Miro and J. Siu, *Creating Healthy Communities: Tools and Actions to Foster Environments for Healthy Living* (Vancouver: Smart Growth BC, 2009); Kent, Thompson, and Jalaludin, *Healthy Built Environments* (see n. 184 above).

193 Sainsbury, "Ethical Considerations," 39–48 (see n. 180 above).

194 Berland, "Foundations for a Healthier Built Environment" (see n. 188 above); Kent and Thompson, "Health and the Built Environment" (see n. 180 above).
195 S. Galea, J. Aherne, S. Rudenstine, et al., "Urban Built Environment and Depression: A Multilevel Analysis," *Journal of Epidemiology and Community Health* 59, 10 (2005): 822–27.
196 R. Jackson, "Environment Meets Health, Again," *Science* 315, 5817 (2007): 1337.
197 L.B. Ford, "Climate Change and Health in Canada," *McGill Journal of Medicine* 12, 1 (2009): 78–84.
198 P. Epstein and E. Mills, *Climate Change Futures: Health, Ecological and Economic Dimensions* (Cambridge, MA: Harvard Center for Health and the Global Environment, 2005).
199 Health Canada, *Climate Change and Health and Well-Being: A Policy Primer* (Ottawa: Minister of Public Works and Government Services, 2001).
200 Ibid.
201 S.M. Bernard et al., "The Potential Impacts of Climate Variability and Change on Air-Pollution Related Health Effects in the United States," *Environmental Health Perspectives* 109, Supp. 2 (2001): 199–209.
202 P. Wayne, S. Foster, J. Connolly, et al., "Production of Allergenic Pollen by Ragweed Is Increased in CO_2 Enriched Atmospheres," *Annals of Allergy, Asthma, and Immunology* 88 (2002): 279–82.
203 K. Emanuel, "Increasing Destructiveness of Tropical Cyclones over the Past 30 Years," *Nature* 436 (2005): 686–88; T.R. Knutson and R.E. Tuleya, "Impact of CO_2-Induced Warming on Simulated Hurricane Intensity and Precipitation: Sensitivity to the Choice of Climate Model and Convective Parameterization," *Journal of Climate* 17 (2004): 3477–95.
204 D.F. Charron, "Potential Impacts of Climate Change on the Epidemiology of Zoonotic Diseases in Canada," *Canadian Journal of Public Health* 93, 5 (2002): 334–35.
205 Public Health Agency of Canada, "West Nile Virus: Human Surveillance" (2014), http://www.phac-aspc.gc.ca/wnv-vwn/mon-hmnsurv-archive-eng.php#a2008_12.
206 Federal, Provincial and Territorial Advisory Committee on Population Health, *Toward a Healthy Future: Second Report on the Health of Canadians* (Ottawa: Health Canada, 1999).

Chapter 3: The Environmental Burden of Disease

1 R. Samuel McLaughlin Centre for Population Health Risk Assessment, *Workshop Proceedings on the Environmental Burden of Disease* (Ottawa: McLaughlin Centre/ Health Canada, 2007).
2 D. Briggs, "Environmental Pollution and the Global Burden of Disease," *British Medical Bulletin* 68 (2003): 1–24.
3 C. Chociolko, R. Copes, and J. Rekart, *Needs, Gaps, and Opportunities Assessment for the National Collaborating Centre for Environmental Health* (Vancouver: NCCEH, 2006).
4 A. Prüss-Üstün, C. Mathers, C. Corvalán, and A. Woodward, *Assessing the Environmental Burden of Disease at National and Local Levels: Introduction and Methods*, Environmental Burden of Disease Series, No. 1 (Geneva: World Health Organization,

2003); D. Kay, A. Prüss, and C. Corvalán, *Methodology for Assessment of Environmental Burden of Disease* (Geneva: World Health Organization, 2000).

5 K.R. Smith, C. Corvalán, and T. Kjellstrom, "How Much Global Ill Health Is Attributable to Environmental Factors?" *Epidemiology* 10 (1999): 573–84.

6 J.M. Melse and A.E.M. de Hollander, "Human Health and the Environment" (background document for the OECD *Environmental Outlook,* ch. 21) (Paris: OECD, 2001).

7 A. Prüss-Üstün and C. Corvalán, *Preventing Disease through Healthy Environments: Towards an Estimate of the Environmental Burden of Disease* (Geneva: World Health Organization, 2006).

8 World Health Organization, *Ambient (Outdoor) Air Quality and Health,* Fact Sheet No. 313 (Geneva: WHO, 2014); World Health Organization, *Household Air Pollution and Health,* Fact Sheet No. 292 (Geneva: WHO, 2014).

9 F. Valent, D. Little, R. Bertollini, L.E. Nemer, et al., "Burden of Disease Attributable to Selected Environmental Factors and Injuries among Children and Adolescents in Europe," *Lancet* 363 (2004): 2032–39.

10 P. Landrigan, C. Schechter, J. Lipton, M. Fahs, and J. Schwartz, "Environmental Pollutants and Disease in American Children: Estimates of Morbidity, Mortality, and Costs for Lead Poisoning, Asthma, Cancer, and Developmental Disabilities," *Environmental Health Perspectives* 110, 7 (2002): 721–28; I. Mathews and S. Parry, *The Burden of Disease Attributable to Environmental Pollution* (Cardiff: University of Wales College of Medicine, 2005).

11 K. Davies and D. Hauge, *Economic Costs of Diseases and Disabilities Attributable to Environmental Contamination in Washington State* (Seattle: Collaborative for Health and Environment, 2005); R. Massey and F. Ackerman, *Costs of Preventable Childhood Illness: The Price We Pay for Pollution* (Medford, MA: Global Development and Environment Institute, Tufts University, 2003); K. Shuler, S. Nordbye, S. Yamin, and C. Ziebold, *The Price of Pollution: Cost Estimates of Environment-Related Disease in Minnesota* (Minneapolis: Institute for Agricultural and Trade Policy/Minnesota Center for Environmental Advocacy, 2006).

12 World Health Organization, *Country Profile of Environmental Burden of Disease: Canada* (Geneva: WHO, 2007), http://www.who.int/quantifying_ehimpacts/national/countryprofile/canada.pdf.

13 Prüss-Üstün et al., *Assessing the Environmental Burden of Disease* (see n. 4 above).; Kay et al., *Methodology for Assessment of Environmental Burden of Disease* (see n. 4 above).

14 Smith et al., "How Much Global Ill Health Is Attributable to Environmental Factors?," 573–84 (see n. 5 above).

15 Prüss-Üstün and Corvalán, *Preventing Disease through Healthy Environments* (see n. 7 above).

16 Ibid.

17 World Health Organization, *Country Profile of Environmental Burden of Disease: Canada* (see n. 12 above).

18 World Health Organization, *Country Profile of Environmental Burden of Disease: Country Profiles – Sources and Explanations* (Geneva: WHO, 2007), http://www.who.int/quantifying_ehimpacts/countryprofilesexplanatoryandsources_updated.pdf.

19 D.R. Boyd and S.J. Genuis, "The Environmental Burden of Disease in Canada: Respiratory Disease, Cardiovascular Disease, Cancer, and Congenital Affliction," *Environmental Research* 106 (2008): 240–49.

20 Statistics Canada, *Leading Causes of Death,* Report 84–215-X. (Ottawa: Statistics Canada, 2012).

21 Melse and de Hollander, "Human Health and the Environment" (see n. 6 above).

22 Prüss-Üstün and Corvalán, *Preventing Disease through Healthy Environments* (see n. 7 above).

23 Health Canada, *Respiratory Disease in Canada* (Ottawa: Health Canada, 2001).

24 Canadian Institute for Health Information, Canadian Lung Association, Health Canada, and Statistics Canada, *Respiratory Disease in Canada* (Ottawa: Health Canada, 2001).

25 Ontario Medical Association, *The Illness Costs of Air Pollution: 2005–2026 Health and Economic Damage Estimates* (Toronto: Ontario Medical Association, 2005).

26 Statistics Canada, *Leading Causes of Death* (see n. 20 above); Canadian Institute for Health Information, *Hospital Morbidity Database 2000/01: Tabular Reports* (Ottawa: CIHI, 2002).

27 C.A. Pope III, R.T. Burnett, G.D. Thurston, et al., "Cardiovascular Mortality and Long-Term Exposure to Particulate Air Pollution: Epidemiological Evidence of General Pathophysiological Pathways of Disease," *Circulation* 109 (2004): 71–77; A. Prüss-Üstün, L.J. Fewtrell, P. Landrigan, and J.L. Ayuso-Mateos, "Lead Exposure," in *Comparative Quantification of Health Risks,* ed. M. Ezzatti, A.D. Lopez, A. Rodgers, et al. (Geneva: World Health Organization, 2004); M. Concha-Barrientos, D. Campbell-Lendrum, and K. Steenland, *Occupational Noise: Assessing the Burden of Disease from Work-Related Hearing Impairment at National and Local Levels,* Environmental Burden of Disease Series, No. 9 (Geneva: World Health Organization, 2004).

28 Canadian Cancer Society, Statistics Canada, and Public Health Agency of Canada, *Canadian Cancer Statistics 2015* (Toronto: Canadian Cancer Society, 2015).

29 Cancer Care Ontario, *Insight on Cancer: Environmental Exposures and Cancer* (Toronto: Canadian Cancer Society, Ontario Division, 2005).

30 S. Janssen, G. Solomon, and T. Schettler, *Chemical Contaminants and Human Disease: A Summary of Evidence* (Bolinas, CA: Collaborative on Health and the Environment, 2004), http://ww2.protectingourhealth.org/corethemes/links/2004 -0203spreadsheet.htm; Y.M. Coyle, "The Effect of Environment on Breast Cancer Risk," *Breast Cancer Research and Treatment* 84 (2004): 273–88.

31 L. Fritschi, G. Benke, A.M. Hughes, A. Kricker, et al., "Occupational Exposure to Pesticides and Risk of Non-Hodgkin's Lymphoma," *American Journal of Epidemiology* 162, 9 (2005): 849–57.

32 E.G. Knox, "Childhood Cancers and Atmospheric Carcinogens," *Journal of Epidemiology and Community Health* 59, 2 (2005): 101–5.

33 S.A. Huchcroft, Y. Mao, and R. Semenciw, "Cancer and the Environment: Ten Topics in Environmental Cancer Epidemiology in Canada," *Chronic Disease in Canada* 29, Supp. 1 (2010): 1–8.

34 S.C. Darby, D. Hill, A. Auvinen, et al., "Radon in Houses and Risk of Lung Cancer: Collaborative Analysis of Data from 13 European Case-Control Studies," *British Medical Journal* 330 (2005): 223–26; D. Krewski, J.H. Lubin, J.M. Zielinski, et al.,

"Residential Radon and Risk of Lung Cancer: A Combined Analysis of 7 North American Case-Control Studies," *Epidemiology* 16, 2 (2005): 137–45.

35 There will be an estimated 20,900 deaths from lung cancer in Canada in 2015. Thus 9–15 percent of 20,900 equals a range of 1,800–3,130. Canadian Cancer Institute, National Cancer Institute of Canada, and Public Health Agency of Canada, *Canadian Cancer Statistics 2015* (Toronto: Canadian Cancer Society, 2015), http://www. cancer.ca/en/cancer-information/cancer-101/canadian-cancer-statistics-publication/ past-editions-canadian-cancer-statistics/?region=bc.

36 National Research Council, Board of Biological Effects of Ionizing Radiation of the National Academy of Sciences, *BEIR VI Report: The Health Effects of Exposure to Indoor Radon* (Washington, DC: National Academies Press, 1999); World Health Organization, *Air Quality Guidelines for Europe*, 2nd ed. (Copenhagen: WHO Regional Office for Europe, 2000).

37 National Cancer Institute, "Radon and Cancer" (2014), http://www.cancer.gov/ cancertopics/factsheet/Risk/radon.

38 M. de Groh and H. Morrison, "Environmental Tobacco Smoke and Deaths from Coronary Heart Disease in Canada," *Chronic Disease in Canada* 23, 1 (2002): 13–16.

39 Canadian Cancer Society, Statistics Canada, and Public Health Agency of Canada, *Canadian Cancer Statistics 2015* (see n. 28 above).

40 A.J. Cohen, H.R. Anderson, B. Ostro, K.D. Pandey, et al., "The Global Burden of Disease Due to Outdoor Air Pollution," *Journal of Toxicology and Environmental Health* 68, 13–14 (2005): 1301–7.

41 A. Almaskut, P.J. Farrell, and D. Krewski, "Statistical Methods for Estimating the Environmental Burden of Disease in Canada, with Applications to Mortality from Fine Particulate Matter," *Environmetrics* 23 (2012): 329–44.

42 Auditor General of Canada, "Ozone Protection: The Unfinished Journey," in *Report to Parliament* (1997), http://www.oag-bvg.gc.ca.

43 Canadian Cancer Society, Statistics Canada, and Public Health Agency of Canada, *Canadian Cancer Statistics 2015* (see n. 28 above).

44 International Agency for Research on Cancer, "Arsenic in Drinking-Water," *IARC Monographs on the Evaluation of Carcinogenic Risks to Humans* 84 (2004): 39–267; K.P. Cantor, C.F. Lynch, M.E. Hildesheim, M. Dosemeci, et al., "Drinking Water Source and Chlorination Byproducts. I. Risk of Bladder Cancer," *Epidemiology* 9 (1998): 21–28.

45 K. Kasim, P. Levallois, K.C. Johnson, et al., "Chlorination Disinfection By-Products in Drinking Water and the Risk of Adult Leukaemia in Canada," *American Journal of Epidemiology* 163, 2 (2006): 116–26; C. Infante-Rivard, E. Olson, L. Jacques, and P. Ayotte, "Drinking Water Contaminants and Childhood Leukemia," *Epidemiology* 12 (2000): 13–19; W.D. King and L.D. Marrett, "Case-Control Study of Bladder Cancer and Chlorination By-Products in Treated Water (Ontario, Canada)," *Cancer Causes Control* 7, 6 (1996): 596–604.

46 Congenital anomalies include approximately 450 cases of Down syndrome, 200 cases of neural tube defects, 100 cases of anencephaly, 400 to 500 cases of orofacial clefts (cleft lip or cleft palate), and 100 cases of spina bifida. Public Health Agency of Canada, *Canadian Perinatal Health Report, 2008* (Ottawa: Minister of Health, 2008); Canadian Institute for Health Information, *Health Indicators 2005* (Ottawa:

CIHI, 2005); Federal, Provincial, and Territorial Advisory Committee on Population Health, *Statistical Report on the Health of Canadians* (Ottawa: Statistics Canada, 1999).

47 Public Health Agency of Canada, ibid.

48 S.J. Genuis, "The Chemical Erosion of Human Health: Adverse Environmental Exposure and In-Utero Pollution – Determinants of Congenital Disorders and Chronic Disease," *Journal of Perinatal Medicine* 34, 3 (2006): 185–95.

49 Ibid.; A. Ohlsson and P. Shah, *Determinants and Prevention of Low Birth Weight: A Synopsis of the Evidence* (Edmonton: Institute of Health Economics, 2008).

50 M. Vinceti, S. Rovesti, M. Bergomi, et al., "Risk of Birth Defects in a Population Exposed to Environmental Lead Pollution," *Science of the Total Environment* 278, 1–3 (2001): 23–30.

51 M.I. Cedergren, A.J. Selbing, O. Lofman, et al., "Chlorination Byproducts and Nitrate in Drinking Water and Risk for Congenital Cardiac Defects," *Environmental Research* 89, 2 (2002): 124–30; B.F. Hwang and J.J. Jaakkola, "Water Chlorination and Birth Defects: A Systematic Review and Meta-Analysis," *Archives of Environmental Health* 58, 2 (2003): 83–91.

52 F.P. Perera, V. Rauh, R.M. Whyatt, et al., "A Summary of Recent Findings on Birth Outcomes and Developmental Effects of Prenatal ETS, PAH, and Pesticide Exposures," *Neurotoxicology* 26, 4 (2005): 573–87.

53 Ibid.

54 J.F. Logman, L.E. de Vries, M.E. Hemels, et al., "Paternal Solvent Exposure and Adverse Pregnancy Outcomes: A Meta-Analysis," *American Journal of Industrial Medicine* 47, 1 (2005): 37–44; K. Khattak, G.K. Moghtader, K. McMartin, et al., "Pregnancy Outcome Following Gestational Exposure to Organic Solvents: A Prospective Controlled Study," *Journal of the American Medical Association* 281, 12 (1999): 1106–9.

55 G. Latini, C. DeFelice, G. Presta, et al., "In Utero Exposure to Di-(2-ethylhexyl) Phthalate and Duration of Human Pregnancy," *Environmental Health Perspectives* 111, 14 (2003): 1783–85.

56 R.P. Bull, B. Ritz, and G.M. Shaw, "Neural Tube Defects and Maternal Residential Proximity to Agricultural Pesticide Applications," *American Journal of Epidemiology* 163, 8 (2006): 743–53; E.M. Bell, I. Hertz-Picciotto, and J.J. Beaumont, "A Case-Control Study of Pesticides and Fetal Death Due to Congenital Anomalies," *Epidemiology* 12, 2 (2001): 148–56.

57 P. Mendola, S.G. Selevan, S. Gutter, and D. Rice, "Environmental Factors Associated with a Spectrum of Neurodevelopmental Deficits," *Mental Retardation and Developmental Disabilities Research Reviews* 8, 3 (2002): 188–97.

58 S.R. Palmer, F.D. Dunstan, H. Fielder, et al., "Risk of Congenital Anomalies after the Opening of Landfill Sites," *Environmental Health Perspectives* 113, 10 (2005): 1362–65; H. Dolk, M. Vrijheid, B. Armstrong, et al., "Risk of Congenital Anomalies Near Hazardous-Waste Landfill Sites in Europe: The EUROHAZCON Study," *Lancet* 352, 9126 (1998): 423–27.

59 T.H. Shepard, *Catalog of Teratogenic Agents*, 9th ed. (Baltimore: Johns Hopkins University Press, 1998); J.L. Schardein, *Chemically Induced Birth Defects*, 3rd ed. (New York: Marcel Dekker, 2000).

60 Genuis, "The Chemical Erosion of Human Health," 185–95 (see n. 48 above); P. Grandjean and P. Landrigan, "Developmental Neurotoxicity of Industrial Chemicals," *Lancet* 368 (2006): 2167–78; E. Fombonne, "Epidemiology of Autism and Other Pervasive Developmental Disorders: An Update," *Journal of Autism and Developmental Disorders* 33 (2003): 365–81; B. Mekdeci and T. Schettler, *Birth Defects and the Environment* (Bolinas, CA: The Collaborative on Health and the Environment, 2004), http://www.healthandenvironment.org/birth_defects/peer_reviewed.

61 National Collaborating Centre for Environmental Health, *Systematic Review of Environmental Burden of Disease in Canada* (Vancouver: NCCEH, 2011), 32.

62 Health Canada, *National Strategic Framework on Children's Environmental Health* (Ottawa: Health Canada, 2010); Health Canada, "Response to Environmental Petition No. 294 Filed by Mr. Frank Woodcock under s. 22 of the Auditor General Act, May 28, 2010" (2010), http://www.oag-bvg.gc.ca/internet/English/pet_294_e_34055.html.

63 S. Judek, B. Jessiman, D. Stieb, and R. Vet, "Estimated Number of Excess Deaths in Canada Due to Air Pollution" (Health Canada and Environment Canada, 2005), http://www.metrovancouver.org/services/air-quality/_layouts/15/WopiFrame.aspx?sourcedoc=/services/air-quality/AirQualityPublications/AirPollutionDeaths.pdf&action=default&DefaultItemOpen=1.

64 Statistics Canada, "Population of Census Metropolitan Areas, Table 051-0034" (2006). The populations of the census divisions in the eight cities included in the Health Canada study, with the full population of the census metropolitan area in parentheses, are:

Quebec City	505,000	(718,000)
Montreal	1,776,000	(3,636,000)
Ottawa	721,000	(1,149,000)
Toronto	2,385,000	(5,304,000)
Hamilton	467,000	(715,000)
Windsor	350,000	(332,000)
Calgary	881,000	(1,060,000)
Vancouver	1,829,000	(2,208,000)
Total	8,915,000	(15,122,000)

The other three cities in the top ten in Canada that were not included in the Health Canada study are Edmonton (1,016,000), Winnipeg (707,000), and London (464,000).

65 Ontario Medical Association, *The Illness Costs of Air Pollution: 2005–2026 Health and Economic Damage Estimates* (Toronto: Ontario Medical Association, 2005).

66 Canadian Medical Association, *No Breathing Room: National Illness Costs of Air Pollution* (Toronto: CMA, 2008).

67 Organisation for Economic Co-operation and Development, *The Cost of Air Pollution: Health Impacts from Road Transport* (Paris: OECD, 2014).

68 Ontario Medical Association, *Smog's Excess Burden on Baby Boomers: Aging Population Most Vulnerable to Smog* (Toronto: Ontario Medical Association, 2006); Ontario Medical Association, *The Illness Costs of Air Pollution* (see n. 65 above).

69 For purposes of this analysis, the word "pesticides" includes insecticides, herbicides, fungicides, rodenticides, and slimicides.

70 Statistics Canada, *Deaths by Cause, Chapter XX, External Causes of Morbidity and Mortality.* Table 102–0540 (Ottawa: Statistics Canada, 2014).

71 IWK Regional Poison Centre, *Annual Statistical Report* (Halifax: IWK Regional Poison Centre, 2002); J.B. Mowry, D.A. Spyker, L.R. Cantilena, et al., "2012 Annual Report of the American Association of Poison Control Centers National Poison Data System," *Clinical Toxicology* 51, 10 (2013): 949–1229.

72 D.R. Boyd, *Northern Exposure: Acute Pesticide Poisonings in Canada* (Vancouver: David Suzuki Foundation, 2007).

73 Ibid.

74 Mowry et al., "2012 Annual Report," 949–1229 (see n. 71 above).

75 M.D. Sanborn, A. Abelsohn, M. Campbell, and E. Weir, "Identifying and Managing Adverse Environmental Health Effects. 3. Lead Exposure," *Canadian Medical Association Journal* 166 (2002): 1287–92.

76 Health Canada, *Risk Management Strategy for Lead* (Ottawa: Health Canada, 2013).

77 T.A. Jusko, C.R. Henderson, B.A. Lanphear, et al., "Blood Lead Concentrations <10 µg/dL and Child Intelligence at 6 Years of Age," *Environmental Health Perspectives* 116, 2 (2008): 243–48.

78 Health Canada, *Report on Human Biomonitoring of Environmental Chemicals in Canada: Results of the Canadian Health Measures Survey Cycle 1 (2007–2009)* (Ottawa: Minister of Health, 2010).

79 E. Richardson, W. Pigott, C. Craig, M. Lawson, and C. Mackie, *North Hamilton Child Blood Lead Study Public Health Report* (Hamilton, ON: Hamilton Public Health Services, 2011); É. Dewailly, P. Ayotte, D. Pereg, S. Déry, et al., *Exposure to Environmental Contaminants in Nunavik: Metals* (Québec City: Institut national de santé publique du Québec/Nunavik Regional Board of Health and Social Services, 2007).

80 Trail Area Health and Environment Committee, "Fall 2012 Blood Lead Results" (2012), http://www.thep.ca/pages/reports/.

81 Statistics Canada. *2015, Population by sex and age group, Table 051-0001.* There are 1.92 million Canadian children aged 0–4 and 384,000 five-year-olds (1.92 million aged 5–9 times 0.2). This makes 2,304,000 children aged five and under, with 1 percent of this group (23,040 children) suffering elevated lead levels.

82 C-Enternet, *2011 Short Report* (Ottawa: Canada's National Integrated Enteric Pathogen Surveillance System, 2012).

83 P. Payment and M.S. Riley, *Resolving the Global Burden of Gastrointestinal Illness: A Call to Action* (Washington, DC: American Academy of Microbiology, 2002).

84 Public Health Agency of Canada, *National Enteric Surveillance Program: Annual Report* (Ottawa: Public Health Agency of Canada, 2011).

85 T. Edge, J.M. Byrne, R. Johnson, et al., "Waterborne Pathogens," in *Threats to Sources of Drinking Water and Aquatic Ecosystem Health in Canada,* ed. Environment Canada (Burlington, ON: National Water Research Institute, 2001).

86 S.E. Majowicz, K. Dore, J.A. Flint, et al. 2004. "Magnitude and Distribution of Acute, Self-Reported Gastrointestinal Illness in a Canadian Community," *Epidemiology and Infection* 132, 4 (2001): 607–17.

87   M.K. Thomas, S.E. Majowicz, P.N. Sockett, et al., "Estimated Numbers of Commu-
     nity Illness Due to *Salmonella, Campylobacter* and Verotoxigenic *Escherichia coli:*
     Pathogen-Specific Community Rates," *Canadian Journal of Infectious Diseases and
     Medical Microbiology* 17, 4 (2006): 229–34.
88   Majowicz et al., "Magnitude and Distribution of Acute, Self-Reported Gastrointes-
     tinal Illness," 607–17 (see n. 86 above).
89   M.K. Thomas, R. Murray, L. Flockhart, et al., "Estimates of the Burden of Foodborne
     Illness in Canada for 30 Specified Pathogens and Unspecified Agents, Circa 2006,"
     Foodborne Pathogens and Disease 10, 7 (2013): 639–48.
90   P.S. Mead, L. Slutsker, V. Dietz, et al., "Food-Related Illness and Death in the United
     States," *Emerging Infectious Diseases Journal* 5, 5 (1999): 1–19.
91   C-Enternet, *2011 Short Report* (see n. 82 above).
92   A. Ravel, J. Greig, C. Tinga, at al., "Exploring Historical Canadian Foodborne Out-
     break Data Sets for Human Illness Attribution," *Journal of Food Protection* 72, 9
     (2009): 1963–76.
93   A. Lukacsovics, M. Hatcher, and A. Papadopolous, *Risk Factors and Surveillance
     Systems for Foodborne Illness Outbreaks in Canada* (Vancouver: National Collab-
     orating Centre for Environmental Health, 2014).
94   C.G. Schuster, A.G. Ellis, W.J. Robertson, et al., "Infectious Disease Outbreaks
     Related to Drinking Water in Canada 1974–2001," *Canadian Journal of Public
     Health* 96, 4 (2005): 254–58.
95   Health Canada, "Environmental Sustainability and Health" (presentation to the Ad
     Hoc Committee on Sustainability and the Environment, on file with author) (2004).
96   J.B. Rose, R.M. Atlas, C.P. Gerba, et al., *Microbial Pollutants in Our Nation's Water:
     Environmental and Public Health Issues* (Washington, DC: American Society for
     Microbiology, 1999).
97   P. Payment, J. Siemiatycki, L. Richardson, et al., "A Prospective Epidemiological
     Study of Gastrointestinal Health Effects Due to the Consumption of Drinking
     Water," *International Journal of Environmental Health Research* 7 (1997): 5–31; P.
     Payment, "Epidemiology of Endemic Gastrointestinal and Respiratory Diseases:
     Incidence, Fraction Attributable to Tap Water and Costs to Society," *Water Science
     and Technology* 35, 11–12 (1997): 7–10.
98   J. Aramini, M. McLean, J. Wilson, et al., "Drinking Water Quality and Health Care
     Utilization for Gastrointestinal Illness in Greater Vancouver," *Canada Communicable
     Disease Report* 26, 24 (2000): 211–14.
99   G. Lim, J. Aramini, M. Fleury, et al., *Investigating the Relationship between Drinking
     Water and Gastroenteritis: Edmonton 1993–1998* (Ottawa: Health Canada, 2002).
100 S.M. Choi, S.D. Yoo, and B.M. Lee, "Toxicological Characteristics of Endocrine-
     Disrupting Chemicals: Developmental Toxicity, Carcinogenicity, and Mutagenicity,"
     Journal of Toxicology and Environmental Health, Part B 7, 1 (2004): 1–32.
101 I. Janssen, "The Public Health Burden of Obesity in Canada," *Canadian Journal of
     Diabetes* 37, 2 (2013): 90–96.
102 L. Hardell, M. Carlberg, K. Hansson Mild, "Pooled Analysis of Two Case-Control
     Studies on Use of Cellular and Cordless Telephones and the Risk for Malignant
     Brain Tumours Diagnosed in 1997–2003," *International Archives of Occupational
     and Environmental Health* 79, 8 (2006): 630–39; M.C. Powell and M.S. Kanarek,

"Nanomaterial Health Effects – Part 1: Background and Current Knowledge," *Wisconsin Medical Journal* 105, 2 (2006): 16–20.

103 P. Epstein and E. Mills, *Climate Change Futures: Health, Ecological and Economic Dimensions* (Cambridge, MA: Harvard Center for Health and the Global Environment, 2005); A.J. McMichael, ed., *Climate Change and Human Health* (Geneva: World Health Organization, 1996); D.F. Charron, "Potential Impacts of Climate Change on the Epidemiology of Zoonotic Diseases in Canada," *Canadian Journal of Public Health* 93, 5 (2002): 334–35; K.H. Bartlett, L. MacDougall, S. Mak, et al., "*Cryptococcus gattii:* A Tropical Pathogen Emerging in a Temperate Climate Zone" (paper presented at the 16th Biometeorology and Aerobiology Conference, Vancouver, 2004), http://ams.confex.com/ams/AFAPURBBIO/techprogram/paper_80027.htm.

104 V.O. Ezenwa, M.S. Godsey, R.J. King, and S.C. Guptill, "Avian Diversity and West Nile Virus: Testing Associations between Biodiversity and Infectious Disease Risk," *Proceedings of the Royal Society B – Biological Sciences* 273 (2006): 109–17.

105 M.D. Anway, C. Leathers, and M.K. Skinner, "Endocrine Disruptor Vinclozolin Induced Epigenetic Transgenerational Adult Onset Disease," *Endocrinology* 147, 6 (2006): s43–s49; T.J. Murray, M.V. Maffini, A.A. Ucci, C. Sonnenschein, and A.M. Soto, "Induction of Mammary Gland Ductal Hyperplasias and Carcinoma in Situ Following Fetal Bisphenol A Exposure," *Reproductive Toxicology* 23, 3 (2006): 383–90.

106 W.V. Welshons, K.A. Thayer, B.M. Judy, C.A. Taylor, et al., "Large Effects from Small Exposures. I. Mechanisms for Endocrine-Disrupting Chemicals with Estrogenic Activity," *Environmental Health Perspectives* 111, 8 (2003): 994–1006.

107 National Collaborating Centre for Environmental Health, *Systematic Review of Environmental Burden,* 40 (see n. 61 above).

108 S.S. Lim, T. Vos, A.D. Flaxman, et al., "A Comparative Risk Assessment of Burden of Disease and Injury Attributable to 67 Risk Factors and Risk Factor Clusters in 21 Regions, 1990–2010: A Systematic Analysis for the Global Burden of Disease Study 2010," *Lancet* 380, 9859 (2012): 2224–60.

109 National Collaborating Centre for Environmental Health, *Systematic Review of Environmental Burden,* 44 (see n. 61 above).

Chapter 4: Environmental Injustices

1 L. Westra and B. Lawson, *Faces of Environmental Racism: Confronting Issues of Global Justice,* 2nd ed. (Oxford: Rowman and Littlefield, 2001).

2 A. Neimanis, H. Castleden, and D. Rainham, "Examining the Place of Ecological Integrity in Environmental Justice: A Systematic Review," *Local Environment* 17, 3 (2012): 349–67.

3 R.D. Bullard, *Dumping in Dixie: Race, Class, and Environmental Quality,* 3rd ed. (Boulder, CO: Westview Press, 2000).

4 S.A. Perlin, K. Sexton, and D.W.S. Wong, "An Examination of Race and Poverty for Populations Living near Industrial Sources of Air Pollution," *Journal of Exposure Science and Environmental Epidemiology* 9 (1999): 29–48.

5 R. McConnell, K. Berhane, L. Yao, M. Jerrett, et al., "Traffic, Susceptibility, and Childhood Asthma," *Environmental Health Perspectives* 114, 5 (2006): 766–72.

6 T.R. Tooke, B. Klinkenberg, and N.C. Coops, "A Geographical Approach to Identifying Vegetation-Related Environmental Equity in Canadian Cities," *Environment and Planning B: Planning and Design* 37, 6 (2010): 1040–56.

7 A. Dale and L.L. Newman, "Sustainable Development for Some: Green Urban Development and Affordability," *Local Environment* 14, 7 (2009): 669–81.

8 L. Westra, *Environmental Justice and the Rights of Indigenous Peoples* (London: Earthscan, 2008).

9 R.D. Bullard, ed., *The Quest for Environmental Justice: Human Rights and the Politics of Pollution* (San Francisco: Sierra Club Books, 2005).

10 US General Accounting Office, *Siting of Hazardous Waste Landfills and Their Correlation with Racial and Economic Status of Surrounding Communities* (Washington, DC: Government Printing Office, 1983).

11 United Church of Christ Commission for Racial Justice, *Toxic Wastes and Race: A National Report on the Racial and Socio-Economic Characteristics of Communities with Hazardous Waste Sites* (New York: United Church of Christ, 1987).

12 Bullard, *Dumping in Dixie* (see n. 3 above).

13 E.J. Ringquist, "Assessing Evidence of Environmental Inequities: A Meta-Analysis." *Journal of Policy Analysis and Management* 24, 2 (2005): 223–47; R.D. Bullard, ed., *Unequal Protection: Environmental Justice and Communities of Color* (San Francisco: Sierra Club Books, 1994).

14 D.L. Anderton, "Environmental Equity in Superfund: Demographics of the Discovery and Prioritization of Abandoned Toxic Sites," *Evaluation Review* 21, 1 (1997): 3–26.

15 E.J. Ringquist, "Environmental Justice: Normative Concerns, Empirical Evidence, and Government Action," in *Environmental Policy: New Directions for the Twenty-First Century*, ed. N. Vig and M. Kraft (Washington, DC: CQ Press, 2003), 272.

16 P. Mohai, B. Kweon, S. Lee, and K. Ard, "Air Pollution around Schools Is Linked to Poorer Student Health and Academic Performance," *Health Affairs* 30, 5 (2011): 852–62.

17 S.A. Perlin, D. Wong, and K. Sexton, "Residential Proximity to Industrial Sources of Air Pollution: Interrelationships among Race, Poverty, and Age," *Journal of the Air and Waste Management Association* 51, 3 (2001): 406–21.

18 V. Been, "What's Fairness Got to Do with It? Environmental Justice and the Siting of Locally Undesirable Land Uses," *Cornell Law Review* 78 (1993): 1001–36; C. Foreman, *The Promise and the Peril of Environmental Justice* (Washington, DC: Brookings Institution, 1998).

19 D.R. Williams and C. Collins, "U.S. Socioeconomic and Racial Differences in Health: Patterns and Explanations," *Annual Review of Sociology* 21 (1995): 349–86.

20 Natural Resources Defense Council, *Hidden Danger: Environmental Health Threats in the Latino Community* (New York: NRDC, 2004).

21 J. Lester, H. Allan, and K. Hill, *Environmental Injustice in the United States: Myths and Realities* (Boulder, CO: Broadview Press, 2001); W. Bowen, *Environmental Justice: Towards Research-Based Decision-Making* (New York: Garland Press, 2001).

22 Bullard, *The Quest for Environmental Justice* (see n. 9 above).

23 M.B. Gerrard and S.R. Foster, eds., *The Law of Environmental Justice: Theories and Procedures to Address Disproportionate Risk*, 2nd ed. (Chicago: American Bar

Association, 2008); S. Bonorris, *Environmental Justice for All: A Fifty State Survey of Legislation, Policies and Cases,* 3rd ed. (Chicago: American Bar Association/ Hastings College of the Law, 2007).

24 Bonorris, ibid.

25 L.W. Cole and S.R. Foster, *From the Ground Up: Environmental Racism and the Rise of the Environmental Justice Movement* (New York: New York University Press, 2001).

26 *Bakersfield Citizens for Local Control v. City of Bakersfield,* 124 Cal. App. 4th 1184 (Cal. Ct. App. 2004); *Eagle Environmental, L.P. v. Commonwealth of Pennsylvania,* 884 A.2d 867 (Pa. 2005); *Colonias Dev. Council v. Rhino Envtl. Svcs., Inc.,* 117 P.3d 939, 948 (2005).

27 R.J. Brulle and D.N. Pellow, "Environmental Justice: Human Health and Environmental Inequalities," *Annual Review of Public Health* 27 (2006): 103–24.

28 Ibid.

29 US Environmental Protection Agency, *EPA Needs to Consistently Implement the Intent of the Executive Order on Environmental Justice,* Evaluation Report No. 2004-P00007 (Washington, DC: US EPA Office of the Inspector General, 2004).

30 US Commission on Civil Rights, *Redefining Rights in America: The Civil Rights Record of the George W. Bush Administration, 2001–2004* (2004), 72–79, https:// www.law.umaryland.edu/marshall/usccr/documents/cr12r24.pdf.

31 US Environmental Protection Agency. *Plan EJ 2014 Progress Report* (Washington, DC: US EPA, 2013); J. Desmond-Harris, "The Environment and Obama: What's Next?" (2013), http://www.theroot.com/blogs/blogging-beltway/environment-and -obama-whats-next.

32 Quoted in B. Mock, "Why Obama's Carbon Regs Will Help Kids of Color Breathe Easier," *Grist,* June 3, 2014, http://grist.org/climate-energy/why-obamas-carbon-regs -will-help-kids-of-color-breathe-easier/.

33 M. Lloyd-Smith and L. Bell, "Toxic Disputes and the Rise of Environmental Justice in Australia," *International Journal of Occupational and Environmental Health* 9 (2003): 14–23; L. McCleod, L. Jones, A. Stedman, R. Day, et al., "The Relationship between Socio-Economic Indicators and Air Pollution in England and Wales: Implications for Environmental Justice," *Regional Environmental Change* 1 (2000): 78–85; R. Haluza-Delay, "Environmental Justice in Canada," *Local Environment* 12, 6 (2007): 557–64; D.A. McDonald, ed., *Environmental Justice in South Africa* (Cape Town: University of Cape Town Press, 2002); J. Curtice, A. Ellaway, C. Robertson, et al., *Public Attitudes and Environmental Justice in Scotland: A Report for the Scottish Executive on Research to Inform the Development and Evaluation of Environmental Justice Policy* (Edinburgh: Scottish Centre for Social Research, 2005).

34 World Health Organization (Regional Office for Europe), *Environmental Inequalities in Europe: An Assessment* (Copenhagen: WHO Regional Office for Europe, 2012).

35 Haluza-Delay, "Environmental Justice in Canada," 557–64 (see n. 33 above).

36 R. Haluza-DeLay and H. Fernhout, "Sustainability and Social Inclusion? Examining the Frames of Canadian English-Speaking Environmental Movement organizations," *Local Environment* 16, 7 (2011): 727–45; A. Gosine, "Myths of Diversity: Canadian Environmentalists Don't Want to Talk about Racism – But Too Often that Means the Uncritical Acceptance of Popular Diversity Myths," *Alternatives* 29, 1 (2003): 12–17.

37 D. Chakravartty, C.L.S. Wiseman, and D.C. Cole, "Differential Environmental Exposures among Non-Indigenous Canadians as a Function of Race/Gender and Race/Ethnicity Variables: A Scoping Review," *Canadian Journal of Public Health* 105, 6 (2014): e438–e444.

38 J.R. Masuda, T. Zupancic, B. Poland, and D. Cole, "Environmental Health and Vulnerable Populations in Canada: Mapping an Integrated Equity-Focused Research Agenda," *Canadian Geographer* 54, 4 (2008): 427–50.

39 D. Draper and B. Mitchell, "Environmental Justice Considerations in Canada," *Canadian Geographer* 45, 1 (2001): 93–98; J. Agyeman, P. Cole, R. Haluza-Delay, and P. O'Riley, eds., *Speaking for Ourselves: Environmental Justice in Canada* (Vancouver: UBC Press, 2009); A. Gosine and C. Teelucksingh, *Environmental Justice and Racism in Canada: An Introduction* (Toronto: Emond Montgomery, 2008). See the Centre for Environmental Health Equity, http://www.sehe.ca.

40 Government of Canada, *Children's Health and the Environment in North America: A First Report on Available Indicators and Measures. Country Report: Canada* (Gatineau, QC: Environment Canada, 2005), 58.

41 J. O'Heany, R. Kusiak, C.E. Duncan, et al., "Blood Lead and Associated Risk Factors in Ontario Children," *Science of the Total Environment* 71, 3 (1988): 477–83.

42 S.H. Wilson, "Genetics and Environmental Health," in *Environmental Health: From Global to Local*, ed. H. Frumkin (San Francisco: Wiley, 2005), 128–42.

43 D. Hattis, A. Russ, R. Goble, et al., "Human Inter-Individual Variability in Susceptibility to Airborne Particles," *Risk Analysis* 21 (2001): 585–99.

44 R. Haluza-Delay, P. O'Riley, P. Cole, and J. Agyeman, "Introduction. Speaking for Ourselves, Speaking Together: Environmental Justice in Canada," in Agyeman et al., *Speaking for Ourselves*, 7 (see n. 39 above).

45 P. Blow, *The Village of Widows: The Story of the Sahtu Dene and the Atomic Bomb* [videorecording] (Peterborough, ON: Lindum Films, 1999); A. Keeling and J. Sandlos, "Environmental Justice Goes Underground: Historical Notes from Canada's Northern Mining Frontier," *Environmental Justice* 2, 3 (2009): 117–25.

46 S.C.B. Gilby, "Variations on a Theme: Environmental Racism and the Adverse Effects of Natural Resource Extraction on the Aboriginal Peoples of Canada," Master of Laws thesis, Dalhousie University, 1996, 136.

47 *Frontenac Ventures Corp. v. Ardoch Algonquin First Nation et al.* (2008) 91 O.R. (3rd) 1 (C.A.); R. Lovelace, "Prologue. Notes from Prison: Protecting Algonquin Lands from Uranium Mining," in Agyeman et al., *Speaking for Ourselves*, ix-xix (see n. 39 above).

48 Royal Commission on Aboriginal Peoples, *The Report of the Royal Commission on Aboriginal Peoples* (Ottawa: The Commission, 1996).

49 Haluza-Delay et al., "Introduction. Speaking for Ourselves, Speaking Together," 13 (see n. 44 above).

50 L. Young, "Alberta Report Finds Fort Chipewayan Has Higher Rates of Three Kinds of Cancer," *Global News*, March 24, 2014, http://globalnews.ca/news/1227635/alberta-report-finds-fort-chipewyan-has-higher-rates-of-three-kinds-of-cancer/.

51 K. Erikson, *A New Species of Trouble: The Human Experience of Modern Disasters* (New York: Norton, 1995).

52 N. Ilyniak, "Mercury Poisoning in Grassy Narrows: Environmental Injustices, Colonialism, and Capitalist Expansion in Canada," *McGill Sociological Review* 4 (2014): 43–66.

53 R.M. Van Wynsberghe, *AlterNatives: Community, Identity and Environmental Justice on Walpole Island* (Toronto: Allyn and Bacon, 2002).

54 J. Carrie, F. Wang, H. Sanei, et al., "Increasing Contaminant Burdens in an Arctic Fish, Burbot (*Lota lota*), in a Warming Climate," *Environmental Science and Technology* 44, 1 (2010): 316–22.

55 S.F. Trainor, A. Goduhn, L.K. Duffy, et al., "Environmental Injustice in the Canadian Far North: Persistent Organic Pollutants and Arctic Climate Impacts," in Agyeman et al., *Speaking for Ourselves*, 144–62 (see n. 39 above).

56 Indian and Northern Affairs Canada, *Canadian Arctic Contaminants Assessment Report II: Human Health* (Ottawa: INAC, Northern Contaminants Program, 2003).

57 Government of Canada, *Children's Health and the Environment in North America* (see n. 40 above).

58 D. Saint-Amour, M.-S. Roy, C. Bastien, et al., "Alterations of Visual Evoked Potentials in Preschool Inuit Children Exposed to Methylmercury and Polychlorinated Biphenyls from a Marine Diet," *Neurotoxicology* 27, 4 (2006): 567–78.

59 P. Plusquellec, G. Muckle, E. Dewailly, et al., "The Relation of Environmental Contaminants Exposure to Behavioral Indicators in Inuit Preschoolers in Arctic Quebec," *Pediatrics* 128, 5 (2011): 873–82; O. Boucher, S.W. Jacobson, P. Plusquellec, et al., "Prenatal Methylmercury, Postnatal Lead Exposure and Evidence of Attention Deficit/Hyperactivity Disorder among Inuit Children in Arctic Quebec," *Environmental Health Perspectives* 120, 10 (2012): 1456–61.

60 E. MacDonald and S. Rang, *Exposing Canada's Chemical Valley: An Investigation of Cumulative Air Pollution Emissions in the Sarnia, Ontario Area* (Toronto: Ecojustice, 2007).

61 World Health Organization, *Global Database of Urban Air Pollution* (Geneva: WHO, 2013).

62 D.N. Scott, "Confronting Chronic Pollution: A Socio-Legal Analysis of Risk and Precaution," *Osgoode Hall Law Journal* 46, 2 (2008): 293–343; D.D. Jackson, "Shelter in Place: A First Nation Community in Canada's Chemical Valley," *Interdisciplinary Environmental Review* 11, 4 (2010): 249–62.

63 C.A. Mackenzie, A. Lockridge, and M. Keith, "Declining Sex Ratio in a First Nation Community," *Environmental Health Perspectives* 113 (2005): 1295–98.

64 M.L. Terrell, K.P. Hartnett, and M. Marcus, "Can Environmental or Occupational Hazards Alter the Sex Ratio at Birth? A Systematic Review," *Emerging Health Threats Journal* 4 (2011), doi: 10.3402/ehtj.v4i0.7109.

65 S. Sabzwari and D.N. Scott, "The Quest for Environmental Justice on a Canadian Aboriginal Reserve," in *Poverty Alleviation and Environmental Law*, ed. Y. Le Bouthillier, M.A. Cohen, J.J. Gonzalez Marquez, A Mumma, and S. Smith (Cheltenham, UK: IUCN Academy of Environmental Law/Edward Elgar, 2012), 88.

66 D.R. Boyd, "No Taps, No Toilets: First Nations and the Constitutional Right to Water in Canada," *McGill Law Journal* 57, 1 (2011): 81–134.

67 Commissioner of the Environment and Sustainable Development, "Chapter 5: Drinking Water in First Nations Communities," in *Report of the Commissioner of the*

Environment and Sustainable Development to the House of Commons (Ottawa: Office of the Auditor General of Canada, 2005).

68 Health Canada, "First Nations and Inuit Health: Drinking Water and Wastewater" (2014), http://www.hc-sc.gc.ca/fniah-spnia/promotion/public-publique/water-eau -eng.php; M. Mascarenhas, "Where the Waters Divide: First Nations, Tainted Water, and Environmental Justice in Canada," *Local Environment* 12, 6 (2007): 565–77.

69 M. Clark, "Shigellosis and First Nations Communities," *Health Policy Research Bulletin* 4: (2002) 15–18, 26.

70 Arctic Council, *Impacts of a Warming Arctic: Arctic Council Impact Assessment* (Cambridge: Cambridge University Press, 2004).

71 S. Theriault, "The Food Security of the Inuit in Times of Change: Alleviating the Tension between Conserving Biodiversity and Access to Food." *Journal of Human Rights and the Environment* 2, 2 (2011): 136–56.

72 S.F. Trainor, F.S. Chapin III, H.P. Huntington, G. Kofinas, and D.C. Natcher, "Arctic Climate Impacts and Cross-Scale Linkages: Environmental Justice in Canada and the United States," *Local Environment* 14, 6 (2007): 630.

73 Inuit Circumpolar Conference, "Petition to the Inter-American Commission on Human Rights Seeking Relief from Violations Resulting from Global Warming Caused by Acts and Omissions of the United States" (2005), http://earthjustice.org/ sites/default/files/library/legal_docs/petition-to-the-inter-american-commission -on-human-rights-on-behalf-of-the-inuit-circumpolar-conference.pdf.

74 Theriault, "The Food Security of the Inuit," 136–56 (see n. 71 above).

75 H. McCurdy, "Africville: Environmental Racism," in L. Westra and P.S. Wenz, eds. *Faces of Environmental Racism: Confronting Issues of Global Justice* (Lanham, MD: Rowman and Littlefield, 1995), 75–92; J. Nelson, *Razing Africville: A Geography of Racism* (Toronto: University of Toronto Press, 2008).

76 Gilby, "Variations on a Theme" (see n. 46 above).

77 L. Deacon and J. Baxter, "No Opportunity to Say No: A Case Study of Procedural Environmental Injustice in Canada," *Journal of Environmental Planning and Management* 56, 5 (2012): 1–17.

78 A. Nabalamba, G.K. Warriner, and K. McSpurren, "Social Justice and Environmental Equity: Distributing Environmental Quality," *Environments* 29, 1 (2001): 85–98.

79 M. Buzzelli and M. Jerrett, "Comparing Proximity Measures of Exposure to Geo-statistical Estimates in Environmental Justice Research," *Environmental Hazards* 5 (2003): 13–21; M. Buzzelli and M. Jerrett, "Racial Gradients of Ambient Air Pollution Exposure in Hamilton, Canada," *Environment and Planning A* 36 (2004): 1855–76.

80 S. Kershaw, S. Gower, C. Rinner, and M. Campbell, "Identifying Inequitable Exposure to Toxic Air Pollution in Racialized and Low Income Neighbourhoods to Support Pollution Prevention," *Geospatial Health* 7, 2 (2013): 274.

81 Canadian Institute for Health Information, *Urban Physical Environments and Health Inequalities* (Ottawa: CIHI, 2011).

82 T.H. Oiamo, I.N. Luginaah, D.O. Atari, and K.M. Gorey, "Air Pollution and General Practitioner Access and Utilization: A Population Based Study in Sarnia, 'Chemical Valley,' Ontario," *Environmental Health* 10: 71 (2011), doi:10.1186/1476-069X-10-71.

83 P.J. Veugelers and J.R. Read, "Health Deficiencies in Cape Breton County, Nova Scotia, Canada, 1950–1995," *Epidemiology* 10, 5 (1999): 495–99.

84 M. Barlow and E. May, *Frederick Street: Life and Death on Canada's Love Canal* (Toronto: HarperCollins, 2000); T.W. Lambert, L. Guyn, and S.E. Lane, "Development of Local Knowledge of Contamination in Sydney, Nova Scotia: Environmental Health Practice from an Environmental Justice Perspective," *Science of the Total Environment* 368, 2–3 (2006): 471–84.

85 T.W. Lambert and S.E. Lane, "Lead, Arsenic, and Polycyclic Aromatic Hydrocarbons in Soil and House Dust in the Communities Surrounding the Sydney, Nova Scotia, Tar Ponds," *Environmental Health Perspectives* 112, 1 (2004): 35–41.

86 M. Buzzelli, *Environmental Justice in Canada: It Matters Where You Live* (Ottawa: Canadian Policy Research Networks, 2008).

87 F. Handy, "Income and Air Pollution in Hamilton, Ontario," *Alternatives* 6 (1977): 18–24.

88 M. Buzzelli, M. Jerrett, R. Burnett, and N. Finkelstein, "Spatiotemporal Perspectives on Air Pollution and Environmental Justice in Hamilton, Canada, 1985–1996," *Annals of the Association of American Geographers* 93, 3 (2003): 557–73; M. Jerrett, R. Burnett, P. Kanaroglou, et al., "A GIS-Environmental Justice Analysis of Particulate Air Pollution in Hamilton, Canada," *Environment and Planning A* 33 (2001): 955–73; Buzzelli and Jerrett, "Comparing Proximity Measures of Exposure," 13–21 (see n. 79 above).; Buzzelli and Jerrett, "Racial Gradients of Ambient Air Pollution Exposure," 1855–76 (see n. 79 above).

89 S. Rang, F. de Leon, J. Foulds, et al., *An Examination of Pollution and Poverty in the Great Lakes Basin* (Toronto: Canadian Environmental Law Association/ Environmental Defence, 2008); K. Okamoto, "Tower Neighbourhood Revitalization in Toronto and Canadian Environmental Justice Politics," *Environmental Justice* 6, 2 (2013): 41–47; M. Ollevier and E. Tsang, *Environmental Justice in Toronto* (report prepared for the City of Toronto, 2007).

90 M. Buzzelli and M. Jerrett, "Geographies of Susceptibility and Exposure in the City: Environmental Inequity of Traffic-Related Air Pollution in Toronto," *Canadian Journal of Regional Science* 30, 2 (2007): 195–210.

91 Okamoto, "Tower Neighbourhood Revitalization," 41–47 (see n. 89 above).

92 D.L. Crouse, N.A. Ross, and M.S. Goldberg, "Double Burden of Deprivation and High Concentrations of Ambient Air Pollution at the Neighbourhood Scale in Montréal, Canada," *Social Science and Medicine* 69, 6 (2009): 971–81.

93 U. Thompson and S. Caquard, "Compiling a Geographic Database to Study Environmental Injustice in Montreal: Process, Results, and Lessons," in *Mapping Environmental Issues in the City: Arts and Cartography Cross Perspectives*, ed. S. Caquard et al. (Berlin: Springer-Verlag, 2011), 10–29; N.A. Ross, S. Tremblay, and K. Graham, "Neighbourhood Influences on Health in Montréal, Canada," *Social Science and Medicine* 59, 7 (2004): 1485–94.

94 J.G. Su, T. Larson, T. Gould, M. Cohen, and M. Buzzelli, "Transboundary Air Pollution and Environmental Justice: Vancouver and Seattle Compared," *GeoJournal* 75, 6 (2010): 595–608.

95 T.R. Tooke, B. Klinkenberg, and N.C. Coops, "A Geographical Approach to Identifying Vegetation-Related Environmental Equity in Canadian Cities," *Environment and Planning B: Planning and Design* 37, 6 (2010): 1040–56.

96 J. Wandel, M. Riemer, W. De Gómez, et al., *Homelessness and Global Climate Change: Are We Ready? A Report from the Study on the Vulnerability to Global Climate Change of People Experiencing Homelessness in Waterloo Region* (Waterloo, ON: University of Waterloo, 2010).

97 B. Ramin and T. Svoboda, "Health of the Homeless and Climate Change," *Journal of Urban Health* 86, 4 (2009): 654–64.

98 D.L. Powell and V. Stewart, "Children: The Unwitting Target of Environmental Injustices," *Pediatric Clinics of North America* 48, 5 (2001): 1291–1305.

99 D. Wigle, *Child Health and the Environment* (Oxford: Oxford University Press, 2003).

100 P.J. Landrigan and R.A Etzel, eds., *The Textbook of Children's Environmental Health* (Oxford: Oxford University Press, 2014).

101 Wigle, *Child Health and the Environment* (see n. 99 above); D.T. Wigle, T.E. Arbuckle, M.C. Turner, et al., "Epidemiologic Evidence of Relationships between Reproductive and Child Health Outcomes and Environmental Chemical Contaminants," *Journal of Toxicology and Environmental Health B, Critical Reviews* 11, 5–6 (2008): 373–517.

102 US EPA, *America's Children and the Environment: Measures of Contaminants, Body Burdens, and Illnesses* (Washington, DC: US EPA, 2003).

103 Public Health Agency of Canada, "Childhood Cancer (Ages 0–14)" (n.d.), http://www.phac-aspc.gc.ca/cd-mc/cancer/childhood_cancer-cancer_enfants-eng.php.

104 Health Canada, *Persistent Environmental Contaminants and the Great Lakes Basin Population: An Exposure Assessment*, Cat. No. H46–2/98–218E (Ottawa: Minister of Public Works and Government Services, 1998).

105 D.R. Boyd, *Northern Exposure: Acute Pesticide Poisonings in Canada* (Vancouver: David Suzuki Foundation, 2007).

106 L.K. Wolf, "The Crimes of Lead," *Chemical and Engineering News* 92, 5 (2014): 27–29.

107 Commission on Life Sciences, *Scientific Frontiers in Developmental Toxicology and Risk Assessment* (Washington, DC: National Academy of Sciences, 2000).

108 Lung Association of Saskatchewan, "Influence of Family Income on Hospital Visits for Asthma among Canadian School Children," *Thorax* 57, 6 (2002): 513–17.

109 The Canadian Partnership for Children's Health and the Environment includes the Canadian Association of Physicians for the Environment, Canadian Child Care Federation, Canadian Environmental Law Association, Environmental Health Clinic at Women's College Hospital, Environmental Health Institute of Canada, Learning Disabilities Association of Canada, Ontario College of Family Physicians, Pollution Probe, South Riverdale Community Health Centre, and Toronto Public Health. http://www.healthyenvironmentforkids.ca.

110 T. Hancock, "Children's Environmental Health," in *The Health of Canada's Children: A CICH Profile*, 3rd ed. (Ottawa: CICH, 2000).

111 Commission for Environmental Cooperation, *Making the Environment Healthier for Our Kids: An Overview of Environmental Challenges to the Health of North America's Children* (Montreal: Commission for Environmental Cooperation, 2002), 4.

112 Emphasis in original. When the memo became public in February 1992, Brazil's then-secretary of the environment, Jose Lutzenburger, offered the following re-

sponse to Summers: "Your reasoning is perfectly logical but totally insane ... Your thoughts [provide] a concrete example of the unbelievable alienation, reductionist thinking, social ruthlessness and the arrogant ignorance of many conventional 'economists' concerning the nature of the world we live in."

113 A. Prüss-Üstün and C. Corvalan, *Preventing Disease through Healthy Environments: Towards an Estimate of the Environmental Burden of Disease* (Geneva: World Health Organization, 2006).

114 K. Chatham-Stephens et al., "Burden of Disease from Toxic Waste Sites in India, Indonesia, and the Philippines in 2010," *Environmental Health Perspectives* 121, 7 (2013): 791–96.

115 Y.T. Hwang, D.M.W. Frierson, and S.M. Kang, "Anthropogenic Sulphate Aerosol and the Southward Shift of Tropical Precipitation in the Late 20th Century," *Geophysical Research Letters* 40, 11 (2013): 2845–50.

116 A. Prüss-Üstün, S. Bonjour, and C. Corvalan, "The Impact of the Environment on Health by Country: A Meta-Synthesis," *Environmental Health* 7: 7 (2008), doi:10.1186/1476-069X-7-7

117 World Health Organization, *Household Air Pollution and Health,* Fact Sheet No. 292 (Geneva: WHO, 2014).

118 World Health Organization, *Ambient (Outdoor) Air Quality and Health,* Fact Sheet No. 313 (Geneva: WHO, 2014).

119 L. Fewtrell et al., *Lead: Assessing the Environmental Burden of Disease* (Geneva: World Health Organization, 2003).

120 L. Goldman and N. Tran, *Toxics and Poverty: The Impact of Toxic Substances on the Poor in Developing Countries* (Washington, DC: World Bank, 2002); Food and Agriculture Organization and United Nations Environment Programme, *Pesticide Poisoning: Information for Advocacy and Action* (Geneva: UNEP, 2004).

121 A.J. McMichael et al., eds., *Climate Change and Human Health* (Geneva: World Health Organization, 2003); Global Humanitarian Forum, *Human Impact Report: Climate Change – The Anatomy of a Silent Crisis* (2009), http://www.ghf-ge.org.

122 D.L. Davies, "Short-Term Improvements in Public Health from Global Climate Policies on Fossil Fuel Combustion: An Interim Report," *Lancet* 350, 9088 (1997): 1341–49.

123 Mining Watch Canada is an NGO that monitors the overseas activities of Canadian mining firms. See http://www.miningwatch.ca. Canadian Broadcasting Corporation, "The Ugly Canadians," *The National,* July 6, 1998.

124 K. Straif, L. Benbrahim-Tallaa, R. Baan, et al., "A Review of Human Carcinogens – Part C: Metals, Arsenic, Dusts, and Fibres," *Lancet Oncology* 10, 5 (2009): 453–54; M.A. Silverstein, L.S. Welch, and R. Lemen, "Developments in Asbestos Cancer Risk Assessment," *American Journal of Industrial Medicine* 52, 11 (2009): 850–58; International Agency for Research on Cancer, "Asbestos," *IARC Monographs on the Evaluation of Carcinogenic Risks to Humans* 1987, Suppl. 7 (1987): 106–16.

125 World Health Organization, *Elimination of Asbestos-Related Disease* (Geneva: WHO, 2006).

126 International Labour Organization, "Resolution Concerning Asbestos: Adopted by the 95th Session of the International Labour Conference, June 2006," UNEP/FAO/RC/COP.3/INF/17.

127 Office of the Auditor General of Canada, "Canada's Policies on Chrysotile Asbestos Exports" (response by the Minister of Foreign Affairs to Environment Petition no. 179) (Ottawa: Office of the Auditor General of Canada, 2006).

128 A. Attaran, D.R. Boyd, and M.B. Stanbrook, "Asbestos Mortality: A Canadian Export," *Canadian Medical Association Journal* 179, 9 (2009): 871.

129 Ibid.

130 Office of the Auditor General of Canada, "Canada's Policies on Chrysotile Asbestos Exports" (see n. 127 above).

131 A. Nikiforuk, "Alberta's Tar Sands Pollution Refugees," *The Tyee*, March 2, 2013, http://thetyee.ca/News/2013/03/02/Tar-Sand-Pollution-Refugees/.

132 S. Wakefield and J. Baxter, "Linking Health Inequality and Environmental Justice: Articulating a Precautionary Framework for Research and Action," *Environmental Justice* 3, 3 (2010): 95–102.

133 J. Masuda, B. Poland, and J. Baxter, "Reaching for Environmental Health Justice: Canadian Experiences for a Comprehensive Research, Policy and Advocacy Agenda in Health Promotion," *Health Promotion International* 25, 4 (2010): 453–63.

134 Buzzelli and Jerrett, "Racial Gradients of Ambient Air Pollution Exposure," 1873 (see n. 79 above).

135 J. Masuda and A. Crabtree, "Environmental Justice in the Therapeutic Inner City," *Health and Place* 16, 4 (2010): 656–65.

Chapter 5: The Economic Costs of the Environmental Burden of Disease

1 Canadian Institute for Health Information, *National Health Expenditure Trends 1975 to 2012* (Ottawa: CIHI, 2012).

2 Ibid.

3 Ibid.

4 Ibid.

5 M. Jerrett, J. Eyles, C. Dufournaud, and S. Birch, "Environmental Influences on Healthcare Expenditures: An Exploratory Analysis from Ontario, Canada," *Journal of Epidemiology and Community Health* 57, 5 (2003): 334–38.

6 Canadian Institute for Health Information, *Health Care Cost Drivers: The Facts* (Ottawa: CIHI, 2011).

7 Conference Board of Canada, *Health Matters: An Economic Perspective* (Ottawa: Conference Board of Canada, 2013).

8 S. Brandt, L. Perez, N. Künzli, et al., "Costs of Childhood Asthma Due to Traffic-Related Pollution in Two California Communities," *European Respiratory Journal* 40 (2012): 363–70.

9 K. Knowlton, M. Rotkin-Ellman, L. Geballe, et al., "Six Climate Change-Related Events in the United States Accounted for About $14 Billion in Lost Lives and Health Costs," *Health Affairs* 30, 11 (2011): 2167–76.

10 Health Canada, *Economic Burden of Illness in Canada, 1998* (Ottawa: Health Canada, 2002).

11 Ibid.

12 D.R. Boyd and S.J. Genuis, "The Environmental Burden of Disease in Canada: Respiratory Disease, Cardiovascular Disease, Cancer, and Congenital Affliction," *Environmental Research* 106 (2008): 240–49.

13 Direct costs in 2000 are from the Public Health Agency of Canada, *Investing in Prevention: The Economic Perspective* (Ottawa: Public Health Agency of Canada, 2009). These costs were adjusted to 2010 in Conference Board of Canada, *Health Matters.* The 2010 costs were then adjusted to 2014 dollars to incorporate inflation by using the Bank of Canada's Inflation Calculator (http://www.bankofcanada.ca/rates/related/inflation-calculator/). A basket of goods and services that cost $100 in 2010 would have cost $108.00 in April 2014. This is a conservative approach because Canadian health care expenses have risen faster than inflation. Canadian Institute for Health Information, *National Health Expenditure Trends, 1975 to 2013* (Ottawa: CIHI, 2013).

14 Indirect costs in 2000 are from the Public Health Agency of Canada, *Investing in Prevention: The Economic Perspective* (Ottawa: Public Health Agency of Canada, 2009). These costs were adjusted to 2010 in Conference Board of Canada, *Health Matters.* The 2010 costs were then adjusted to 2014 dollars to incorporate inflation by using the Bank of Canada's Inflation Calculator (http://www.bankofcanada.ca/rates/related/inflation-calculator/). A basket of goods and services that cost $100 in 2010 would have cost $108.00 in April 2014. This is a conservative approach because Canadian health care expenses have risen faster than inflation. Canadian Institute for Health Information, *National Health Expenditure Trends, 1975 to 2013* (see n. 13 above).

15 L.G. Chestnut and P. De Civita, *Economic Valuation of Mortality Risk Reduction: Review and Recommendations for Policy and Regulatory Analysis* (Ottawa: Government of Canada Policy Research Initiative, 2009).

16 Ibid.

17 F. Bellavance, G. Dionne, and M. Lebeau, "The Value of a Statistical Life: A Meta-Analysis with a Mixed Effects Regression Model," *Journal of Health Economics* 28 (2009): 444–64.

18 The Boyd and Genuis study reported a range of premature deaths from 10,000 to 24,600. For purposes of the VSL calculation, the midpoint of this range (17,300 premature deaths) was used.

19 Organisation for Economic Co-operation and Development, *Environmental Outlook* (Paris: OECD, 2001).

20 T. Muir and M. Zegarac, "Societal Costs of Exposure to Toxic Substances: Economic and Health Costs of Four Case Studies That Are Candidates for Environmental Causation," *Environmental Health Perspectives* 109, Suppl 6 (2001): 885–903.

21 Health Canada, "Environmental Sustainability and Health" (presentation to the Ad Hoc Committee on Sustainability and the Environment, 2004).

22 Ontario Ministry of Environment, *Trans-Boundary Air Pollution in Ontario* (Toronto: Ontario Ministry of Environment, 2005).

23 Ontario Medical Association, *The Illness Costs of Air Pollution: 2005–2026 Health and Economic Damage Estimates* (Toronto: Ontario Medical Association, 2005).

24 Canadian Medical Association, *No Breathing Room: National Illness Costs of Air Pollution* (Ottawa: CMA, 2008).

25 Ibid.

26 D. Sawyer, S. Stiebert, and C. Welburn, *Evaluation of Total Cost of Air Pollution Due to Transportation in Canada* (Ottawa: Marbek Resource Consultants Ltd., 2007).

27 Converted US$27.3 billion at an exchange rate of US$1 = Cdn$1.25. OECD, *The Cost of Air Pollution: Health Impacts from Road Transport* (Paris: OECD, 2014).

28 DSS Management Consultants Inc. and RWDI Air Inc., *Cost Benefit Analysis: Replacing Ontario's Coal-Fired Electricity Generation* (prepared for the Ontario Ministry of Energy, 2005).

29 K. Anderson, T. Weis, B. Thibault, et al., *A Costly Diagnosis: Subsidizing Coal Power with Albertans' Health* (Edmonton: Pembina Foundation/Asthma Society of Canada/ Canadian Association of Physicians for the Environment/Lung Association, Alberta and Northwest Territories/Pembina Institute, 2013).

30 Toronto Public Health, *Air Pollution Burden of Illness from Traffic in Toronto* (City of Toronto, 2007).

31 A.J. Pappin and A. Hakami, "Source Attribution of Health Benefits from Air Pollution Abatement in Canada and the United States: An Adjoint Sensitivity Analysis," *Environmental Health Perspectives* 121 (2013): 572–79.

32 A. Hakami, quoted in Carleton University News Release, "Carleton Research Casts Sobering Light on Costs of Air Pollution," March 18, 2013, http://newsroom. carleton.ca/2013/03/18/carleton-research-casts-sobering-light-on-health-costs -of-air-pollution/.

33 European Environment Agency, *Environment and Health* (Copenhagen: European Environment Agency, 2005).

34 J. Brandt, J. Silver, J. Christensen, et al., "Health Cost Externalities of Air Pollution in Europe," *Atmospheric Chemistry and Physics Discussions* 13 (2013): 5923–59.

35 World Health Organization, Regional Office for Europe, *Economic Cost of the Health Impact of Air Pollution in Europe: Clean Air, Health, and Wealth* (Copenhagen: WHO, 2015).

36 B. Lewis, "Draft Pollution Law Seeks to Tackle Lethal European Air," *Reuters*, December 18, 2013, http://www.reuters.com/article/2013/12/18/us-eu-air-idUSBRE 9BH0DE20131218.

37 L. Trasande, R.T. Zoeller, U. Hass, et al. "Estimating Burden and Disease Costs of Exposure to Endocrine-Disrupting Chemicals in the European Union," *Journal of Clinical Endocrinology and Metabolism* (2015), doi: 10.1210/jc.2014-4324.

38 F. Haucke and U. Bruckner, "First Approaches to the Monetary Impact of Environmental Health Disturbances in Germany," *Health Policy* 94 (2010): 34–44.

39 M.S. Andersen and D.O. Clubb, "Understanding and Accounting for the Costs of Inaction," in *Late Lessons from Early Warnings: The Precautionary Principle* (Copenhagen: European Environment Agency, 2013), 596–612.

40 T. Yang, K. Matus, S. Paltsev, and J. Reilly, *Economic Benefits of Air Pollution Regulation in the USA: An Integrated Approach* (Boston: Massachusetts Institute of Technology, 2004).

41 P. Landrigan, C. Schechter, J. Lipton, et al., "Environmental Pollutants and Disease in American Children: Estimates of Morbidity, Mortality, and Costs for Lead Poisoning, Asthma, Cancer, and Developmental Disabilities," *Environmental Health Perspectives* 110, 7 (2002): 721–28.

42 L. Trasande and Y. Liu, "Reducing the Staggering Costs of Environmental Disease in Children, Estimated at $76.6 Billion in 2008," *Health Affairs* 30, 5 (2011): 863–70.

43 D.C. Bellinger, "A Strategy for Comparing the Contributions of Environmental Chemicals and Other Risk Factors to Neurodevelopment of Children," *Environmental Health Perspectives* 120, 4 (2012): 501–7.

44 L. Trasande, P.J. Landrigan, and C. Schecter, "Public Health and Economic Consequences of Methyl Mercury Toxicity to the Developing Brain," *Environmental Health Perspectives* 113, 5 (2005): 590–96.

45 R. Massey and F. Ackerman, *Costs of Preventable Childhood Illness: The Price We Pay for Pollution,* GDAE Working Paper 03–09 (Medford, MA: Tufts University, 2003).

46 Brandt et al., "Costs of Childhood Asthma," 363–70 (see n. 8 above).

47 Trasande and Liu, "Reducing the Staggering Costs," 867 (see n. 42 above).

48 D.M. Uhlmann, "Environmental Law, Public Health and the Values Conundrum," *Michigan Journal of Environmental and Administrative Law* 3, 2 (2014): 231–42.

49 W. Harrington, *Grading Estimates of the Benefits and Costs of Federal Regulations: A Review of Reviews* (Washington, DC: Resources for the Future, 2006).

50 Knowlton et al., "Six Climate Change-Related Events," 2167–76 (see n. 9 above).

51 S. Embrey, J.V. Remais, and J Hess, "Climate Change and Ecosystem Disruption: The Health Impacts of the North American Rocky Mountain Pine Beetle Infestation," *American Journal of Public Health* 102, 5 (2012): 818–27.

52 I. Janssen, "Health Care Costs of Physical Inactivity in Adults," *Applied Physiology, Nutrition and Metabolism* 37 (2012): 803–6.

53 UN Millennium Ecosystem Assessment, *Ecosystems and Human Well-Being: Synthesis* (Washington, DC: Island Press, 2005).

54 Dolf de Groot, quoted in D.C. Holzman, "Accounting for Nature's Benefits: The Dollar Value of Ecosystem Services," *Environmental Health Perspectives* 120, 4 (2012): A152–A157.

55 S.S. Myers and J.A. Patz, "Emerging Threats to Human Health from Global Environmental Change," *Annual Review of Environmental Research* 34 (2009): 223–52.

56 One Health Commission, "Health and Ecosystems: Analysis and Linkages" (2014), https://www.onehealthcommission.org/en/one_health_resources/whos_who_in_one_health/health__ecosystems_analysis_of_linkages_heal/.

57 OECD, *Costs of Inaction on Key Environmental Challenges* (Paris: OECD, 2008), 49.

58 W. Harrington, R.D. Morgenstern, R. Brotzman, et al., *An Ex Post Perspective on the Costs of Hazardous Air Pollutant Regulations* (Washington, DC: US EPA, 2006); W. Harrington, R.D. Morgenstern, and P. Nelson, "On the Accuracy of Regulatory Cost Estimates," *Journal of Policy Analysis and Management* 19, 2 (2000): 297–322; Stockholm Environment Institute, *Costs and Strategies Presented by Industry during the Negotiations of Environmental Regulations* (Stockholm: Stockholm Environmental Institute, 1999).

59 B. Jessiman and R. Burnett, "Sulphur in Gasoline," in *Health and the Environment: Critical Pathways,* Issue 4 (Ottawa: Health Canada, 2002).

60 G. Jenkins, C.-Y. Kuo, and A. Ozbafli, *Cost-Benefit Analysis Case Study on Regulations to Lower Sulphur in Gasoline,* Queen's Economics Department Working Paper No. 1134 (Kingston, ON: Queen's University, 2007).

61 Government of Canada, "Regulatory Impact Analysis Statement for the *Reduction of Carbon Dioxide Emissions from Coal-Fired Generation of Electricity Regulations,* SOR/2012–167," *Canada Gazette,* August 30, 2012.

62 Environment Canada, "Economic Issues: Human Health Costs" (2013), http://www.ec.gc.ca/air/default.asp?lang=En&n=085A22B0-1.

63 Environment Canada and Health Canada, "Regulatory Impact Analysis Statement for Draft Multi-Sector Air Pollutants Regulations," *Canada Gazette*, June 7, 2014.

64 Health Canada, *Risk Management Strategy for Lead* (Ottawa: Health Canada, 2013).

65 Marbek Resource Consultants, *Cost-Benefit Analysis for Cleaner Source Water* (prepared for the Canadian Council of Ministers of the Environment) (Ottawa: Marbek Resource Consultants Ltd., 2007).

66 S.D. Grosse, T.D. Matte, J. Schwartz, et al., "Economic Gains Resulting from the Reduction in Children's Exposure to Lead in the United States," *Environmental Health Perspectives* 110 (2002): 563–69.

67 US EPA, *Benefits and Costs of the Clean Air Act, 1970 to 1990* (Washington, DC: US EPA, 1997).

68 L.G. Chestnut and D.M. Mills, "A Fresh Look at the Benefits and Costs of the US Acid Rain Program," *Journal of Environmental Management* 77 (2005): 252–66.

69 US EPA, *Regulatory Impact Analysis for the Final Clean Air Interstate Rule* (Washington, DC: US EPA, 2005).

70 US EPA, *Draft Regulatory Impact Analysis: Tier 3 Motor Vehicle Emission and Fuel Standards* (Washington, DC: US EPA, 2013).

71 US EPA, *The Benefits and Costs of the Clean Air Act from 1990 to 2020: Final Report* (Washington, DC: US EPA, 2011).

72 US EPA, *Report to Congress: Highlights of the Diesel Emissions Reduction Program* (Washington, DC: US EPA, 2009).

73 E. Gould, "Childhood Lead Poisoning: Conservative Estimates of the Social and Economic Benefits of Lead Hazard Control," *Environmental Health Perspectives* 117, 7 (2009): 1162–67.

74 Office of Management and Budget, *2013 Draft Report to Congress on the Benefits and Costs of Federal Regulations* (Washington, DC: OMB, 2013).

75 Ibid.

76 M. Bellanger, C. Pichery, D. Aerts, et al., "Economic Benefits of Methylmercury Exposure Control in Europe: Monetary Value of Neurotoxicity Prevention," *Environmental Health* 12: 3 (2013), doi:10.1186/1476-069X-12-3.

77 O. Chanel, S. Henschel, P.G. Goodman, et al., "Economic Valuation of the Mortality Benefits of a Regulation on SO_2 in 20 European Cities," *European Journal of Public Health* (February 24, 2014), doi:10.1093/eurpub/cku018.

78 Health and Environment Alliance and Health Care without Harm, *Acting Now for Better Health – A 30% Reduction Target for EU Climate Policy* (Brussels: Health and Environment Alliance/Health Care without Harm, 2010).

79 D.A Chokshi and T.A Farley, "The Cost-Effectiveness of Environmental Approaches to Disease Prevention," *New England Journal of Medicine* 367, 4 (2012): 295–97.

80 Ibid., 297.

81 B. Milstein, J. Horner, P. Briss, et al., "Why Behavioral and Environmental Interventions Are Needed to Improve Health at Lower Cost," *Health Affairs* 30, 5 (2011): 823–32.

82 Ibid., 824.

83 Jerrett et al., "Environmental Influences on Healthcare Expenditures," 334–38 (see n. 5 above).

84 Ibid.

85 N.D. Woods, D.M. Konisky, and A.O'M. Bowman, "You Get What You Pay for: Environmental Policy and Public Health," *Publius* 39, 1 (2009): 95–116.

86 P.K. Narayan and S. Narayan, "Does Environmental Quality Influence Health Expenditures? Empirical Evidence from a Panel of Selected OECD Countries," *Ecological Economics* 65, 2 (2008): 367–74.

87 Conference Board of Canada, *Critical Steps for Canada – Environmental Health Lessons across Borders: Australia, Sweden and California* (Ottawa: Conference Board of Canada, 2009).

88 D. Buck and S. Gregory, *Improving the Public's Health: A Resource for Local Authorities* (London: The King's Fund, 2013); M. Kinver, "Green Spaces Can Save NHS Billions," *BBC News: Science and Environment* (2013), http://www.bbc.co.uk/news/science-environment-24806994.

89 S. Ambec, M.A. Cohen, S. Elgie, and P. Lanoie, "The Porter Hypothesis at 20: Can Environmental Regulation Enhance Innovation and Competitiveness?" *Review of Environmental Economics and Policy* 7, 1 (2013): 2–22; P. Ekins and S. Speck, eds., *Environmental Tax Reform (ETR): A Policy for Green Growth* (Oxford: Oxford University Press, 2011).

90 R. Smith, *Pollution in Canada: A Review of the Literature and Initial Estimate of the Costs* (Ottawa: Sustainable Prosperity, 2014).

91 European Environmental Agency, *Late Lessons from Early Warnings: The Precautionary Principle* (Copenhagen: European Environmental Agency, 2001), 3–4.

Chapter 6: Environmental Health Law and Policy

1 Germany (Federal Government), *Perspectives for Germany: A National Sustainable Development Strategy* (Berlin, 2002); Swedish Environmental Objectives Council, *Sweden's Environmental Objectives: Are We Getting There?* (Stockholm: Swedish Environmental Objectives Council, 2004); United Kingdom (Government), *One Future – Different Paths: The UK's Shared Framework for Sustainable Development* (London, 2005).

2 Sweden (Ministry of the Environment), *The Swedish Environmental Objectives: Interim Targets and Action Strategies (Summary of Gov. Bill 2000/01:130)* (Stockholm, 2001), 2, http://www.regeringen.se/content/1/c4/11/97/2aa978ad.pdf.

3 D.R. Boyd, *The Environmental Rights Revolution: A Global Study of Constitutions, Human Rights and the Environment* (Vancouver: UBC Press, 2011).

4 D.R. Boyd, *The Right to a Healthy Environment: Revitalizing Canada's Constitution* (Vancouver: UBC Press, 2012).

5 J. Borrows, *Canada's Indigenous Constitution* (Toronto: University of Toronto Press, 2010).

6 Environment Canada, Department of Foreign Affairs and International Trade, Health Canada, and Department of Justice, "Government of Canada's Response to Environmental Petition 163 Filed by Mr. David R. Boyd" (Ottawa: Office of the Auditor General of Canada, 2006).

7 Boyd, *The Environmental Rights Revolution* (see n. 3 above).

8   D.R. Boyd, "The Implicit Constitutional Right to a Healthy Environment," *Review of European Community and International Environmental Law* 20, 2 (2011): 171–79.

9   Boyd, *The Environmental Rights Revolution* (see n. 3 above).

10 Boyd, *The Right to a Healthy Environment* (see n. 4 above).

11 *Mossville Environmental Action Now v. United States* (2010), Petition 242–05. Admissibility Decision, Report No. 43/10, March 17, 2010.

12 Boyd, *The Environmental Rights Revolution* (see n. 3 above).

13 *Beatriz Silvia Mendoza et al. v. National Government et al. (Damages stemming from contamination of the Matanza-Riachuelo River)*, M. 1569, July 8, 2008, Supreme Court of Argentina.

14 C. Jeffords and L. Minkler, "Do Constitutions Matter? The Effect of Constitutional Environmental Rights Provisions on Environmental Performance" (paper delivered at the Yale University/UNITAR Conference on Human Rights and the Environment, New Haven, CT, September 5–7, 2014); Boyd, *The Environmental Rights Revolution* (see n. 3 above).

15 World Health Organization, National Environmental Health Action Plans (NEHAPS) (n.d.), http://www.who.int/heli/impacts/nehaps/en/.

16 Institute of Medicine, *The Future of Public Health* (Washington, DC: National Academies Press, 1988).

17 National Research Council, *Pesticides in the Diets of Infants and Children* (Washington, DC: National Academies Press, 1993).

18 US Department of Health and Human Services, *Healthy People 2010* (Washington, DC: US Government Printing Office, 2000).

19 For details of the US environmental health efforts, see the website of the National Center for Environmental Health at http://www.cdc.gov/nceh.

20 US Department of Health and Human Services, *Healthy People 2010* (see n. 18 above).

21 US Department of Health and Human Services, *Healthy People 2020* (Washington, DC: DHHS, 2010), http://www.healthypeople.gov.

22 Ibid.

23 US Department of Health and Human Services, *Healthy People 2020 Leading Health Indicators: Progress Update* (Washington, DC: DHHS, 2014).

24 Australian Institute of Environmental Health, *The National Environmental Health Strategy* (Canberra: Commonwealth of Australia, 1999).

25 M. Stoneham, J. Dodds, and K. Buckett, "Policy in the Government Context," in *Environmental Health in Australia and New Zealand*, ed. N. Cromar, S. Cameron, and H. Fallowfield (Melbourne: Oxford University Press, 2004), 127–41.

26 European Commission, *The European Environment and Health Action Plan 2004–2010*, COM(2004) 416 Final (Brussels, 2004).

27 Council of the European Union, *Renewed EU Sustainable Development Strategy* (Brussels, 2006).

28 Commission of the European Communities, *Together for Health: A Strategic Approach for the EU: 2008–2013*, COM(2007) 630 Final (Brussels, 2007).

29 Commission of the European Communities, *Mid Term Review of the European Environment and Health Action Plan 2004–2010*, COM(2007) 314 Final (Brussels, 2007).

30 Cabinet Committee for the Economic Union, *Human Health and the Environment: A Strategy for Reducing Human Health Risks from Environmental Hazards* (report of Committee decision) (Ottawa: CCEU, 1999).

31 *Lavesta Area Group v. Alberta (Energy and Utilities Board)*, 2007 ABCA 194 (CanLII).

32 Bill 111, An Act to End Environmental Racism, introduced by NDP MLA Lenore Zann.

33 Health Canada, *National Strategic Framework on Children's Environmental Health* (Ottawa: Health Canada, 2010), http://www.hc-sc.gc.ca/ewh-semt/alt_formats/hecs -sesc/pdf/pubs/contaminants/Framework_children-cadre_enfants/Framework_ children-cadre_enfants-eng.pdf.

34 K. Boothe and K. Harrison, "The Influence of Institutions on Issue Definition: Children's Environmental Health Policy in the United States and Canada," *Journal of Comparative Policy Analysis* 11, 3 (2009): 287–307.

35 A. Gore, Press conference at the Children's National Medical Center regarding Executive Order 13045: "Reduce Environmental Health and Safety Risks to Children," April 21, 1997.

36 L. Kiefer, J. Frank, E. Di Ruggiero, et al., "Fostering Evidence-Based Decision-Making in Canada: Examining the Need for a Canadian Population and Public Health Evidence Centre and Research Network," *Canadian Journal of Public Health* May-June 2005, I-1–I-19.

37 S.M. Teutsch, "Considerations in Planning a Surveillance System," in *Principles and Practice of Public Health Surveillance*, ed. S.M. Teutsch and R.E. Churchill (New York: Oxford University Press, 2000), 17–29.

38 Pew Environmental Health Commission, *America's Environmental Health Gap: Why the Country Needs a Nationwide Health Tracking Network* (Baltimore: Johns Hopkins School of Hygiene and Public Health, 2000), http://healthyamericans. org/reports/files/healthgap.pdf; M.A. McGeehin, J.R. Qualters, and A.S. Niskar, "National Environmental Public Health Tracking Program: Bridging the Information Gap," *Environmental Health Perspectives* 112, 14 (2004): 1409–13; J. Litt, N. Tran, K.C. Malecki, et al., "Mini-Monograph: Identifying Priority Health Conditions, Environmental Data, and Infrastructure Needs: A Synopsis of the Pew Environmental Health Tracking Project," *Environmental Health Perspectives* 112, 14 (2004): 1414–18.

39 US Centers for Disease Control and Prevention, "National Environmental Public Health Tracking Program" (2014), http://www.cdc.gov/nceh/tracking/.

40 US Centers for Disease Control and Prevention, *CDC's Strategy for the National Environmental Public Health Tracking Program, Fiscal Years 2005–2010* (Atlanta: CDC, 2005).

41 US Centers for Disease Control and Prevention, *CDC's National Environmental Public Health Tracking Program: National Network Implementation Plan* (Atlanta: CDC, 2006).

42 US Centers for Disease Control and Prevention, *Keeping Track, Promoting Health* (Atlanta: CDC, 2006).

43 World Health Organization Regional Office for Europe, "Environment and Health Information System" (n.d.), http://www.enhis.org.

44 D. Haines, "Environmental Health Surveillance, Biomonitoring and Indicators" (presentation at National Policy Consultation on Children's Health and the Environment, Edmonton, April 18–19, 2007).

45 Commission for Environmental Cooperation, *Children's Health and the Environment in North America: A First Report on Available Indicators and Measures* (Montreal: Commission for Environmental Cooperation, 2006).

46 W. Leiss, cited in T. Schrecker, "Using Science in Environmental Policy: Can Canada Do Better?" in *Governing the Environment: Persistent Challenges, Uncertain Innovations,* ed. E. Parson (Toronto: University of Toronto Press, 2001).

47 Public Health Agency of Canada, *Report on Plans and Priorities: 2014–2015* (Ottawa: Public Health Agency of Canada, 2014).

48 A. Lukacsovics, M. Hatcher, and A. Papadopolous, *Risk Factors and Surveillance Systems for Foodborne Illness Outbreaks in Canada* (Vancouver: National Collaborating Centre for Environmental Health, 2014).

49 C. Stephen, H. Artsob, W.R. Bowie, et al., "Perspectives on Emerging Zoonotic Disease Research and Capacity Building in Canada," *Canadian Journal of Infectious Diseases and Medical Microbiology* 15 (2004): 339–44.

50 Environment Canada, "National Air Pollution Surveillance Program" (2014), http://www.ec.gc.ca/rnspa-naps/Default.asp?lang=En&n=5C0D33CF-1.

51 M.M. Loh, J.I. Levy, J.D. Spengler, E.A. Houseman, and D.H. Bennett, "Ranking Cancer Risks of Organic Hazardous Pollutants in the United States," *Environmental Health Perspectives* 115, 8 (2007): 1160–68.

52 Canadian Council of Ministers of the Environment, Water Quality Task Group, *A Canada-Wide Framework for Water Quality Monitoring* (Winnipeg: Canadian Council of Ministers of the Environment, 2006), app. 1.

53 Environment Canada, *Data Sources and Methods for the Freshwater Quality Indicator* (Ottawa: Environment Canada, 2013).

54 D.R. O'Connor, *Report of the Walkerton Inquiry (Part 2): A Strategy for Safe Drinking Water* (Toronto: Queen's Printer, 2002), Recommendation 36.

55 Canadian Council of Ministers of the Environment, *A Canada-Wide Framework for Water Quality Monitoring* (see n. 52 above).

56 Environment Canada, "About Fresh Water Quality Monitoring and Surveillance" (2013), http://www.ec.gc.ca/eaudouce-freshwater/default.asp?lang=En&n=50947E1B-1.

57 D. McAmmond, *Food and Nutrition Surveillance in Canada: An Environmental Scan* (report prepared for Health Canada) (2000), 25.

58 R.J. Haines, *Farm to Fork: A Strategy for Meat Safety in Ontario* (report of the Meat Regulatory and Inspection Review) (Toronto: Queen's Printer, 2004).

59 Health Canada, *Canadian Community Health Survey, Cycle 2.2 Nutrition* (Ottawa: Health Canada, 2004).

60 First Nations Environmental Contaminants Program, http://environmental contaminants.ca/.

61 Government of Canada, "Northern Contaminants Program" (2015), http://www.science.gc.ca/default.asp?lang=En&n=7A463DBA-1.

62 R. Smith, "Testimony before the Standing Committee on the Environment and Sustainable Development," June 12, 2006 (transcript), 18.

63 Environment Canada, _Guide for Reporting to the National Pollutant Release Inventory_ (Ottawa: Environment Canada, 2005).
64 K. Harrison and W. Antweiler, "Incentives for Pollution Abatement: Regulation, Regulatory Threats, and Non-Governmental Pressures," _Journal of Policy Analysis and Management_ 22, 3 (2003): 361–82.
65 Ibid.
66 A.K. Chambers, M. Strosher, T. Wooten, J. Moncrieff, and P. McCready, "Direct Measurement of Fugitive Emissions of Hydrocarbons from a Refinery," _Journal of the Air and Waste Management Association_ 58 (1047): 1047–56.
67 Standing Committee on the Environment and Sustainable Development, _Pesticides: Making the Right Choice for Human Health and the Environment_ (Ottawa: House of Commons, 2000).
68 _Pest Control Products Sales Information Reporting Regulations_, SOR/2006-261.
69 Public Health Agency of Canada, "West Nile Virus: Protect Yourself" (n.d.), http://www.phac-aspc.gc.ca/wn-no/index-eng.php; M.A. Drebot, R. Lindsay, I.K. Barker, et al., "West Nile Virus Surveillance and Diagnostics: A Canadian Perspective," _Canadian Journal of Infectious Diseases and Medical Microbiology_ 14, 2 (2003): 105–14.
70 B. Parfitt, "Untracked Toxic Waste Seeps Out of Sight," _Georgia Straight,_ January 18, 2007; M. Jacott, C. Reed, and M. Winfield, _The Generation and Management of Hazardous Wastes and Transboundary Hazardous Waste Shipments between Mexico, Canada and the United States_ (Austin: Texas Center for Policy Studies, 2001).
71 US Centers for Disease Control and Prevention, _Fourth National Report on Human Exposure to Environmental Chemicals_ (Atlanta: CDC, 2009).
72 Ibid.
73 A.M. Calafat, X. Ye, L.Y. Wong, J.A. Reidy, and L.L. Needham, "Exposure of the US Population to Bisphenol A and 4-_tertiary_-Octylphenol: 2003–2004," _Environmental Health Perspectives_ 116, 1 (2007): 39–44.
74 A.M. Calafat, L.Y. Wong, Z. Kuklenyik, J.A. Reidy, and L.L. Needham, "Polyfluoroalkyl Chemicals in the US Population: Data from the National Health and Nutrition Examination Survey (NHANES) 2003–2004 and Comparisons to NHANES 1999–2000," _Environmental Health Perspectives_ 115, 11 (2007): 1596–1602.
75 B.C. Blount, L. Valentin-Blasini, J.D. Osterloh, J.P. Mauldin, and J.L. Pirkle, "Perchlorate Exposure of the US Population, 2001–2002," _Journal of Exposure Science and Environmental Epidemiology_ 10 (2006): 1–8.
76 M. Wilhelm, U. Ewers, and C. Schulz, "Revised and New Reference Values for Some Persistent Organic Pollutants (POPs) in Blood for Human Biomonitoring in Environmental Medicine," _International Journal of Hygiene and Environmental Health_ 206 (2003): 223–29.
77 Environmental Defence Canada, _Toxic Nation: A Report on Pollution in Canadians_ (Toronto: EDC, 2005).
78 Health Canada, _Report on Human Biomonitoring of Environmental Chemicals in Canada: Results of the Canadian Health Measures Survey Cycle 1, 2007–2009_ (Ottawa: Health Canada, 2010).

79　Health Canada, *Second Report on Human Biomonitoring of Environmental Chemicals in Canada: Results of the Canadian Health Measures Survey Cycle 2, 2009–2011* (Ottawa: Health Canada, 2013).

80　Health Canada, "Maternal-Infant Research on Environmental Chemicals" (2013), http://www.mirec-canada.ca.

81　Government of Alberta, *Chemicals in Serum of Children in Southern Alberta 2004–2006* (Edmonton: Alberta Biomonitoring Program, 2010).

82　B. Bienkowski and M. Cone, "Frogs Feminized, but Atrazine's Effects on People Unknown," *Environmental Health News,* June 17, 2013, http://www.environmental healthnews.org/ehs/news/2013/atrazine-health.

83　D.B. Barr, P. Panuwet, J.V. Nguyen, S. Udunka, and L.L. Needham, "Assessing Exposure to Atrazine and Its Metabolites Using Biomonitoring," *Environmental Health Perspectives* 115 (2007): 1474–78.

84　Pew Environmental Health Commission, *America's Environmental Health Gap* (see n. 38 above).

85　C.G. Schuster, A.G. Ellis, W.J. Robertson, et al., "Infectious Disease Outbreaks Related to Drinking Water in Canada 1974–2001," *Canadian Journal of Public Health* 96, 4 (2005): 254–58.

86　Ibid.

87　R. Copes, "What Physicians Can Do to Prevent Illnesses Related to Drinking Water," *Canadian Medical Association Journal* 175, 9 (2006): 1057.

88　Public Health Agency of Canada, *Laboratory Surveillance Data for Enteric Pathogens in Canada: Annual Summary 2005* (Winnipeg: Public Health Agency of Canada, 2007), 86.

89　Ibid., 98.

90　Health Canada and Environment Canada, "Response to Environmental Petition 201: Environmental Health in Canada. Filed by David R. Boyd under s. 22 of the Auditor General Act" (Ottawa: Office of the Auditor General of Canada, 2007).

91　D.R. Boyd, *Northern Exposure: Acute Pesticide Poisonings in Canada* (Vancouver: David Suzuki Foundation, 2007).

92　M. Durigon, C. Elliott, R. Purssell, and T. Kosatsky, "Canadian Poison Control Centres: Preliminary Assessment of Their Potential as a Resource for Public Health Surveillance," *Clinical Toxicology* 51, 9 (2013): 886–91.

93　D. Daws and D.A. Kent, "Poisoning in British Columbia," *British Columbia Medical Journal* 48, 1 (2006): 35.

94　Health Canada, *Proposal to Develop a Network for Health Surveillance in Canada* (Ottawa: Health Canada, 1999), 48.

95　K.C. Johnson, "Status Report: National Enhanced Cancer Surveillance System: A Federal-Provincial Collaboration to Examine Environmental Cancer Risks," *Chronic Diseases in Canada* 21, 1 (2000): 34–35.

96　R.D. Barr, M.L. Greenberg, A.K. Shaw, and L.M. Mery, "The Canadian Childhood Cancer Surveillance and Control Program (CCCSCP): A Status Report," *Pediatric Blood and Cancer* 50, Supp 2 (2008): 518–19.

97　Public Health Agency of Canada, "Canadian Perinatal Surveillance System" (n.d.), http://phac-aspc.gc.ca/rhs-ssg/index-eng.php.

98 Public Health Agency of Canada, "FoodNet Canada: An Overview" (2013), http://www.phac-aspc.gc.ca/foodnetcanada/overview-apercu-eng.php.

99 K.S. Gehle, J.L. Crawford, and M.T. Hatcher, "Integrating Environmental Health into Medical Education," *American Journal of Preventive Medicine* 41, 4S3 (2011): S296–S301.

100 P.J. Landrigan and R.A Etzel, "New Frontiers in Children's Environmental Health," in *The Textbook of Children's Environmental Health*, ed. P.J. Landrigan and R.A Etzel (Oxford: Oxford University Press, 2014), 561.

101 McAmmond, *Food and Nutrition Surveillance in Canada*, 37 (see n. 57 above).

102 S.R. Hilts, S.E. Bock, T.Y. Oke, et al., "Effect of Interventions on Children's Blood Lead Levels," *Environmental Health Perspectives* 106, 2 (1998): 79–83; R. Lorenzana, R. Troast, M. Mastriano, et al., "Lead Intervention and Pediatric Blood Lead Levels at Hazardous Waste Sites," *Journal of Toxicology and Environmental Health Part A* 66, 10 (2003): 871–93.

103 M.E. Campbell, C.E. Gardner, J.J. Dwyer, et al., "Effectiveness of Public Health Interventions in Food Safety: A Systematic Review," *Canadian Journal of Public Health* 89, 3 (1998): 197–202.

104 D.C. Cole, L. Vanderlinden, J. Leah, et al., "Municipal Bylaw to Reduce Cosmetic/Non-Essential Pesticide Use on Household Lawns – A Policy Implementation Evaluation," *Environmental Health* 10: 74 (2011), doi:10.1186/1476-069X-10-74.

105 National Collaborating Centre for Environmental Health, http://www.ncceh.ca.

106 *Canadian Institutes of Health Research Act*, S.C. 2000, c. 6, s. 4(d)(ii).

107 Health Canada and Environment Canada, "Response to Environmental Petition 201" (see n. 90 above).

108 Canadian Institutes of Health Research, "CIHR Estimated Expenditures in Research Related to the Environment Funding Database" (personal emails received from Caroline Shewchuk, Data Production Specialist, Evaluation and Analysis, Corporate Affairs Portfolio, Canadian Institutes of Health Research, March 19, 2007).

109 K. Davies, *Identifying National Research Priorities for the Environmental Influences on Health: Context and Options* (Ottawa: Canadian Institutes of Health Research, 2002).

110 J. Frank and E. de Ruggiero, *Mapping and Tapping the Wellsprings of Health Strategic Plan 2002–2007* (Ottawa: Canadian Institutes of Health Research, Institute of Population and Public Health, 2002).

111 P.J. Landrigan and R.A Etzel, eds., *The Textbook of Children's Environmental Health* (Oxford: Oxford University Press, 2014).

112 Norwegian Institute of Public Health, "Norwegian Mother and Child Cohort Study" (2010), http://www.fhi.no/eway/default.aspx?pid=240&trg=Main_6664&Main_6664=6894:0:25,7372:1:0:0:::0:0.

113 US Department of Health and Human Services, *Growing Up Healthy: An Overview of the National Children's Study* (Washington, DC: DHHS, 2004).

114 G. Oster and D. Thompson, "Estimated Effects of Reducing Dietary Saturated Fat Intake on the Incidence and Costs of Coronary Heart Disease in the United States," *Journal of the American Dietetic Association* 96, 2 (1996): 127–31; National Heart, Lung, and Blood Institute, National Institutes of Health, and Department of

Health and Human Services, *Framingham Heart Study: 50 Years of Research Success* (Bethesda, MD: National Heart, Lung, and Blood Institute, 2002).

115 J.N. Lavis, S.E. Ross, G.L. Stoddart, et al., "Do Canadian Civil Servants Care about the Health of Populations?" *American Journal of Public Health* 93, 4 (2003): 658–63.

116 K. Keough, "The Third Amyot Lecture: How Science Informs the Decisions of Government," *Canadian Journal of Public Health* 93, 2 (2002): 104–8.

117 L. Kiefer, J. Frank, E. Di Ruggiero, et al., "Fostering Evidence-Based Decision-Making in Canada: Examining the Need for a Canadian Population and Public Health Evidence Centre and Research Network," *Canadian Journal of Public Health* 96, 3 (May–June 2005): I-1–I-19.

118 C. Chociolko, R. Copes, and J. Rekart, *Needs, Gaps, and Opportunities Assessment for the National Collaborating Centre for Environmental Health* (Vancouver: NCCEH, 2006).

119 Davies, *Identifying National Research Priorities for the Environmental Influences on Health* (see n. 109 above).

120 Public Health Agency of Canada, "Departmental Performance Report 2006–2007" (2007), http://www.tbs-sct.gc.ca/dpr-rmr/2006-2007/inst/ahs/ahs01-eng.asp#_Toc177793130; Canadian Public Health Association, "Policy Resolutions: Motion No. 1, Children's Environmental Health" (1999), http://www.cpha.ca/uploads/resolutions/1999_e.pdf; Commissioner of the Environment and Sustainable Development, "Chapters 3 and 4: Managing Toxic Substances," in *Report to the House of Commons* (Ottawa: Office of the Auditor General of Canada, 1999); International Joint Commission, *Ninth Biennial Report on Great Lakes Water Quality* (Ottawa: International Joint Commission, 1998); National Round Table on the Environment and the Economy, *Managing Potentially Toxic Substances in Canada* (Ottawa: NRTEE, 2001); Royal Society of Canada, *Implications of Global Change for Human Health: Final Report of the Health Issues Panel of the Canadian Global Change Program*, Incidental Report Series IR95–2 (Ottawa: Royal Society of Canada, 1995).

121 National Institute of Environmental Health Sciences, http://www.niehs.nih.gov/.

122 National Institute of Environmental Health Sciences, "Fiscal Year 2015 Budget" (2014), https://www.niehs.nih.gov/about/congress/justification/2015/2015_congressional_508.pdf.

123 National Center for Environmental Health, "2012 Budget Information" (2013), http://www.cdc.gov/nceh/information/2012budget.htm.

124 Swedish Environmental Protection Agency, *Swedish Consumption and the Environment* (Stockholm: Swedish Environmental Protection Agency, 2011), 6.

125 Ibid., 73.

126 Royal Norwegian Ministry of Finance, *Norway's Strategy for Sustainable Development* (Oslo: Royal Norwegian Ministry of Finance, 2008).

127 Organisation for Economic Co-operation and Development, Development Co-operation Directorate, "Aid Statistics" (2014), http://www.oecd.org/dac/stats/.

128 Ibid.

129 D. Leblanc, "CIDA Funds Seen to Be Subsidizing Mining Firms," *Globe and Mail*, January 29, 2012.

130 National Energy Board, *Factors and Scope of the Factors for the Environmental Assessment Pursuant to the Canadian Environmental Assessment Act, 2012* (Calgary: National Energy Board, 2014).

131 Canadian Heritage, "Canada's Second UN Universal Periodic Review: Response of Canada to the Recommendations" (2013), http://www.pch.gc.ca/eng/1357245757204/1357245878778.

132 L.M. Collins, "Environmental Rights on the Wrong Side of History: Revisiting Canada's Position on the Human Right to Water," *RECIEL* 19, 3 (2010): 351–65.

133 World Health Organization, "Health and Environment Linkages Initiative" (2014), http://www.who.int/heli/en/.

134 Canada's Coalition to End Global Poverty, *Protecting Our Common Future: An Assessment of Canada's Fast Track Climate Financing* (2013), http://www.chf.ca/documents/Studies_And_Reports/Protecting_our_common_future.pdf.

135 Ibid.

Chapter 7: A Comparative Analysis of Environmental Health Laws and Policies

1 Environment Canada, "Backgrounder: Canadian Ambient Air Quality Standards" (2013), http://ec.gc.ca/default.asp?lang=En&n=56D4043B-1&news=A4B2C28A-2DFB-4BF4-8777-ADF29B4360BD.

2 D.R. Boyd, *Unnatural Law: Rethinking Canadian Environmental Law and Policy* (Vancouver: UBC Press, 2003), 243–45.

3 Canadian Environmental Law Association and Ontario College of Family Physicians, *Environmental Standard Setting and Children's Health* (Toronto: CELA/Ontario College of Family Physicians, 2000).

4 US Environmental Protection Agency, "Regulatory Actions: Ground-Level Ozone" (2014), http://www.epa.gov/groundlevelozone/actions.html.

5 T. Gunton and K.S. Calbrick, *The Maple Leaf in the OECD: Canada's Environmental Performance* (study prepared for the David Suzuki Foundation) (Vancouver: David Suzuki Foundation/School of Resource and Environmental Management, Simon Fraser University, 2010).

6 Environment Canada, *Turning the Corner: An Action Plan to Reduce Greenhouse Gas Emissions and Air Pollution* (Ottawa: Environment Canada, 2007).

7 Environment Canada and Health Canada, "Regulatory Impact Analysis Statement for Draft Multi-Sector Air Pollutants Regulations," *Canada Gazette* 148, 23 (June 7, 2014).

8 Ibid.

9 Environment Canada, "Backgrounder: Canadian Ambient Air Quality Standards" (see n. 1 above).

10 European Union, *Directive 2008/50/EC of the European Community and of the Council of 21 May 2008 on Ambient Air Quality and Cleaner Air for Europe.*

11 The US EPA's *Control of Hazardous Air Pollutants from Mobile Sources* (*Federal Register* 72, 37 2007:8428) requires benzene concentrations in gasoline to be less than 0.62 percent by 2011, whereas Canada's *Benzene in Gasoline Regulations* (SOR/97-493) allows benzene concentrations ranging from 1.0 to 1.5 percent.

12 US EPA, "Diesel Fuel Regulations and Standards" (2014), http://www.epa.gov/otaq/fuels/dieselfuels/regulations.htm.

13 D.R. Boyd, *Radon: The Unfamiliar Killer* (Vancouver: David Suzuki Foundation, 2006).

14 G. Akerblom, *Radon Legislation and National Guidelines* (Stockholm: Swedish Radiation Protection Institute, 1999).

15 World Health Organization, *WHO Handbook on Indoor Radiation: A Public Health Perspective* (Geneva: World Health Organization, 2009).

16 S. Darby, D. Hill, and R. Doll, "Radon: A Likely Carcinogen at All Exposures," *Annals of Oncology* 12 (2001): 1341-51.

17 US EPA, "Radon" (2014), http://www.epa.gov/radon.

18 For information on Canada's National Radon Action Campaign, see http://www.takeactiononradon.ca/.

19 World Health Organization, *Air Quality Guidelines for Europe*, 2nd ed. (Copenhagen: WHO Regional Office for Europe, 2000).

20 World Health Organization, *International Radon Project: Survey on Radon Guidelines, Programmes and Activities – Final Report* (Geneva: WHO, 2007).

21 Akerblom, *Radon Legislation and National Guidelines* (see n. 14 above).

22 R.J. Magee, D. Won, and E. Lusztyk, *Indoor Air Quality Guidelines and Standards* (Ottawa: National Research Council of Canada, 2005).

23 Pollution Probe, *Healthy Indoors: Achieving Healthy Indoor Environments in Canada* (Toronto: Pollution Probe, 2002).

24 I. Morton and S. Hills, *Promoting Solutions for Healthy Indoor Environments* (Ottawa: Healthy Indoors Partnership, 2005).

25 Federal-Provincial-Territorial Committee on Drinking Water, *From Source to Tap: Guidance on the Multi-Barrier Approach to Safe Drinking Water* (Winnipeg: Canadian Council of Ministers of the Environment, 2004).

26 World Health Organization, *Guidelines for Drinking-Water Quality*, 3rd ed. (Geneva: WHO, 2004).

27 D.R. O'Connor, *Report of the Walkerton Inquiry, Part 2* (Toronto: Queen's Printer, 2002), 156.

28 Ibid., 149.

29 D. Krewski, J. Balbus, D. Butler-Jones, et al., "Managing Health Risks from Drinking Water: A Report to the Walkerton Inquiry," *Journal of Toxicology and Environmental Health Part A* 65 (2002): 1635–1823.

30 European Union, *EU Council Directive 1998/93/EC of 3 November 1998 on the Quality of Water Intended for Human Consumption*.

31 G. Dunn, K. Bakker, and L. Harris, "Drinking Water Quality Guidelines across Provinces and Territories: Jurisdictional Variation in the Context of Decentralized Water Governance," *International Journal of Environmental Research and Public Health* 11, 5 (2014): 4634–51.

32 R. Christensen, *Waterproof III: Canada's Drinking Water Report Card* (Vancouver: Ecojustice, 2011).

33 The number of national drinking water quality guidelines incorporated into or exceeded by provincial and territorial regulations is as follows (enforceable except where noted): Newfoundland and Labrador, 93 (not binding); Nova Scotia, 93; New

Brunswick, 93 (not binding); Prince Edward Island, 94 (not binding); Quebec, 71; Ontario, 82; Manitoba, 90; Saskatchewan, 56; Alberta, 72; British Columbia, 94 (not binding); Northwest Territories and Nunavut, 94; Yukon, 27. Dunn et al., "Drinking Water Quality Guidelines" (see n. 31 above).

34 S.E. Hrudey and E.J. Hrudey, *Safe Drinking Water: Lessons from Recent Outbreaks in Affluent Nations* (London: IWA Publishing, 2004), ch. 3.

35 In both the United States and Australia, 95 percent of samples must be zero for total coliforms (compared with 90 percent for Canada).

36 *US Surface Water Treatment Rule* (1989) and *Interim Enhanced Surface Water Treatment Rule* (1998), 40 C.F.R. SS. 141.170–141.173.

37 Christensen, *Waterproof III* (see n. 32 above).

38 Health Canada, *Guidelines for Canadian Drinking Water Quality: Summary Table* (Ottawa: Health Canada, 2014).

39 Ibid.

40 US Agency for Toxic Substances and Disease Registry, "Toxicological Profile for Di(2-ethylhexyl)phthalate (DEHP)" (2002), http://www.atsdr.cdc.gov.

41 World Health Organization, *Guidelines for Drinking-Water Quality* (see n. 26 above).

42 US EPA, "Primary Drinking Water Regulations, enacted pursuant to the *Safe Drinking Water Act*" (2009), http://www.epa.gov/safewater/mcl.html#mcls.

43 National Health and Medical Research Council and National Resource Management Ministerial Council, *Australian Drinking Water Guidelines* (Canberra: NHMRC/ NRMMC, 2011).

44 Canada – *Food and Drug Regulations*, C.R.C. 870, as amended; United States – Food and Drug Administration, "Beverages: Bottled Water. Final Rule," *Federal Register* 70, 110 (June 9, 2005): 33694.

45 M. Sears, C.R. Walker, and P. Claman, "Pesticide Assessment: Protecting Public Health on the Home Turf," *Paediatrics and Child Health* 11, 4 (2006): 229–34.

46 Health Canada, *Pest Control Products Sales Report 2010* (Ottawa: Health Canada, 2014).

47 Ontario Ministry of Agriculture and Food, *Survey of Pesticide Use in Ontario, 2008* (Toronto: Ontario Ministry of Agriculture and Food, 2010).

48 N. Bachand and L. Gue, *Pesticide-Free? Oui! 2011 Progress Report: A Comparison of Provincial Cosmetic Pesticide Bans* (Vancouver: David Suzuki Foundation and Equiterre, 2011).

49 World Health Organization, *The WHO Recommended Classification of Pesticides by Hazard* (Geneva: WHO, 2010).

50 Food and Agriculture Organization and World Health Organization, "CODEX Pesticide Residues in Food Online Database" (2014), http://www.codexalimentarius. net/pestres/data/index.html?lang=en.

51 T.B. Hayes, V. Khoury, A. Narayan, et al., "Atrazine Induces Complete Feminization and Chemical Castration of African Clawed Frogs," *Proceedings of the National Academy of Sciences (U.S.)* 107, 10 (2010): 4712–16; T.B. Hayes, A. Collins, M. Lee, et al., "Hermaphroditic, Demasculinized Frogs after Exposure to the Herbicide, Atrazine, at Low Ecologically Relevant Doses," *Proceedings of the National Academy of Sciences (U.S.)* 99 (2002): 5476–80.

52 Another study confirms that EU MRLs are generally stronger than American MRLs. P. Thorbek and K. Hyder, "Relationship between Physicochemical Properties and Maximum Residue Levels and Tolerances of Crop-Protection Products for Crops Set Out by the U.S.A, European Union, and Codex," *Food Additives and Contaminants* 23, 8 (2006): 764–76.

53 Canadian Food Inspection Agency, *National Chemical Residue Monitoring Program, 2009–2010 Annual Report* (Ottawa: CFIA, 2012).

54 M. Griffith-Greene, "Pesticide Traces in Some Tea Exceed Allowable Limit," *CBC News*, March 8, 2014, http://www.cbc.ca/news/canada/pesticide-traces-in-some -tea-exceed-allowable-limits-1.2564624.

55 US Department of Agriculture, "Pesticide Data Program: Annual Summary Calendar Year 2013" (2014), http://www.ams.usda.gov/AMSv1.0/pdp/.

56 Ibid.

57 US Food and Drug Administration, *Pesticide Monitoring Program: 2011 Pesticide Report* (Washington, DC: FDA, 2014).

58 Ibid.

59 European Food Safety Authority, "The 2010 European Union Report on Pesticide Residues in Food," *EFSA Journal* 11, 3 (2013): 3130.

60 UN Environment Programme, *Global Chemicals Outlook* (Nairobi: UNEP, 2013).

61 K. Fulcher and H. Gibb, "Setting the Research Agenda on Chemicals," *International Journal of Environmental Research and Public Health* 11 (2014):1049–57.

62 T. Grant, "Asbestos Imports Rising in Canada Despite Health Warnings," *Globe and Mail*, March 27, 2015.

63 *Asbestos Products Regulation* (SOR/2007–260).

64 *Ingredient Disclosure List* (SOR/88–64), *Hazardous Products Act*, R.S.C. 1985, c.H-3.

65 *Asbestos Mines and Mills Release Regulations*, SOR/90–341.

66 European Council, *Directive 1976/769/EEC on the Approximation of the Laws, Regulations, and Administrative Provisions of the Member States Relating to Restrictions on the Marketing and Use of Certain Dangerous Substances and Preparations, as amended by Commission Directive 1999/77/EC of 26 July 1999.*

67 M.J. White, *Asbestos and the Future of Mass Torts*, National Bureau of Economic Research Working Paper 10308 (Cambridge, MA: National Bureau of Economic Research, 2004).

68 US EPA, "Asbestos: General" (Region 6 Office, n.d.), http://www.epa.gov/region6/ 6pd/asbestos/asbgenl.htm.

69 *Code of Federal Regulations*, Title 40, Part 61, "National Emission Standards for Hazardous Air Pollutants."

70 National Occupational Health and Safety Commission (NOHSC), "Amendment to Schedule 2 of the *National Model Regulations for the Control of Workplace Hazardous Substances*" (Washington, DC: NOHSC, 1994).

71 US Agency for Toxic Substances and Disease Registry, "Toxicological Profile for DEHP" (see n. 40 above).

72 US National Academy of Sciences, *Phthalates and Cumulative Risk Assessment: The Tasks Ahead* (Washington, DC: National Academies Press, 2008).

73 Health Canada, "Health Canada Advises Parents and Caregivers of Very Young Children to Dispose of Soft Vinyl (PVC) Teethers and Soft Vinyl (PVC) Rattles," Advisory 1998-85 to Parents and Caregivers, November 16, 1998.

74 Environment Canada and Health Canada, *Canadian Environmental Protection Act Priority Substances List Assessment Report: Bis(2-ethylhexyl) Phthalate* (Ottawa: Environment Canada/Health Canada, 1994).

75 Health Canada Expert Advisory Panel on DEHP in Medical Devices, *Final Report* (Ottawa: Health Canada, 2002).

76 *Phthalate Regulations,* SOR/2010–298.

77 *Registration, Evaluation, Authorisation and Restriction of Chemicals ("REACH") Regulations* (EC Regulation No. 1907/2006, as amended).

78 European Commission, *Decision 1999/815/EC Pursuant to Council Directive 92/59/ EEC on General Product Safety.*

79 Australian Competition and Consumer Commission, "Permanent Ban on Children's Products Containing More than 1% DEHP," *Consumer Protection Notice No. 11 of 2011* (2011).

80 Australian Committee for Chemicals Scheduling, "Standard for the Uniform Scheduling of Medicines and Poisons," app. C (2012).

81 Environmental Working Group, *PFCs – A Family of Chemicals that Contaminate the Planet* (Washington, DC: EWG, 2003).

82 Organisation for Economic Co-operation and Development, *Hazard Assessment of Perfluorooctane Sulfonate (PFOS) and Its Salts* (Paris: OECD, 2002).

83 K. Kannan, S. Corsolini, J. Falandysz, et al., "Perfluorooctanesulfonate and Related Fluorochemicals in Human Blood from Several Countries," *Environmental Science and Technology* 38, 17 (2004): 4489–95; Environmental Defence Canada, *Toxic Nation: A Report on Pollution in Canadians* (Toronto: EDC, 2005).

84 C. Schulte, "PFOA – Possible Sources and Regulatory Needs," European Commission Workshop on PFOA, May 4, 2010 Brussels.

85 *Regulations Amending the Prohibition of Certain Toxic Substances Regulations, 2005 (Four New Fluorotelomer-Based Substances);* Environment Canada and Health Canada, "Notice, under s. 84(5) of the *Canadian Environmental Protection Act, 1999,* of Ministerial Prohibition," *Canada Gazette* I, 139, 6 (February 5, 2005); Environment Canada and Health Canada, "Notice, under s. 84(5) of the *Canadian Environmental Protection Act, 1999,* of Ministerial Prohibition," *Canada Gazette* I, 138, 29 (July 18, 2004).

86 *Perfluorooctane Sulfonate Virtual Elimination Act,* S.C. 2008, c-13; *Perfluorooctane Sulfonate and Its Salts and Certain Other Compounds Regulations,* SOR/2008 –178.

87 *Regulations Amending the Prohibition of Certain Toxic Substances Regulations, 2012, Canada Gazette* I (April 4, 2015).

88 Environmental Defence Canada, *Regulation of PFCs Gaining Momentum* (Toronto: EDC, 2006).

89 US EPA, "Perfluorooctanoic Acid (PFOA) and Fluorinated Telomers" (n.d.), http:// www.epa.gov/oppt/pfoa/.

90 C. Hogue, "DuPont Settles PFOA Case for $107.6 Million," *Chemical and Engineering News* 83, 10 (2005): 9.

91 US EPA, *Regulatory Action on PFAS/LCPFAC Compounds* (Washington, DC: US EPA, 2012).

92 European Union, *Directive 2006/122/EC of 12 December 2006 on the Restriction of the Environmentally Harmful Substance PFOS*. See also European Parliament and Council of the European Union, *Regulation 757/2010 of 24 August 2010 Amending EC Regulation 850/2004 on Persistent Organic Pollutants*.

93 L. Vierke, C. Staude, A. Biegel-Engler, et al., "Perfluorooctanoic Acid (PFOA) – Main Concerns and Regulatory Development in Europe from an Environmental Point of View," *Environmental Sciences Europe* 24: 16 (2012).

94 Australian National Industrial Chemicals Notification and Assessment Scheme, "Perfluorooctanoic Acid (PFOA) and Its Derivatives," NICNAS Alert No. 4: Existing Chemicals (2004).

95 E. Setton, P. Hystad, K. Poplawski, et al., "Risk-Based Indicators of Canadians' Exposure to Environmental Carcinogens," *Environmental Health* 12 (2013): 15.

96 World Health Organization (Europe), *WHO Guidelines for Indoor Air Quality* (Geneva: WHO, 2010).

97 *On-Road Vehicle and Engine Emissions Regulations*, SOR/2003–2.

98 Health Canada, "Cosmetic Ingredient Hotlist" (2013), http://www.hc-sc.gc.ca/cps -spc/cosmet-person/hot-list-critique/hotlist-liste-eng.php.

99 *Hazardous Products Act*, R.S.C. 1985 c. H-3.

100 World Health Organization (Europe), *WHO Guidelines for Indoor Air Quality* (see n. 96 above).

101 European Union, *Council Directive 1999/13/EC of 11 March 1999 on the Limitation of Emissions of Volatile Organic Compounds Due to the Use of Organic Solvents in Certain Activities and Installations*.

102 European Union, *Regulation Concerning the Making Available on the Market and Use of Biocidal Products*, Regulation No. 528, May 22, 2012.

103 Harmonised Standard EN 13986: 2004, "Wood-Based Panels for Use in Construction – Characteristics, Evaluation of Conformity, and Marking."

104 Denmark, *Chemical Substances and Products Act*, Act No. 878 of 2010, June 26, 2010. See also SUBSPORT (Substitution Support Portal), "Specific Substances Alternatives Assessment: Formaldehyde" (2013), http://www.subsport.eu/.

105 *Formaldehyde Standards for Composite Wood Products Act*, enacted as Title VI of *Toxic Substances Control Act*, 15 U.S.C. 2697 (2010).

106 *Federal Food, Drug, and Cosmetic Act*, 21 U.S. Code 9, ss. 301–99.

107 *Poison Standard 2014*, http://www.comlaw.gov.au/Details/F2014L01343.

108 Product Safety Australia, "Unsafe Cosmetics Recalled Over Formaldehyde," October 29, 2010.

109 T. McDonald, "A Perspective on the Potential Health Risks of PBDEs," *Chemosphere* 46, 5 (2002): 745–55; P.O. Darnerud, "Toxic Effects of Brominated Flame Retardants in Man and Wildlife," *Environment International* 29, 6 (2003): 841–53; I. Branchi, F. Capone, E. Alleva, et al., "Polybrominated Diphenyl Ethers: Neurobehavioral Effects Following Developmental Exposure," *Neurotoxicology* 24, 3 (2003): 449–62.

110 J.B. Herbstman, A. Sjodin, M. Kurzon, et al., "Prenatal Exposure to PBDEs and Neurodevelopment," *Environmental Health Perspectives* 118, 5 (2010): 712–19.

111 J.J. Ryan, *Polybrominated Diphenyl Ethers in Human Milk: Occurrence Worldwide* (Ottawa: Health Canada, 2004).

112 Environmental Defence Canada, *Polluted Children, Toxic Nation: A Report on Pollution in Canadian Families* (Toronto: EDC, 2006).

113 A. Picard and A. Favaro, "Common Foods Laced with Chemical," *Globe and Mail*, February 14, 2005.

114 *Polybrominated Diphenyl Ethers Regulations*, SOR/2008-218.

115 *Regulations Amending the Prohibition of Certain Toxic Substances Regulations, 2012* (see n. 87 above).

116 European Union, *Directive 2003/11/EC of the European Parliament and of the Council, 6 February 2003, Amending for the 24th Time Council Directive 76/769/EEC Relating to Restrictions on the Marketing and Use of Certain Dangerous Substances and Preparations (Pentabromodiphenyl Ether, Octabromodiphenyl Ether).*

117 European Union, *Directives 2002/95/EC and 2011/65/EU of the European Parliament and of the Council, 27 January 2003 and 8 June 2011, on the Restriction of the Use of Certain Hazardous Substances in Electrical and Electronic Equipment.*

118 Norwegian Pollution Control Authority, "Ban on Deca-BDE," No. 2401 (2008).

119 A. Schecter, O. Päpke, K.C. Tung, et al., "Polybrominated Diphenyl Ether Flame Retardants in the US Population: Current Levels, Temporal Trends, and Comparison with Dioxins, Dibenzofurans and Polychlorinated Biphenyls," *Journal of Occupational and Environmental Medicine* 47, 3 (2005): 199–211.

120 T.A. McDonald, "Polybrominated Diphenyl Ether Levels among United States Residents: Daily Intake and Risk of Harm to the Developing Brain and Reproductive Organs," *Integrated Environmental Assessment and Management* 1 (2005): 343–54.

121 D. Fischer, K. Hooper, M. Athanasiadou, et al., "Children Show Highest Levels of Polybrominated Diphenyl Ethers in a California Family of Four: A Case Study," *Environmental Health Perspectives* 114, 10 (2006): 1581–84.

122 US EPA, "PBDEs: Significant New Use Rule," *Federal Register* 78, 71 (April 24, 2006): 23341–42.

123 US EPA, "Deca-BDE Phase-Out Initiative" (2009), http://www.epa.gov/oppt/existing chemicals/pubs/actionplans/deccadbe.html.

124 F. Harden, J. Muller, and L. Toms, *Organochlorine Pesticides (OCPs) and Polybrominated Diphenyl Ethers (PBDEs) in the Australian Population: Levels in Human Milk* (Canberra: Australian Environment Protection and Heritage Council, 2005).

125 National Industrial Chemicals Notification and Assessment Scheme, *Polybrominated Flame Retardants (PBFRs): Priority Existing Chemical Assessment Report No. 20* (Canberra: Commonwealth of Australia, 2001).

126 Ecojustice and Canadian Environmental Law Association, "Petition to the Commissioner of Environment and Sustainable Development: Implementation of CEPA 1999, s. 75(3) and EU REACH" (April 15, 2014).

127 A. Salamova and R.A. Hites, "Discontinued and Alternative Brominated Flame Retardants in the Atmosphere and Precipitation from the Great Lakes Basin," *Environmental Science and Technology* 45, 20 (2011): 8698–706.

128 National Industrial Chemicals Notification and Assessment Scheme, *Priority Existing Chemical Assessment Report: Hexabromocyclododecane* (Canberra: Commonwealth of Australia, 2012).

129 Environment Canada, *National Inventory Report 1990–2011: Greenhouse Gas Sources and Sinks in Canada* (Ottawa: Environment Canada, 2013).

130 D. Burtraw and M. Woerman, *US Status on Climate Change Mitigation* (Washington, DC: Resources for the Future, 2012).

131 J. Simpson, M. Jaccard, and N. Rivers, *Hot Air: Meeting Canada's Climate Change Challenge* (Toronto: McClelland and Stewart, 2007).

132 *Pembina Institute for Appropriate Development v. Alberta Utilities Commission and Maxim Power Corp.* (2011) ABCA 302.

133 European Union, *Directive 2009/29/EC of 23 April 2009 Amending Directive 2003/87/EC so as to Improve and Extend the Greenhouse Gas Emission Allowance Trading Scheme of the Community; Directive 2009/31/EC of 23 April 2009 on the Geological Storage of Carbon Dioxide; Directive 2009/125/EC of 21 October 2009 Establishing a Framework for the Setting of Ecodesign Requirements for Energy-Related Products; Decision No. 406/2009/EC of 23 April 2009 on the Efforts of Member States to Reduce Their Greenhouse Gas Emissions to Meet the Community's Greenhouse Gas Emission Reduction Commitments Up to 2020; Directive 2009/28/EC of the European Parliament and of the Council of 23 April 2009 on the Promotion of the Use of Energy from Renewable Sources; Directive 2010/31/EU of 19 May 2010 on the Energy Performance of Buildings.*

134 S. Chase, "Tories' 'Recession' Threat Based on Old Numbers," *Globe and Mail,* September 11, 2008, A1.

135 European Union, *Directive 2003/87/EC of 13 October 2003 Establishing a Scheme for Greenhouse Gas Emission Allowance Trading.*

136 European Union, *Directive 2008/101/EC of 19 November 2008 Amending Directive 2003/87/EC so as to Include Aviation Activities in the Scheme for Greenhouse Gas Emission Allowance Trading within the Community; Directive 2009/29/EC of 23 April 2009 Amending Directive 2003/87/EC so as to Improve and Extend the Greenhouse Gas Emission Allowance Trading Scheme of the Community.*

137 European Union, *Directive 2003/96/EC of 27 October 2003 Restructuring the Community Framework for the Taxation of Energy Products and Electricity.*

138 International Council on Clean Transportation, *Global Comparison of Light Duty Vehicle Fuel Economy/GHG Emissions Standards* (Washington, DC: International Council on Clean Transportation, 2012).

139 See Natural Resources Canada's description of the EcoAction program for renewables, including a list of the projects funded, at http://www.nrcan.gc.ca/ecoaction/14145.

140 *Duncan Hunter National Defense Authorization Act for Fiscal Year 2009,* Public Law 110-417, October 14, 2008; *Food, Conservation, and Energy Act of 2008,* Public Law 110-234.The *American Recovery and Reinvestment Act 2009* built on the *Energy Improvement and Extension Act 2008,* the *Energy Storage and Technology Advancement Act 2007,* and the *Energy Policy Act 2005.*

141 European Union, *Directive 2009/28/EC of 23 April 2009 on the Promotion of the Use of Energy from Renewable Sources and Amending and Subsequently Repealing Directives 2001/77/EC and 2003/30/EC.*

142 Ibid.

143 T. Townshend, S. Fankhauser, R. Aybar, et al., eds., *The GLOBE Climate Legislation Study: A Review of Climate Change Legislation in 33 Countries*, 3rd ed. (London: Globe International, 2013), 4.

144 J. Burck, F. Marten, and C. Balss, *The Climate Change Performance Index: Results 2014* (Bonn: Germanwatch and Climate Action Network Europe, 2014), 6.

145 J.J. West, S.J. Smith, R.A. Silva, et al., "Co-Benefits of Mitigating Global Greenhouse Gas Emissions for Future Air Quality and Human Health," *Nature Climate Change* 3 (2013): 885–89.

146 S. Elgie, "Statutory Structure and Species Survival: How Constraints on Cabinet Discretion Affect Endangered Species Listing Outcomes," *Journal of Environmental Law and Practice* 19, 1 (2008): 1–31.

147 D.L. Vanderzwaag and J.A. Hutchings, "Canada's Marine Species at Risk: Science and Law at the Helm, but a Sea of Uncertainties," *Ocean Development and International Law* 36, 3 (2005): 219–59.

148 S. Otto, S. McKee, and J. Whitton, "Saving Species Starts at the Top: Where Is Our Environment Minister?" *Globe and Mail*, August 14, 2013.

149 European Union, *Directive 92/43/EEC of 21 May 1992 on the Conservation of Natural Habitats and Wild Flora and Fauna;* European Union, *Directive 2009/147/EC of 30 November 2009 on the Conservation of Wild Birds;* Australia, *Environment Protection and Biodiversity Conservation Act 1999*, Act No. 91 of 1999; Mexico, *General Law of Ecological Equilibrium and Environmental Protection*, Norma Oficial Mexicana NOM-059-ECOL-2001 (2001).

150 S. Nixon, D. Page, S. Pinkus, et al., *Failure to Protect: Grading Canada's Species at Risk Laws* (Vancouver: Ecojustice, 2012).

151 G. Bates, *Environmental Law in Australia*, 6th ed. (Chatswood, NSW: Reed International Books, 2009).

152 K.E. Gibbs and D.J. Currie, "Protecting Endangered Species: Do the Main Legislative Tools Work?" *PLoS ONE* 7, 5 (2012): e35730, doi:10.1371/journal.pone.0035730.

153 *Medicine Hat and LGX Oil and Gas v. Canada (Minister of Environment)* (2014) Federal Court, Trial Division Application T-12-14.

154 S. Elgie, "Evidence," in *Hearings on Bill C-5, the Species at Risk Act* (Standing Committee on Environment and Sustainable Development, June 7, 2001).

155 World Bank, "Terrestrial Protected Areas (% of Total Land Area)" (2014), http://data.worldbank.org/indicator/ER.LND.PTLD.ZS.

156 Canadian Parks and Wilderness Society, *How Deep Did Canada Dare? Assessing National Progress towards Marine Protection to December 2012* (Ottawa: Canadian Parks and Wilderness Society, 2013).

157 *Environment Protection and Biodiversity Conservation Act 1999*, Act No. 1 of 1999, art. 269AA.

158 *Western Canada Wilderness Committee et al. v. Minister of Fisheries and Oceans et al.* (2014) Federal Court 148.

159 Ibid., para. 85.

160 Species at Risk Registry, http://www.sararegistry.gc.ca/.

161 S. Wojciechowski, S. McKee, C. Brasard, et al., "SARA's Safety Net Provisions and the Effectiveness of Species at Risk Protection on Non-Federal Lands," *Journal of Environmental Law and Practice* 22, 3 (2011): 203–22.

162 See s. 77(1.1) of the *Species at Risk Act.*
163 K. Suckling, N. Greenwald, and T. Curry, *On Time, On Target: How the Endangered Species Act Is Saving America's Wildlife* (Tucson, AZ: Center for Biological Diversity, 2012); P.F. Donald, F.J. Sanderson, I.J. Burfield, et al., "International Conservation Policy Delivers Benefits for Birds," *Nature* 317, 5839 (2010): 810–13.
164 Dr. John Conly, quoted in M. Munro, "As Canada Dawdles, Denmark Shows the World How to Stop Mass Medicating Animals," *Saskatoon Star Phoenix,* April 18, 2014.

Chapter 8: Canada's Failure to Make Polluters Pay

1 Canada's Ecofiscal Commission, *Smart, Practical, Possible: Canada's Options for Greater Economic and Environmental Prosperity* (Montreal: Canada's Ecofiscal Commission, 2014), http://ecofiscal.ca/reports/report/.
2 Organisation for Economic Co-operation and Development, *The Polluter-Pays Principle: OECD Analyses and Recommendations* (Paris: OECD, 1992).
3 OECD, *Taxation, Innovation and the Environment* (Paris: OECD, 2010).
4 T. Sterner and L.H. Isaksson, "Refunded Emission Payments: Theory, Distribution of Costs, and Swedish Experience of NOx Abatement," *Ecological Economics* 57 (2006): 93–106.
5 P. Ekins and S. Speck, eds., *Environmental Tax Reform (ETR): A Policy for Green Growth* (Oxford: Oxford University Press, 2011).
6 Sustainable Prosperity, *Options for Managing Industrial Air Pollution in Canada: The Use of Market-Based Instruments* (Ottawa: Sustainable Prosperity, 2011).
7 *Canadian Environmental Protection Act, 1999,* S.C. 1999, c. 33; *Environmental Protection Act,* R.S.O. 1990, c. E.19.
8 *Imperial Oil Ltd. v. Quebec (Minister of the Environment),* [2003] 2 S.C.R. 624, para. 23.
9 Principle 16, *Rio Declaration,* UN Conference on Environment and Development, June 13, 1992, UN Doc. A/CONF.151/5/Rev.1 (1992), 31 I.L.M. 874.
10 OECD, "Database on Instruments Used for Environmental Policy: Taxes, Fees, Charges" (2014), http://www2.oecd.org/ecoinst/queries/.
11 KPMG International, "KPMG Green Tax Index 2013" (2013), http://www.kpmg.com/greentax.
12 Ekins and Speck, *Environmental Tax Reform* (see n. 5 above). For other examples of ecological tax shifting, see D.R. Boyd, *Unnatural Law: Rethinking Canadian Environmental Law and Policy* (Vancouver: UBC Press, 2003), 321–25.
13 OECD, *Eco-Efficiency* (Paris: OECD, 1998).
14 D.R. Boyd, *Canada vs. Sweden: An Environmental Face-off* (Victoria: Eco-Research Chair in Environmental Law and Policy, 2002).
15 Canada's Ecofiscal Commission, *Smart, Practical, Possible,* 21 (see n. 1 above).
16 OECD, *Comparisons of CO$_2$-Related Tax Rate Differentiation in Motor Vehicle Taxes* (Paris: OECD, 2014).
17 Canada Revenue Agency, "Excise Tax on Fuel Inefficient Vehicles" (2007), http://www.cra-arc.gc.ca/gncy/bdgt/2007/xcs-eng.html.
18 Canada Revenue Agency, "Excise Tax on Fuel Inefficient Vehicles. 2012 – List of Vehicles and Associated Tax Rates" (2012), http://www.cra-arc.gc.ca/E/pub/et/etsl64/list/lst_vh-2012-eng.pdf.

19 US EPA, *Vehicles Subject to the Gas Guzzler Tax for Model Year 2013* (2013), http://www.epa.gov/fueleconomy/guzzler/420b13037.pdf.

20 Australian Taxation Office, *Luxury Car Tax* (Canberra: Australian Taxation Office, 2013).

21 Unless otherwise noted, all dollar amounts are in Canadian dollars.

22 OECD, *Comparisons of CO_2-Related Tax Rate Differentiation* (see n. 16 above).

23 J. Mintz and N. Olewiler, *A Simple Approach for Bettering the Environment and the Economy: Restructuring the Federal Fuel Excise Tax* (Ottawa: Sustainable Prosperity, 2008), 2.

24 BC Ministry of Finance, *Tax Bulletin: Tax Rates on Fuels,* Bulletin MFT-CT 005 (Victoria: BC Ministry of Finance, 2013); Natural Resources Canada, *Fuel Focus: Understanding Gasoline Markets in Canada and Economic Drivers Influencing Prices, 2011 Annual Review* (Ottawa: Natural Resources Canada, 2012).

25 OECD, "Database on Instruments Used for Environmental Policy" (see n. 10 above).

26 Technical Committee on Business Taxation, *Report of the Technical Committee on Business Taxation* (Ottawa: Department of Finance, 1998), P.1.11, http://publications.gc.ca/collections/Collection/F32-5-1998E.pdf.

27 OECD, *Taxing Energy Use: A Graphical Analysis* (Paris: OECD, 2013).

28 Ibid.

29 Mintz and Olewiler, *A Simple Approach for Bettering the Environment and the Economy* (see n. 23 above).

30 OECD, *Taxation, Innovation and the Environment* (see n. 3 above).

31 OECD, *Climate and Carbon: Aligning Prices and Policies* (Paris: OECD, 2013).

32 T. Flannery, R. Beale, and G. Hueston, *The Critical Decade: International Action on Climate Change* (Australia: Climate Commission, 2012).

33 A. Radia, "Harper Government Praises Australia Over Repealing of Carbon Tax," Yahoo News, November 13, 2013, https://ca.news.yahoo.com/blogs/canada-politics/harper-government-praises-australian-government-efforts-repeal-carbon-181702013.html.

34 Finland Ministry of the Environment, "Excise Duty and Strategic Stockpile Fee Rates as of 1 January 2012" (2013), http://ec.europa.eu/environment/enveco/resource_efficiency/pdf/Task%203%20report.pdf.

35 Royal Norwegian Ministry of the Environment, *Norwegian Climate Policy,* Report No. 21 (2011–2012) (Oslo: Royal Norwegian Ministry of the Environment, 2012), 4.

36 Royal Norwegian Ministry of Finance, *Main Features of the Tax Programme for 2013* (Oslo: Royal Norwegian Ministry of Finance, 2012), http://www.statsbudsjettet.no/Upload/Statsbudsjett_2013/dokumenter/pdf/skatt_eng.pdf.

37 Ibid.

38 Ministry of the Environment Sweden, "Twenty Years of Carbon Pricing in Sweden" (2012), http://www.ceps.eu/files/MinistrySweden.pdf.

39 Ibid.

40 *Finance Act 2013,* c. 29, s. 199.

41 World Bank, *Putting a Price on Carbon with a Tax* (Washington, DC: World Bank, 2014).

42 *Finance Act 2010,* No. 5 of 2010, Public Acts of Ireland.

43 S. Speck et al., "Environmental Taxes and ETRs in Europe: The Current Situation and a Review of the Modelling Literature," in *Environmental Tax Reform (ETR): A Policy for Green Growth,* ed. P. Ekins and S. Speck (Oxford: Oxford University Press, 2011), ch. 5.

44 Switzerland, Federal Office for the Environment, "Reduction Objective for 2012 Not Achieved; Increase in Carbon Tax on Fossil Fuels in 2014" (press release, Bern, July 3, 2013), http://www.bafu.admin.ch/dokumentation/medieninformation/00962/index.html?lang=de&msg-id=49576.

45 *Act on Environmental and Resource Taxes,* No. 129/2009, Statutes of Iceland.

46 European Union, "Chapter 16 – Taxation," in *Screening Report: Iceland* (2011), http://ec.europa.eu/enlargement/pdf/iceland/key-documents/screening_report_16_is_internet_en.pdf.

47 L. Davies, "Carbon Tax Ruled Unconstitutional," *The Guardian,* December 30, 2009.

48 Reuters, "French Carbon Tax to Yield 4 Billion Euros in 2016," September 21, 2013, http://www.reuters.com/article/2013/09/21/france-energy-idUSL5N0HH04K20130921.

49 Globe International, *The Globe Climate Legislation Study* (see n. 54 above).

50 *Clean Energy Act 2011,* Commonwealth of Australia Consolidated Acts, No. 131 (2011), s. 100.

51 R. McGuirk, "Australian Carbon Tax to Be Repealed by Incoming Conservative Government," *Globe and Mail,* September 8, 2013.

52 Government of Australia, "An Overview of the Clean Energy Legislative Package" (Canberra: Government of Australia, 2011).

53 T. Flannery, R. Beale, and G. Hueston, *The Critical Decade: International Action on Climate Change* (Canberra: Climate Commission, 2012).

54 Globe International, *The Globe Climate Legislation Study: A Review of Climate Change Legislation in 33 Countries,* 3rd ed. (London: Globe International, 2013).

55 *Framework Act on Low Carbon Green Growth,* Statutes of South Korea.

56 Center for Climate and Energy Solutions, *Options and Considerations for a Federal Carbon Tax* (Arlington, VA: Center for Climate and Energy Solutions, 2013), http://www.c2es.org/publications/options-considerations-federal-carbon-tax.

57 World Bank, *Putting a Price on Carbon with a Tax* (Washington, DC: World Bank, 2014).

58 BC Ministry of Finance, *Myths and Facts about the Carbon Tax* (Victoria: BC Ministry of Finance, 2013).

59 M.S. Anderson and P. Ekins, eds., *Carbon-Energy Taxation: Lessons from Europe* (Oxford: Oxford University Press, 2009); M.S. Anderson, "Europe's Experience with Carbon-Energy Taxation," *Sapiens* 3, 2 (2010), http://sapiens.revues.org/1072; J. Sumner, L. Bird, and H. Smith, *Carbon Taxes: A Review of Experiences and Policy Design Considerations* (Golden, CO: US National Renewable Energy Laboratory, 2009); S.-L. Hsu, *The Case for a Carbon Tax: Getting Past Our Hangups to Effective Climate Policy* (Washington, DC: Island Press, 2011).

60 S. Elgie and J. McClay, *BC's Carbon Tax Shift after Five Years: An Environmental and Economic Success Story* (Ottawa: Sustainable Prosperity, 2013).

61 Ibid.

62 OECD, *Taxing Energy Use*, 24 (see n. 27 above).

63 World Bank, *Putting a Price on Carbon with a Tax* (see n. 57 above).

64 OECD, *Taxing Energy Use* (see n. 27 above).

65 P. Soderholm, *Extending the Environmental Tax Base: Prerequisites for Increased Taxation of Natural Resources and Chemical Compounds* (Stockholm: Swedish Environmental Protection Agency, 2004), http://www.naturvardsverket.se/Om -Naturvardsverket/Publikationer/ISBN/5400/91-620-5416-3/.

66 Sweden Chemical Inspectorate, *Ordinance on Fees for Pesticides*, No. 2013 (2013), 63. http://www.kemi.se/en/Content/Pesticides/Charges/.

67 E. Spikkerud, *Pesticide Taxation in Norway* (Oslo: Norwegian Food Safety Authority, 2012).

68 D. Pearce and P. Koundouri, *Fertilizer and Pesticide Taxes for Controlling Non-Point Water Pollution* (Washington, DC: World Bank, 2003).

69 Danish Ministry of the Environment, *Protect Water, Nature, and Human Health: Pesticides Strategy 2013–2015* (Copenhagen: Danish Ministry of the Environment, 2012).

70 Denmark, *Law Regarding a Change in the Tax on Pesticides and Biocides*, No. 594, dated June 18, 2012.

71 OECD, *Water Policy and Agriculture: Meeting the Challenge* (Paris: OECD, 2012), 84.

72 Canada Revenue Agency, *GST/HST Info Sheet: Fertilizer and Pesticides*, GI-048 (2008), http://www.cra-arc.gc.ca/E/pub/gi/gi-048/gi-048-e.pdf.

73 *Permit Fees Regulation*, B.C. Reg. 299/92 (Schedules B and C), pursuant to the *Environmental Management Act*, S.B.C. 2003, c.-53; *Fees Regulation*, N.S. Reg. 68/2013, pursuant to the *Environment Act*, S.N.S. 1994–95, c. 1.

74 Ecotec Research, *Study on the Economic and Environmental Implications of the Use of Environmental Taxes and Charges in the European Union and Its Member States* (Brussels: Ecotec Research, 2001), http://ec.europa.eu/environment/enveco/ taxation/.

75 L. Hoglund Isaksson, "Abatement Costs in Response to the Swedish Charge on Nitrogen Oxide Emissions," *Journal of Environmental Economics and Management* 50 (2005): 102–20.

76 US EPA, *The United States Experience with Economic Incentives for Protecting the Environment* (Washington, DC: US EPA, 2001).

77 Alabama, Alaska, Delaware, Hawaii, Kentucky, Maine, Massachusetts, Pennsylvania, Rhode Island, Utah, and Virginia.

78 Arizona, Arkansas, Colorado, Connecticut, Florida, Kansas, Minnesota, Missouri, Nevada, New York, North Carolina, Ohio, Oregon, South Carolina, South Dakota, Tennessee, Vermont, and Washington.

79 California, Indiana, Louisiana, Maryland, Montana, New Jersey, Oklahoma, Texas, West Virginia, and Wisconsin.

80 US EPA, *The United States Experience with Economic Incentives* (see n. 76 above).

81 *Clean Air Act*, 42 USC, s. 7661a(b).

82 South Coast Air Quality Management District, *Rule 301: Permitting and Associated Fees* (2014), http://www.aqmd.gov/docs/default-source/rule-book/reg-iii/rule-301. pdf?sfvrsn=10.

83 Ibid.

84 *Superfund Amendments and Reauthorization Act of 1986,* Public Law 99–499, October 17, 1986.

85 J.L. Ramseur, M. Reisch, and J.E. McCarthy, *Superfund Taxes or General Revenues: Future Funding Issues for the Superfund Program* (Report to Congress) (Washington, DC: Congressional Research Service, 2008).

86 US EPA, *International Experiences with Economic Incentives for Protecting the Environment* (Washington, DC: US EPA, 2005).

87 M. Faure, "Effectiveness of Environmental Law: What Does the Evidence Tell US?" *William and Mary Environmental Law and Policy Review* 36, 2 (2012): 293–336.

88 "Directive 2004/35/CE of the European Parliament and of the Council of 21 April 2004 on Environmental Liability with Regard to the Prevention and Remedying of Environmental Damage," *Official Journal L.* 143 (April 30, 2004): P.0056–P.0075.

89 France (Minister of Economy and Finance), "General Tax on Polluting Activities" (circular of April 9, 2013), NOR: BUDD1307144C.

90 Ibid.

91 OECD, *Household Water Pricing in OECD Countries* (Paris: OECD, 1999).

92 *Charges for Industrial and Commercial Water Users,* Ontario Reg. 450/07, as amended.

93 *Water Regulation,* B.C. Reg. 204/88.

94 OECD, *Inventory of Estimated Budget Support and Tax Expenditures for Fossil Fuels, 2013* (Paris: OECD, 2013).

95 International Monetary Fund, *Energy Subsidy Reform: Lessons and Implications* (Paris: IMF, 2013).

96 International Energy Agency, *Energy Prices and Taxes* (Paris: IEA, 2014).

97 Commissioner of the Environment and Sustainable Development, "Chapter 2: Financial Assurances for Environmental Risks," in *Report to Parliament* (Ottawa: Office of the Auditor General of Canada, 2012), 2.

98 Ibid.

99 *Energy Safety and Security Act,* S.C. 2015, c. 4.

100 J. Firestone, "Enforcement of Pollution Laws and Regulations: An Analysis of Forum Choice," *Harvard Environmental Law Review* 27 (2003): 105–76.

101 J. Tosun, "Environmental Monitoring and Enforcement in Europe: A Review of Empirical Research," *Environmental Policy and Governance* 22, 6 (2012): 437–48.

102 Faure, "Effectiveness of Environmental Law," 293–336 (see n. 87 above).

103 S. Bell and D. McGillivray, *Environmental Law,* 6th ed. (Oxford: Oxford University Press, 2006).

104 Faure, "Effectiveness of Environmental Law," 293–336 (see n. 87 above).

105 Boyd, *Unnatural Law* (see n. 12 above); A.L. Girard, S. Day, and L. Snider, "Tracking Environmental Crime through CEPA: Canada's Environment Cops or Industry's Best Friend?" *Canadian Journal of Sociology* 35, 2 (2010): 219–41; Commissioner of the Environment and Sustainable Development, "Enforcement of the Canadian Environmental Protection Act, 1999," in *Report of the Commissioner of the Environment and Sustainable Development to the House of Commons* (Ottawa: Office of the Auditor General of Canada, 2011), ch. 3; Ecojustice, *Getting Tough on Environmental Crime? Holding the Federal Government to Account on Environmental Crime* (Ottawa: Ecojustice, 2011).

106 Tom McMillan, quoted in Boyd, *Unnatural Law,* 101 (see n. 12 above).
107 Girard et al., "Tracking Environmental Crime through CEPA," 219–41 (see n. 105 above).
108 Toronto Public Library, "Circulation and Collection Use (Including Fines and Fees) Policy Recommendations 2013" (April 29, 2013).
109 K. Timoney and P. Lee, *Environmental Incidents in Northeastern Alberta's Bitumen Sands Region, 1996–2012* (Edmonton: Global Forest Watch, 2013).
110 Boyd, *Unnatural Law* (see n. 12 above).
111 Commissioner of the Environment and Sustainable Development, "Enforcement of the Canadian Environmental Protection Act, 1999"; Ecojustice, *Getting Tough on Environmental Crime?*
112 R. Esworthy, *Federal Pollution Control Laws: How Are They Enforced?* (Report for Congress) (Washington, DC: Congressional Research Service, 2013).
113 US EPA, "Compliance and Enforcement: Annual Results 2011" (2012), http://www.epa.gov/compliance/enforcement/annual-results/eoy2011.pdf.
114 US Department of Justice, "BP Exploration and Production Inc. Pleads Guilty, Is Sentenced to Pay Record $4 Billion for Crimes Surrounding Deepwater Horizon Incident" (press release, January 29, 2013).
115 US EPA, "Compliance and Enforcement: Annual Results 2011" (see n. 113 above).
116 D. Fumano, "Environment Ministry Continues to Shield Water Act Violators," *Province,* October 8, 2013.
117 Government of Canada, *Public Accounts of Canada 1983–2012, Volume II* (1983–2012) (spreadsheets on file with author).
118 Provincial Governments, *Public Accounts* (1988–2012) (spreadsheets on file with author).
119 OECD, *Economic Surveys: Canada* (Paris: OECD, 2012).
120 OECD, *Taxing Energy Use* (see n. 27 above).
121 Ekins and Speck, *Environmental Tax Reform (ETR)* (see n. 5 above).
122 Canada's Ecofiscal Commission, *Smart, Practical, Possible* (see n. 1 above).

Chapter 9: Why Does Canada Lag Behind?

1 J.B. Moyle, trans., *The Institutes of Justinian* (Oxford: Clarendon Press, 1913).
2 World Commission on Environment and Development, *Our Common Future* (Oxford: Oxford University Press, 1987), 330.
3 J. Rockstrom, W. Steffen, K. Noone, et al., "A Safe Operating Space for Humanity," *Nature* 461, 24 (2009): 472–75; C. Folke, "Respecting Planetary Boundaries and Reconnecting to the Biosphere," in *State of the World 2013: Is Sustainability Still Possible?* ed. Worldwatch Institute (Washington, DC: Island Press, 2013), 19–27.
4 P. Victor, *Managing without Growth: Slower by Design, Not Disaster* (Cheltenham, UK: Edward Elgar, 2008); T. Jackson, *Prosperity without Growth* (London: Sustainable Development Commission, 2009).
5 S. Wood, G. Tanner, B.J. Richardson, "Whatever Happened to Canadian Environmental Law?" *Ecology Law Quarterly* 37 (2010): 981–1040.
6 M. M'Gonigle and L. Takeda, "The Liberal Limits of Environmental Law: A Green Legal Critique," *Pace Environmental Law Review* 30, 3 (2013): 1005–1115.

7   J. Oliver, "Natural Resources: Canada's Advantage, Canada's Opportunity" (notes for remarks at Canaccord Genuity Corporation, Toronto, September 4, 2012), http://www.nrcan.gc.ca/media-room/speeches/2012/3357.

8   Natural Resources Canada, "Assessing the Economic Impact of the Energy and Mining Sectors," Energy and Mines Ministers Conference, Charlottetown, September 2012.

9   J. Stanford, "A Cure for Dutch Disease: Active Sector Strategies for Canada's Economy" (technical paper for Alternative Federal Budget) (Ottawa: Canadian Centre for Policy Alternatives, 2012).

10 Ibid.

11 D. Davidson and N. Mackendrick, "State-Capital Relations in Voluntary Environmental Improvement," *Current Sociology* 55, 5 (2007): 674–95.

12 D.R. Boyd, *Unnatural Law: Rethinking Canadian Environmental Law and Policy* (Vancouver: UBC Press, 2003), 253–54.

13 D. Cayley-Daoust and R. Girard, *Big Oil's Oily Grasp* (Ottawa: Polaris Institute, 2012).

14 Canadian Council of Chief Executives, *Kananaskis 2011: Building an Agenda for a Sound Energy Future* (submission to the Conference of Energy and Mines Ministers, 2011).

15 A. Kwasniak, "The Eviscerating of Federal Environmental Assessment in Canada," *University of Calgary Faculty of Law Blog* (March 31, 2009), http://ablawg.ca/2009/03/31/the-eviscerating-of-federal-environmental-assessment-in-canada/; Boyd, *Unnatural Law* (see n. 12 above).

16 K. Badenhausen, "Best Countries for Business," *Forbes Magazine*, October 3, 2011, http://www.forbes.com/lists/2011/6/best-countries-11_Canada_CHI019.html.

17 Letter to Peter Kent, Environment Minister and Joe Oliver, Natural Resources Minister, dated December 12, 2011, from the Canadian Petroleum Products Institute, Canadian Association of Petroleum Producers, Canadian Gas Association, and Canadian Energy Pipeline Association (on file with author).

18 Cayley-Daoust and Girard, *Big Oil's Oily Grasp* (see n. 13 above).

19 R.B. Gibson, "In Full Retreat: The Canadian Government's New Environmental Assessment Law Undoes Decades of Progress," *Impact Assessment and Project Appraisal* 30, 3 (2012): 179–88.

20 W. Everson, "Testimony before House of Commons Standing Committee on Environment and Sustainable Development," *Evidence*, 3rd Session, 40th Parliament (November 15, 2010); T. Huffaker, "Testimony before House of Commons Standing Committee on Environment and Sustainable Development," *Evidence*, 3rd Session, 40th Parliament (November 15, 2010).

21 Huffaker, ibid.

22 Everson, "Testimony" (see n. 20 above).

23 D.R. Boyd, *The Right to a Healthy Environment: Revitalizing Canada's Constitution* (Vancouver: UBC Press, 2012).

24 *An Act to Establish a Canadian Environmental Bill of Rights*, Bill C-634, introduced by NDP MP Linda Duncan on October 29, 2014, in the 41st Parliament, 2nd Session.

25 R.S. Haszeldine, "Carbon Capture and Storage: How Green Can Black Be?" *Science* 325, 5948 (2009): 1647–52.

26 Royal Norwegian Ministry of Finance, *Norway's Strategy for Sustainable Development* (Oslo: Royal Norwegian Ministry of Finance, 2008).

27 Ibid.

28 Royal Norwegian Ministry of Finance, "The Government Pension Fund" (2014), https://www.regjeringen.no/en/topics/the-economy/the-government-pension-fund/id1441/. For the Fund's current market value, see http://www.nbim.no/en/.

29 Conference Board of Canada, "How Canada Performs" (2015), http://www.conferenceboard.ca/hcp/default.aspx.

30 M. Anderson, "How Ottawa Sabotaged Our Kyoto Pledge in 2002," *The Tyee*, October 4, 2006.

31 S. McCarthy, "Oil Industry Successfully Lobbied Ottawa to Delay Climate Regulations, Emails Show," *Globe and Mail*, November 8, 2013.

32 L. Whittingdon, "New Oil and Gas Regulations Would Be 'Crazy', Harper Says," *Toronto Star*, December 9, 2014.

33 S. McCarthy, "Ottawa Scales Back Oversight of Offshore Drilling," *Globe and Mail*, November 6, 2013.

34 M. De Souza, "Canada Says Oil, Gas Industry Organized PR Strategy for Oilsands," *Postmedia News*, August 9, 2011.

35 D.R. Boyd, A. Attaran, and M. Stanbrook, "Asbestos Mortality: A Canadian Export," *Canadian Medical Association Journal* 179, 9 (2008): 871–72.

36 Boyd, *Unnatural Law* (see n. 12 above).

37 E.M. Noam, *Who Owns the World's Media*, Columbia Business School Research Paper 13–22 (New York: Columbia Business School, 2013).

38 *Adbusters Media Foundation v. Canadian Broadcasting Corporation et al.* (2009) BCCA 148 (CanLII).

39 N. Oreskes and E.M. Conway, *Merchants of Doubt: How a Handful of Scientists Obscured the Truth on Issues from Tobacco Smoke to Global Warming* (New York: Bloomsbury, 2011).

40 J. Doyle, "Goodbye Tony Burman, Hello CBC Lite," *Globe and Mail*, June 21, 2007.

41 D. Winseck, "Media and Internet Concentration in Canada, 1984–2011" (2012), http://dwmw.wordpress.com/2012/11/26/media-and-internet-concentration-in-canada/.

42 D. Gutstein, *Not a Conspiracy Theory: How Business Hijacks Democracy* (Toronto: Key Porter Books, 2009), 292.

43 D. Michaels, *Doubt Is Their Product: How Industry's Assault on Science Threatens Your Health* (Oxford: Oxford University Press, 2008).

44 G. Markowitz and D. Rosner, *Deceit and Denial: The Deadly Politics of Industrial Pollution* (Berkeley: University of California Press, 2002).

45 Michaels, *Doubt Is Their Product* (see n. 43 above).

46 J. Bakan, *Just Words: Constitutional Rights and Social Wrongs* (Toronto: University of Toronto Press, 1997).

47 A. Reynolds, B. Reilly, and A. Ellis, *Electoral System Design* (Stockholm: International Institute for Democracy and Electoral Assistance, 2006).

48 P. Russell, *Two Cheers for Minority Government* (Toronto: Emond Montgomery, 2008).

49 Wood et al., "Whatever Happened to Canadian Environmental Law?" 981–1040 (see n. 5 above).

50 D. Savoie, *Governing from the Centre: The Concentration of Power in Canadian Politics* (Toronto: University of Toronto Press, 1999).

51 J. Simpson, *The Friendly Dictatorship* (Toronto: McClelland and Stewart, 2001).

52 E. May, *Losing Confidence: Power, Politics, and the Crisis in Canadian Democracy* (Toronto: McClelland and Stewart, 2009), 8.

53 A. Nikiforuk, *Tar Sands: Dirty Oil and the Future of a Continent* (Vancouver: Greystone Books, 2010).

54 K. Stewart, "Federal Environment Minister's Door Opens Wide to Big Oil" (Greenpeace, 2012), http://www.greenpeace.org/canada/en/Blog/federal-environment -ministers-door-opens-wide/blog/41962/.

55 Quoted in S. Chase, "Peter Kent's Green Agenda: Clean Up Oil Sands' Dirty Reputation," *Globe and Mail,* January 6, 2011.

56 A. Johnston, *Legal Backgrounder: Bill C-43 a Threat to Environmental Safety and Democracy* (Vancouver: West Coast Environmental Law, 2014).

57 Quoted in J. Gailus, "An Act of Deception: Fiction Upstages Fact in the Environmental Assessment of Alberta's Oil Sands," *Alternatives Journal* 38, 5 (2012), http:// www.alternativesjournal.ca/energy-and-resources/act-deception.

58 Quoted in ibid.

59 N. Snow, "Alberta Premier Wants Full, Reasoned Debate on Keystone XL," *Oil and Gas Journal,* April 9, 2013, http://www.ogj.com/articles/print/volume-111/issue-4b/ general-interest/alberta-premier-wants-full-reasoned.html.

60 P. Koring, "Kent Finds Canada's Green Record Is a Tough Sell in Washington," *Globe and Mail,* April 10, 2013.

61 Wood et al., "Whatever Happened to Canadian Environmental Law?" 981–1040 (see n. 5 above).

62 K. Harrison, *Passing the Buck: Federalism and Canadian Environmental Policy* (Vancouver: UBC Press, 1995).

63 T.A. Murray, *The Prevention of the Pollution of Canada's Surface Waters* (Ottawa: Canada's Commission of Conservation, 1912).

64 Canada, *House of Commons Debates* (February 14, 1969), 5524.

65 D. Gibson, *Constitutional Jurisdiction over Environmental Management in Canada* (Ottawa: Government of Canada, 1970), 57.

66 P. Muldoon, *Environment and the Constitution: Submission to the Standing Committee on the Environment* (Toronto: Canadian Environmental Law Association, 1991).

67 *Friends of the Oldman River Society v. Minister of Transport et al.,* [1992] 1 S.C.R. 3, para. 86.

68 Harrison, *Passing the Buck* (see n. 62 above).

69 S. Elgie, "Kyoto, the Constitution and Carbon Trading: Waking a Sleeping BNA Bear (or Two)," *Review of Constitutional Studies* 13, 1 (2007): 67–129.

70 A.R. Lucas and J. Yearsley, "The Constitutionality of Federal Climate Change Legislation," *Journal of Environmental Law and Policy* 23 (2011): 205–36.

71 *Interprovincial Co-operatives Limited et al. v. R.,* [1976] 1 S.C.R. 477.

72 *Fowler v. R.,* [1980] 2 S.C.R. 213; *Northwest Falling Contractors v. R.,* [1980] 2 S.C.R. 292.

73 *R. v. Crown Zellerbach,* [1988] 1 S.C.R. 401.

74 *Friends of the Oldman River Society* (see n. 67 above).

75 *114957 Canada Ltée (Spraytech, Société d'arrosage) v. Hudson (Town)*, [2001] 2 S.C.R. 241.

76 *R. v. Hydro-Québec*, [1997] 3 S.C.R. 213.

77 Canadian Press, "Taseko Asks Federal Court to Quash Minister's Decision on Rejected B.C. Gold Mine," *Vancouver Sun*, March 26, 2014.

78 *Medicine Hat and LGX Oil and Gas v. Canada (Minister of Environment)* (2014) Federal Court, Trial Division Application T-12-14.

79 M. Illical and K. Harrison, "Protecting Endangered Species in the US and Canada: The Role of Negative Lesson Drawing," *Canadian Journal of Political Science* 40 (2007): 367–94.

80 W. Amos, K. Harrison, and G. Hoberg, "In Search of a Minimum Winning Coalition: The Politics of Species-at-Risk Legislation in Canada," in *Politics of the Wild: Canada and Endangered Species*, ed. K. Beazley and R. Boardman (Oxford: Oxford University Press, 2001), 156.

81 *Nuclear Safety and Control Act*, S.C. 1997, c. 9.

82 Boyd, *Unnatural Law* (see n. 12 above).

83 D. Ludwig, R. Hilborn, and C. Walters, "Uncertainty, Resource Exploitation, and Conservation: Lessons from History," *Science* 260, 5104 (1993): 17–36.

84 G. Scudder, *Biodiversity Conservation and Protected Areas in British Columbia* (Vancouver: UBC Centre for Biodiversity Research, 2003).

85 *Species at Risk Act*, S.C. 2002, c. 29.

86 D.R. Boyd, *Wild by Law: A Report Card on Laws Governing Canada's Parks and Protected Areas, and a Blueprint for Making these Laws More Effective* (Victoria: POLIS Project on Ecological Governance, 2002).

87 Boyd, *Unnatural Law*, ch. 5.3, "Marine Biodiversity" (see n. 12 above).

88 Editorial Board, "Frozen Out," *Nature* 483, 6 (2012): 6.

89 M. De Souza, "Stephen Harper's Tories Downplay Climate Knowledge of New Environment Canada Boss," *Postmedia News*, October 19, 2012, http://o.canada.com/news/politics-and-the-nation/environment-canadas-new-top-bureaucrat-cant-say-what-causes-climate-change/.

90 Organisation for Economic Co-operation and Development, *Voluntary Approaches for Environmental Policy: Effectiveness, Efficiency, and Usage in the Policy Mixes* (Paris: OECD, 2003).

91 I. Matsukawa, "The Effects of Information on Residential Demand for Electricity," *Energy Journal* 25, 1 (2004): 1–17; B. Shui and H. Dowlatabadi, "Consumer Lifestyle Approach to US Energy Use and the Related CO_2 Emissions," *Energy Policy* 33, 2 (2005): 197–208; J. Eto, S. Kito, L. Shown, et al., "Where Did the Money Go? The Cost of the Performance of the Largest Commercial Sector DSM Programs," *Energy Journal* 21, 2 (2000): 23–49.

92 D. Loughran and J. Kulick, "Demand-Side Management and Energy Efficiency in the United States," *Energy Journal* 25, 1 (2004): 19–43; F. Wirl, *The Economics of Conservation Programs* (Boston: Kluwer, 1997).

93 A. Chandra, S. Gulati, and M. Kandlikar, "Green Drivers or Free Riders: An Analysis of Tax Rebates for Hybrid Vehicles," *Journal of Environmental Economics and Management* 60, 2 (2010): 78–93.

94 A. Jaffe, R. Newell, and R. Stavins, "Technological Change and the Environment," in *Handbook of Environmental Economics,* vol. 1, ed. K.G. Maler and J.R. Vincent (Amsterdam: Elsevier, 2003).

95 P. Portney and R. Stavins, eds., *Public Policies for Environmental Protection* (Washington, DC: Resources for the Future, 2000), 33.

96 Ibid.

97 M. Jaccard, N. Rivers, and M. Horne, *The Morning After: Optimal Greenhouse Gas Policies for Canada's Kyoto Obligations and Beyond,* C.D. Howe Institute Commentary No. 197 (Toronto: C.D. How Institute, 2004), http://www.cdhowe.org.

98 European Environment Agency, *Environmental Taxes: Recent Developments in Tools for Integration* (Luxembourg: European Environmental Agency, 2000); A. Jordan, R.K. Wurzel, and A.R. Zito, *"New" Instruments of Environmental Governance? National Experiences and Prospects* (London: Frank Cass, 2003).

99 "Syncrude to Pay $3M Penalty for Duck Deaths," *CBC News,* October 22, 2010, http://www.cbc.ca/news/canada/edmonton/syncrude-to-pay-3m-penalty-for-duck -deaths-1.906420.

100 *R. v. Bloom Lake General Partner Limited (2014),* http://www.ec.gc.ca/alef-ewe/default.asp?lang=En&n=87E31737-1.

101 *Sandy Pond Alliance to Protect Canadian Waters v. Canada* (2013) FC 1112, October 31, 2013, para. 88.

102 Friends of the Earth Canada, *Standing on Guard: Environmental Rights in Canada, 2009* (Ottawa: Friends of the Earth Canada, 2009), 2.

103 R. Hazell and B. Worthy, "Assessing the Performance of Freedom of Information," *Government Information Quarterly* 27, 4 (2010): 352–59.

104 Centre for Law and Democracy, *Right to Information Ratings* (Halifax: Centre for Law and Democracy, 2013), http://www.rti-rating.org/index.php.

105 *Jobs, Growth and Long-term Prosperity Act,* S.C. 2012, c. 19.

106 West Hawk Associates, *Green Canada: Eco-Literacy of Canadians and Benefits/ Barriers to Pro-Environment Behavior* (report prepared for Environment Canada) (2009), http://www.westhawk.com/portfolio/GreenCanada.pdf.

107 Royal Bank of Canada, "Canadian Water Attitudes Survey" (2011), http://www.rbc.com/bluewater.

108 Royal Bank of Canada, "Canadian Water Attitudes Survey" (2009), http://www.rbc.com/bluewater.

109 A. Turcotte, M.L. Moore, and J. Winter, "Energy Literacy in Canada," *University of Calgary Public Policy Research Paper* 5, 32 (2012): 1–47.

110 M. De Souza, "Canadians in Dark on Kyoto Protocol, Most Unaware PM Withdrew: Poll," *Vancouver Sun,* November 6, 2013.

111 S. Shepherd and A.C. Kay, "On the Perpetuation of Ignorance: System Dependence, System Justification, and the Motivated Avoidance of Socio-Political Information," *Journal of Personality and Social Psychology* 102, 2 (2012): 264–80.

112 R.W. Scholz, *Environmental Literacy in Science and Society: From Knowledge to Decisions* (Cambridge: Cambridge University Press, 2011).

113 M. De Souza, "Opposition Brands Canada Revenue Agency Spending on Audits of Charities a 'Witch Hunt,'" *Postmedia News,* October 11, 2013.

114 *Friends of the Oldman River Society v. Minister of Transport et al.* (see n. 67 above); *R. v. Hydro-Québec* (see n. 76 above); *Ontario v. Canadian Pacific,* [1995] 2 S.C.R. 1031; *114957 Canada Ltée (Spraytech, Société d'arrosage) v. Hudson (Town),* [2001] 2 S.C.R. 241; *British Columbia v. Canadian Forest Products Ltd.,* [2004] 2 S.C.R. 74; *Imperial Oil Ltd. v. Quebec (Minister of Environment),* [2003] 2 S.C.R. 624.

115 *R. v. Sault Ste. Marie,* [1978] 2 S.C.R. 1299, 1326.

116 *R. v. Sparrow,* [1990] 1 S.C.R. 1075.

117 *Friends of the Oldman River Society v. Minister of Transport et al.,* 16–17 (see n. 67 above).

118 *R. v. Hydro-Québec,* para. 85 (see n. 76 above).

119 *114957 Canada Ltée (Spraytech, Société d'arrosage) v. Hudson (Town),* para. 1 (see n. 114 above).

120 *Imperial Oil Ltd. v. Quebec (Minister of Environment)* (see n. 114 above).

121 *British Columbia v. Canadian Forest Products Ltd.,* para. 155 (see n. 114 above).

122 *St. Lawrence Cement Inc. v. Barrette,* [2008] 3 S.C.R. 392.

123 *Castonguay Blasting v. Ontario (Minister of the Environment),* [2013] 3 S.C.R. 323.

124 *Ontario v. Canadian Pacific,* [1995] 2 S.C.R. 1031, para. 55; *R. v. Hydro-Québec,* para. 124 (see n. 76 above); *Imperial Oil Ltd. v. Quebec (Minister of Environment),* para. 20 (see n. 114 above); *Montréal (City) v. 2952-1366 Québec Inc.,* [2005] 3 S.C.R. 141, para. 99.

125 D.R. Boyd, *Vancouver 2020: A Bright Green Future. An Action Plan for Becoming the World's Greenest City by 2020* (Vancouver: City of Vancouver, 2009).

126 Town of Oakville, *Health Protection Air Quality By-law,* No. 2010–035 (2010).

127 See the David Suzuki Foundation website, http://bluedot.ca.

128 J.W. Kingdon, *Agendas, Alternatives, and Public Policies,* 2nd ed. (Ann Arbor: University of Michigan Press, 1995).

129 T. Schrecker, "Using Science in Environmental Policy: Can Canada do Better?" in *Governing the Environment: Persistent Challenges, Uncertain Innovation,* ed. E. Parson (Toronto: University of Toronto Press, 2001).

Chapter 10: A Preventive and Precautionary Approach

1 Canadian Medical Association, *Determining the Impact of Chemical Contamination on Human Health* (Ottawa: CMA, 2010); American Academy of Pediatrics, "Pesticide Exposure in Children: Policy Statement," *Pediatrics* 130, 6 (2012): e1757–63; D. Wigle, *Child Health and the Environment* (Oxford: Oxford University Press, 2003); Commission for Environmental Cooperation, *Children's Health and the Environment in North America: A First Report on Available Indicators and Measures* (Montreal: Commission on Environmental Cooperation, 2006); H. Frumkin, ed., *Environmental Health: From Global to Local,* 2nd ed. (San Francisco: John Wiley and Sons, 2010).

2 M. Stoneham, J. Dodds, and K. Buckett, "Policy in the Government Context," in *Environmental Health in Australia and New Zealand,* ed. N. Cromar, S. Cameron, and H. Fallowfield (Melbourne: Oxford University Press, 2004), 131.

3 D.R. Boyd, *Greenest City: Quick Start Recommendations* (Vancouver: Greenest City Action Team, 2009); D.R. Boyd, *Vancouver 2020: A Bright Green Future. An*

Action Plan for Becoming the World's Greenest City by 2020 (Vancouver: City of Vancouver, 2009).

4 D.R. Boyd, *Prescription for a Healthy Canada: Towards a National Environmental Health Strategy* (Vancouver: David Suzuki Foundation, 2007).

5 Conference Board of Canada, *Critical Steps for Canada: Environmental Health Lessons Across Borders – Australia, Sweden, and California* (Ottawa: Conference Board of Canada, 2009).

6 Canadian Public Health Association, *Global Change and Public Health: Addressing the Ecological Determinants of Health* (Ottawa: Canadian Public Health Association, 2015).

7 D.R. Boyd, *Sustainability within a Generation: A New Vision for Canada* (Vancouver: David Suzuki Foundation, 2004), http://www.davidsuzuki.org.

8 Environment Canada, "National Environmental Objectives" (draft, 2005). Document on file with author.

9 Swedish Environmental Objectives Council, *For the Sake of Our Children: Sweden's National Environmental Quality Objectives, a Progress Report* (Stockholm: Swedish Environmental Protection Agency, 2005).

10 Commonwealth of Massachusetts, Department of Environmental Protection, *Toxics Use Reduction Information Release* (Boston: Commonwealth of Massachusetts, 2014); Toxics Use Reduction Institute, *Trends in the Use and Release of Carcinogens in Massachusetts* (Lowell, MA: TURI, 2013).

11 European Union, *Directive 2003/15/EC of the European Parliament and of the Council, 27 February 2003 Relating to Cosmetic Products.*

12 Environment Canada, *Planning for a Sustainable Future: A Federal Sustainable Development Strategy for Canada 2013–2016* (Ottawa: Environment Canada, 2013), 36.

13 Ibid., 37.

14 Ibid., 67.

15 A. Abelsohn, J. Frank, and J. Eyles, "Environmental Public Health Tracking/ Surveillance in Canada: A Commentary," *Healthcare Policy* 4, 3 (2009): 37–52.

16 Ibid., 49.

17 Pew Environmental Health Commission, *America's Environmental Health Gap: Why the Country Needs a Nationwide Health Tracking Network* (Baltimore: Johns Hopkins School of Hygiene and Public Health, 2000).

18 Government of Canada, *Children's Health and the Environment in North America: A First Report on Available Indicators and Measures. Country Report: Canada* (Gatineau, QC: Environment Canada, 2005), 57.

19 See Pew Environmental Health Commission, *America's Environmental Health Gap* (see n. 17 above).; US Centers for Disease Control and Prevention, *CDC's Strategy for the National Environmental Public Health Tracking Program* (Atlanta: CDC, 2005); M. Ono, Y. Honda, Y. Moriguchi, et al., "Environmental Health Surveillance System in Japan: Air Pollution and Children's Health," *Epidemiology* 17, 6 (2006): 262–63.

20 A.-E. Vermette, P.-A. Dube, and S. Gosselin, "La toxicovigilance: une vigie des menaces à la santé d'origine chimique," *Bulletin d'Information Toxicologique* 30, 1 (2014): 14–37.

21 Government of Canada, *Children's Health and the Environment in North America,* 56 (see n. 18 above).

22 L. Gammie, "Review of Issue #5 – Drinking Water Standards," in *Managing Health Risks from Drinking Water: A Background Paper for the Walkerton Inquiry* (prepared on behalf of the Ontario Water Works Association and the Ontario Municipal Water Association), ed. D. Krewski, J. Balbus, D. Butler-Jones, et al., http://www. archives.gov.on.ca/en/e_records/walkerton/part2info/partieswithstanding/pdf/ OWWA5.pdf.

23 Commission for Environmental Cooperation, *Children's Health and the Environment in North America* (see n. 1 above). See also Government of Canada, *Children's Health and the Environment in North America* (see n. 18 above).

24 J.B. Mowry, D.A. Spyker, L.R. Cantilena, J.E. Bailey, and M. Ford, "2012 Annual Report of the American Association of Poison Control Centers National Poison Data System," *Clinical Toxicology* 51, 10 (2013): 949–1229.

25 Canadian Association of Poison Control Centres, http://www.capcc.ca.

26 M. Durigon, C. Elliott, R. Purssell, and T. Kosatsky, "Canadian Poison Control Centres: Preliminary Assessment of Their Potential as a Resource for Public Health Surveillance," *Clinical Toxicology* 51, 9 (2013): 886–91.

27 National Institute for Occupational Safety and Health, *Pesticide-Related Injury and Illness Surveillance: A How-To Guide for State-Based Programs,* NIOSH publication 2006–102 (Cincinnati, OH: NIOSH, 2006), http://www.cdc.gov/niosh/docs/ 2006-102/pdfs/2006-102.pdf.

28 A. Lukacsovics, M. Hatcher, and A. Papadopolous, *Risk Factors and Surveillance Systems for Foodborne Illness Outbreaks in Canada* (Vancouver: National Collaborating Centre for Environmental Health, 2014).

29 US Centers for Disease Control and Prevention, *CDC's Strategy for the National Environmental Public Health Tracking Program* (see n. 19 above); P. Gosselin and C.M. Furgal, "Challenges and Directions for Environmental Public Health Indicators and Surveillance," *Canadian Journal of Public Health* 93, 5 (2002): S5-S8.

30 Wigle, *Child Health and the Environment,* 20 (see n. 1 above).

31 C. Chociolko, R. Copes, and J. Rekart, *Needs, Gaps, and Opportunities Assessment for the National Collaborating Centre for Environmental Health* (Vancouver: NCCEH, 2006), 37.

32 F. Capra, *The New Facts of Life* (Berkeley: Center for Ecoliteracy, 2008), http://www. ecoliteracy.org/essays/new-facts-life.

33 Royal Norwegian Ministry of Finance, *Norway's Strategy for Sustainable Development* (Oslo: Royal Norwegian Ministry of Finance, 2008).

34 Health Canada and the Lung Associations of Ontario and New Brunswick, "Take Action on Radon" (2013), http://www.takeactiononradon.ca/.

35 For example, see the US Environmental Protection Agency's Surf Your Watershed website at http://cfpub.epa.gov/surf/locate/index.cfm, or the EPA's Envirofacts website at http://www.epa.gov/enviro/index.html.

36 Canadian Environmental Health Atlas, http://www.ehatlas.ca/.

37 Canadian Medical Association, *Determining the Impact of Chemical Contamination,* 6 (see n. 1 above).

38 R. Villela, N. Dimnik, A. Ray, et al., "Medical Students' Attitudes about Cosmetic Pesticides before and after an Ecosystem Health Seminar: A Pilot Study," *EcoHealth* 5, 3 (2008): 275–77.

39 National Collaborating Centre for Environmental Health, *Environmental Health Degree Programs/Courses in Canada* (Vancouver: NCCEH, 2013).

40 See https://www.cma.ca/En/Pages/online-cme-courses.aspx.

41 Canadian Medical Association, *Determining the Impact of Chemical Contamination*, 5 (see n. 1 above).

42 C. Jeffords and L. Minkler, "Do Constitutions Matter? The Effect of Constitutional Environmental Rights Provisions on Environmental Performance" (paper delivered at the Yale University/UNITAR Conference on Human Rights and the Environment, New Haven, CT, September 5–7, 2014); D.R. Boyd, *The Environmental Rights Revolution: A Global Study of Constitutions, Human Rights and the Environment* (Vancouver: UBC Press, 2012).

43 Canadian Bar Association, *Report of the Canadian Bar Association Committee on Sustainable Development in Canada: Options for Law Reform* (Ottawa: Canadian Bar Association, 1990).

44 National Round Table on the Environment and the Economy, *Developing Ambient Air Quality Objectives for Canada: Advice to the Minister of Environment* (Ottawa: NRTEE, 2008).

45 D.R. Boyd, "Elements of an Effective Environmental Bill of Rights," *Journal of Environmental Law and Practice*, 2015, in press.

46 For updates, the David Suzuki Foundation has created a website, http://bluedot.ca.

47 *Emergency Planning and Community Right-to-Know Act*, 42 US Code 116, ss. 301–13.

48 European Union, *Regulation on the Classification, Labelling, and Packaging of Substance and Mixtures: Regulation (EC) No 1272/2008 of the European Parliament and of the Council of 16 December 2008*.

49 *Hazardous Products Act*, R.S.C. 1985, c. H-3; *Controlled Product Regulations*, SOR 88–66.

50 City of Toronto, *Environmental Reporting and Disclosure Bylaw*, Municipal Code ch. 423 (2008), http://www.toronto.ca/legdocs/municode/1184_423.pdf.

51 Toronto Public Health, *Tracking and Reducing Chemicals in Toronto: ChemTRAC Annual Report, 2011 Reporting Year* (Toronto: Toronto Public Health, 2013).

52 Ontario Task Force on the Primary Prevention of Cancer, *Recommendations for the Primary Prevention of Cancer* (Toronto: Queen's Printer, 1995).

53 D.R. O'Connor, *Report of the Walkerton Inquiry* (Toronto: Queen's Printer, 2002).

54 National Round Table on the Environment and the Economy, *Developing Ambient Air Quality Objectives* (see n. 44 above).

55 M.S. Friedman, K.E. Powell, L. Hutwagner, et al., "Impact of Changes in Transportation and Commuting Behaviors during the 1996 Summer Olympic Games in Atlanta on Air Quality and Childhood Asthma," *JAMA* 285, 7 (2001): 897–905.

56 S. Henschel, R. Atkinson, A. Zeka, et al., "Air Pollution Interventions and Their Impact on Public Health," *International Journal of Public Health* 57, 5 (2012): 757–68.

57   J.M. Samet, J. Spengler, and C. Mitchell, "Indoor Air Pollution," in *Environmental and Occupational Medicine,* ed. William N. Rom (Philadelphia: Lippincott-Raven Publishers, 1998).

58   Radon Working Group, *Report of the Radon Working Group on a New Radon Guideline for Canada* (submitted to the Federal-Provincial-Territorial Radiation Protection Committee) (Ottawa: Health Canada, 2006).

59   A. Juneau, "The Federal Gas Tax Transfer to Municipalities: An Insider Perspective," *Public Sector Digest,* Summer 2012, 48–51.

60   O'Connor, *Report of the Walkerton Inquiry, Part 2,* 336 (see n. 53 above).

61   US Environmental Protection Agency, *Water Distribution System Analysis: Field Studies, Modeling, and Management: A Reference Guide for Utilities* (Washington, DC: US EPA, 2005).

62   Canada's Ecofiscal Commission, *Smart, Practical, Possible: Canada's Options for Greater Economic and Environmental Prosperity* (Montreal: Canada's Ecofiscal Commission, 2014), http://ecofiscal.ca/reports/report/.

63   Technical Committee on Business Taxation, *Report of the Technical Committee on Business Taxation* (Ottawa: Department of Finance, 1998), 9.16, http://publications. gc.ca/collections/Collection/F32-5-1998E.pdf.

64   Green Budget Coalition, *Recommendations for Budget 2005* (Ottawa: Green Budget Coalition, 2005), http://greenbudget.ca/.

65   Commission on the Reform of Ontario's Public Services, "Chapter 13: Environment and Natural Resources" in *Public Services for Ontarians: A Path to Sustainability and Excellence* (Toronto: Ontario Ministry of Finance, 2012).

66   Commissioner of the Environment and Sustainable Development, "Chapter 3: Federal Contaminated Sites and their Impacts," in *Spring Report to Parliament* (Ottawa: Office of the Auditor General of Canada, 2012).

67   National Round Table on the Environment and the Economy, *Achieving 2050: A Carbon Pricing Policy for Canada (Advisory Note)* (Ottawa: NRTEE, 2009); Pembina Institute and David Suzuki Foundation, *Climate Leadership, Economic Prosperity* (Edmonton: Pembina Institute, 2009).

68   Health Canada, *Pest Control Products Sales Report for 2011* (Ottawa: Health Canada, 2014).

69   G. Wossink and T.A. Feitshans, "Pesticide Policies in the European Union," *Drake Journal of Agricultural Law* 5 (2000): 223–47.

70   I. Parry, D. Heine, E. Lis, and S. Li, *Getting Energy Prices Right: From Principles to Practice* (Washington, DC: International Monetary Fund, 2014).

71   Ontario Task Force on the Primary Prevention of Cancer, *Recommendations* (see n. 52 above).

72   Organisation for Economic Co-operation and Development, *Taxation, Innovation and the Environment* (Paris: OECD, 2010).

73   "Bergen Ministerial Declaration on Sustainable Development," *Yearbook on International Environmental Law* 1 (1990): 429-31. Endorsed by the Supreme Court of Canada: *114957 Canada Ltee (Spraytech, Societe d'arrosage) v. Town of Hudson* (2001), 40 C.E.L.R. (N.S.) 1 (S.C.C.).

74   *Canadian Environmental Protection Act, 1999,* S.C. 1999, c. 33, s. 2(1)(a); *Canada Oceans Act,* S.C. 1996, c. 31, Preamble; Canada *Species at Risk Act,* S.C. 2002, c. 29,

Preamble and s. 38; New Brunswick *Clean Air Act,* S.N.B. 1997, c. C-5.2, s. 2(h); Nova Scotia *Endangered Species Act,* S.N.S. 1998, c. 11, ss. 2(1)(h) and 11(1); Nunavut *Wildlife Act,* S.Nu. 2003, c. 26, ss. 1(2)(e), 130(3), 132(1)(e), 132(2), and 134(2)(b).

75 European Environment Agency, *Late Lessons from Early Warnings 1898–1998* (Copenhagen: European Environment Agency, 2002).

76 *Weir v. Minister of Health,* 2011 FC 1322, November 21, 2011.

77 *Equiterre and David Suzuki Foundation v. Health Canada,* 2013. For information on this case, see http://www.ecojustice.ca/cases/federal-pesticide-litigation.

78 N. Mortillaro, "Enjoying That Apple? European Union Thinks It Contains Carcinogens," *Global News,* April 29, 2014, http://globalnews.ca/news/1295658/enjoying -that-apple-it-could-be-toxic-european-union-believes/.

79 The Canadian Cancer Society's position is posted on its website at http://www. cancer.ca/en/prevention-and-screening/be-aware/harmful-substances-and -environmental-risks/?region=bc. The Learning Disabilities Association of Canada's position is reflected on its website at http://www.ldac-acta.ca/media-releases/48 -unprecedented-coalition-of-18-health-and-environment-groups-band-together -to-support-bc-ban-on-lawn-and-garden-chemicals.

80 Canadian Medical Association, "Resolution GC04-50 – Combined Fertilizer/ Pesticides" (approved August 18, 2004).

81 M. Christie, *Private Property Pesticide By-laws in Canada: Population Statistics by Municipality* (Ottawa, 2010), http://www.healthyenvironmentforkids.ca/sites/ healthyenvironmentforkids.ca/files/BylawList.pdf.

82 *114957 Canada Ltee (Spraytech, Societe d'arrosage) v. Town of Hudson* (see n. 73 above).

83 A.K. Todd, *Changes in Urban Stream Water Pesticide Concentrations One Year after Cosmetic Pesticide Ban* (Toronto: Ontario Ministry of Environment, Environmental Monitoring and Reporting Branch, 2010).

84 Statistics Canada, *Households and the Environment 2007* (Ottawa: Statistics Canada, 2009).

85 *Pesticides Management Code,* R.S.Q. 2003, c. P-9.3, r.0.01.

86 American Academy of Pediatrics Council on Environmental Health, "Policy Statement: Pesticide Exposure in Children," *Pediatrics* 130, 6 (2012): e1757–e1763.

87 Ibid.

88 Auditor General of Canada, "Chapter 4: Canada's Food Recall System," in *Fall 2013 Report to Parliament* (Ottawa: Office of the Auditor General of Canada, 2013).

89 KPMG LLP, *Chemicals Management Plan: Horizontal Evaluation* (Ottawa: Health Canada/Environment Canada, 2011).

90 The European Union has created a Substitution Support Portal, a website offering extensive practical and legal information regarding the application of the substitution principle. See http://www.subsport.eu/.

91 Lowell Center for Sustainable Production, *Decabromodiphenylether: An Investigation of Non-Halogen Substitutes in Electric Enclosure and Textile Applications* (Lowell: University of Massachusetts, 2005).

92 Toxics Use Reduction Institute, *Five Chemicals Alternatives Assessment Study* (Lowell, MA: TURI, 2006).

93 Ontario Task Force on the Primary Prevention of Cancer, *Recommendations,* 29 (see n. 52 above).

94 Swedish Ministry of Environment, *New Guidelines on Chemicals Policy: Non-Hazardous Products* (Stockholm: Ministry of Environment, 2000).

95 P. Grandjean and P.J. Landrigan, "Neurobehavioural Effects of Developmental Toxicity," *Lancet Neurology* 13, 3 (2014): 330–38; P. Grandjean and P.J. Landrigan, "Developmental Neurotoxicity of Industrial Chemicals," *Lancet* 368, 9553 (2006): 2167–78.

96 A. Bergman, J.J. Heindel, S. Jobling, K.A. Kidd, and R.T. Zoeller, *State of the Science: Endocrine Disrupting Chemicals 2012: Summary for Policymakers* (Geneva: UN Environmental Programme/World Health Organization, 2013).

97 L.N. Vandenberg, T. Colborn, T.B. Hayes, et al., "Hormones and Endocrine-Disrupting Chemicals: Low-Dose Effects and Non-Monotonic Dose Responses," *Endocrine Review* 33, 3 (2012): 378–455.

98 Bergman et al., *State of the Science* (see n. 96 above).

99 For example, see European Commission, *Regulation 358/2014 of 9 April 2014 Amending Annexes II and V to Regulation (EC) No 1223/2009 of the European Parliament and of the Council on Cosmetic Products.*

100 Canadian Strategy for Cancer Control, National Committee on Environmental and Occupational Exposures, *Prevention of Occupational and Environmental Cancers in Canada: A Best Practices Review and Recommendations* (2006), http://s.cela.ca/files/uploads/BPReport_Final_May2006.pdf.

101 E. Brown Weiss, *In Fairness to Future Generations: International Law, Common Patrimony, and Intergenerational Equity* (Tokyo: United Nations University, 1989), 37–38.

102 *Canada National Parks Act,* S.C. 2000, c. 32.

103 R.D. Torrie, T. Bryant, M. Beer, et al., *An Inventory of Low Carbon Energy for Canada* (David Suzuki Foundation and Canadian Academy of Engineering, 2013).

104 Commissioner of the Environment and Sustainable Development, *Meeting Canada's 2020 Climate Change Commitments* (Ottawa: Office of the Auditor General of Canada, 2012).

105 J.E. Aldy and R.N. Stavins, *Using the Market to Address Climate Change: Insights from Theory and Experience,* Working Paper No. 17488 (Cambridge, MA: National Bureau of Economic Research, 2011).

106 D. Sawyer and P. Gass, *Climate Policy Year in Review and Trends, 2013: Regulating Carbon Emissions in Canada* (Winnipeg: International Institute for Sustainable Development, 2014); National Round Table on the Environment and the Economy, *Getting to 2050: Canada's Transition to a Low Emission Future* (Ottawa: NRTEE, 2007); National Round Table on the Environment and the Economy, *Achieving 2050: A Carbon Pricing Policy for Canada* (Ottawa: NRTEE, 2009); J. Simpson, M. Jaccard, and N. Rivers, *Hot Air: Meeting Canada's Climate Change Challenge* (Toronto: McClelland and Stewart, 2007).

107 Intergovernmental Panel on Climate Change, Working Group II, "Chapter 11: Human Health: Impacts, Adaptation, and Co-Benefits," in *Climate Change 2014: Impacts, Adaptation and Vulnerability (Fifth Assessment Report)* (New York: Cambridge University Press, 2014).

108 D. McCollum, N. Bauer, K. Calvin, A. Kitous, and K. Riahi, "Fossil Resource and Energy Security Dynamics in Conventional and Carbon Constrained Worlds," *Climatic Change* 123 (2013): 413–26.

109 European Union, *Energy Performance of Buildings Directive,* No. 244/2012 of January 16, 2012.

110 T. Gomes, "The Impact of Sovereign Wealth Funds on International Financial Stability," Bank of Canada Discussion Paper No. 2008-14 (Ottawa: Bank of Canada, 2008); U.S. Das, A. Mazarei, and H. van der Horn, *Economics of Sovereign Wealth Funds: Issues for Policy Makers* (Washington, DC: International Monetary Fund, 2010).

111 M. Drohan, *The 9 Habits of Highly Effective Resource Economies: Lessons for Canada* (Ottawa: Canadian International Council, 2012).

112 Norges Bank Investment Management, "The Fund's Market Value" (2014), http://www.nbim.no/.

113 P. MacKinnon, *A Futures Fund for Saskatchewan: A Report to Premier Brad Wall on the Saskatchewan Heritage Initiative* (Saskatoon: Government of Saskatchewan, 2013).

114 Quebec Minister of Finance and Economy, "Actions to Reduce the Debt" (2014), http://www.finances.gouv.qc.ca/en/page.asp?sectn=36&contn=347.

115 J. Munson, "No Sovereign Wealth Fund for Canada's Resources, Oliver Says" (October 12, 2012), http://www.ipolitics.ca/2012/10/12/no-sovereign-wealth-fund -for-canadas-resources-says-oliver/.

116 M. Drohan, "Learn from Alberta's Mistake: Provinces Should Save Resources," *Canadian Business,* March 18, 2013, http://www.canadianbusiness.com/economy/learn -from-albertas-mistake/.

117 MacKinnon, *A Futures Fund for Saskatchewan* (see n. 113 above).

118 A.B. Klass and L.-Y. Huang, *Restoring the Trust: Water Resources and the Public Trust Doctrine* (Washington, DC: Center for Progressive Reform, 2009).

119 R. Pentland, *Public Trust Doctrine: Potential in Canadian Water and Environmental Management* (Victoria: POLIS Project on Ecological Governance, 2009).

120 O.M. Brandes and R. Christensen, *The Public Trust and a Modern BC Water Act,* Legal Issues Brief 2010-1 (Victoria: POLIS Water Sustainability Project, 2010).

121 *British Columbia v. Canadian Forest Products Ltd.,* [2004] 2 S.C.R. 374.

122 J. Borrows, *Canada's Indigenous Constitution* (Toronto: University of Toronto Press, 2010).

123 C. Wood and R. Pentland, *Down the Drain: How We Are Failing to Protect Our Water Resources* (Vancouver: Greystone Books, 2013).

124 M. Barlow, *Blue Future: Protecting Water for People and the Planet Forever* (Toronto: Anansi, 2013).

125 M. Prieur, "De l'urgente necessité de reconnaître le principe de non regression en droit de l'environnement," *IUCN Academy of Environmental Law E-Journal* 1 (2011): 26–45.

126 D.R. Boyd, *The Right to a Healthy Environment: Revitalizing Canada's Constitution* (Vancouver: UBC Press, 2012).

127 C. Dhillon and M.G. Young, "Environmental Racism and First Nations: A Call for Socially Just Public Policy Development," *Canadian Journal of Humanities and Social Sciences* 1, 1 (2010): 23–37.

128 Bill C-469, *Canadian Environmental Bill of Rights.*

129 World Health Organization (Regional Office for Europe), *Environmental Health Inequalities in Europe: An Assessment* (Copenhagen: WHO Regional Office for Europe, 2012).

130 J. Kemm, J. Parry, and S. Palmer, *Health Impact Assessment: Concepts, Theory, Techniques, Applications* (Oxford: Oxford University Press, 2004).

131 L. Zajac, E. Sprecher, P.J. Landrigan, and L. Trasande, "A Systematic Review of US State Environmental Legislation and Regulation with Regard to the Prevention of Neurodevelopmental Disabilities and Asthma," *Environmental Health* 8 (2009): 9–21.

132 Canadian Institute for Health Information, *Urban Physical Environments and Health Inequalities: A Scoping Review of Interventions* (Ottawa: CIHI, 2012).

133 US Environmental Protection Agency, *Creating Equitable, Healthy, and Sustainable Communities: Strategies for Advancing Smart Growth, Environmental Justice, and Equitable Development* (Washington, DC: US EPA, 2013).

134 S.J. Rothenberg and J.C. Rothenberg, "Testing the Dose-Response Specification in Epidemiology: Public Health and Policy Consequences for Lead," *Environmental Health Perspectives* 113, 9 (2005): 1190–95.

135 S.N. Tsekrekos and I. Buka, "Lead Levels in Canadian Children: Do We Have to Review the Standard?" *Paediatrics and Child Health* 10, 4 (2005): 215–20.

136 L.K. McAllister, *Making Law Matter: Environmental Protection and Legal Institutions in Brazil* (Stanford, CA: Stanford University Press, 2008).

137 V. Passos de Freitas, "The Importance of Environmental Judicial Decisions: The Brazilian Experience," in *Symposium of Judges and Prosecutors of Latin America: Environmental Compliance and Enforcement,* ed. M.E. Di Paola (Buenos Aires: Fundacion Ambiente y Recursos Naturales, 2003), 62.

138 McAllister, *Making Law Matter* (see n. 136 above).

139 M. Haddock, *Environmental Tribunals in British Columbia* (Victoria: Environmental Law Centre, 2011).

140 Ibid., 13.

141 G. Pring and C. Pring, *Greening Justice: Creating and Improving Environmental Courts and Tribunals* (Washington, DC: Access Initiative/World Resources Institute, 2010).

142 G. Pring and K. Pring, "Specialized Environmental Courts and Tribunals at the Confluence of Human Rights and the Environment," *Oregon Review of International Law* 11, 2 (2010): 301–29.

143 B.J. Preston, "The Land and Environment Court of New South Wales: Moving towards a Multi-Door Courthouse," *Australasian Dispute Resolution Journal* 19 (2008): 72–82.

144 G. Pring and C. Pring, *Greening Justice* (see n. 141 above).

145 Ibid., 110.

146 Supreme Court of the Philippines, *Rules of Procedure for Environmental Cases* (Manila: Supreme Court of the Philippines, 2010).

147 Ibid., Rule 3, Sec. 3.
148 Royal Norwegian Ministry of Finance, *Norway's Strategy for Sustainable Development*, 15 (see n. 33 above).
149 Grandjean and Landrigan, "Neurobehavioural Effects of Developmental Toxicity," 330–38 (see n. 95 above); Grandjean and Landrigan, "Developmental Neurotoxicity of Industrial Chemicals," 2167–78 (see n. 95 above).
150 S. Anderson and M. Perez-Rocha, *Mining for Profits in International Tribunals: Lessons for the Trans-Pacific Partnership* (Washington, DC: Institute for Policy Studies, 2013).
151 UN Conference on Trade and Environment, "Recent Developments in Investor-State Dispute Settlement" (Geneva: UNCTAD, 2014), http://unctad.org/en/publications library/webdiaepcb2014d3_en.pdf.
152 *Lone Pine Resources Inc. v. The Government of Canada* (2013), Notice of Arbitration, September 6, 2013, http://www.italaw.com/cases/1606 (United Nations Commission on International Trade Law).
153 UN Conference on Trade and Environment, "Recent Developments in Investor-State Dispute Settlement" (see n. 151 above).
154 J. Hunka, "Calgary-Based Mining Company Suing Costa Rica for More than $1 Billion," *Global News*, October 4, 2013, http://globalnews.ca/news/883756/calgary -based-mining-company-suing-costa-rica-for-more-than-1-billion/.
155 D.R. Boyd, *Unnatural Law: Rethinking Canadian Environmental Law and Policy* (Vancouver: UBC Press, 2003).
156 Australia Department of Foreign Affairs and Trade, "Gillard Government Policy Statement: Trading Our Way to More Jobs and Prosperity" (Canberra, 2011).
157 Janet M. Eaton, "Australia's Rejection of Investor-State, from AUSFTA to the Gillard Government's Trade Policy and the Implications for Canada" (December 31, 2013), http://www.commonfrontiers.ca/Single_Page_Docs/PDF_Docs/Jan08_14 -AUSFTA-paper.pdf.

Chapter 11: Systemic Changes in Pursuit of Sustainability

1 W. McDonough and M. Braungart, *Cradle to Cradle: Remaking the Way We Make Things* (New York: North Point Press, 2002).
2 J. Rockstrom, W. Steffen, K. Noone, et al., "A Safe Operating Space for Humanity," *Nature* 461, 24 (2009): 472–75.
3 Cited in C. Lochhead, "Critics Question Desirability of Relentless Economic Growth," *San Francisco Chronicle*, January 4, 2014.
4 Ibid.
5 D. Jolly, "G.D.P. Seen as Inadequate Measure of Economic Health," *New York Times*, September 14, 2009; J. Stiglitz, A. Sen, and J.P. Fitoussi, *Report by the Commission on the Measurement of Economic Performance and Social Progress* (2009), http://www.stiglitz-sen-fitoussi.fr/documents/rapport_anglais.pdf.
6 T. Jackson, *Prosperity without Growth: Economics for a Finite Planet* (London: Earthscan, 2009), 168.
7 New Economics Foundation, *The Happy Planet Index 2012 Report: A Global Index of Sustainable Well-being* (London: New Economics Foundation, 2012).

8 R. Boarini and M.M. D'Ercole, "Going beyond GDP: An OECD Perspective," *Fiscal Studies* 34, 3 (2013): 289–314.

9 World Bank, *China 2030: Building a Modern, Harmonious and Creative High-Income Society* (Washington, DC: World Bank, 2012).

10 M. Anielski, *The Economics of Happiness: Building Genuine Wealth* (Gabriola, BC: New Society, 2007).

11 The European Union has a comprehensive website about alternatives to GDP: http://ec.europa.eu/environment/beyond_gdp/index_en.html.

12 Canadian Index of Wellbeing, "How Are Canadians Really Doing?" (2012), https://uwaterloo.ca/canadian-index-wellbeing/.

13 Ibid.

14 P.A. Victor, *Managing without Growth: Slower by Design, Not Disaster* (Cheltenham, UK: Edward Elgar, 2008), 183.

15 Jackson, *Prosperity without Growth* (see n. 6 above).

16 McDonough and Braungart, *Cradle to Cradle* (see n. 1 above).

17 D.R. Boyd, *Unnatural Law: Rethinking Canadian Environmental Law and Policy* (Vancouver: UBC Press, 2003), ch. 10.

18 Royal Norwegian Ministry of Finance, *Norway's Strategy for Sustainable Development* (Oslo: Royal Norwegian Ministry of Finance, 2008), 13.

19 Swedish Environmental Protection Agency, *Swedish Consumption and the Environment* (Stockholm: Swedish Environmental Protection Agency, 2011).

20 R. Heinberg, *The Party's Over: Oil, War, and the Fate of Industrial Societies* (Gabriola Island, BC: New Society, 2003); B. Lomborg, *The Skeptical Environmentalist: Measuring the Real State of the World* (Cambridge: Cambridge University Press, 2001).

21 World Commission on Environment and Development, *Our Common Future* (New York: Oxford University Press, 1987).

22 K.-H. Robert, *The Natural Step Story: Seeding a Quiet Revolution* (Gabriola Island, BC: New Society, 2002).

23 European Commission, *Towards a Circular Economy: A Zero Waste Programme for Europe* (Brussels: European Commission, 2014); Japan, *Law for the Promotion of Efficient Use of Resources*, Act no. 48 of April 26, 1991; China, *Circular Economy Promotion Law*, passed in the 4th meeting of the Standing Committee of the 11th National People's Congress on August 29, 2008.

24 M.Z. Jacobson and M.A. Delucchi, "Providing All Global Energy with Wind, Water, and Solar Power, Part I: Technologies, Energy Resources, Quantities, and Areas of Infrastructure and Materials," *Energy Policy* 39 (2009): 1154–69.

25 T. Mai, D. Sandor, R. Wiser, and T. Schneider, *Renewable Electricity Futures Study: Executive Summary*, NREL/TP-6A20–52409-ES (Golden, CO: National Renewable Energy Laboratory, 2012).

26 Union of Concerned Scientists, *Ramping Up Renewables: Energy You Can Count On* (Cambridge, MA: Union of Concerned Scientists, 2013).

27 Australian Energy Market Operator, "100 Per Cent Renewables Study: Executive Briefing" (2013), http://www.environment.gov.au/climate-change/publications/aemo-modelling-outcomes.

28 G. Parkinson, "Renewables Now Cheaper than Coal and Gas in Australia" (2013), http://reneweconomy.com.au/2013/renewables-now-cheaper-than-coal-and-gas-in -australia-62268.

29 Ibid.

30 Ibid.

31 World Wildlife Fund, Ecofys, and Office of Metropolitan Architecture, *The Energy Report: 100% Renewable Energy by 2050* (Gland, Switzerland: WWF, 2011).

32 S. Nicola, "Renewables Meet Record 27 Percent of German Electricity Demand," *Bloomberg News*, May 9, 2014, http://www.bloomberg.com/news/2014-05-09/ renewables-meet-record-27-percent-of-german-electricity-demand.html.

33 K. Kroh, "Germany Sets New Record, Generating 74% of Power Needs from Renewable Energy," *Climate Progress*, May 13, 2014, http://thinkprogress.org/climate/ 2014/05/13/3436923/germany-energy-records/.

34 Organisation for Economic Co-operation and Development, *Green Growth: Germany* (Paris: OECD, 2013).

35 Germany, Ministry for the Environment, *Gross Employment from Renewable Energy in Germany* (Berlin: Ministry for the Environment, 2012), http://www.germany. info/contentblob/3146650/Daten/3903428/BMU_GrosEmploymentRE2011_DD. pdf.

36 US Energy Information Administration, "Country Reports" (2014), http://www.eia. gov/countries/index.cfm.

37 J. Murray, "Wind Power Was Spain's Top Source of Electricity in 2013," *The Guardian,* January 6, 2014, http://www.theguardian.com/environment/2014/jan/06/wind -power-spain-electricity-2013.

38 R. ten Hoedt, "After the Gold Rush: Japan's Second Solar Boom," *Energy Post,* May 15, 2014, http://www.energypost.eu/goldrush-japans-second-solar-boom/.

39 Union of Concerned Scientists, *Ramping Up Renewables* (see n. 26 above).

40 L.T. Johnson, S. Yeh, and C. Hope, "The Social Cost of Carbon: Implications for Modernizing Our Electricity System," *Journal of Environmental Studies and Sciences* 3, 4 (2013): 369–75.

41 International Energy Agency, *Energy Technology Perspectives 2014: Harnessing Electricity's Potential* (Paris: IEA, 2014), http://www.iea.org/publications/freepublications/ publication/EnergyTechnologyPerspectives_ES.pdf.

42 R.D. Torrie, T. Bryant, M. Beer, et al., *An Inventory of Low-Carbon Energy for Canada* (Vancouver: Trottier Energy Futures Project, 2013).

43 Natural Resources Canada, "About Renewable Energy" (2014), https://www.nrcan. gc.ca/energy/renewable-electricity/7295.

44 UN Sustainable Development Solutions Network, *Pathways to Deep Decarbonization. Interim Report: Canada Chapter* (New York: Sustainable Development Solutions Network, 2014).

45 Global Wind Energy Council, *Global Wind Report: Annual Market Update 2014* (Brussels: Global Wind Energy Council, 2015).

46 Renewing Futures, *Meeting the Human Resources Needs of Canada's Renewable Electricity Industry* (Ottawa: Renewing Futures, 2013), http://www.renewingfutures.ca/ CMFiles//EHRCrffr.pdf.

47 *Green Energy and Green Economy Act,* S.O. 2009, c. 12.

48 "Tesla Model S Sets All-Time Norway Car Sales Record," *Gas2,* April 2, 2014, http://gas2.org/2014/04/02/tesla-model-s-sets-all-time-norway-car-sales-record/.

49 R. Everett, G. Boyle, S. Peake, and J. Ramage, eds., *Energy Systems and Sustainability: Power for a Sustainable Future,* 2nd ed. (Oxford: Oxford University Press, 2012).

50 D.R. Boyd, *The Right to a Healthy Environment: Revitalizing Canada's Constitution* (Vancouver: UBC Press, 2012).

51 *State v. Acheson,* 1991, 2 SA 805 (Nm).

52 T. Hayward, *Constitutional Environmental Rights* (Oxford: Oxford University Press, 2005).

53 See ss. 16–23 of the *Canadian Charter of Rights and Freedoms.*

54 D. Marrani, "The Second Anniversary of the Constitutionalisation of the French Charter for the Environment: Constitutional and Environmental Implications," *Environmental Law Review* 10, 1 (2008): 9–27; D. Marrani, "Human Rights and Environmental Protection: The Pressure of the Charter for the Environment on French Administrative Courts," *Sustainable Development Law and Policy* 10, 1 (2009): 52–57.

55 *Ontario v. Canadian Pacific,* [1995] 2 S.C.R. 1031 at 1076.

56 Canadian Bar Association, *Report of the Canadian Bar Association Committee on Sustainable Development in Canada: Options for Law Reform* (Ottawa: Canadian Bar Association, 1990), 27.

57 Angus Reid, "David Suzuki Foundation: Segmentation Study" (2012). On file with the author.

58 D.D. Bridge and A. Laytner, trans., *The Animals' Lawsuit against Humanity: An Illustrated 10th Century Iraqi Fable* (Louisville, KY: Fons Vitae, 2005).

59 J. Borrows, *Canada's Indigenous Constitution* (Toronto: University of Toronto Press, 2010), 243–44.

60 J.S.Y. Henderson, "First Nations' Legal Inheritances in Canada: The Mikmaq Model," *Manitoba Law Journal* 23, 1 (1996): 1–31.

61 C. Stone, "Should Trees Have Standing? Toward Legal Rights for Natural Objects," *Southern California Law Review* 45, 2 (1972): 450–501; *Sierra Club v. Morton,* 405 U.S. 727 (1972).

62 Stone, ibid., 450–501.

63 Ecuador Constitution, Art. 71.

64 *R.F. Wheeler and E.G. Huddle v. Attorney General of the State of Loja* [2011] Judgment No. 11121-2011-0010, March 30, 2011, Loja Provincial Court of Justice.

65 Bolivia, *Law on the Rights of Mother Earth,* Law no. 71 of December 2010.

66 *Te Urewera Act 2014,* New Zealand Public Act No. 51, July 27, 2014.

67 Australian Associated Press, "Push for Queensland Reef to Have Legal Identity," *Daily News,* February 2, 2014, http://thenewdaily.com.au/news/2014/02/04/push-qld-reef-legal-identity/.

68 Community Environmental Legal Defense Fund, "Rights-Based Local Laws Drafted by CELDF" (2014), http://celdf.org/resources-ordinances.

69 New Zealand Electoral Commission, "Referenda" (2014), http://www.elections.org.nz/voting-system/referenda.

70 A. Lijphart, *Patterns of Democracy: Government Forms and Performance in Thirty-Six Countries* (New Haven, CT: Yale University Press, 1999).

71 "Fair Elections Act: Slow it Down Mr. Polievre," *Globe and Mail,* March 9, 2014; "Fair Elections Act: If Evidence Voted, This Bill Would Die," *Globe and Mail,* March 31, 2014.

72 J. Mander, *The Capitalism Papers: Fatal Flaws of an Obsolete System* (Berkeley, CA: Counterpoint, 2012).

73 Bill C-586, *An Act to Reform the Canada Elections Act and the Parliament of Canada Act (Candidacy and Caucus Reforms).* Passed 2nd Reading in the House of Commons on September 24, 2014.

74 J. Smith, ed., *The Democratic Dilemma: Reforming the Canadian Senate* (Montreal and Kingston: McGill-Queen's University Press, 2009).

75 *Reference re Senate Reform,* 2014, SCC 32 (CanLII).

76 *BCE v. 1976 Debentureholders,* [2008] 3 S.C.R. 560 at para. 40.

77 An excellent overview of benefit corporations is available at http://www.bcorporation. net/.

78 W.H. Clark and L. Vranka, "White Paper: The Need and Rationale for the Benefit Corporation: Why It Is the Legal Form That Best Addresses the Needs of Social Entrepreneurs, Investors, and, Ultimately, the Public" (2013), http://www.benefit corp.net/storage/documents/Benecit_Corporation_White_Paper_1_18_2013.pdf.

79 M.R. Deskins, "Benefit Corporation Legislation, Version 1.0 – A Breakthrough in Stakeholder Rights?" *Lewis and Clark Law Review* 15 (2011): 1047. See http://www. benefitcorp.net/state-by-state-legislative-status.

80 "B Corp Community" (2014), http://www.bcorporation.net/b-corp-community.

81 Sustainable Prosperity, "Benefit Corporations" (2012), http://www.sustainable prosperity.ca/dl894&display.

82 T.S. Carter and T.L.M. Man, "Canadian Registered Charities: Business Activities and Social Enterprise – Thinking Outside the Box" (paper presented at the National Center on Philanthropy and the Law Annual Conference at New York University School of Law, October 24, 2008).

83 Parliamentary Special Committee on Co-operatives, "Status of Co-operatives in Canada" (Ottawa: Public Works and Government Services Canada, 2012), http://www. parl.gc.ca/content/hoc/Committee/411/COOP/Reports/RP5706528/cooprp01/ cooprp01-e.pdf.

84 R. Wilkinson and K. Pickett, *The Spirit Level: Why Greater Equality Makes Societies Stronger* (New York: Bloomsbury, 2009).

85 S. Motesharrei, J. Rivas, and E. Kalnay, "Human and Nature Dynamics (HANDY): Modeling Inequality and Use of Resources in the Collapse or Sustainability of Societies," *Ecological Economics* 101 (2014): 90–102, doi:10.1016/j.ecolecon.2014. 02.014.

86 Conference Board of Canada, "How Canada Performs" (2014), http://www.conference board.ca/hcp/details/society.aspx.

87 Ibid.

88 Canadian Centre for Policy Alternatives, *Outrageous Fortune* (Ottawa: Canadian Centre for Policy Alternatives, 2014).

89 Ernst & Young, "2014–15 Worldwide Personal Tax Guide" (2014), http://www.ey.
    com/GL/en/Services/Tax/Worldwide-personal-tax-guide---Country-list; Deloitte,
    "Deloitte International Tax Source: Tax Guides and Highlights" (2015), https://www.
    dits.deloitte.com/Administration/ManageHomePage/Popup.aspx?ChildPage=
    Country%20Guides%20and%20Highlights.

90 D.A. Green and J.R. Kesselman, eds., *Dimensions of Inequality in Canada* (Van-
    couver: UBC Press, 2006).

91 OECD, *Growing Unequal? Income Distribution and Poverty in OECD Countries –
    Country Note: Canada* (Paris: OECD, 2009).

92 Canadian Centre for Policy Alternatives, *What Can Governments Do about Can-
    ada's Growing Gap? Canadian Attitudes towards Income Inequality* (Ottawa: Can-
    adian Centre for Policy Alternatives, 2007).

93 Human Security Report Project, *Human Security Report 2013: The Decline in Global
    Violence: Evidence, Explanation, and Contestation* (Vancouver: Human Security
    Press, 2013); L. Themnér and P. Wallensteen, "Armed Conflict, 1946–2012," *Journal
    of Peace Research* 50, 4 (2013): 509–21; S. Pinker, *The Better Angels of Our Nature:
    Why Violence Has Declined* (Cambridge, MA: Harvard University Press, 2011).

94 C. Clark and J. Torobin, "Tough Choices for Defence Spending," *Globe and Mail*,
    October 25, 2010, http://www.theglobeandmail.com/news/national/time-to-lead/
    tough-choices-for-defence-spending/article1215484/.

95 S. Chase, "New Warships to Cost More than $100 Billion, Ottawa Estimates," *Globe
    and Mail*, November 13, 2013.

96 S. Evans, *The Green Republic: A Conservation History of Costa Rica* (Austin: Uni-
    versity of Texas Press, 1999).

97 Central Intelligence Agency, *The World Factbook* (Washington, DC: CIA, 2014),
    https://www.cia.gov/library/publications/the-world-factbook/.

98 New Economics Foundation, *The Happy Planet Index: 2012 Report, a Global Index
    of Sustainable Well-being* (London: New Economics Foundation, 2012).

99 Jackson, *Prosperity without Growth* (see n. 6 above).

Chapter 12: The Time for Action Is Now

1 S.A. Rauch and B.P. Lanphear, "Prevention of Disability in Children: Elevating the
   Role of Environment," *The Future of Children* 22, 1 (2012): 193–217; A. Bérubé,
   "Toward an Economic Analysis of the Environmental Burden of Disease among
   Canadian Children," *Journal of Toxicology and Environmental Health Part B:
   Critical Reviews* 10, 1–2 (2007): 131–42.

2 Conference Board of Canada, "How Canada Performs" (2015), http://www.conference
   board.ca/hcp/default.aspx.

3 Organisation for Economic Co-operation and Development, *Total Expenditure on
   Health Care Per Capita* (Paris: OECD, 2014).

4 Conference Board of Canada, "How Canada Performs" (see n. 2 above).

5 M. Munro, "As Canada Dawdles, Denmark Shows the World How to Stop Mass
   Medicating Animals," *Saskatoon Star Phoenix*, April 18, 2014, http://o.canada.com/
   news/national/as-canada-dawdles-denmark-shows-the-world-how-to-stop-mass
   -medicating-animals.

6 D. Meironyte, K. Noren, and A. Bergman, "Analysis of Polybrominated Diphenyl Ethers in Swedish Human Milk, a Time-Related Trend Study, 1972–1997," *Journal of Toxicology and Environmental Health Part A* 58, 6 (1999): 329–41.

7 P.O. Darnerud, M. Aune, S. Atuma, et al., "Time Trend of Polybrominated Diphenyl Ether (PBDE) Levels in Breast Milk from Uppsala, Sweden, 1996–2001," *Organohalogen Compounds* 58 (2002): 233–36.

8 L. Hardell and M. Eriksson, "Is the Decline of the Increasing Incidence of Non-Hodgkin Lymphoma in Sweden and Other Countries a Result of Cancer Preventive Measures?" *Environmental Health Perspectives* 111, 14 (2003): 1704–6.

9 S.D. Cohen, *Multinational Corporations and Foreign Direct Investment: Avoiding Simplicity, Embracing Complexity* (New York: Oxford University Press, 2007).

10 New Economics Foundation, *The Happy Planet Index 2012 Report: A Global Index of Sustainable Well-being* (London: New Economics Foundation, 2012).

11 G. Koop, R. McKitrick, and L. Tole, "Air Pollution, Economic Activity and Respiratory Illness: Evidence from Canadian Cities, 1974–1994," *Environmental Modeling and Software* 25, 7 (2010): 873–85.

12 D. Michaels, *Doubt Is Their Product: How Industry's Assault on Science Threatens Your Health* (Oxford: Oxford University Press, 2008).

13 G. Markowitz and D. Rosner, *Deceit and Denial: The Deadly Politics of Industrial Pollution* (Berkeley: University of California Press, 2003).

14 W. Block, ed., *Economics and the Environment: A Reconciliation* (Vancouver: Fraser Institute, 1990).

15 UN Environment Programme, "The Ozone Layer: Protecting Our Atmosphere for Generations to Come" (2012), http://www.unep.org/NEWSCENTRE/default. aspx?DocumentId=2698&ArticleId=9326.

16 D.M. Uhlmann, "Environmental Law, Public Health and the Values Conundrum," *Michigan Journal of Environmental and Administrative Law* 3, 2 (2014): 231–42.

17 D.A Chokshi and T.A Farley, "The Cost-Effectiveness of Environmental Approaches to Disease Prevention," *New England Journal of Medicine* 367, 4 (2012): 295–97; B. Milstein, J. Horner, P. Briss, et al., "Why Behavioral and Environmental Interventions Are Needed to Improve Health at Lower Cost," *Health Affairs* 30, 5 (2011): 823–32.

18 T.A. Myers, M.C. Nisbet, E.W. Maibach, and A.A. Leiserowitz, "A Public Health Frame around Climate Change Arouses Positive Emotions," *Climatic Change* 113 (2012): 1105–12.

19 S. Ambec, M.A. Cohen, S. Elgie, and P. Lanoie, "The Porter Hypothesis at 20: Can Environmental Regulation Enhance Innovation and Competitiveness?" *Review of Environmental Economics and Policy* 7, 1 (2013): 2–22.

Index